THE LOST PALACE

The British Embassy in Berlin

THE LOST PALACE

The British Embassy in Berlin

Julia Toffolo

First published in Great Britain in 2017 by
The Book Guild Ltd
9 Priory Business Park
Wistow Road, Kibworth
Leicestershire, LE8 0RX
Freephone: 0800 999 2982
www.bookguild.co.uk
Email: info@bookguild.co.uk
Twitter: @bookguild

Typeset by Park Studio, London (www.park-studio.com)

Printed and bound in Great Britain by CPI Group (UK) Ltd, Croydon, CR0 4YY

ISBN 978 1910878 330

British Library Cataloguing in Publication Data.
A catalogue record for this book is available from the British Library.

CONTENTS

Acknowledgements

Many people have given me help and encouragement in this endeavour. I would particularly like to thank Sir Michael Arthur; Helen Davis of the Sissinghurst Archive; Daniel Herrmann; Charles Malet; and Dr Mark Pottle for their help in various capacities. Thanks also go to Mark Bertram; Roger Golding, Penny Johnson and other former colleagues at the UK Government Art Collection; Sir Simon McDonald; my business partner Freda Matassa; Professor Patrick Salmon; and Sir John and Lady Ann Tusa, all of whom read earlier drafts of the book and provided invaluable comments and support. My thanks also go to former GAC colleague Philippa Martin, whose specialist knowledge of Lord Leighton's *oeuvre* first directed me towards the story of the British Embassy in Berlin. Linda Lundin of Park Studio designed the book.

I have made efforts to contact relevant copyright holders for permission to quote from or to reproduce images. If I have quoted from or reproduced copyright material without proper acknowledgement, I apologise and will fully acknowledge errors and/or omissions in any future edition of this book.

I thank the following for their help in locating and/or in reproducing and quoting from original and copyright material: Her Majesty Queen Elizabeth II (for extracts from Queen Victoria's Journals); the Architectural Museum at Berlin Technical University (for August Orth material); His Grace The Duke of Bedford (for extracts from *Lord William Russell and his Wife 1815–1846* by Georgiana Blakiston); the Birmingham Museum of Art, Alabama, USA (for John Singer Sargent's portrait of Lady D'Abernon); Virginia Bonham-Carter (for the Asquith/Bonham-Carter Archive); the British Library (for the D'Abernon Papers); the Bodleian Library at the University of Oxford and Sir Henry Rumbold (for the Rumbold Papers); the Churchill Archives Centre at the University of Cambridge (for the Sir Eric Phipps Papers and the Sir Cecil Spring-Rice Papers); Krystyna Kirkpatrick (for *The Inner Circle* by Sir Ivone Kirkpatrick); Sir Henry Rumbold and Francis Farmar (for Rumbold Family Papers and for their friendly encouragement); my former colleagues at the UK Government Art Collection (for GAC Files); Nicholas Mosley, Lord Ravensdale (for material from Irene Ravensdale's diary); Adam Nicolson, 5th Baron Carnock and Juliet Nicolson (for *Diplomacy* by Harold Nicolson; *Portrait of a Marriage* by Nigel Nicolson; *Vita and Harold: the Letters of Vita Sackville-West and Harold Nicolson* and *Harold Nicolson Diaries and Letters*, both edited by Nigel Nicolson) and the photograph of Vita and her two sons taken at Long Barn; David Pryce-Jones (for *Unity Mitford: A Quest*); the British Architectural Library at the Royal Institute of British Architects; Sir Henry Rumbold and Francis Farmar for extracts and a photograph from the Rumbold Family Papers; and Michael Smith (for *Foley: The Spy who Saved 10,000 Jews*).

The extract from *Lord Randolph Churchill* by Winston Churchill (Macmillan 1906) is quoted with permission of Curtis Brown, London, on behalf of the Estate of Winston S. Churchill (© The Estate of Winston S. Churchill). Extracts from *Sir Horace Rumbold: Portrait of a Diplomat 1869–1941* by the late Sir Martin Gilbert (Heinemann 1973) are quoted with permission of A.P. Watt at United Agents on behalf of Martin Gilbert (www.martingilbert.com), with thanks to Lady Esther Gilbert. Extracts from *The Diary of Edward Goschen 1900-1914* (edited by H.D. Howard, Royal Historical Society, Camden Fourth Series, 1980) and from 'Money, Morals and the Pillars of Bismarck's Society' by Fritz Stern, *Central European History* (Volume III No.1/2, 1970) are quoted with permission of Cambridge University Press. Extracts from *The Red Count: The Life and Times of Harry Kessler* by Laird M. Easton (University of California Press, © 2002) are quoted by permission of the Regents of the University of California. The extracts from the English translation of *The English House* by Hermann Muthesius are quoted with permission of Frances Lincoln Ltd, © 2007. Extracts from Crown Copyright documents are quoted by courtesy of The Controller of Her Majesty's Stationery Office at The National Archives.

I had the idea for this book more than seven years ago, and would especially like to thank Florian Eames, without whose everlasting patience, support and encouragement it may never have come about.

Julia Toffolo
London, May 2017

INTRODUCTION

On 21 February 1934 German Chancellor Adolf Hitler attended a lunch party at the British Embassy in Berlin. To 1930s' tastes, the imposing building he entered was very old-fashioned. Its grand, florid and historiated decoration dated back to the final years of the Kingdom of Prussia, when, under the stewardship of Hitler's historic predecessor Otto von Bismarck, Berlin had become the capital of a unified Germany. Five-and-a-half years later Sir Nevile Henderson, the final British Ambassador before the start of the Second World War, left the building for the nearby Reich Chancellery to submit to Hitler the British ultimatum, triggering the start of hostilities between the two countries, hostilities that were to result in the destruction of much of the German capital, including the British Embassy.

Like so much of the pre-1945 vanished city of Berlin, this building exists now only in the imagination. Now a new, very different British Embassy occupies exactly the same location at 70 Wilhelmstrasse, close to Berlin's historic main avenue Unter den Linden and next door to the rebuilt Adlon Hotel. A spectacular piece of multi-coloured contemporary architecture by an acclaimed British architect, this new Embassy symbolises Britain's confidence in the reunification of Germany after fifty years of the Cold War's icy grip on Eastern Europe. The British Ambassador's symbolic return to Berlin, on 3 September 1999, was on the sixtieth anniversary of the start of the Second World War that followed Sir Nevile Henderson's ultimatum to Adolf Hitler. On that date I too was in Berlin, installing works of art in the Ambassador's Residence.

I worked at the UK Government Art Collection from 1991 to 2013 as its first Registrar and later its Deputy Director, keeping track of, devising and installing art displays in diplomatic buildings worldwide. Over time I became fascinated by the history that had taken place within the walls of these buildings, the notion of them as repositories of memories of political, diplomatic, social and cultural events, their walls witnesses to the thousands of people who have worked in them or who visited the buildings as guests. The history of the British Embassy and the nearby buildings in the government quarter in Berlin is particularly interesting, a microcosm of Berlin's endless capacity for change and reinvention as, from the 1870s, the city and country passed through monarchy, civil war, republic, fascist dictatorship, near destruction, division into two political halves, communist dictatorship, reunification and return to democracy. Down the years the people who lived and worked in the Embassy found themselves spectators and major players in these events; events that shaped not only the history of Germany but the course of world history.

As the first British Ambassador to a united Germany, Lord Odo Russell acquired the former Palais Strousberg at 70 Wilhelmstrasse for use as an embassy in 1876. The doyen of the diplomatic corps in Berlin, Russell and his successors in the years before early August 1914 presided over the glamorous Berlin winter 'season', a long-lost world of imperial balls and complicated court protocol. At the head of a 'Family Embassy', the British Ambassador enjoyed close and friendly relations with the German Imperial Family, while the Embassy became a welcome refuge for Queen Victoria's daughter Vicky, the Prussian Crown Princess and her beloved husband, Fritz. Their son Wilhelm's well-documented eccentricities occasionally took centre stage in the 'Family Embassy' itself. Few could imagine that within a few short years those close family relationships were to descend into an unthinkable European war as, attacked by a howling mob on 4 August 1914, the Embassy was suddenly to become the very focal point of German hatred against the British.

Situated in the heart of Berlin's government district, the Embassy was always at physical risk from the political instability that followed the Great War. But after 1920 something of the pre-August 1914 allure returned to the building when the guests of Lord D'Abernon and his glamorous wife included representatives of the democratic republic that rose from the ashes of that war, as the Embassy became the centre of frantic attempts to regenerate the country's crippled economy. A host of cultural figures, including Charlie Chaplin, John Galsworthy, Albert Einstein and the 'Bloomsbury Set' were embassy guests during the German capital's extraordinary cultural renaissance during the 'roaring twenties', only for political and economic events once more to transform Germany and its Government into, as Ambassador Horace Rumbold described it, 'a lunatic asylum'. In the final six-and-a-half years of its active life, many of the Embassy's official guests were necessarily members of the totalitarian and merciless Government that took control of Germany in 1933. Facing the daily challenge of living and working in this ever more frightening political world, it was the job of the Embassy's staff to manage and channel Britain's increasingly fraught diplomatic relations with Nazi Germany while being powerless to prevent the slide into another world war, a war which would destroy the building.

Told from the point of view of the Ambassadors' representational duties and the day-to-day experiences of their staff, researching this story has been a challenge. There are very few photographs of the Embassy's interior. Oral history is now no longer an option: I am unaware of anyone who experienced the building as an adult who is still with us. Reliance upon personal memoirs and diaries has obvious limitations and can only ever paint an incomplete picture. Documentation relating to social events naturally tends to be ephemeral; anything of this type is generally not retained for very long in embassies at the best of times and was in any case unlikely to survive the events of the Second World War. The loss, almost certainly at that time, of many decades' worth of red leather-bound visitors' books (still in use in diplomatic residences) is much to be mourned, as are the Ministry of Works' files on the building, which were probably disposed of after 1945 as no longer worth keeping. That anything at all of this nature has survived is thanks to Sir Eric Phipps, Ambassador to Berlin early in the Nazi era and who, fortunately for posterity, was a hoarder of invitations, seating plans, photographs and press cuttings, retained amongst his official papers.

Using these and other sources it has been possible to reconstruct something of the building's internal appearance, atmosphere and of the social events that took place over the course of the seven decades it proudly stood on Wilhelmstrasse. Of course none of it can be told without briefly recounting historical events, but this is not a history of Germany, Berlin, or of British–German relations over the same period: there is, after all, plenty of such information available elsewhere. It is instead the story of a building that was on the very doorstep of, and occasionally at the centre of, those events. That story begins, however, not with a diplomat but with the Embassy's builder: one of the most remarkable men in Germany's industrial and economic history, the infamous 'Railway King' – Bethel Henry Strousberg.

Note on Monetary Values
Providing modern equivalents of historical monetary values is notoriously difficult. Nevertheless not to make the attempt would remove, I believe, something from the full appreciation of this narrative. Based on Bank of England inflation statistics, *as an extremely rough guide indeed* I would therefore suggest that £1 in the 1870s and 1880s today equates to very approximately £100–£150 and in the 1920s, £50–£100. When making any conversion it is also vital to bear in mind the immense changes over time in the relative values of goods and services, the price of 'real estate' being an excellent example.

CHAPTER 1
BETHEL HENRY STROUSBERG: 'THE GREATEST MAN IN GERMANY'

There was the house. There was the furniture. There were the carriages, the horses, the servants with the livery coats and powdered heads, and the servants with the black coats and unpowdered heads. There were the gems, and the presents, and all the nice things that money can buy.
Anthony Trollope, *The Way We Live Now* (1875), Chapter IV

I know, from life and from history, something you have not thought of: often, the outward and visible material signs and symbols of happiness and success only show themselves when the process of decline has already set in. The outer manifestations take time – like the light of that star up there, which may in reality be already quenched, when it looks to us to be shining its brightest.
Senator Thomas Buddenbrook, Thomas Mann, *Buddenbrooks: The Decline of a Family* (1902, English Translation by H.T. Lowe-Porter 1924), Part Seven, Chapter VI

Sunday, 13 March 1870 was Bethel Henry Strousberg's silver wedding anniversary, an ideal opportunity to show off his recently completed palatial residence at 70 Wilhelmstrasse in Berlin. While the street was thronged with his guests' carriages, Strousberg's luxurious rooms were packed with guests and well-wishers from the great and the good in the Prussian capital who marvelled at the mounds of expensive and elaborate anniversary presents, tokens of acclaim for the Prussian 'Railway King'. Amongst the gifts was a silver model of St Bride's Church in London where Strousberg and his English wife had married in 1845, he aged twenty-one and she just sixteen. Mingling with the VIPs he had striven so much to impress, Strousberg could have every reason to feel satisfied with his achievements. Central Europe bristled with his properties, industrial concerns and businesses, making him one of the wealthiest men in Prussia. Through the building and financing of its railways, he had helped bring about the rapid industrial transformation of Germany.[1]

But Strousberg had a secret. Amongst the pillars of Prussian society who gathered to toast him that day in the lavish surroundings of the Palais Strousberg, how many could have guessed that at the age of twenty-three, in England, he had been found guilty of embezzlement and sentenced to imprisonment with hard labour? He had been unlucky. In July 1847, sailing under the assumed name of Bartholdi, Strousberg absconded from his adopted country on the SS *Washington*, sailing out of Southampton for the United States, carrying money that had been entrusted to him by three building societies to deposit at a bank. Just a day out of port, and only because the wrong grade of coal had been loaded for the steamer's boilers, the ship was forced to turn back for Southampton. Waiting for Strousberg as the ship steamed back to the docks was a member of one of the defrauded societies, suspicious about the young man's absence and who had made his way to the port acting on a hunch. Strousberg was promptly arrested, tried and convicted.

It was not the first time that Bethel Henry Strousberg had made a strategic decision to change his name: Baruch Hirsch Strausberg was born on 20 November 1823, in Neidenberg* in East Prussia. The Strausbergs were a moderately prosperous and long-established merchant Jewish family, but at the age of fifteen Baruch decided to try his chances in the City of London, where some of his family ran a small business importing Continental fancy goods. Anglicising his name, converting from Judaism to Christianity and marrying Mary Ann Swan (the daughter of a City linen draper), the burning ambition of the reborn 'Bethel Henry Strousberg' was to climb to the top of the British social ladder almost from the bottom.

Released from prison, Strousberg made a living from writing and publishing, establishing two business magazines and turning himself into an expert in the insurance market. But this period of good fortune and respectability lasted only until the embezzlement episode resurfaced to threaten Strousberg's carefully honed reputation. So, in another gamble, in 1855 he returned with his wife and growing family to his native Prussia, settling in its capital, Berlin. Although he had never been to the city before he soon established several business ventures there, based on his British and German specialist knowledge and language skills. On the basis of his past achievements, in 1857 he applied for, and was awarded, a doctorate from the University of Jena.

Strousberg then got the lucky break of his life. Assisting with a specialised legal opinion, he was introduced to Lord Bloomfield, the British Minister† to Berlin, who began to consult him in a number of other legal matters. Through Bloomfield Strousberg made contact with several British investors and contractors involved with railway construction, a new economic boom industry in Prussia. Strousberg recognised the future when he saw it, and set about building up a complicated network of deals to finance these inevitably extremely expensive operations. When the money began to flow in, he used the profits to do something different, boldly cutting out the middle man not only by financing, but actually creating the associated railway supply industries – blast furnaces, collieries, steelworks and locomotive factories – many of which had up until then not existed in Prussia in an advanced form. What became a highly successful industrial empire could therefore offer a complete railway construction package of expertise, labour and materials.

Strousberg's self-belief and drive had brought him a considerable distance from his unpromising social beginnings and criminal record. But he needed more: to demonstrate that he had a rightful place in the highest echelons of Prussian society. He was not alone in this endeavour – so did many of his fellow *nouveaux riches*, the industrialists and bankers who were making their fortunes through Germany's rapid economic growth, and, like them, Strousberg set out to obtain a landed estate. In

---

* Now Nidzica in Poland.
† The status of the British Legation in Berlin was raised to that of full embassy in 1862 (see Chapter 2).

1868 he acquired the lordship of Zbirow,‡ not far from Prague, using the fashionable Berlin architect August Orth to improve and extend the buildings. Orth was also employed on several purely industrial projects for Strousberg, amongst them the huge Berlin terminus§ for the Berlin–Görlitz railway, originally intended for the planned rail line from Vienna. This station's large scale was to set the standard for future railway termini in what was shortly to become the buzzing new capital of Germany, whose rapid growth was being funded from the profits from the new industries and railways funded by new joint-stock companies.

As his wealth expanded exponentially, Strousberg moved his family into increasingly grander houses in Berlin, but by the mid-1860s he decided he wanted something better: a new house, built to his own specifications and where he could indulge in some serious conspicuous consumption. And in contrast to industrialist contemporaries like August Borsig, who had built his large villa in the middle of a park near to his own locomotive factory in the Berlin suburb of Moabit, Strousberg wanted his residence to be located in the very centre of political and financial Berlin. The site that he chose was on the west side of Wilhelmstrasse, one block south from the street's junction with Unter den Linden.

This area of Berlin had been laid out as a new town in the late seventeenth century by the Elector Friedrich Wilhelm of Prussia. It had a classical grid pattern of streets based on the main east–west processional artery of the city running from the Royal Schloss through to the Pariser Platz,¶ the Brandenburg Gate** and beyond, through the Tiergarten,†† its avenue of lime trees giving the road on the eastern side of the Brandenburg Gate the name Unter den Linden. In homage to the area's royal developer, streets cutting through Unter den Linden on a rough north–south axis were given the names Friedrichstrasse and Wilhelmstrasse. As the years progressed the large elegant aristocratic townhouses lining Wilhelmstrasse were gradually converted into government offices as Berlin became the capital of Germany, making 'Wilhelmstrasse' the political centre of the city: its 'Whitehall'. At 76 Wilhelmstrasse, for example, was the Prussian Foreign Ministry and home of Otto von Bismarck, and at 77 was the Radziwill Palace, later to become the Reich Chancellery. Just to the east of Wilhelmstrasse lay Behrenstrasse with its huge banking houses and a couple of streets south, on Jägerstrasse, was the German State Bank. Strousberg's chosen site was thus the equivalent of building a huge new house virtually next door to Downing Street in London and within an easy stroll of the Bank of England: it was a political and economic expression of Strousberg's self-regard – and undoubted position – as by then one of the richest, most powerful and influential men in Germany.

The site fronted directly on to Wilhelmstrasse, but, hemmed in by other buildings both to the north and south, it was relatively small, its width some 37.8 metres and its maximum depth 45.6 metres.[2] While buildings on the same side

‡ Now Zbiroh, Czech Republic. The castle is now a hotel.
§ The station was badly damaged in the Second World War and demolished in 1962.
¶ The square was given this name in 1814 after the overthrow of Napoleon.
** The Brandenburger Tor dates from the 1790s, a major gate in Berlin's city walls that were removed in the 1860s as Berlin expanded.
†† Literally 'Animal/Beast Garden', a huge, semi-wild public park that had served as a hunting ground for the Prussian royal family in the sixteenth century.

1. In 1870, at the height of his power and influence Bethel Henry Strousberg was portrayed with his family and pets by the artist Ludwig Knaus.

of the street boasted long gardens backing on to the Tiergarten to the west, the site had no garden to speak of. Strousberg was far more interested in the house itself. Again, he employed August Orth as his architect, demanding a building in a rich, historical and flamboyant style that was typical of the new buildings funded by the new moneyed classes that were going up in Berlin at the time (and which were for many of those with older money the object of ridicule and disdain). Building began in 1867 and was completed the following year. It cost Strousberg a total of 900,000 marks.[3]*

The house had two principal storeys plus an attic floor and a half-sunken basement. Classically inspired, it featured a central two-storeyed shallow portico supported by four sandstone columns with Corinthian capitals. Above the portico was a pediment with a large sculpted frieze depicting five classical statues including a central winged figure in the centre and a female figure with a caduceus, an ancient symbol of commerce. It was not a particularly restrained message to passers-by, but then Strousberg had never been known for his subtlety: far from looking like a family villa, the Palais Strousberg made the kind of urban statement normally associated with public and political buildings, museums, theatres, opera houses and banks. Grand, luxurious and fitted with ultra-modern technology, it strove to demonstrate that Strousberg had 'arrived'.

---

* Roughly £45,000 at the time. The house's interior appearance in Strousberg's time is described at the end of this Chapter.

By the end of 1869, Strousberg's mansion was ready for his family to move into. Flatteringly, he was able to welcome to his new home no less a figure than Otto von Bismarck, then Minister-President of the Kingdom of Prussia, while the cultured Crown Prince Friedrich and Crown Princess Victoria came to inspect his art collection. According to one account, the railway entrepreneur even opened the house to the public once a week, 'when admiring crowds walked through its interior, casting envious eyes on the rich English carpets and other magnificent adornments.'[4] It was the height of Strousberg's career, and during his silver wedding celebrations the *Berliner Börsen-Zeitung* commented that his acclaim was 'clear recognition from the widest possible circles of the man's enormous importance', 'evidence of the extent to which trade and industry are in this day and age able to elevate those who take the lead in these areas with intelligence and willpower'.[5] It was not to last.

***

'Strousberg is undoubtedly the greatest man in Germany. The chap will be the German Kaiser next. … His guiding principle is to swindle investors, while acting fairly towards suppliers and other industrialists,' Friedrich Engels remarked to Karl Marx in 1869.[6] Indeed, Strousberg's success was based on business methods that operated on the edge of legality and financial probity, and his complicated and interlinked method of financing backed up by small investors came under heavy criticism. Often operating simultaneously, his various schemes involved financing projects before receiving payment, rendering him dangerously vulnerable to cash-flow problems. Mirroring what had happened during the 'railway bubble' in Great Britain in the 1840s, speculation on railway shares dominated the German stock markets in the 1860s as the aristocracy (even Bismarck) and thousands of more lowly investors all clamoured for their share of the spoils.

In 1868 Strousberg had chosen to involve himself in building a new railway system in Romania. It was a venture for which he put together a consortium of investors that included several prominent Prussian aristocrats, but ran into logistical and financial problems that became so serious as to endanger the German economy itself. The project had numerous expensive unforeseen logistical problems, and, with the Romanian Government threatening to default on its own payments, Strousberg suddenly found himself in deep financial trouble. Using some of the money earmarked for the Romanian project to shore up some of his other ventures, his business problems multiplied when railways were commandeered for military purposes during the Franco-Prussian War of 1870–71. It was an ironic twist, as railways were to be crucial in contributing to Prussia's victory against France and therefore its future prosperity and success.

Forced to ask Bismarck for an enormous state loan, in early 1871 Strousberg defaulted on the interest on his Romanian ventures. As share values plummeted, some of the industrialist's more influential shareholders asked Bismarck for government assistance. In the latter part of that year Bismarck appointed two prominent bankers – Adolf von Hansemann and his own personal banker and close associate Gerson von Bleichröder – to manage the crisis in a series of initiatives that would not be settled until the end of the decade.[7] Intimately connected with the

Rothschild banking dynasty, the influential Bleichröder had himself been involved in railway promotion in Germany and had brokered France's huge reparation payments to Prussia after her defeat in the Franco-Prussian War. By the early 1870s Bleichröder's riches dwarfed even Strousberg's: by far the richest man in Berlin, he owned a huge palatial townhouse on Behrenstrasse, the city's banking street.

Strousberg's financial house of cards was now collapsing. On 7 February 1873, in the lower house of the Prussian Parliament the liberal politician Eduard Lasker denounced the 'Strousberg system', the unregulated *laissez-faire* system of awarding railway concessions and building railways that was leading to economic turmoil,[8] 'the cause of the deepest demoralization and corruption all over the country.'[9] It caused a national sensation. That May, the Austrian stock market crashed, to be followed on 28 October by no fewer than twenty-eight Prussian banks and the entire Berlin Stock Exchange. Their savings and investments suddenly worthless, many were ruined, shareholders now liable for the losses of the companies in which they had invested. By early 1874, sixty-one banks, one hundred and sixteen industrial enterprises and four railway companies were bankrupt, thousands of workers in Strousberg's various industrial concerns had lost their jobs, and many of his personal creditors had lost their investments. The *Gründerkrach*[*] followed the *Gründerzeit*[†] that had in part been fuelled by France's huge reparation payments and heralded a long-term industrial and agricultural depression.

Not for the last time in Germany, one of the by-products of this economic crash was an outpouring of vitriolic anti-Semitism, Jewish bankers and industrialists first in the line of fire as scapegoats. Despite his earlier conversion to Christianity, Strousberg was counted amongst them, 'the Semite' who had 'filled the Augean Stable with rubbish and depravity.'[10] As creditors within his complicated network of businesses angrily demanded payment, Strousberg now decided to accept a huge loan from the newly established Commercial Loan Bank in Moscow. It was a fatal decision, for the bank – which had, suspiciously, approached Strousberg to make the offer – was a sham, its directors falsifying accounts to stay in business.

In October 1875 Strousberg accepted an invitation to go to Russia to put his affairs with the Commercial Loan Bank in order; an opportunity, he hoped, also to increase the size of his loan. This already stood at a massive seven million roubles, encouraging the Russian Government to investigate: on 14 October 1875 Strousberg was on his way to St Petersburg from Moscow when, once again, he was detained to help the authorities with their enquiries. The Commercial Loan Bank was sealed and ceased trading, its directors arrested and charged with making reckless loans to Strousberg without proper financial security and with publishing false accounts to cover risky transactions. Strousberg followed the bank's directors into custody and was faced with bankruptcy proceedings. By now he owed the staggering sum of some seventy-four million marks[‡] to unsecured creditors and, as of 19 October 1875, was declared bankrupt in Berlin and in Prague.

Strousberg spent a year in imprisonment in Moscow, passing the time by writing his best-selling financial apologia *Dr. Strousberg und sein Wirken*, published in

---

[*] 'Founders' Crash'.
[†] 'Founders' Age', the economic conditions that had helped create the creation of a unified Germany.
[‡] Very approximately £4,000,000 at the time.

Berlin in 1876. Blaming Lasker's speech in the Prussian Parliament as the *coup de grâce* that had financially finished him off, he accused the politician in no uncertain terms: 'The attack you made on me in parliament has wounded my honour, sacrificed me to contempt and scorn, embittered my life and ruined my family. And by bringing about material damages, it has indirectly led to my current misfortune.'[11] At his trial in Moscow in October that year Strousberg was found guilty of damaging the Commercial Loan Bank by obtaining seven million roubles from them without sufficient security, as well as offering bribes. Ordered to be deported from Russia, for bureaucratic reasons Strousberg was forced to remain in detention until Chancellor Bismarck himself intervened in the affair. But, at least on a public basis, the railway king showed little remorse, stating in his memoirs that 'My calculations may have been false, but they were made with the best intentions and in all good faith,'[12] and certainly on the basis of the evidence presented and of his memoirs many were to come to the conclusion even at the time that he was not, in fact, the 'vulgar swindler he has been often called.'[13]

Strousberg's numerous businesses and possessions were sold to attempt to settle at least some of his massive debts and pay something to his creditors. For a man who had risen so high from unpromising beginnings, this aspect of his fall must have very difficult to bear, particularly as, stuck 1,800 kilometres from Berlin in detention in Moscow, he was powerless to prevent it. In 1873 he had already had to sell his Palais Strousberg art collection, described as 'not only the most extensive of all the private art collections in Berlin, but also, in terms of its intrinsic value, by far the most important', originating from 'the modern schools of painting in Germany, France and Belgium.'[14]§ Strousberg's next humiliation was the public sale of his grand coach and four black horses (a gift from the Prince of Romania), on site in the covered yard of the Palais Strousberg, while his treasured libraries from 70 Wilhelmstrasse and the Schloss Zbirow were auctioned off in June 1876 and May 1882. One of the jewels in Strousberg's crown was of course 70 Wilhelmstrasse itself, and parties interested in purchasing it were rumoured to include members of the Prussian royal family, testament to the grandeur, luxury and convenient location of the building. On 2 March 1876 Bleichröder brokered a deal for its sale for 900,000 marks[15] (considerably above its estimate of 600,000 marks).[16]

As part of his efforts to sort out the fiasco of the Romanian railway finances on behalf of the German Government, Bleichröder had to extricate several prominent Prussian aristocrats from the financial holes into which they had dug themselves with their investments in Strousberg's ventures. Amongst them were the Duke of Ujest¶ and the Duke of Ratibor,** who became the successful 'purchasers' of 70 Wilhelmstrasse. Bleichröder had already lent them a considerable amount of money against the somewhat unreliable security of Strousberg's Romanian railway shares, and it is conceivable that Strousberg's Berlin house was in fact purchased

§ An example of the paintings in Strousberg's art collection was *Weekday in Paris* (1869) by Adolph Menzel, purchased from the collection by the banker Adolf von Liebermann and since 1935 in the Kunstmuseum, Düsseldorf (4433). Strousberg also commissioned art: in 1870 he, his wife and seven children were portrayed by the fashionable artists Ludwig Knaus and Gustav Graef. With money in racehorses, Strousberg was also portrayed on horseback by Carl Steffeck.
¶ Now Ujazd in Poland.
** Now Racibórz in Poland.

by Bleichröder himself, in order to be given to the dukes as a disposable asset which they could sell on at a later stage and/or from which a substantial rental income could be made.

Chancellor Bismarck's later account of Bleichröder's part in all the Strousberg affair's 'bloodletting … on German capital'[17] seems (typically) cynical and patronising, given that the banker counted on Bismarck as a friend:

> Our greatest lords and our bootblacks believed that Strousberg would present them with a gold mine, and a great many risked the best part of what they possessed, believing the promises of this adventurer. All that is buried now in the Rumanian mud and, one fine day, two dukes, one general who is an aide-de-camp, a half-dozen ladies-in-waiting, twice that many chamberlains, a hundred coffee-house owners and all the cabmen of Berlin found themselves totally ruined. The Emperor took pity on the dukes, the aide-de-camp, the ladies-in-waiting, and the chamberlains, and charged me with pulling them out of the trouble. I appealed to Bleichröder who, on condition of getting a title of nobility, which as a Jew he valued, agreed to rescue the Duke of Ratibor, the Duke of Ujest, and General Count Lehndorf; two dukes and an aide-de-camp saved – frankly, that is worth the 'von' bestowed on the good Bleichröder. But the ladies-in-waiting, the cabmen and the others were left drowning....[18]

Loyally, the Dukes of Ujest and Ratibor (and/or Bleichröder) did much to support Strousberg's family during his period of imprisonment in Moscow. The bankrupt industrialist finally crossed the border back into Germany on 12 September 1877. Two of Strousberg's sons had married daughters of his former associates British railway entrepreneurs Joseph Bray and George Barclay Bruce, and his family stood by him. One of his sons was even able to buy back one of Strousberg's auctioned-off businesses, and, in a small way, Strousberg returned to publishing. In his memoirs he insisted that 'The loss of my resources, indeed of every vestige of my property, affects me but little,'[19] but its effect on his nearest and dearest may well have been greater: his wife Mary Ann died in September 1882 aged only fifty-three, following a severe stroke.

Strousberg had triumphed over adversity in his earlier days, but now luck finally deserted him. Having experienced the extremes of near-poverty, forced labour and imprisonment as well as immense influence, wealth and luxury, Strousberg's life ended in his sixty-first year on 31 May 1884 in frugal circumstances in a residential hotel in Taubenstrasse in Berlin, after a heart attack. August Orth attended his former client's modest funeral at the Matthiaskirche in Schöneberg, Berlin, on 4 June. Bismarck's final opinions on Strousberg were clear: 'he was a man of extraordinary energy and fertility of mental resources; and had his moral and intellectual faculties been anything like equally balanced, his life's tale would doubtless have been very different.'[20]

Strousberg's Palace in Berlin

The Berlin press were fascinated with the Palais Strousberg and its technology, and based on their accounts and other sources it is possible to describe the interior appearance of 70 Wilhelmstrasse in Strousberg's day. The building featured the latest technology, including gas lighting (with moveable shades in some of the reception rooms) and central heating throughout. Steam power was used to produce hot water for the kitchens, scullery, laundry and bathrooms.

The building's imposing two-storey entrance/staircase hall, lit by a skylight, featured a tinkling fountain in the middle. The deep-red carpet and upholstery made a dramatic contrast with the classical columns and dramatic horseshoe-shaped staircase all made from white scagliola, white marble and biscuit porcelain. Upstairs, on the first-floor landing, opposite the front doorway, was the entrance to the master bedroom.

On the ground floor to the left there was a sequence of ornate reception rooms with tall ceilings, beginning with a large drawing room, its windows looking out on to the street. This led to a music room, square in shape with an apse in each of the four corners, a painted frieze by Friedrich Schaller above and lit by a skylight. A removable wooden wall to the right could be folded away into an internal light well providing a small stage for musicians or other performances, allowing the room also to operate as a ballroom, concert hall or theatre. This was followed by a circular drawing room, again with apses in the corners, followed by a 'winter garden' overlooking a rear courtyard with a central fountain. Beyond the winter garden, at the rear of the house, was a raised terrace overlooking the courtyard and part of the rear garden of the Palais Redern on the corner of Unter den Linden.

Retracing one's steps to the circular drawing room, to the left was a huge, lofty dining room decked out with heavy neo-Renaissance furniture and silverware and with two semi-circular apses to the east and west, the latter projecting into the rear courtyard. Further on to the right was a billiard room and to the left, a picture gallery. While many of the rooms were hung with paintings, the picture gallery

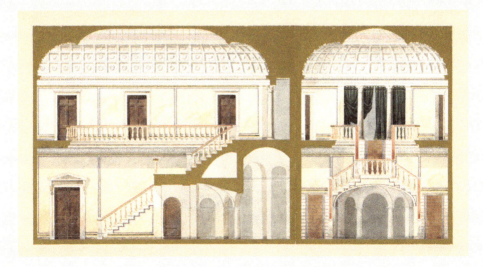

2. A cross-section of the staircase hall of the Palais Strousberg by August Orth (1876).

itself was spectacular, displaying some two hundred works from Strousberg's collection of contemporary French and German art.

Visitors wishing to see the railway king in his business capacity turned right from the entrance hall into a waiting room decorated with hunting trophies and weapons. Beyond was Strousberg's office looking out on to Wilhelmstrasse, with green walls and a large desk and bookcase, a large brownish red marble fireplace on the right, the mantelpiece covered in family photographs. A door to the left of the fireplace led to another of the building's highlights: a galleried library containing over 3,000 volumes, the bookshelves made from walnut, the room featuring a ceiling painting by Wilhelm Peters and lit by a skylight. To the right of the fireplace a door led to a bedroom, the railway king's bolthole away from his wife and family upstairs. Behind the four-poster bed was a safe, the inner sanctum of Strousberg's business empire and big enough to 'hold the shares in all of the railways in the Strousberg empire and a multitude of securities[21]'.

On the first floor was a breathtakingly massive master bedroom, its size and shape corresponding to the dining room below. Here the main colour of the walls and upholstery was green, with the beds hidden away in curtained-off niches with separate dressing rooms. The house was fitted with deluxe modern conveniences, the *pièce de résistance* being an elaborate and luxurious bathroom with hot and cold running water, the walls decorated with imitation Pompeian red frescoes, and a marble floor. Half the room was taken up with a huge sunken bath with a shower bath next to it, and even a separate bath and sauna (running water and water closets were truly luxurious features for Germany at the time). There were five guest rooms and bedrooms for Strousberg's large family, as well as a schoolroom, playroom and accommodation for the children's nanny and governess.

Some of the servants' bedrooms were on the attic floor, but their daily working area was the half-sunken large cellar, where the kitchens, laundry, larders and more bedrooms were found, together with a large servants' hall immediately beneath the entrance/staircase hall, surrounded by other facilities. To the right (north) of the house, were stables and coach house for the all-important carriage and horses; a separate door directly on to Wilhelmstrasse led to a covered coachway that also served as the 'tradesman's entrance' with a further door leading to the 'backstairs' to all floors. On the cellar floor there was also a grotto, bowling lane and aquarium.

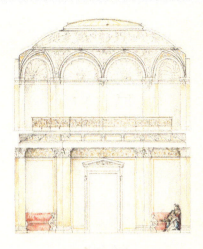

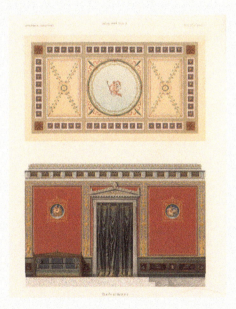

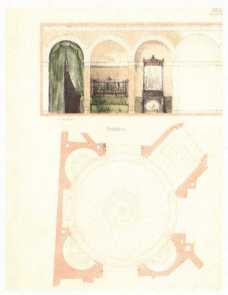

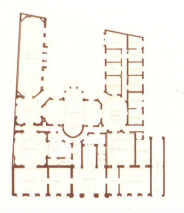

Clockwise from middle left: 3. Design for the ceiling and one of the walls in the main bathroom at the Palais Strousberg by August Orth (1869). 4. Cross-sections of the library and music room of the Palais Strousberg by August Orth (dated 12 February 1867); 5. A plan and cross-section of the 'boudoir' at the Palais Strousberg by August Orth (1876); 6. Ground floor plan of the Palais Strousberg by August Orth (1867) showing his planned subdivided front drawing room (bottom left), a feature that was incorporated only later in the history of the house.

CHAPTER 2
1871–1878: 'ONE OF THE FINEST MANSIONS IN BERLIN'

Broadly speaking our diplomatic missions abroad have three tasks: to negotiate with the foreign Government concerned; to explain Britain and British policy to the Government and people; and finally to interpret the country in which they live to the British Government.
Sir Ivone Kirkpatrick, *The Inner Circle* (1959), Chapter III

The social activitites of an envoy are also of importance. He is expected to maintain a style commensurate with the dignity of the country he represents. He is expected to entertain frequently, to give large official dinner-parties and balls and to invite officials, colleagues and men of business to constant informal meals. He is required to cultivate the intimacy of persons of eminence or influence in the country in which he resides; to display a lively interest in local industries, art, sport and letters; to visit the provinces and acquaint himself with industrial and agricultural conditions; and to keep in friendly contact with those of his countrymen who share his exile.
Harold Nicolson, *Diplomacy* (1939), Chapter VIII

'My visit to Berlin was quite successful – I took Loftus' Embassy and paid the first quarter in advance – bought what he left of his furniture for £1085 – got a few servants and came back here well pleased with what I had done.'[1]

Having been appointed British Ambassador to Berlin, Odo Russell arrived in the new capital of the unified Germany in September 1871, his main task in this first brief visit to secure a building where the British could operate an embassy.

For centuries British diplomatic representation had been dominated by a small group of very wealthy aristocratic families, generations of whom entered the profession and intermarried. Odo Russell was a prime example. His father, Major-General Lord William Russell, was the middle son of the 6th Duke of Bedford and brother of the 7th Duke. One of the richest families in England, the Russells' fortune dated back to the time of King Henry VIII and included the Bloomsbury Estates, large tracts of highly profitable land in London as well as Woburn Abbey in Bedfordshire, the imposing 'stately home' where Odo Russell was to be proud to entertain and impress visiting German VIPs. For generations this great Whig family had filled major roles at the centre of the British Establishment; the 4th Duke had served as the British Ambassador to Paris in 1762–63 and had negotiated the peace treaty that had ended the Seven Years War, while Odo's uncle Lord John Russell served as Prime Minister and Foreign Secretary.

7. Odo Russell photographed on 2 September 1864 by Camille Silvy, taken during the period Russell was the British Envoy to the Holy See in Rome.

Odo's mother, Elizabeth Ann Rawdon, was educated and highly intelligent. She married Lord William Russell in 1817 and Russell family pride and tradition were important to her. Writing to a friend, she explained the choice of her youngest son's unusual name: 'I took refuge in the middle ages & the family annals & found the first Norman adventurer of the Roussels who came over with the Conqueror was Odo de Roussel, so here is his name revived, good man, 800 years after an ungrateful forgetfulness of his posterity.'[2] Odo was born in January 1829 and was for the most part brought up abroad: his father served as Minister to Lisbon and Minister to Württemburg before becoming the British Minister to Berlin in 1835. He was proud of the work he accomplished there, boasting to Lord John Russell in December 1838 that 'My political position here is perfect. I doubt whether any English Minister ever stood so well at the Court of Berlin as I do. When I came here I had cruel uphill work to keep my ground. I am now at the top of the tree.'[3] But unfortunately for him, in an age when the Government's political colour had great influence over diplomatic appointments, when a Tory administration took power in 1841 Russell's achievements did not prevent him from being removed from his posting and replaced.

Many of Odo Russell's childhood memories from the 1830s were of the elegant neoclassical Berlin of Karl Friedrich Schinkel, as their French tutor took him and his two brothers Hastings and Arthur to museums, botanical gardens, private art collections and the famous Berlin porcelain factory.[4] Given their parental background and upbringing, it was hardly surprising that Odo and his brothers shared formidable linguistic talents, and, although he had been taught at home and never attended university, Odo's 'knowledge extended also to the literature of the four languages which he spoke with easy facility.'[5]* In 1849, at the age of twenty, he followed his father into the diplomatic service as an attaché at the British Embassy in Vienna. He slowly ascended the diplomatic ranks, gaining experience in London, Constantinople, Washington and Rome, all the while acquiring an

* While Odo's extensive exposure to Continental Europe in the formative years of his youth gave him an impressive understanding of European languages, it may also, paradoxically, have harmed his career. When in 1880 the Crown Princess mentioned him to her mother, Queen Victoria, as a possible successor to Earl Granville as Foreign Secretary, the Queen replied that 'No one can think more highly of Lord Odo than I do – but he has a good deal that is foreign in him' (Queen Victoria to the Crown Princess, 12 October 1880, *Beloved Mama: Private Correspondence of Queen Victoria and the German Crown Princess, 1878–1885* (ed. Roger Fulford, p. 90).

enviable reputation in the Foreign Office for the clarity and level-headedness of his dispatches.

Odo had a large head and suffered from 'liverishness' but, although describing himself unflatteringly (as well as inaccurately) as 'a middle-aged fat man of 40 wearing spectacles and having no money and no prospects'[6] in May 1868 he married Lady Emily Theresa Villiers, fourteen years his junior. One of Alexandra of Denmark's bridesmaids at her marriage to the Prince of Wales in 1863, Emily too came from an influential 'diplomatic' family: she was the daughter of the 4th Earl of Clarendon, Secretary of State for Foreign Affairs; her younger brother was to become Ambassador to Brussels, while her eldest sister married Lord Derby, Secretary of State for the Colonies and later Governor-General of Canada.

In November 1870 W. E. Gladstone, the Prime Minister, sent Odo to the German army headquarters at Versailles on a special diplomatic mission: to take part in discussions with Prussia's Minister-President Otto von Bismarck over Russia's refusal to continue to comply with certain articles of the 1856 Treaty of Paris that had ended the Crimean War. It was the beginning of a beneficial relationship that was to last for over a decade, for, despite Bismarck's powerful and irascible personality, Russell found himself able to build up a kind of special understanding and mutual respect[†] with him that no other diplomat was to enjoy. In January 1871 the negotiations resulted in a London conference on the neutrality of the Black Sea ports. Odo remained in Versailles, within earshot of the bombardment of Paris by the besieging Prussian army.

At this point the British Ambassador to the Prussian Court in Berlin was Lord Augustus Loftus, who had presented his credentials in February 1866. He too had a Berlin background, having entered the diplomatic service as Secretary to Odo's father thirty years before. He had however proved unpopular with the British royal family, especially Queen Victoria's daughter, the Prussian Crown Princess, who, at least at first, described him as 'personally disagreeable, pompous, indiscreet and very <u>forward</u>'[7] and, cuttingly, 'not gifted by Heaven with intellect.'[8] Nor did Bismarck take to him. In retrospect, and surely inspired by a need to defend himself against the powerful international figures arrayed against him at the time, Loftus claimed that it was he who had suggested there should be a change of British Ambassadors in 1871. Not unjustly, he reasoned that the advent of the German Empire called for a fresh political relationship with the new regime and that his responsibilities for the wellbeing of French prisoners of war in Prussia during the Franco-Prussian War had tainted him politically in Berlin. In any event the new regime gave a perfect excuse for the appointment of a new Ambassador, as all diplomatic representatives were required to re-present their credentials to the new German Emperor.[9] The important appointment went to Odo Russell.

Lord Lyons was later to remark to the Foreign Secretary Earl Granville that 'The Corps Diplomatique acquiesced in the appointment of [Russell] though it

---

† At one stage Russell 'went out on a limb' and called Bismarck's bluff by implying that Great Britain might go to war, a threat for which the British had little appetite and which he had no official permission to issue, but the bluff worked (Karina Urbach, *Bismarck's Favourite Englishman: Lord Odo Russell's Mission to Berlin*, pp. 61–2).

was over the heads of many of his seniors because of his personal qualities and of his successful experience in the United States, Rome, and the Foreign Office.'[10] Russell himself believed that he had been promoted over the heads of no fewer than thirty-two senior diplomats.[11] For him, it was a (perhaps childhood) dream come true, a posting for which he had longed for many years, a fact which his wife Emily was very aware of. 'It is curious, isn't it, that he should be going to grapple with Bismarck which is what he said he wished to do beyond everything – and this before he is Ambassador in Berlin', she had presciently remarked in 1870 when Gladstone had sent him to Versailles.[12]

Russell arrived in Berlin officially to start his ambassadorship on 16 February 1872 and presented his credentials to the new German Emperor that April.

***

The 'embassy' (or 'legation', if the post concerned did not have full ambassadorial status) was at this stage any suitable building where the ambassador or minister (in the case of a legation) could operate in the host country's capital – or wherever a host country's government was located. Traditionally, ambassadors had to set up the embassy building and household (including servants and transport) using a lump sum provided by the British Government for this purpose, usually requiring anything above and beyond this to be met from the ambassador's own means. When his appointment came to an end, an ambassador had to pack everything up again, sometimes, but not always, passing on the building, furniture and archives etc. to his successor to take over on his departure. Subordinate to the ambassador was appointed a secretary who acted as deputy in his absence and various attachés. Often living and dining with the ambassador and his family, attachés were young men expected to pay their own way. The diplomatic service was unsurprisingly therefore inevitably staffed by those who had access to private means, as Odo described to his brother:

> Dips must live with the richest in the land – every attaché expects a mission in a few years – he enters Diplomacy – travels to his post … he has already anticipated on his first quarter – journey, furniture, linen – he is not paid. After 2 years he is transferred – sale at a loss or carriage of furniture to the new post, journey, outfit, leave to go home to see his family – two journeys – The uncertainty of expenses in diplomacy is fatal to the steadiest attaché.[13]

His comments echo those of his diplomatic predecessors in the Russell family. Sent to France to negotiate the 1763 Treaty of Paris, the 4th Duke of Bedford found that what was expected of him was a drain even on his wealth, describing the posting as 'this ruinous embassy.'[14] (The job did, however, have its compensations: on their departure from Paris King Louis XV presented the Duke and Duchess with a stunning 183-piece Sèvres dinner service that remains one of the highlights of a visit to Woburn Abbey.) Several decades later the observations made by Odo's diplomat father about the demands that his representational duties made upon his means were scathing: 'I gave dinners, concerts, &c., in short bored & ruined myself pro bono publico & then learnt that I was abused for stinginess by some, for ostentation by others, for a fool by all.'[15]

Changes were, however, afoot: the diplomatic service very gradually became more professionalised, entrance examinations were established and successful attachés were given some official financial remuneration. Separate funds began to be granted for running the political, or chancery, element of the embassy's work, rather than these costs being met from one lump sum supplemented by an ambassador's own means. In 1861 the Milnes Commission introduced a ranking system amongst the attachés of First, Second and Third Secretaries. Only gradually did the percentage of noblemen in the service decline, however, as did the duration of individual ambassadorial postings, a state of affairs that was to change only in the early twentieth century.*

In 1870 the British Government actually owned only two buildings operating as embassies on a permanent basis – an imposing purpose-built one at Constantinople (1808; rebuilt in the late 1840s after a fire), and Paris, a magnificent eighteenth-century town house on the rue du Faubourg Saint-Honoré purchased by the 1st Duke of Wellington from the Bonaparte family in 1814. Although Berlin was raised in status from a legation to an embassy in 1862, it did not have a permanent building in the city. In keeping with a general aversion on the part of HM Treasury towards spending large amounts of money on buildings abroad, it was considered preferable to rent (rather than purchase) a house or apartment, and, to ensure maximum value for money, preferable that any rent should be negotiated on a long lease basis. While Odo's father Lord William Russell's Embassy in Berlin had been located at 21 Unter den Linden, the Embassy Russell had secured in the city from his predecessor Loftus was an apartment in a large mid-century house on the corner of Leipzigerstrasse and Leipziger Platz. This prime site was a short way to the east of the busy Potsdamer Platz, and was later to become the site of Wertheim's huge department store. The apartment was rented from Count Arnim, the German Ambassador to Paris and later to Constantinople, the British sharing the building with the Turkish representative to the Court of Prussia.

One recurring theme in the history of British diplomatic buildings is the plaintive cry of an ambassador back to London that not enough heed is being taken to secure embassy and residence accommodation commensurate with the ambassador's own local judgement of the importance of Great Britain's standing in the eyes of the country to which he is posted. In contrast, the most important issue for the Treasury back in London has always been the financial costs of such missions in the light of their perceived (immediate, rather than long-term) practical value to HM Government. Concerned to save money and spend it frugally, the Treasury has always struggled with a Foreign Office anxious to prove the necessity of such expenditure to help promote Great Britain's standing overseas.

The British Government's traditional parsimony abroad extended even to the amount of money Odo Russell spent in his representational work. Like his father, he was expected to foot the bill himself for much of these duties – parties, luncheons, dinners, etc., where less formal, but equally important 'soft' diplomacy could take place. As a member of one of Britain's richest families he had the financial means to do so, but only via his eldest brother Hastings, who became 9th Duke of Bedford two months after Odo's arrival in Berlin in 1872. His brother's help in this regard

---

* Most diplomatic postings nowadays last three to five years, depending on circumstances.

was to prove essential for Russell in Berlin: Odo and Emily informed Lord Derby that they could not 'do the necessary cost of receptions etc. at Berlin on the salary allowed, and had last year to draw £5,000 from the Duke of Bedford to meet their expenses.'[16] Following the formal presentation of his credentials Russell hosted two unavoidable diplomatic *entrée* receptions in Berlin on 5 and 6 April 1872 and duly submitted[17] two large bills to the Foreign Office to cover his expenditure. The Foreign Office rejected most of their content on the basis of the amounts claimed when compared to Russell's colleagues in other posts. But the Office had failed to take into account his local obligations to what was a new imperial regime or the fact that the unusually large number of diplomatic representatives in Berlin (from the various German principalities) required a proportionate increase in diplomatic entertaining duties and expenses. To add to his costs, in 1878 Russell reported that he had spent £3,935.16s.5d. on 'state carriages, horses, liveries, uniforms, &c', as these things were 'an indispensable portion of diplomatic representation.'[18]

The penny-pinching attitude extended to staff allowances. A few months after his arrival in Berlin Russell suffered a recurrence of one of his perennial medical complaints. Writing to the Foreign Secretary on 2 July 1872 he reported that 'a very severe cold in my lungs and liver has so far interfered with my general health' and that he needed to take the 'cure' in the spa town of Karlsbad* for a few weeks, leaving the Second Secretary Plunkett as Chargé d'Affaires during his absence.[19] Although his position as Chargé was officially recognised by London, it was made clear to Lord Odo† that Plunkett would be granted an allowance of £1 per day for the additional responsibilities, an amount Russell evidently did not regard as sufficient. 'I should not be doing my duty if I hesitated to state that your Lordship's innovation will cause surprise and disappointment among the rising members of the Profession', he informed Granville.[20] Nevertheless, Russell introduced Plunkett as Chargé d'Affaires to the President of the Imperial Chancery and he was duly delivered of 'the Archives, Cyphers and Plate of Her Majesty's Embassy'[21] repeating the ceremony in which the Ambassador himself had taken part earlier that year.

***

It was at the Embassy on Leipzigerstrasse that Arthur Nicolson arrived in February 1874 in the junior post of Third Secretary to work with Russell and his colleagues. Shortly afterwards the British Ambassador took his shy new young member of staff to his first court ball and pointed out a small group of men standing together. They were the Emperor Wilhelm I, Minister of War Albrecht von Roon, Field Marshal Helmuth von Moltke, and Otto von Bismarck. Imparting his lifelong enthusiasm as a diplomat for the history taking place around him, Russell told Nicolson 'There you can observe the makers of modern Germany.'[22] Not all of it was, however, quite so exhilarating: amidst fears of a renewed war between Germany and France Nicolson was kept very busy on the routine work of the time deciphering telegrams

---

* Now Karlovy Vary in the Czech Republic.
† Queen Victoria granted Odo the courtesy title of 'Lord Odo Russell' after his elder brother Hastings became Duke of Bedford not long after Odo's arrival in Berlin.

and, in the pre-typewriter age, undertaking some of the more tedious of a junior diplomat's duties, no matter what promise he might show: laboriously copying despatches by hand.‡

The greatest of Odo Russell's four 'makers of modern Germany' was Otto von Bismarck. Having risen through the ranks of the Prussian Landtag and its diplomatic service, in 1862 Bismarck became Prussia's Minister-President; his speech to the Landtag in September of that year was prophetic when, referring to the future of the German kingdom, he declared that 'The great questions of the day will not be settled by speeches and majority decisions … but by blood and iron.' Three wars against common enemies, culminating in the Franco-Prussian War of 1870–71, resulted in the unification of the formerly disparate German states. The German Imperial Constitution of 16 April 1871 to all intents and purposes established a confederation of sovereign principalities working together in a German Empire, with Prussia, the dominant power both in terms of land mass and population, effectively at its head, a development that overturned the balance of European powers that had been in place for the previous six decades. While the Prussian Head of State (and therefore, effectively, of Germany) was the Hohenzollern King, now German Emperor (or Kaiser§) Wilhelm I, day-to-day government responsibility really lay in the hands of Chancellor Otto von Bismarck. The Emperor's main residence was in the nearby military town of Potsdam, but much imperial ceremonial took place at the Royal Schloss, or Palace, located in Berlin, at the eastern end of Unter den Linden.¶

8. 'One of the makers of modern Germany': Otto von Bismarck photographed by Numa Blanc for an 1860s/1870s *carte de visite*.

This was a new and exciting world of German and international politics, with a new, booming capital fed by massive war reparation payments from France and (thanks to Strousberg and his fellow entrepreneurs) fast becoming an extremely

‡ Attachés and secretaries wrote letters and despatches by hand, signed by the sender. Sometimes particularly long despatches were written by several different hands. The ability to write legibly was for obvious reasons an important asset in the diplomatic service, and one for which subsequent readers of these documents have to be particularly grateful.
§ For the sake of consistency, the term 'Emperor' will be used in this book rather than *Kaiser*.
¶ This building was badly damaged in the Second World War and demolished by the East German Government in 1950. In the 1970s part of the area the Palace had occupied was taken up by the vast and unappealing Palast der Republik, which was in 2006–8 itself demolished, leaving the huge site empty. Following considerable public debate as to the future of this highly symbolic site at the centre of Berlin, a replica of the exterior of the old *Schloss* is being built, housing a multi-purpose interior.

powerful industrial city. The new Imperial German Government regarded it important for Great Britain to conduct its diplomatic business in a building of a size and dignity proportionate not only with its status as the colonial and industrial superpower of the era but one which also reflected Germany's new international status and its royal and imperial dynastic ties with Great Britain. In reality however it seemed to the Germans that the British appeared to take little interest in German affairs, traditionally placing Paris higher than Berlin in their international diplomatic rankings. In the years immediately following Germany's sound defeat of its Continental rival in the Franco-Prussian War, the Germans took this as a slight to their prestige, as Odo Russell explained in 1874:

> …since Berlin has become the Capital and great centre of activity of all the leading men from the twenty-seven states composing Germany, and since Germany has become a great and powerful Empire of which the Princess Royal of Great Britain will be the future Empress, the British Embassy has also naturally increased in importance, and the result is that surprise – not to say envy – is keenly felt and constantly expressed by those leading Statesmen of Germany that it should be looked upon, and actually be inferior in rank to the British Embassy in Paris, because they fail to understand why Her Majesty's Government give France a higher rank than Germany among European Nations.[23]

In contrast, the Germans placed the British higher than the French.

For the British Embassy to occupy an apartment in a building in a shopping street, rented from Count Arnim and shared with the Turks, was simply not good enough. '[N]othing lay dearer to [Russell's] heart than the desire to promote a better and friendlier understanding between the two nations,'[24] and mindful of the German administration's dim view of Britain's diplomatic accommodation in Berlin, Russell began to battle with the British Government to secure a more commodious and suitable embassy. 'You cannot be expected to ruin yourself for public appearance and if the Treasury will not lodge you suitably, no reproach can be attached to you for being inadequately lodged,' Edmund Hammond, the Permanent Under-Secretary for Foreign Affairs, had tried to reassure Russell,[25] who from early on in his ambassadorship voiced his frustrations about the apartment he had taken on from Loftus.

'The Emperor, the Crown Prince, and many of the leading Statesmen and Members of Parliament often ask why England does not own an Embassy House in Berlin', Russell told the Foreign Secretary in February 1873.[26] It was a theme to which he returned again and again the following year, describing the British Government's Embassy as based in a 'lodging house' in correspondence with the new Foreign Secretary: 'to the often expressed surprize of the Imperial Family, who wish the British Embassy in the Capital of Germany, as a family Embassy, not to work below other English Embassies abroad or foreign Embassies at Berlin. I have endeavoured to overcome this impression by representing on a larger scale than was the case before the establishment of the Empire', he added, while taking the opportunity to remind Lord Derby that, at the same time, 'there is of course a limit to my private means which I cannot overstep…'[27]

At this period houses for British embassies and legations usually had to be of sufficient size to accommodate not only the business functions of an embassy, but also rooms suitable for entertaining guests from the host country and accommodation for the ambassador (or minister), his family and servants.[28] Finding such a house in the booming new capital of Germany, where property prices and rents were rising so fast, was no easy task. But, as Russell pointed out to the Foreign Office in London, the issue had to be faced and a decision had to be taken. And there was a deadline to consider: repeatedly he reminded the Foreign Secretary that the lease of the property from Count Armin was due to terminate on 1 October 1876 and that the conversations he had on the subject with his landlord and his co-tenant the Turkish representative were not promising. Armin was intending either to cash in by selling his house or by vastly increasing the rent: Leipzigerstrasse was fast becoming the most important commercial centre in Berlin and as such bankers and financial companies were anxious to acquire the building and its garden for speculative building ventures.[29] In January 1873 Arnim had told the British he was prepared to sell his house to them at 500,000 thalers* (£75,000 at the time),[30] a price which he raised three months later to 750,000 thalers (£112,500).[31]

Over the course of 1873 and 1874 Russell received several offers from individuals to sell houses and/or land for a new embassy, but the Treasury's response did not waiver. '[T]he Lords Commissioners of Her Majesty's Treasury are not disposed to purchase an Embassy House in Berlin, that Their Lordships would only be induced to do so, if they could save annual expenditure thereby, and that they think it probable that prices at Berlin are at the present moment exceptionally inflated.'[32] One potential vendor, Simon Cohn, became so frustrated at the Government's failure to accept what he considered a generous offer to sell his house to the British that he called on Russell and huffily told him that 'he intended to renew his offer direct to Mr. Gladstone with whom he felt it would be easier to treat than with Her Majesty's Embassy.'[33] Russell agreed with London that house prices were high in Berlin, but they were hardly likely to decrease, even considering the financial crisis that was by now engulfing the country. In late 1873 the Treasury informed Russell that the equivalent of £45,000 was the maximum they could envisage in purchasing a property. Russell's response was withering. Minor powers such as the Grand Duchy of Baden were purchasing embassy buildings, while 'The decision of Their Lordships summarily to reject any renewed proposal to negotiate upon a basis of more than £45,000 will, I fear, be the cause of inconvenience to my successors, – to Her Majesty's Government, – and to the Public Service, and of expense to the Country in future.'[34]

On 5 October 1874 the British Embassy relayed breaking news to the Foreign Office in London: their landlord had been arrested and thrown in prison, on charges relating to documents that had mysteriously gone missing from the German Embassy in Paris. Arnim's independent and colourful behaviour as German Ambassador to France had set him at odds with Bismarck, who saw him as a political rival; although later released on bail, following several trials and facing personal ruin, Arnim went into exile abroad. Understandably, he wished to settle

---

* Before German unification, each German state operated its own separate currency, the most common being the thaler, which remained official currency in Germany until 1908, existing concurrently with the German mark, established as the single German currency; at this period one thaler approximated to roughly three marks.

the issue of the purchase of his house, and once more he offered it to the British Government in its entirety for the equivalent of £90,000. The Treasury refused.[35]

Time was running out. In March 1875 the Lords of the Treasury recommended that a representative from the Board of Works visit Berlin in order to provide an objective report on the advisability of either continuing to rent or of purchasing a new site on which to build. Accordingly, consultant surveyor Charles Stephenson visited the city that spring.[36] In the meantime Russell was instructed to approach Arnim yet again to discover whether he might relent and extend the lease. On 30 April Arnim agreed – at a cost of £3,600 per annum, a sum which the Treasury urged Russell to negotiate for the usual ten years. That fell through when Arnim refused to lower the price or rent out the entire house.[37] But now Russell urged the rent of another house, bringing to the Foreign Secretary's attention a property that Stephenson had inspected and which he had heard was to be let out. Russell had also seen it and 'thought it without exception the house best suited for Her Majesty's Embassy in every respect I had yet seen in Berlin,'[38] valuing it at £75,000.[39] It was Strousberg's palatial residence on Wilhelmstrasse.

Strousberg had actually already offered to sell the house to Russell at a sum of 600,000 thalers (£90,000)[40] as early as April 1872, but Russell had felt bound to refuse the offer, 'since I felt quite sure that the Chancellor of the Exchequer could not recommend the purchase of an Embassy House upon such terms to the House of Commons.'[41] The new owners, the Dukes of Ujest and Ratibor, were willing to sell the property for about £60,000 (400,000 thalers). Russell's endeavours to secure a lease evidently proved troublesome, however, and were apparently resolved only with the help of the Emperor himself. 'His Majesty has given many proofs of real personal interest in Her Majesty's Embassy, and the representation of Great Britain at Berlin; and on hearing of the difficulties which stood in the way of securing so good a house as No 70 Wilhelmstrasse, His Majesty was graciously pleased to speak in our favour and the settlement was at once effected.' The owners agreed to make necessary alterations and improvements, together with a ten-year lease.[42]

'It has been a long troublesome and anxious affair,' Russell wrote to his friend the Chief Clerk of the Foreign Office on 3 June. '… I have paid off the rent of this apartment and hope to leave it this quarter, as the lease of the new House begins on the 1st of July, instead of on the 1st of October to which I hope you won't object, otherwise I shall have to pay it out of my pocket!'[43] At the time Strousberg himself was of course incarcerated in Moscow, but, given his extensive British connections, he might have felt that the occupation of his palatial former home in Berlin by the British Establishment for use as their representative base in his homeland represented a certain symmetry – or irony, in view of his British criminal record.

Russell made the decision that he and his family would occupy the entirety of the former Palais Strousberg rather than share the accommodation with the embassy staff and offices, so he paid 3,300 marks per annum rental for some rooms for use as offices in separate premises on the nearby Pariser Platz.[44] Moving into 70 Wilhelmstrasse, he and his wife Emily began to use its suite of ornate rooms for representational purposes.

***

9. The façade of 70 Wilhelmstrasse in a photograph taken in about 1870.

The first group of major diplomatic events that were to prove the representational worth of the house and certainly test the mettle of the Embassy's domestic staff were those associated with the Congress of Berlin, hosted by Bismarck to settle international interests in the Balkans following the recent Russo–Turkish War. That this major international conference was held in Berlin was testimony to the new German capital's growing diplomatic importance, the Congress's delegates featuring a cross-section of the most powerful representatives from Europe, Turkey and Russia. Chancellor Bismarck chaired the sessions, with Great Britain represented by the Prime Minister Lord Beaconsfield* and Foreign Secretary the Marquess of Salisbury, attended by a future Prime Minister, the young Arthur Balfour (acting as his uncle Lord Salisbury's private secretary). As Britain's diplomatic representative in Berlin, Russell's role was to play host to his distinguished British guests, smooth things over and act as a general intermediary during the discussions.

Beaconsfield left London for Berlin on 8 June 1878 on a leisurely trip by rail, arriving on the 11th. Russell had invited both the Prime Minister and Salisbury to stay in the Embassy; neither however accepted. Interspersing his visit to Berlin with short stays with the German imperial family in Potsdam, Beaconsfield instead lodged at the luxurious and first grand hotel in Berlin, the Kaiserhof, on Wilhelmplatz.† He was by this time an international celebrity, his novels bestsellers

---

* Benjamin Disraeli had been created the Earl of Beaconsfield in 1876.
† A town square on Wilhelmstrasse further to the south of the Embassy, on the eastern side of the street opposite the junction with Vossstrasse; following the changes to the area after the destruction of the Second World War, it no longer exists. The Kaiserhof Hotel lay at the south-east corner of the square, in front of the small Zeitenplatz. The hotel had been badly damaged by a major fire in October 1875 just days after its glamorous opening, and was subsequently quickly rebuilt.

10. One of the sessions of the Congress of Berlin as portrayed by *The Illustrated London News* on 22 June 1878. Odo Russell sits at the left-hand table.

with his literary admirers including Chancellor Bismarck himself. His reputation as a statesman was no less impressive: in November 1875 the German Ambassador to Great Britain, Count Münster, had described him in no uncertain terms as 'the greatest leader and parliamentary tactician in the history of England.'[45] But even Beaconsfield's lauded accomplishments had their limitations, and Russell's own diplomatic skills were soon needed to ensure the smooth running of the Congress (from the British point of view). The problem was that the Prime Minister spoke bad French, and with such a heavy English accent as to be barely understandable, if not downright comical.[46] Concerned that he might embarrass his country, the British delegates asked Russell for help. Early on in the proceedings, after an appeal from Beaconsfield's trusted private secretary, Montagu Corry, Russell managed to catch the Prime Minister just before he went to bed. Using flattery, Russell persuaded him to give his speeches in English instead, on the basis that the delegates from the other powers would naturally wish to appreciate his renowned skill as an orator in his native language. Beaconsfield acquiesced.[47]

The Congress was held in Bismarck's official residence, the former Radziwill Palace at 77 Wilhelmstrasse, a short walk from the Embassy. Officially opened on Thursday 13 June, the Congress's sessions were to continue until the signing of the Treaty of Berlin a month later on 13 July. The main talks took place in one of the largest rooms in the Palace, in which had been installed a large horseshoe-shaped table at which the 'plenipotentiaries' sat for discussions. But despite the international importance of the events and of the VIPs who attended the talks, the overall atmosphere in the capital was restrained: following Karl Nobiling's attempt on the Emperor's life on 2 June, Berlin was in a state of melancholic anticipation of Wilhelm's imminent death (which did not, in the event, come to pass). His son Friedrich acted as Regent, with court protocol preventing the imperial family from attending all but a few formal receptions. Additionally, the main Berlin Court winter 'season' was by this stage of the year long past. Nevertheless, there were a number of official and diplomatic receptions for the delegates and other VIPs, and each participating country gave its own party in their respective embassy or in hotels.

The Russells worked hard at their representational duties during the Congress, giving dinners and suppers for the principal delegates, welcoming 'diplomatic and fashionable society to the splendid halls of the British Embassy every Monday night.'[48] On 12 June Beaconsfield attended a dinner there, describing it as 'one of the finest mansions in Berlin'[49] and over the next few weeks he attended a gala banquet at the Royal Palace, dinners with the Emperor and his family and with the Bismarcks, and numerous banquets given by the French, Italians, Turks and Austrians. Much of what spare time he had was spent in Strousberg's former library in the Embassy.[50] In London, *The Graphic* magazine attempted to convey to its British readers something of the atmosphere of the diplomatic receptions in Berlin that summer:

> It is not all work and no play, even at the Berlin Congress, and although there is not so much waltzing as at a similar assemblage in Vienna in years gone by, there is no lack of receptions or dinners. At one time we hear of the Congress breaking up early because a certain Ambassador has a dinner, while on another day the sitting is curtailed because some of the Plenipotentiaries have been invited to the Crown Prince's table at 6 p.m. Scarcely an evening passes without some Ambassadorial reception taking place and in some cases as, for instance, at the British Embassy, an official 'evening' is given one evening a week. Our illustration represents the first of these receptions given by Lord and Lady Odo Russell, at which all the Plenipotentiaries, save Prince Bismarck and Prince Gortchakoff, were present. The scene in question was deprived of some of the brilliancy which usually attends such occasions, as, owing to the Court mourning*, the ladies' dresses were of sombre hue, although many of the guests were in uniform.[51]

'She is quite out and out the leader of fashion in Berlin – plays her part admirably'[52] was how Beaconsfield described his hostess, Lady Emily Russell, following an evening reception at the British Embassy on 24 June. His description of the nature and importance of diplomatic parties, based on his experiences that evening, remains as true today as it was then: 'It is absolutely necessary to go to these receptions, but the late hours try me. I begin to die at ten o'clock and should like to be buried before midnight. But, in a Congress, absence from any influential assembly of human beings is a mistake. So much more than the world imagines is

* King George of Hanover (1819-1878) had died on 12 June and had been buried in St George's Chapel, Windsor, on the 24th.

done by personal influence.'[53] Even so, the stresses and strains of the talks, the endless evening receptions and fine dining took their toll on the Prime Minister who was seventy-three and already suffering from ill health. Confined to bed for several days in early July by an attack of gout, he was in such a bad way that a doctor was summoned. Beaconsfield was, however, well enough to attend Bleichröder's magnificent banquet for the Congress delegates at his palatial home* five minutes away from the Embassy on 3 July. Amidst the gilded spendours[54] of his residence, the banker and the Prime Minister struck up a particular and lasting friendship.

Beaconsfield was again too indisposed to attend the final Congress banquet held on 13 July in the spectacular White Hall of the Royal Schloss. But the signing of the Treaty of Berlin was regarded as his personal triumph, achieving peace with Russia without war, and he was now hailed as a world statesman – certainly Bismarck regarded him as his equal at the negotiating table, in bluff and counter-bluff. On Friday 21 June Beaconsfield had been due to attend a large dinner at the Embassy when, while he was dressing in the Kaiserhof Hotel, the German Chancellor called on him and, highly unusually, asked him to dine at his home instead. But the German Chancellor's attempts to catch the British Prime Minister unawares and engage in some one-to-one summitry with him were to no avail: Beaconsfield had called Bismarck's bluff at that vital stage in the negotiations by threatening to leave Berlin. He had got the measure of the German Chancellor as early as 1862 when he had witnessed Bismarck in London candidly outlining aggressive plans for uniting Germany through a mixture of war with Austria and political chicanery. 'Take care of that man! He means what he says.' Beaconsfield presciently told the Austrian envoy to Great Britain.[55]

The Congress over, Beaconsfield returned to England on the cross-Channel train service, arriving at Charing Cross Station in London to a rapturous welcome on 16 July and later famously proclaiming from a first floor window of 10 Downing Street to the crowds below that he had brought back 'peace with honour'. For his part, Odo Russell had turned out to be one of the stars of the Congress. Acting as the Prime Minister's and Foreign Secretary's trusted and experienced trilingual aide at the talks, he smoothed things over and made things happen behind the scenes. Together with his wife he hosted glamorous parties for international heads of state in the new, spacious, British Embassy so conveniently located near the Congress's location on Wilhelmstrasse. In recognition of his contribution, in March 1881 Beaconsfield's successor as Prime Minister, W.E. Gladstone, was to grant Odo Russell a peerage as Baron Ampthill.[†] Earlier, family pressures had induced him to reject a peerage from Beaconsfield himself: Russell's brother, the Duke of Bedford, had misgivings as to whether it was appropriate for a 'Whig' ambassador to accept such an honour from a 'Tory' Prime Minister.[56] Odo was unamused by the invidious position in which he had been placed by his family: '… I confess that a seat in the House of Lords is the height of my ambition if I live long enough not to die in harness abroad.'[57] But he had had to refuse it, particularly

---

* 36 Behrenstrasse.
† A village (now a small town) near Woburn Abbey. The Duke of Bedford also provided his brother and family with a home there, Ampthill House.

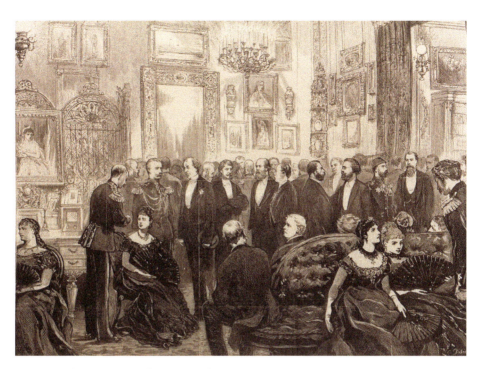

11. *The Graphic*'s illustration of a reception for Plenipotentiaries held at the British Embassy during the Congress of Berlin, published on 29 June 1878. Emily Russell is the second figure seated from the left, Lord Beaconsfield stands next to her, and Odo Russell stands behind the middle of the sofa.

annoyingly given the huge amount of money he had been expected to spend on entertaining during the Congress, partly to meet the expectations of the Crown Prince and Princess as a public mark of the close dynastic relationship between the two countries. 'The Congress puts me to unexpected expense in this summer season. Constant receptions … and an open house … When the feast of nations is over I must ask for some compensation if it is not offered by HMG,'[58] Russell had wearily told his brother, the Duke of Bedford, who generously gave him £1,000 towards his expenditure.

Despite its international success, Lord Salisbury's personal experience of the Congress had been less than enjoyable. His trip to Berlin from London was delayed by bad weather in the Channel, and while Beaconsfield appreciated the hot summer weather in Berlin ('a midsummer night's dream'[59]), for Salisbury the '[h]eat here is extreme, – the place detestable. At Potsdam there are mosquitoes – here there are minor Powers. I don't know which is worst.'[60]

12. Odo Russell as caricatured by 'Spy' (Sir Leslie Ward) in *Vanity Fair*, 28 July 1877.

CHAPTER 3
1878–1884: THE DOYEN OF THE BERLIN DIPLOMATIC CORPS

On 12 June 1879 Charles Lowe, *The Times* foreign correspondent in Berlin and regular Embassy visitor, sent to London a florid account of the celebrations for the golden wedding anniversary of the German Emperor and Empress, describing a lavish, long and formal ceremony in the White Hall of the Royal Schloss where the corps diplomatique assembled to congratulate the imperial couple. The senior-ranking diplomat at the Imperial Court – the Doyen[*] – was the British Ambassador and so Russell (and his wife) took precedence: Lady Emily, as Doyenne, led the ambassadors' wives in to greet the Emperor and Empress, followed by Lord Odo, 'wearing his crimson sash and lately acquired Order of St. George,'[†] with all members of the embassy staff.[1]

It was the Emperor and Bismarck who had requested that Russell should assume the role of Doyen at Berlin, 'because The Crown Princess is of the English royal family.'[2] The position demanded attendance at every function at Court, engaging much of Russell's time over and above his regular duties on behalf of Great Britain, and his description of his expected obligations during an average day goes a long way to explaining why he often felt exhausted:

> At one o' clock I drive in state to the Palace to congratulate the Emperor on his 76th birthday. At five o'clock I dine again in uniform at Bismarck's with the whole diplomatic body and propose to the health of His Majesty. At eight o'clock 'en gala' I go to the Empress' reception and concert which lasts from 8 to 1.30 am if not 2 am. To this last affair Emily goes with me to head the circle of the diplomatic ladies as doyenne, 'notre doyenne' as they call her.[3]

The Embassy was the focal point for British representation in Berlin, and there was plenty of gossip and events there for Lowe to report. At the height of the Berlin season on 8 February 1880 the Russells hosted a 'most brilliant ball party' to which some 350 people were invited. The Emperor and Empress themselves arrived at about half past nine that evening, together with several other members of the German royal family. The Emperor led Lady Emily, and Lord Odo the Empress, into the ballroom, 'where, under a kind of canopy, seats had been arranged for the Imperial guests'. Later at supper the imperial couple sat at the same table as the Russells. While the Empress left immediately after supper, the Emperor stayed until nearly one o'clock the following morning, the last of the guests not leaving before half past three.[4]

---

[*] The first in precedence of the diplomatic corps attached to a foreign government or court.
[†] Probably that of St Michael and St George; the order was founded in 1818 for 'extraordinary or non-military service in a foreign country'.

13. The Emperor Friedrich III when Crown Prince at the Court Ball in 1878, by Anton von Werner, painted in 1895. Amongst Fritz's cultured company in the painting are the distinguished pathologist Hermann Hemholtz and painters Adolf von Menzel (in the doorway to right) and Ludwig Knaus.

The Doyenne, Lady Emily Russell, spoke German fluently and was, as Beaconsfield had remarked, a consummate hostess. But her responsibilities were sometimes accompanied by considerable discomfort. 'I ... do not know how I shall get through the winter at Berlin at all with this terrible climate, suffocating rooms, impossibility to go out so often, and late hours ...' the Crown Princess told her mother, Queen Victoria, about the rigorous demands of her own royal duties. '... Emily Russell can stand it no better than I can. She spends days in bed with racking headaches after these interminable dinners and soirées and yet she is a thorough 'cosmopolitan' and likes Society and going out so much and is always so civil and amiable to everyone.'[5] Emily had been plagued by these headaches for some time: on 30 January 1873 she had a bad attack of neuralgia, but duty demanded she attend 'the first great Court Reception or Drawingroom [sic] ... because her absence, as Doyenne of the Diplomatic Body, might have caused some inconvenience to Their Majesties.'[6] Her efforts were, at least, appreciated: hearing she was unwell, the Emperor sent Lady Emily a personal note (written by a courtier) thanking her for her attendance, hoping 'that the fatigue has not been too much for her Ladyship. His Majesty charges me to express to Lady Odo Russell His best thanks, as well as those of The Empress, and hopes that her Ladyship will be soon quite recovered.'[7]

Not only were there the events at home and at Court to endure, but contemporary etiquette also demanded the 'paying of calls': 'I find that last year 1,870 Gentlemen and 908 Ladies called ... making a total of 2,778 visits Emily had to return driving day after day to drop cards at their houses. It is not enormous, but it takes time to accomplish and omissions are unavoidable now and then,' Odo reported to his brother.[8] Sometimes the behaviour of even the most senior of embassy guests was a diplomatic trial to endure. The Chancellor's son Herbert von Bismarck, himself a diplomat, was a regular in British Embassy circles, but had an unpredictable temper and, as Charles Lowe recalled, a 'brusqueness of manner which ... rendered him far more fit for the career of a dragoon than of a diplomatist.'[9] Perhaps his fiery personality had evolved as a defence mechanism against his father's own uncontrollable rages against those who crossed him, both the cause and symptom of the Chancellor's numerous psychosomatic illnesses. On one occasion in May 1880, during a dinner at the Embassy hosted by Lady Emily at which Herbert's mother, Princess Bismarck, was also present, there was a disagreement over the amount of fresh air required by the hostess and guests. Herbert suddenly lost

14. & 15. Vicky and Fritz gave this pair of portraits by Viktor Stauffer (after the originals by Heinrich von Angeli) to Odo Russell's brother Hastings, 9th Duke of Bedford in 1881; they remain on display at Woburn Abbey.

his temper with the embassy servants over their delay in opening the windows as his mother had requested. Much to Herbert's embarrassment, this juicy piece of gossip was duly reported in the press, but Russell apologised in case the servants had treated him with less respect than the Chancellor's son might have expected.[10]

More happily, in December Russell reported to the Foreign Secretary that the Crown Prince and Princess had visited the Embassy several times.[11] Crown Prince Friedrich Wilhelm ('Fritz') had married Queen Victoria's eldest child, Victoria ('Vicky'), in January 1858. Undoubtedly a love match, it also had a strong geopolitical background: Victoria and Albert's dreams for the future were for a Germany ruled by an enlightened and cultured German emperor and British empress, their daughter. Russell had first met the couple in Rome in 1862 when serving as British Minister to the Holy See, and his close friendship with them was an important element of his role in Berlin; he frequently welcomed them to the Embassy, where their younger children played with the Russells' own four sons and two daughters. The royal and imperial friendship with the Russell family was close: in 1878 the Crown Prince and Princess were guests at Woburn Abbey, and in 1881 Fritz was to present the Duke of Bedford with portraits of himself and Vicky.* Strong-minded and highly intelligent, the Crown Princess treated the Embassy as a refuge, a little piece of England where she could temporarily escape from 'the sullenness and stiffness and perpetual 'official' life'[12] of the Court, and from German politicians, Bismarck in particular. The latter distrusted Vicky's and

* The portraits are by Viktor Stauffer after Heinrich von Angeli, and hang in Queen Victoria's Bedroom at Woburn Abbey. Also part of the Woburn Abbey collections and on display in the same room is a small etching by Queen Victoria of her eldest daughter, later the Crown Princess, when a baby, which she presented to the Duchess of Bedford in August 1841 after her visit to Woburn with Prince Albert the Prince Consort, and photographs of Fritz, and Vicky and Queen Victoria.

the Empress Augusta's liberal leanings and influence over the Emperor and Crown Prince, about which, owing to their birth and status, he of course could do very little.

Bismarck's overtly negative attitude towards the Empress Augusta was an embarrassment in Berlin's diplomatic circles. Despite the shortcomings of the Embassy on Leipzigerstrasse the Emperor and Empress had paid the British Government and Lord Odo Russell the compliment of paying a number of calls there. Indeed, on 5 March 1873 that building had been the first foreign Embassy in which the new 'imperial' couple chose to dine, '[T]he honour thus conferred on Her Majesty's Embassy is considered as a gracious desire to mark publicly the cordial feelings of respectful affection The Emperor and Empress of Germany entertain for Her Majesty the Queen,'[13] Russell proudly reported to London. Bismarck had however previously confessed to Russell that that he had spoken to the Empress only twice since the Franco-Prussian War. Now he found that, horror of horrors, according to protocol he would have to sit next to her at the dinner. Shortly beforehand he sent his excuses, blaming an attack of lumbago. 'Prince Bismarck often expresses his hatred to [sic] the Empress in such strong language that my husband is placed in a very difficult position…' Lady Emily later confided to Queen Victoria.[14]

In November 1881 the embassy staff celebrated Vicky's brother the Prince of Wales's birthday; the Crown Prince and Princess and their children were also there 'looking so happy and cheerful and well disposed towards H.M. Govt. at home.'[15] Close ties between the British and German royal families formed the bedrock of British diplomatic relations in Berlin, and the attempt on Queen Victoria's life at Windsor on 2 March 1882 created an outpouring of sympathy; the imperial family, court dignitaries, members of the Government, the diplomatic corps and all sections of Berlin society visiting the Embassy to leave cards and make personal expressions of sympathy and thanks that the Queen was safe.[16]

***

16. The powerful Berlin banker Gerson von Bleichröder as portrayed by Oskar Begas in 1871.

Russell had been assisted by the Jewish banker Gerson von Bleichröder in trying to find a more suitable embassy house for the British and, specifically, in procuring the Palais Strousberg for the purpose. He already enjoyed a close relationship with the banker, whom he probably first encountered at Versailles. The Ambassador even entrusted some of his own money to him for investment, and often met him on a social basis. In October 1872 Bleichröder had become British Consul-General in Berlin, an unpaid and honorific, but prestigious post.

The historic position of British Consul, separate from and subordinate to members of the diplomatic service proper, was that of representing British interests overseas, usually in terms of trade, and gradually, in some parts of the world, with additional *de facto* responsibility for the interests of locally based British subjects. In many places, foreign nationals, rather than native British subjects,[17] sought and were employed for these duties. Sir Francis Oppenheimer, of German extraction himself, who in 1900 succeeded his father as British Consul-General in Frankfurt, candidly described why this was so in Germany: 'The popularity, the desirability of the appointment in German eyes is easily understood. The office carried with it an official status and title, a handsome uniform and, as the appointment is honorary and unpaid, the chance in due course of an order or decoration – all of which are dear to the German mind.'[18]

Russell reported to the Foreign Office in London that although the British Embassy could manage the necessary work and, strictly, it was probably unnecessary to replace the deceased former holder of the position, Freiherr Viktor von Magnus (another banker), he recommended that Bleichröder should be given the position. Russell told Lord Granville that he 'entirely agreed' with him that

> very great advantages to the commercial and industrial interests of England can be obtained by the appointment of a Person of wealth and consideration to the Town of Berlin to whom native official and commercial authorities are more readily accessible than to Diplomacy. He thinks that no one could better realise these advantages than the banker Baron Bleichröder, who is not only the Rothschild of Berlin, but also one of Prince Bismarck's most intimate friends and advisers in financial and commercial matters. Baron Bleichröder, who holds an exceptionally good position in Berlin society, is often personally consulted by the Emperor and the Crown Prince and is generally trusted and respected by the governing and commercial classes of Prussia.[19]

The banker again demonstrated his close relationship with the British by donating no less than 30,000 marks for a new English church in Berlin, a long-held ambition on the part of Russell and the Crown Princess. For many years British marriage ceremonies had had to be held in a 'specially prepared chamber'[20] in the Embassy, and regular worship by the English-speaking community in the city had taken place in undignified hired hotel rooms or in the gatehouse of the Monbijou Palace just north of the river Spree. But Berlin's rapid expansion made this solution inadequate to meet increasing demand. To commemorate the Crown Prince and Princess's silver wedding anniversary in 1883, money was raised to pay for a dedicated church* in the grounds of the Monbijou Palace with funding from British donors and Vicky, who also donated some church plate. She laid the foundation stone and time capsule at a ceremony on 24 May 1884 (Queen Victoria's birthday), attended by members of the imperial family, several court officials, members of the British Embassy, and the English congregation in Berlin.[21] Following further solicitation on the part of the Crown Princess, Bleichröder was also to fund the church's organ. Dedicated to St George, with a small spire and surrounded by a small English-style churchyard, the church evoked 'a pleasant memory of home,'[22] and was to serve the Embassy and English speaking community in Berlin until the Second World War.

---

* The architect was Julius Carl Rachsdorff, who also built Berlin Cathedral.

***

The Palais Strousberg was evidently a great success as an embassy, if only for its large, flexible and imposing entertaining spaces which had done much to aid recent British diplomatic efforts on the international stage. However, the accommodation issue had still not been resolved on a long-term basis, as the British did not own the building. A real chance to do so was however to come in October 1883. Russell relayed to Lord Granville the promising news that the Duke of Ujest had now become the building's the sole owner[23] and wished to realise his asset by selling the freehold, at cost price – an amount which on 13 November the Treasury reported to the Board of Works amounted to £64,375. Russell's argument to Granville made good financial sense:

> The sum asked is large, but if a continuance of the lease be thought preferable to the purchase of the freehold, HMG will have paid a still larger sum in rent alone in less than twenty-five years … After nearly twelve years residence [in Berlin], I can safely assert that it is impossible to find another house in Berlin as an Embassy as good in every respect as the present one …. In the interests of economy, of the Public Service, and of my successors, I would therefore recommend the Duke of Ujest's offer to your Lordship's consideration.[24]

Russell recommended that the Treasury or Board of Works send out a 'competent person' to inspect the house and negotiate with Ujest's representative. This was Robert Boyce, Architect and Surveyor at the Board of Works, who completed his report in early December. Boyce had spent nearly ten years in Shanghai designing a number of buildings suitable for British representatives in the Far East (including the Legation Residence at Tokyo) and had become the principal architect and surveyor for the British Government's foreign estate.[25] Although Granville seemed convinced by Russell's arguments, and consequently recommended purchase to HM Treasury in London, the Treasury characteristically informed the Board of Works that it would entertain the proposal only if it was 'beyond question' of great advantage.[26]

Boyce's extensive report on the Embassy was, in most respects, favourable to the suggestion of purchase. He described the building's elevation as

> Classic – good proportions, with columns in front supporting a large enriched pediment rising the whole height of the front. In the Basement the kitchens, pantries, and other offices connected therewith – and also the stables. The entire is dry and apparently wholesome … and I may note that the kitchen and pantry were the cleanest and freest from smell and best ordered of any I have inspected.[27]

An important concern for all large houses in cities was the location of the stables. Here Boyce was able to provide reassurances that they were 'completely, as far as exhalations are concerned, sealed from the dwelling house', but even so he had to admit that 'at times some traces of them are perceptible in the part of the Basement next the covered court.'[28]

In general, Boyce was well satisfied with the house:

> The Ground or Principal Floor contains all the reception rooms, Dining Room, Ambassador's Study, and Library. The Entrance Hall and

Staircase, all of which latter is in white marble and the walls, columns and pilasters in excellent scagliola. The rooms are beautifully decorated as befits a first class Embassy House. Much of this, however, has been done at Lord Amphtill's expense … The Bedroom Floor over this affords ample accommodation for a large family, good light and air, the principal bedroom being of magnificent size and arrangement. The Attic floor also gives complete accommodation for the Ambassador's servants – cheerful, healthy rooms … Regarding the sanitary arrangements, they are fairly good, indeed very good for a Berlin house of its date, no cause of complaint occurring during the present occupancy. The drainage at the back end of the premises where the surface is lowest is not so satisfactory, frequent cleanings are required, but I am of opinion that this admits of remedy…. Such is the present structural state and condition of the property, and, so far as I am capable of judging, I consider the house sound and well built, and I have no hesitation in saying that it is 'adaptable for an Ambassador's Residence'.[29]

So far, so good, but Boyce felt that circumstances were also propitious to construct a purpose-built Residence in Berlin, the most economical solution in the long term. There were 'two or three excellent sites now in the market', one of them sited in the Tiergarten, to the west of the Brandenburg Gate, 'in my opinion, a superior position to the present'. On the other hand, if 70 Wilhelmstrasse could be acquired at a 'fair' price ('i.e. a price judged by what it would cost to build one') then its purchase should go ahead.[30]

Boyce's conclusion therefore was that the Duke of Ujest should be told that the British Government was willing to consider purchasing the house from him, but only for a sum that it would cost to build a new residence, a sum which he calculated should be £45,000, given that alterations would be necessary:

To any one who sees the house as it now appears, so beautifully decorated, it may appear very cheap at this price, it is therefore necessary to point out that almost all of this has been done at Lord Amphill's expense – his Lordship having expended on fittings and furniture since his appointment to Berlin upwards of £1,200!* He has had to have doors made to fit the door openings in the principal rooms, as they were without any, the previous occupier contenting himself with portieres.[31†]

All in all Boyce recommended offering £51,700 (£50,000 purchase plus £1,500 alterations and £200 legal expenses), to set against £55,000 to build a completely new Residence from scratch. Boyce reckoned that a new house would be able to be better equipped as regards 'Stables, ventilation, drainage, complete circuit for carriages &c'. While 'the space under the glass roof affords good standing room for six or more carriages', the ability for horses and carriages to undertake a 360° turn

---

* This would appear to be a mistake: in April 1878 Russell reported that his total expenditure on furniture for both the Leipzigerstrasse property and 70 Wilhelmstrasse amounted to more than £10,400 (£6,050.8s.6d on the former and £4,360.16s on additional items for the latter) [*Correspondence respecting the Repairs and the Supply and Maintenance of Furniture at Certain of Her Majesty's Embassies and Legations*, Foreign Office, February 1879, TNA, WORK 10/255].

†*Portières* – door curtains – were popular in Germany at the time, and can be seen in drawings and early photographs of 70 Wilhelmstrasse.

17. The rear courtyard of the Palais Strousberg as seen in a photograph taken in about 1870.

was, probably owing to the narrowness of the site, impossible at 70 Wilhelmstrasse. However, as Boyce had been assured, such an arrangement was apparently not uncommon in Berlin and the embassy servants were used to it.[32]

It was no surprise that Russell was keen for HM Government to accept Ujest's offer but HM Treasury was, as ever, equally keen to avoid spending money overseas. Not unreasonably, as the Ambassador had pointed out to Granville on 20 October, 'We might have saved a lot of money if we had purchased [the house] 8 years ago, as I recommended at the time.' He was neither the first nor the last British Ambassador, by any means, to deplore the British Government's short-term aversion to spending public money, a decision that would inevitably require greater expenditure at a later date*. He continued to plead that 'The acquisition of an Embassy by H.M. Govt. would, I believe, gratify the Imperial Family as well as the German Govt. to judge by their frequent queries on the subject, but the Treasury will probably object to the price.'[33]

He was right. In January the Duke of Ujest rejected Boyce's recommended offer, explaining that while he had no wish to make a profit out of the transaction, he could hardly justify allowing the British Government to acquire the building at a heavy loss to himself.[34] Their offer rejected and the end of the original ten year lease in sight, HM Treasury recommended purchasing the site Boyce had identified in the Tiergarten so that a purpose-built embassy could be erected. Russell countered that while the asking price for that site might superficially appear a bargain, 'The reason for which it has hitherto been unsaleable is, that a house built

---

* See, for example, Sir Nevile Henderson's remarks on the subject fifty years later (Chapter 16).

on it would be shut in between the walls of two very high lodging houses and an extensive block of very high lodging houses at the back, so that from three sides it would be deprived of light and air.'[35] Boyce's response was that the surrounding houses at the Tiergarten site were not as an apparently undignified location as Ampthill had described, but were similar to the smart 'chambers' of flats then being built in London.[36] He now cited one of the additional problems of 70 Wilhelmstrasse was itself one of light: although 'a view into a neighbouring yard is afforded from the upper windows of servants' rooms at the back, ... even this is liable to be shut out at any time;[†] there is no right of light so that, as a matter of fact, this house is only open on the street front.'[37]

A by now very despondent Russell pointed out that no further work needed to be done to the house until he left post, and, as for compensation, on leaving Berlin he intended

> to sell my fixtures and furniture by public auction, unless my successor wishes to purchase any portion of them at a valuation.... In my previous correspondence on the subject I have urged the purchase of the Duke of Ujest's house in the interest both of the public service and of economy 1st because it has proved, after eight years experience to be unexceptionable in every respect, and that there is not a better Embassy House to be found in Berlin. And 2ndly because building an Embassy House in Berlin will cost considerably more in the end than buying a ready made one.[38]

Boyce regarded the Embassy's lack of a garden as a problem. It was true that the absence of a garden to act as an additional entertaining and sporting space for six months of the year with an opportunity to show off British horticultural style and expertise, particularly at the Monarch's Birthday celebration every June, made 70 Wilhelmstrasse comparatively unusual in the Foreign Office estate.[‡] But Russell reasoned (by now with more than a hint of desperation) that the surrounding topography made up for this:

> Like the German Embassy in London,[§] Her Majesty's Embassy in Berlin is admirably situated one door from the Linden Ally [sic] in the Wilhelm Strasse, close to the Imperial Palaces, the Foreign Office, and the Foreign Secretaries [sic] House, the Chancellor's Palace, all the principal public offices of the Empire, and the Foreign Embassies. The gardens of these public buildings form the back of the Wilhelm Strasse, and the tops of their trees can be seen from the bedroom windows of the Embassy looking into the central light and ornamental area or small courtyard in the House, whilst the right side of the House the windows of the picture gallery, billiard room, school room, Bedrooms and first rate servants rooms, overlook the <u>neighbours courtyard,</u> which is large, light and airy with trees in it overhanging a fountain at its centre[¶] and all of

---

† He was correct in this prediction: this area was later to be taken up by the buildings and terrace of the new Adlon Hotel – see Chapter 7.

‡ For example, the British Embassies in Constantinople (now the British Consulate-General) and Paris have always had extensive gardens.

§ Then at 9 Carlton House Terrace.

¶ This was the back garden of the Palais Redern, on the corner of Unter den Linden, and the future site of the Adlon Hotel.

this must have escaped Mr. Boyce's memory since he reports 'as a matter of fact this house is only open on the street front'.[39]

Russell urged Boyce to return to Berlin, as there was a great difference between opinions that could possibly be gathered in a week and those 'in 12 yrs of Berlin affairs' as he had enjoyed. Diplomatic influence still exercised a real influence on the press and the public and he reiterated that 'a lowering of the Standard of Representation hitherto authorized by Her Majesty's Government in a country the reigning families and international interests of which are so closely related would not be favourably interpreted by public opinion.'[40]

As a compromise, Russell was asked to consider the possibility of renewing the lease of 70 Wilhelmstrasse with whoever purchased the house, but even if this proved possible, it was likely to be at a higher sum than before. Perhaps by now tired of the struggle, the Ambassador wearily told Granville that

> Since I learn from Your Lordship's present instruction that my opinion has no weight with the Lords Commissioners of Her Majesty's Treasury, it is useless for me to insist any further on what I have urged all along with conscientious conviction and some local experience, that while Their Lordships decline to purchase the very best Embassy House in the very best situation in Berlin, they will save nothing by building an inferior house in a less suitable site, and I regret their Lordships decision both in the interest of economy and of public service, of Your Lordship's office and of my successors.[41]

But all was not yet lost. Used to dealing with far less important missions and personnel in the Far East, Boyce had misjudged both the situation and the individual with whom he was dealing on site, the internationally respected diplomat and Doyen of the Berlin diplomatic corps, for, in early July, the First Commissioner of Works overruled him and wrote to the Treasury: '…I beg leave to acquaint your Lordships that, in the face of Lord Ampthill's strongly expressed opinion – an opinion which, as I learn privately, is endorsed by the German Ambassador in London – I cannot advise your Lordships any longer to resist purchasing the Berlin Embassy House from the Duke of Ujest.'[42] However, he protected Boyce's professional reputation (and that of the Board of Works) by pointing out that 'Your Lordships will remember that this Department has pointed out that considerable expenditure will probably become necessary sooner or later on the sanitary arrangements of the house.'[43] Ujest accepted £61,375 for the freehold of 70 Wilhelmstrasse. Russell had won: the house he had fought so hard for the British Government to acquire as its embassy in Berlin, and on which he had spent so much of his own and his family's money, was now permanently on the British Government's Estate.

***

At this moment of triumph Russell was at the top of his professional game, his diplomatic experience and abilities lionised by the British Establishment. 'It is difficult for the ordinary Englishman, but little acquainted with the intricacies of foreign politics, to estimate the full value to his country of a really tried and able diplomatist,' the magazine *Vanity Fair* had opined in 1883:

We possess but few, very few, such – men not only inspiring the fullest confidence in their own countrymen and in foreign Governments alike, but well acquainted with the persons and characters of European statesmen, and thoroughly conversant with European policy; men of tried temper, tact and discretion, and commanding other tongues as completely as their own. To an Empire such as Great Britain, possessing but a limited military force, and yet having vital interests to defend in every quarter, the presence of one such man in the councils of Europe may be worth an additional corps d'armée; and such a man is Lord Odo Russell.[44]

In August 1884, a month after his victory over the Board of Works and HM Treasury, Russell retired to his country villa in Potsdam, bought for him by Bleichröder in 1875.[45] The area would have brought back his childhood memories from the 1830s: his father, Lord William Russell, had acquired a country house a mile from Potsdam where Odo and his brothers had spent happy days playing amongst the surrounding lakes. It was where he had spent his ninth birthday, 20 January 1838, during an exceptionally harsh winter. His villa, where he had a magnificent library, was close to the Imperial Palace of Sansscouci, on a hill overlooking the town. Russell was in the habit of spending most of his time there once the court season was over every year at Easter, conducting essential representational embassy business in Potsdam and commuting into Berlin when required until returning to the city on a permanent basis in late summer every year.[46]

On 19 August Russell visited Foreign Minister Count Hatzfeldt at the Foreign Office on Wilhelmstrasse, but on returning to Potsdam that evening he began to feel unwell. He had noticed that since about May, his long-standing 'liver' problems had seemed to worsen. Normally, as Charles Lowe later explained, he treated this by taking his annual 'cure' at Karlsbad (the change of water, diet and above all opportunity for some relaxation presumably made a medical difference), but this year he had been unable to do so.[47] The Ambassador struggled back into Berlin the following day, but the day after that he felt so ill that he had to ask his deputy Sir Charles Scott to stand in for him at the Embassy.[48]

Confined to bed in Potsdam, Russell became so poorly he could not communicate with London in person, and on 23 August Scott wrote to Granville to report that the Ambassador was very ill from 'another sharp liver attack.'[49] The following day he seemed to rally a little but that evening took a turn for the worse: it was peritonitis, fatal in an age before competent surgical procedures and antibiotics. His condition quickly worsened as, racked by appalling pain, an internal abscess burst and perforated his intestines. Extremely concerned, the Empress sent her personal physician to attend the Ambassador. This doctor's prognosis that the case was 'a dangerous one' reached the embassy staff only at ten o'clock the following morning. Scott rushed to Potsdam as fast as he could, but he was too late. After a few hours, mercifully, 'of almost complete absence of pain and, except during a slight interval, in full possession of his consciousness,'[50] Russell died at eleven o'clock in the morning of Monday, 25 August. He was not yet fifty-six.

CHAPTER 4
1884–1885: 'AN APPANAGE OF THE BEDFORD FAMILY'

That same morning, having despatched her personal physician to Russell's bedside, the worried Empress decided to call on his Potsdam villa in person. But, like Charles Scott, she was too late, able to do nothing other than to offer comfort to Emily, inconsolable and 'prostrated with grief'.[1] Lady Ampthill was not alone: the Doyen's sudden death deeply shocked the Foreign Office in London and the diplomatic community in Berlin. Charles Scott reported to the Foreign Secretary:

> From every quarter private and official expressions of sympathy have been presented both at Potsdam and at Her Majesty's Embassy, and the Press, of every shade of opinion testifies to the great loss which the two countries have sustained by the death of a diplomatist whose unremitting efforts have during 13 years been directed to strengthening and maintaining the friendly relations between the two Governments.[2]

Even so, the Foreign Office baulked at Scott's on-the-spot decision to follow local custom and purchase suits of mourning clothes for the two Chancery servants, at a cost of 200 marks (approximately £10):

> Mr Scott speaks of it being the usual custom on such occasions, but the only occasions which we recognize are a) the death of the Sovereign or b) the death of the Sovereign to whom the Minister is accredited … and therefore while it seems quite proper that the two Chancery Servants should have been put into mourning, it would be desirable the charge should have Treasury sanction.[3]

In 1873 Vicky had told Queen Victoria that her husband 'particularly wishes me to say how much Lord Odo is appreciated here – and how excellent in every respect the position is which he and Emily have made for themselves. They are as much respected as they are popular, and consequently are treated by all as your representatives should!'[4] Three years later she described Lord Odo as 'certainly a pearl not only among diplomatists but among men, and dear Emily is quite his counterpart in every way. They possess universal respect, confidence, and good will, which is such a pleasure to see, as alas! it is not always the excellent and the worthy who succeed in the world, and who are liked by all.'[5] Indeed, for as well as an internationally respected diplomat and the senior ambassador in Berlin, by all accounts Odo was a kind, thoughtful and genial figure, and most of the people who met him and recorded their thoughts seem to have liked him. Charles Scott believed 'that never has there been such universal and genuine mourning for a foreign statesman than is felt in all circles here at the untimely death of Her Majesty's Ambassador at this Court.'[6] His diplomatic colleagues and imperial family mourned his loss and condoled with his grieving widow and family,[7] laying wreaths on his coffin at his Potsdam villa. The Empress Augusta went so far as to state that it was 'a national loss to both countries …. Lord Ampthill will never be forgotten by us or by Germany.'[8]

Vicky and Fritz in particular were devastated. Odo 'was [the Crown Princess's] dearest friend who was ever so kind and true to her, whose home was the only one she could go to for help and comfort,'[9] while she must also have appreciated the easy proximity of Emily, her friend and bridesmaid. 'You do not know what this means for the Crown Princess and myself. We shall have to begin a new life now,'[10] Vicky's gloomy husband melodramatically informed the newly arrived attaché James Rennell Rodd; indeed, Rodd recounted that, poignantly, Fritz not only laid a wreath upon Russell's coffin, but also took 'a rosebud from it away with him to keep.'[11] For the Crown Prince and Princess the Embassy had been a place 'where they could escape from the artificialities of Court life and be simple human beings,'[12] where they could temporarily remove themselves from what they regarded as the crushingly reactionary attitude of the Court. In fairness, Vicky's often-expressed strong opinions on the superiority of almost everything in her native England understandably irritated many at that Court, who also believed she exercised an unwelcome liberal and unpatriotic influence over her Prussian husband. Confiding in her mother, Vicky admitted that she hated the 'frigidness and bitterness of the people here,'[13] and (in her experience) for example their cruel treatment of animals: on one occasion an overenthusiastic local *jäger* shot, killed and mutilated her late son's pet cat in the grounds of the Neues Palais in Potsdam, leaving her heartbroken.[14]

Emily wanted her husband's remains to return to England, and the German Emperor himself provided a royal hearse and two royal carriages in full state[15] for the former Ambassador's coffin to process slowly from his villa to the Potsdam Railway Station on Friday, 29 August, where 'every attention and mark of respect, compatible with Lady Ampthill's wish to maintain throughout the strictest privacy, was paid to His Excellency's memory.'[16] The embassy staff, the Emperor and Empress, and other ambassadors and members of the Imperial Court watched sadly as the carriages carrying Odo's remains were coupled on to the train at Charlottenburg Railway Station* for the journey to England. The funeral service at the Bedford family chapel at Chenies† in Buckinghamshire on 3 September was a simple one, but flooded with floral tributes from Queen Victoria, the Prince of Wales and the German imperial family.[17] Back in Berlin, in the English Church of St George that Russell was never to see completed, a specially commissioned west window by William Morris, made to a design by Sir Edward Burne-Jones, featured figures representing Saint George, Peace, Justice, and Saint Michael. The window's upper portion commemorating Lord Ampthill included a design representing souls being received into heaven.

*In 1882 an elevated east–west railway line had been opened along what was then the northern edge of Berlin for both local and long-distance traffic, serving stations Charlottenburg, Zoologischer Garten, Bellevue, Lehrter Bahnhof (now Hauptbahnhof), Friedrichstrasse, Börse (now Hackescher-Markt), Alexanderplatz, Jannowitzbrücke and Schlesicher Bahnhof (now Ostbahnhof); other stations were added later. International trains heading westwards or eastwards could be boarded from several stations along this line and as such were used by arriving and departing diplomatic staff. The lines and stations became part of Berlin's S-Bahn metro system and remain in use today.

† A Russell family home since the early sixteenth century; the Bedford Chapel in the Church of St Michael contains many Russell tombs.

18. Emily, Lady Ampthill during her long widowhood, photographed in 1896 by Alexander Bassano.

'The death of Lord Ampthill is the most serious loss to this country which its Diplomatic Service could have suffered,' dramatically opined *The Spectator* five days after the Ambassador's death.[18] His connections and well-publicised diplomatic abilities certainly made him a difficult act to follow. Despite his family's traditional Whig political leanings, he had managed, more or less successfully, to serve under both Liberal and Conservative Prime Ministers and in more than twelve years in Berlin he had gained an extremely good working relationship not only with the German imperial family, but also with Chancellor Bismarck; perhaps too close, Lord Beaconsfield had initially thought, describing Odo as contenting 'himself with reporting all Bismarck's cynical bravados, which he evidently listens to in an ecstasy of sycophantic wonder.'[19] But, earlier on, at least, in their professional relationship in Berlin, Russell had the measure of Bismarck. On one occasion in the mid-1870s the Chancellor's hand appears to have been at work behind strong rumours of a new war against France: 'Is war in sight?' asked a newspaper article in the spring of 1875, which France took as proof that its old enemy was planning a renewed attack. Russell was convinced that Bismarck was only bluffing, and the Chancellor's refusal to state his intentions defused the situation.[20] But towards the end of his ambassadorship Russell's relationship with the Chancellor cooled, and he faced accusations of failing to appreciate Germany's new ambitions to acquire foreign colonies. At the height of the Arnim affair Russell did however make one observation about Bismarck that was eerily prophetic about a later German Chancellor: Bismarck had '... a deeprooted [*sic*] conviction that his mission on earth is to unite the Germans in Europe, and make them the dominant race in the world – that absolute power is indispensable to him to fulfil his mission, and that to secure absolute power and consolidate his tenure of office against all opposition, the employment of cunning and force are justifiable.'[21]

* * *

The man who would be appointed as the new British Ambassador to Berlin was a topic of some interest in the press. At a distinct risk of stating the blindingly obvious, the leader writer of the popular magazine *The Graphic* was of the opinion that a considerable linguistic ability such as Russell had possessed was a very important requirement for the job: 'All the dispatches issued from the Berlin Chancellery are drawn up in German, and it would be humiliating that a British Ambassador should have to depend upon a secretary for translation of these often astutely worded documents.'[22] In a telling comment upon the social makeup of the diplomatic service of the time, *The Spectator* commented that 'Diplomacy is one of the few professions in which it is still a pure advantage to belong to one of the great families …. it is always an advantage to a diplomatist to be one of the great caste which still commands more confidence abroad and more acceptance in England than any middle-class man can easily create for himself ….'[23]

There were a number of potential candidates. The Prince and Princess of Wales were in favour of Sir Robert Morier, a great friend of Russell's and of the Crown Prince and Princess. He had spent much of his earlier diplomatic career at various German postings, including as an attaché in Berlin at the time of the Crown Prince's marriage to Vicky. A specialist in German affairs, unfortunately for his career his liberal, anti-Prussian stance set him at odds with Chancellor Bismarck, who appears to have blocked the appointment.[24] After some discussion about whether to send Russell's eldest brother, the Duke of Bedford, to Berlin,[25] it was Gladstone, the Prime Minister, who recommended Sir Edward Malet as the most promising candidate, even though the promotion of such a relatively young man would 'ignite the anger of several of his colleagues,'[26] as there were several candidates with greater seniority.

Born on 10 October 1837 while his father Alexander was serving as Secretary at the British Legation in The Hague, Malet was from an ancient Anglo-Norman family steeped in the diplomatic service. He followed his father into the service as an attaché at Frankfurt at the age of seventeen in 1854 and was subsequently posted to Brussels, Buenos Aires, Rio, Washington, Constantinople and Paris. It was in the French capital that he first gained the reputation for maintaining a cool head in a crisis: as Prussian forces shelled the city in 1871 the British embassy staff took refuge in the building's cellars, Malet later being praised for his sang froid by the Ambassador, Lord Lyons. Later he was made agent and Consul-General at Cairo, a posting at a time of political unrest against the British: rioting in June 1882 and a massacre of Europeans at Alexandria sparked military intervention and the British occupation of Egypt. He was 'a remarkable man,' according to Austen Chamberlain, 'and however unexpected the summons of foreign representatives to the Palace, he was always the first to appear, and whatever the hour of the day or night at which the summons reached him, was always immaculately dressed. He was, in fact, a very able diplomatist who stood deservedly high in the estimation of Bismarck and his fellow ambassadors. It was no light task to fill worthily the position just vacated by Lord Ampthill.'[27] Malet became Ambassador to Brussels in 1883, a posting suddenly curtailed by his appointment to replace Russell in Berlin.

Judging from his portraits Malet was a handsome man. Unusually for diplomats of his seniority and experience, he was also unmarried. Women would be prevented from entering the diplomatic service in their own right until 1946, but as wives they had long played an important and usually unsung role in the diplomatic world. The expected (and unpaid) duties and responsibilities of wives were many and varied, corresponding, when their husbands became a head of mission, to those of the mistress of a large household in Britain. Depending on the size of the mission concerned, they included overseeing the Residence's appearance, devising and overseeing entertainments, menus and seating plans, and hiring and overseeing a large complement of staff.

Even with Strousberg's primitive central heating, with its open fires and before the advent of vacuum cleaners and washing machines, keeping the Embassy's rooms heated and clean, especially during the long, freezing winter months in Berlin, would have been an endless, backbreaking job requiring a number of full-time servants, as would the care and maintenance of the main method of transport – horses. British embassy households at this date mirrored the running of aristocratic town and country houses at home, with a hierarchy of servants including liveried footmen, cooks/chefs, stable hands, coachmen, and parlour, laundry, chamber and scullery maids, presided over by a butler and housekeeper. The ambassador and ambassadress might also bring their own lady's maid and valet from Great Britain, as might some of the Embassy's temporary residential guests (or if not, an embassy maid or valet would be assigned for their use).

As in Emily Russell's case, ambassadors' wives were naturally expected to appear at their husband's side in hosting embassy functions. They also attended – sometimes alone – events in other embassies and, indeed, events at the Court to which they were posted, the rituals of which were sometimes very elaborate. In short, wives were expected not only to assist in their husbands' representational duties, but also to present a happy, serene, well-organised and supportive role to their spouses in their postings. Fifty years after Malet's era, the Foreign Office's expectation of diplomatic wives had little changed in essentials:

> In many posts the part played by the wife is fully as important as that of the husband, and in all an immense influence for or against British prestige is exercised by the wife. By this we mean by the wife in her capacity as 'Chefesse'. Women have their own and that a most important part to play in diplomatic life, a part which is quite distinct from that of men but no less essential. We feel that in selecting officers for service abroad … great attention should be paid to this consideration.[28]

What actually went on in private between the Chef de Mission* and his (unpaid) Chefesse when they were both off duty is of course a different matter and for obvious reasons one not often recorded for posterity. Indeed, some wives refused to conform to society's expectations. The role of diplomatic spouse remains to this day a very demanding one, requiring essentially the same traditional skills. A Residence may host several representational events a day, including breakfasts, mid-morning meetings, lunches, tea parties, dinners, receptions and launches. To all intents and purposes the 'job' effectively still does involve running a five star hotel service for VIPs and other guests who may arrive at short notice and whose interests constantly need to be taken into account and managed. It has always required huge reservoirs of self-discipline, organisation, tact, diplomacy (in the general sense of the word), patience, energy and stamina.†

---

* Head of Mission, usually Anglicised by this period to 'Chief'. French was the international language of diplomacy from at least the seventeenth century. Although English has gradually replaced it, many of the phrases remained until at least the first half of the twentieth century and many are still in use (e.g. corps diplomatique, chargé d'affaires, attaché).

† Times are, however, changing. Modern-day spouses (increasingly many of whom are male) nowadays frequently have their own careers and are unwilling to uproot and assume the mantle of traditional, peripatetic, full-time 'hostess'.

In his various postings Malet had managed to do without this close support, but by the time he became Ambassador for the first time, in Brussels in 1883, he was clearly casting around for a wife, and had found one who was to be, in one sense, rather close to home: one of the daughters of Hastings, 9th Duke of Bedford, Odo's niece – Lady Ermyntrude Sackville Russell,* who had attended Ampthill's funeral at Chenies along with the rest of the Russell family. Although she was nineteen years younger than Malet, the Foreign Secretary reassured Queen Victoria that

> Such a marriage would add to his position, and to his means, and would be a resource to the Crown Princess. It is the daughter who likes society. This marriage or rather hope of a marriage ought to be kept an absolute secret as any premature announcement of it might be fatal with the Duke. Otherwise it is difficult to doubt his acquiescence in the wishes of a lady 28 years old, with regard to a man of character, and who has done much successfully in his career.[29]

Malet had already asked the Duke of Bedford for his daughter's hand, but Odo's brother felt unable to commit himself to a decision until the October of 1884. Malet arrived in Berlin that month. Writing to Earl Granville he reported that 'I find the house upside down and I am compelled to live at the Hotel[†] and, with a view to the future, I am most anxious that the necessary repairs should be taken in hand as soon as possible.'[30]

* * *

The purchase of 70 Wilhelmstrasse progressed during the late summer and early autumn of 1884, Malet finally signing the contract for the freehold on 27 November. On 31 March the following year Charles Scott reported to London that the Bank of England had transferred the balance of the purchase price to Bleichröder (acting as the banker) on 29 March, with the Duke of Ujest receiving what he was owed on the 31st.[31] 'My poor sister returns to Berlin on Wednesday or Thursday next and I go with her,' one of Lady Ampthill's brothers[‡] had written to the Chief Clerk of the Foreign Office on 7 September 1884. 'She is very anxious to know whether the Govt will purchase the furniture in the State Rooms &c. If so, she considers it would be of essential advantage that Boyce or someone from the Bd of Works should come out while we are there so that she may get some idea of what will be taken over.'[32] Boyce duly returned to Berlin to catalogue and estimate the value of the typically (for its time) substantial amount of furniture and fittings in each room.[§]

Strousberg's former garden room at the south-west corner of the house (leading on to the raised terrace) and the large internal courtyard garden with a fountain had by this time been partly overlaid by a large ballroom, or the Banqueting Hall as it was sometimes to be known, that could accommodate 600 guests.[33] The

---

* She was one of the daughters of Odo Russell's eldest brother, Hastings, 9th Duke of Bedford and his wife, Elizabeth Sackville (of the family of the Dukes of Dorset), hence Ermyntrude's names. A later member of the family – Vita Sackville-West – will feature later in the Embassy's history (see Chapter 12).
† Presumably the nearby Kaiserhof Hotel.
‡ The Hon. Francis Hyde Villiers.
§ See Chapter 11.

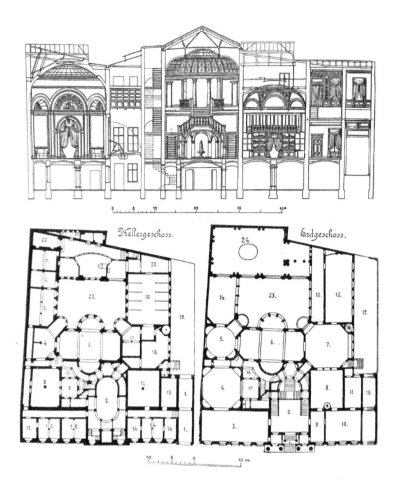

19. Plans of the basement and ground floor of 70 Wilhelmstrasse after alterations to the building, with a cross-section shown above, from *Berlin und seine Bauten* (1896).

architect was again August Orth, whose design for it survives in the Berlin Technical University's architectural archives.[34] Matching the rest of the house in its ornate decoration, the room had paired Corinthian pilasters, its arches supporting a flat ceiling with a skylight. There were several relief carvings in stucco by the sculptor Otto Lessing, and at the northern end of the room, towards Strousberg's former art gallery, can be seen in Orth's design another stucco carving, probably depicting Saint George and the Dragon. There was also a 'minstrels' gallery' on the floor above.

Orth's design for the ballroom differs from his earlier, oval-shaped design that filled in the space over the terrace at the back of the house but left the garden room intact. Interestingly, this earlier, unrealised, design incorporated in the basement underneath a 'Bühne für lebende Bilder etc.'[35] It is dated 21 March

¶ 'Stage for *tableaux vivants*', a popular form of entertainment at this period; in November 1881 it was reported

20. The Embassy's ballroom (looking west) in a photograph dating from the 1880s.

1876, early in the period between the building's sale as one of Strousberg's assets and its formal lease by the British as their Embassy as of 1 July that year. Orth's building application for the revised design of the ballroom bears the same date (1 July 1876[36]) and is amongst a group of surviving designs for 'renovations'* at this period. Given his constant financial worries, it seems unlikely that Lord Odo Russell would have paid for such a large room to be built when the house was held by the British Government only on rental terms. And, considering the equally constant concerns for economy voiced by Her Majesty's Treasury, it seems even more unlikely that the staff of that institution would have even contemplated using public funds for such a purpose. Had the Dukes of Ujest and Ratibor paid for such a room with their own money, Ujest would surely have charged the British Government for it when selling his asset, but the house was offered to the British at its original cost price. In late 1875 and early 1876, when the acquisition of 70 Wilhelmstrasse for use as the British Embassy was under discussion, Russell and Gerson von Bleichröder had exchanged correspondence about plans to extend the building.[37] The banker's generosity to the British in Berlin has already been noted: did he also foot the bill for this major addition to the house?

An issue at this time concerned the current location of the Embassy's offices (Chancery) in Pariser Platz. To save on costs, the Board of Works proposed that, after 31 March 1885 when the lease on that property would have otherwise have

that Lord Dufferin, Ambassador in Constantinople, had presented three *tableaux vivants* at the British Embassy there, 'which have delighted all who had the good fortune to be present' (*The Graphic*, 5 November 1881).
* *Umbau.*

to be renewed, these should be accommodated in 70 Wilhelmstrasse itself, thus combining both the Chancery and Residence in one building, the normal situation at the time in British embassies and legations.† It was proposed that the offices be made from the rooms to the right of the entrance hall, where Strousberg's office had been located, together with the billiard room and library, which Malet had agreed to give up for this purpose. Boyce confidently predicted that once these conversion works had taken place, as well as putting right some structural defects he had identified in March 1884 'to improve … ventilation and sanitary arrangements', 'it is possible that no expenditure on the structure may be requisite for some time to come.'[38]

But his confidence was misplaced. 'I have again to report', he wrote in early January the following year,

> that, after a careful examination of the House, which I was now better able to make, as most of the apartments were vacant, it will be utterly impossible to place the House in a satisfactory state for occupancy, without a considerable addition to what has been already authorised by the Lords Commissioners of Her Majesty's Treasury. This is mainly in consequence of the imperative necessity of immediately remedying some of the structural defects alluded to in my previous report.[39]

Strousberg's famed fondness for innovative bathroom equipment had included a bath disguised as an armchair and a bath tub as a chaise longue.[40] Unfortunately, on closer inspection, it would seem that not all of his legendary 'mod cons' lived up to their reputation or, rather, perhaps, were a 'mod con' too far for the sanitary technology of the time. During one of his return visits to Berlin Boyce had opened the wardrobes in the dressing rooms on either side of the master bedroom only to find two hidden and previously unaccounted-for water closets built inside them. Worryingly, he noted that 'many of the others, particularly two, require entire reconstruction, nor can the drainage be left without examination, and reconstruction if necessary.'[41] Such rare household luxuries in Berlin as running water and water closets provided yet another excuse for the Crown Princess to make an unfavourable comparison between the amenities available in Prussia and in England,[42] but the appeal of Strousberg's luxurious bathroom fittings, according to the German architect Hermann Muthesius (writing two decades later), would in any case have been lost on the British. A bathroom in England, he authoritatively stated, was 'always the simple, plain room dictated by need. Everything is of the best, but the room is fundamentally modest and unpretentious. It is alien to the nature of an Englishman of standing to envelop himself in luxury.'[43]

As part of the required structural works to allow the Chancery to move into the building, Boyce reported that the billiard room would 'have to be altered and divided, a new approach formed, as well as a new staircase to apartments set aside for a Secretary's quarter.'[44] He recommended 'Internal renovation from top to bottom of House, including extensive replastering, repairs to windows, skylights, floor, painting, colouring papering and painting'. By this stage the staff at the Treasury in London may well have started to worry quite how deep the money pit

---

† It was only in the post-Second World War period that the physical separation between Residences and Mission offices became the norm.

Strousberg's mansion was likely to become, but were possibly relieved to learn that Boyce had included 'all plain cheap paper, no expensive paper or wall covering of any kind' in his estimates.[45] The alterations to the Chancery and Secretary's quarters, structural and sanitary and ventilation improvements all added up to the equivalent of some £3,450, plus repairs and additions to furniture. Another £1,900 was required on top of the £3,500 the Treasury had already sanctioned for the work, and even then Boyce was to add that the heating apparatus might well need repair in the following financial year. He had taken the independent decision on the spot to start this work immediately, Malet, 'who is to be married early next year' evidently pressing upon him the need for some urgency in getting the house ready.[46]

Boyce pleaded that he could not possibly have known about all of the house's 'defects' while Ampthill was still living there. It turned out that the sanitary arrangements were in an even worse state than he had reported, and the gas pipes also needed replacing.[47] Malet himself wrote to Earl Granville in early 1885 with further details of Strousberg's disappointing arrangements in this area.[48] A few weeks before there had been an explosion in the kitchens. The cause was a fault in the heating system which, based on a metal coil passing through the kitchen fire, was highly susceptible to fluctuations in the water pressure; occasionally the entire system was brought to a standstill. To add to the woes a 'cesspool' had been discovered directly beneath the kitchen, needing immediate attention.

Malet also requested two rather more cosmetic changes. No doubt with his future bride in mind, the first of these was the division of the long front drawing room – 'the only drawing room available as a day sitting-room for the lady of the house' – into two so as to create an anteroom directly off the hallway, allowing her some privacy when receiving visitors, at a cost of about £50. Interestingly, the assignment of the front of the house into a 'female' reception area (subdivided into two rooms) on the left of the entrance and 'male' reception rooms on the right had already been planned by Orth for Strousberg in the late 1860s.[49] But, while Strousberg's side of the house was indeed kitted out with an anteroom to his study (with suitably 'masculine' decoration), no parallel arrangement seems finally to have been built for his wife.[50] Malet's second request to London was for the creation of a glass awning immediately outside the house, as, somewhat surprisingly, he remarked that 'There is no protection from weather for persons arriving at the front door.'[51]

It would perhaps have been no surprise to Malet that the Office of Works characteristically agreed to pay only for the essential works – repairs to the hot-water system and the renewal of the kitchen drainage (at an estimated £180). Funding for the alteration to the drawing room and the front awning was met with a refusal with the classic excuse that Russell had never requested such work. But Malet pointed out that his predecessor had obviously recognised the need for a room partition because he had placed a large screen* across the room. And, more seriously, 'I may mention that the necessity of dividing the room was first mentioned to me in a high quarter. It was pointed out to me that it was exceedingly

---

* Described by Boyce in his September 1884 list of furniture in the house as a 'Large five fold screen covered with leather' (TNA, WORK 10/488).

inconvenient that there should be no anteroom in which a lady accompanying a Princess could wait during a visit to the Ambassadress, and that she should be compelled to sit in the hall or the Ambassador's room on the other side of it.'[52] At some stage in the house's history this alteration did take place,[53] but, as for the awning, Malet was still plaintively pointing out five years later that the problem had not gone away and that he was having to make use of a 'tent shelter' when guests arrived, at a cost to him of £25 to £35 per annum, expenditure 'which I venture to submit is not a charge which should properly fall to the Ambassador, as it is entirely connected with the State Apartments.'[54] Unfortunately for him, however, it would appear from photographs of the exterior of the building that the permanent glass awning was never erected.

In an age of monarchies diplomatic protocol created the concerns Malet had described that affected the front drawing room, but even so he was later to admit that the house did have its advantages, one being that all of the representational rooms were located on the ground floor:

> I commend this arrangement for all Embassies. One of the every-recurring honours which fall upon Ambassadors is the reception of Sovereigns and Princes, and it is a matter of great convenience to be able to receive them without going downstairs, not as a question of movement from the upper to the ground-floor, but as a matter of etiquette. In the case of Sovereigns the rule is clear – you must receive them at the entrance; but innumerable questions have arisen, in cases where the Ambassador resides on the upper floor, as to how far down the stairs he should come to receive lesser Princes.[55]

As well as converting some of the rooms to the right of the house into the Ambassador's office and Chancery, other areas of the building were altered, either at this period or in successive decades as the Embassy's work expanded and, as staff numbers increased, some areas of the stables downstairs were also converted into offices.[56] It may have been at this time that a gilded metal grille featuring foliate motifs and the British royal coat of arms and motto *Dieu et mon droit* was incorporated into the exterior doors on to the street, and the same design of metal grille used on the first-floor windows, under the portico.

Although Malet was at first unable to live in the Residence, his welcome in Berlin's diplomatic circles was initially warm. Bismarck congratulated the new Ambassador's father on his son's appointment, fondly remembering socialising with his family when serving as a diplomat in Frankfurt over three decades earlier; he looked forward to meeting Malet junior in Berlin.[57] Leaving his deputy Charles Scott as Chargé at the Embassy, Malet was on leave from 26 February to 15 April 1885 for his wedding on 19 March, Lady Ermyntrude Sackville Russell having accepted his marriage proposal (finally approved by her father, the Duke of Bedford). Not without justification, *The Illustrated London News* was later to remark that 'Through her [Lady Ermyntrude] the Embassy has become a kind of appanage[†] of the Bedford family, seeing that her husband's predecessor Lord Odo Russell, who died as Lord Ampthill, was its first diplomatic tenant.'[58]

---

† A natural or customary right or privilege.

CHAPTER 5
1885–1895: 'A Perfect Type of the Trained and Wary Diplomatist'

In the mid-1880s the Berlin embassy staff and their associates included a group of young men who would reach the top echelons of the Foreign Office and British politics. Amongst them was Charles Hardinge, who, at the age of twenty-six arrived in Berlin in early 1885 to take up a posting as Third Secretary. Always stiff, formal and dignified, he was later to achieve the unique record of appointments of Foreign Office Permanent Under-Secretary, Viceroy of India and British Ambassador to Paris. Two years later, in February 1887, a future Chancellor of the Exchequer, Foreign Secretary and Nobel Peace Prize winner arrived in the shape of (Joseph) Austen Chamberlain. Methodically preparing his son for future political office, the politician and former Mayor of Birmingham Joseph Chamberlain had sent his twenty-three-year-old son to Berlin to study the German language and German life, history and politics. Spending a year in the city, Chamberlain remembered how the Malets and the rest of the embassy staff received him with great kindness. Much to the jealousy of his embassy friends, he was invited to dine with Chancellor Bismarck in his Palace (regarded as very unusual, as even ambassadors normally managed to obtain an invitation to dine with the Chancellor only once a year, on the Emperor's birthday).[1]

Five decades later Chamberlain wistfully remembered the days of his youth spent in Berlin and wondered if James Rennell Rodd (who later himself went on to enjoy a distinguished diplomatic career, becoming Ambassador to Rome) remembered 'our parties to the theatres and the suppers afterwards at a small but celebrated oyster bar, were we ate cold partridges and drank Greek wine; or a Sunday at Potsdam with the Scotts, where they had taken a villa by the lake…'. On one of these occasions, an event that seems difficult to reconcile with his later reputation as an elder statesman, Chamberlain was bathing from a boat (rather than from a bathing shed) with his friends, 'with less clothing than was expected'. Suddenly a boating party composed of members of the German royal family appeared, and a 'commotion' resulted. For a fortnight afterwards the road in front of the Scotts' villa was 'picketed by the police.'[2]

Rodd's first diplomatic posting was to Berlin, arriving there in June 1884; when Malet became Ambassador a few short months later after Ampthill's sudden death he asked Rodd to become his private secretary. Rodd remembered Malet as a kindly 'chief', establishing 'a sort of club room for the bachelor members of the staff, who dined with him almost every night.'[3] The unmarried secretaries also had 'a little mess for luncheon at Langlet's, an excellent restaurant kept by a Frenchman, at the corner of the Wilhelm Strasse and the Linden, almost next door to the Embassy' (possibly the same restaurant that Chamberlain remembered). The poet Matthew Arnold, who visited Berlin in November 1885, was asked to become an honorary member of the 'mess'.[4]

Despite all Russell's diplomatic efforts, Malet became Ambassador in Berlin at a time when political sentiments were increasingly turning against Great Britain, a phenomenon that would gradually worsen as time went on. He had set to work on his duties as Ambassador in earnest, using the Embassy's facilities to the full in the shape of the Africa Conference (15 November 1884 – 25 February 1885). Events had moved on from when Russell was told expressly by German Foreign Secretary von Bülow in 1875 that there was 'no wish, or intention, to acquire colonies for Germany on the part of the Emperor or Prince Bismarck.'[5] Germany had come to realise that the acquisition of colonies abroad was a means for European powers to increase their international influence and wealth, and she did not wish to be left behind. At Bismarck's initiative, the Conference was set up to settle rival European claims in the 'Scramble for Africa' and to establish protocols for future colonial development. Malet was the British representative, with specialist experience of some of the affairs of – and perhaps more particularly – British interests in the African Continent, having recently served in Egypt. Amongst the other English-speaking delegates was Henry Morton Stanley, there to advise the King of the Belgians on Belgian possessions in the Congo. On most evenings the British delegates dined with Malet at the Embassy, the party often including Charles Lowe, *The Times* correspondent and sometimes the celebrated Admiral Charles Beresford, on his return from the Upper Nile from his unsuccessful attempt to relieve General Gordon at Khartoum.[6] Another delegate was Lord Rosebery,[*] lodging, as Beaconsfield had done during the Congress of Berlin, at the Kaiserhof Hotel rather than at the Embassy itself. Rodd later remembered that he had 'seldom experienced a more strenuous period than the three months during which [the Conference] sat'[7]: the British delegates, at least, had no separate clerical staff, leaving Rodd and his colleagues to undertake the multiple and tedious necessary copying of documents.

It was a breach of protocol for a diplomat or his wife to take part in formal public events before their official presentation at the court to which their embassy was accredited.[8] But on 18 April 1885, back in Berlin from his honeymoon, Malet was happy to report to the Foreign Secretary that both the German Empress and the Crown Princess had already received Ermyntrude, leaving her free to begin to take part in official receptions organised by the Embassy as Malet's consort. 'I am glad to say that Ermyn seems to take to her public duties as if she were to the manner born,' he proudly reported.[9]

Hardinge remembered the Berlin of 1885, when 'the military show and splendour … were really wonderful …. The streets were always full of officers very well dressed in military uniform and they certainly added greatly to the brightness of the capital.'[10] He remembered balls and diplomatic indiscretions, not the least by Bertie,[†] Prince of Wales in 1885, during one of his many visits to Berlin. In the midst of a diplomatic standoff between Russia and Great Britain after Russia's advance into Afghanistan, Hardinge was shocked to hear the Prince using indiscreet language to the Russian Military Attaché in front of a group of diplomats

---

* In May 1885 he visited Berlin again and met Chancellor Bismarck, later claiming that the renowned German Chancellor frightened him (Marquess of Crewe, *Lord Rosebery*, Vol. I, 240).
† Albert Edward, known to his family as 'Bertie'.

during a big reception in the Embassy.[11] But the close dynastic ties between Great Britain and Germany remained important, and the twenty-fifth anniversary of the Emperor Wilhelm's accession to the throne of Prussia in the following year was a significant diplomatic event for celebration. That January, General Lord Wolseley arrived in Berlin as a special envoy to convey Queen Victoria's official congratulations. It was during this visit that a large military dinner was held in the Embassy's dining room, at which the principal generals in Berlin were guests. On seeing the seating plan in advance, Herbert Bismarck's irascibility again came to the fore when he objected to being seated next to a particular German general. Rodd went to considerable trouble at the last minute to rearrange the tables and seating plan, a stressful task given the importance attached to precedence in protocol at the Berlin Imperial Court. Miraculously, Rodd managed to pull this off, only highly annoyingly to be told by Herbert afterwards that it would not have mattered, since he had confused the general with someone else of the same name.[12] Such irritations apart, for most of the time Herbert Bismarck seems to have got on very well with the embassy diplomatic staff, Hardinge remembering how after balls and parties the young men of the Embassy were in the habit of going to late-night dinners at a 'well known *Brauerei*' where they drank beer and ate sprats, with Herbert generally joining them at midnight or shortly afterwards.[13]

Malet and his staff generally remained on excellent terms with the German imperial family, invited to dine on Queen Victoria's birthday with the Crown Prince and Princess at their main residence, the vast Neues Palais[‡] in Potsdam,[§] as well as to tennis and supper. Despite their concerns for the future on Lord Ampthill's death, Vicky and Fritz continued to find a relaxing refuge at 70 Wilhelmstrasse and were regular visitors, as was Vicky's brother the Prince of Wales, who came to Berlin for the Emperor Wilhelm's ninetieth birthday on 22 March 1887. In a piece of British–German cultural diplomacy, the composer Sir Arthur Sullivan was in the city at the time, conducting his *Golden Legend* at the Berlin Opera House, the Emperor presenting him with a conductor's baton made from ivory and gold. Sullivan was asked to help 'a dilettante theatre performance consisting of a short play and marionettes' in front of the Prince of Wales and several ambassadors.[14]

***

Despite these royal and imperial successes the Embassy itself was not proving to be quite as relaxing a home and workplace as Malet would have hoped. The house's fundamental design was continuing to be problematic, in particular the position of the stables underneath. City dwellers in the past would have been constantly aware of the aroma of horse droppings emanating from stables and everywhere in the streets, so the issue must have been particularly acute to prompt Malet to report it to London. In October 1885 he reported to the new Foreign Secretary that it was impossible to prevent the smells from coming 'into the dwelling rooms and

‡ The 'New Palace' at Potsdam built by Frederick the Great of Prussia in the 1760s, and still in existence.
§ Their Berlin residence was located in a palace on the south side of Unter den Linden opposite the Zeughaus (Arsenal), now the German Historical Museum. Destroyed in the Second World War, it was later rebuilt and is now used for cultural events.

the annoyance especially affects the Chancery which is situated immediately over them. It also affects in a less degree all parts of the house and my own working room is frequently heavily charged with it.'[15] Malet had finally been driven to commission a local engineer, a Mr Grove, to produce a report on the matter. Grove estimated that improvements could be made to the 'ventilating and sanitary arrangements' of the house for some £300, but the only long term solution was to remove the cause of the problem: the horses themselves, and to stable them elsewhere in the city. 'I could, if necessary, fortify my petition by a serious remonstrance from the gentlemen who have to work in the Chancery, as they have repeatedly brought the matter to my notice, but I think that Mr Grove's report is enough to show that the nuisance is serious and dangerous to health.'[16] Grove did not mince his words:

> The stables having been in continual use the masonry, owing to its porous nature, has gradually absorbed, and still continues to absorb the foul airs proceeding from horse-droppings and urine. It has, indeed, now become impregnated with these gases, and in the course of time will become so thoroughly saturated with them that it will be almost impossible to use the rooms situated above for Chancery or dwelling purposes.[17]

As Vicky had complained about palatial buildings in Berlin, the problem was exacerbated by the overall lack of ventilation in the house with its virtually airtight windows and new-fangled central heating. Damning Strousberg's and Orth's space-saving house design, Grove's conclusion was that the stables ought never to have been built under such a house in this manner.

Malet anticipated the inevitable question that would be asked by officials in London: why did his predecessor never complain of these smells? 'I can only reply that the room chiefly affected by it (now the Chancery and First Secretary's room) was at that time the billiard room only used in the evening, when the smell is always less, also that the nuisance is one that has grown up and been intensified by degrees, and that if one lives with a smell, small at the beginning, one perceives it less readily.'[18] Two months went by and nothing happened. In December Malet reminded Lord Salisbury that the smells were 'a source of constant discomfort to my staff and to myself.' Since Berlin was fast filling for the winter season, he urged the acquisition of stables as soon as possible.[19] Mercifully, on 29 January 1886 the Treasury gave permission to the Office of Works to purchase off-site stabling for the horses, but at a rate of no more than £120, the sum Malet had estimated it would cost.[20]

Malet waited another year for news from London about the drainage and sanitary situation. In December 1886 he wrote to the new Foreign Secretary the Earl of Iddesleigh with a new report on the house, urging him to take the matter up with the First Commissioner of Works to authorise the necessary works to make the house 'safely habitable'.[21] Still nothing happened, and by July of 1887 a note of panic began to creep into Malet's pleas:

> During the winter there has been sickness in the house, directly attributable to defective drainage, and in the hot months its condition naturally becomes more dangerous and offensive ... May I, under these circumstances earnestly beg your Lordship to urge the Treasury to give the necessary authorisation immediately, as my leave expires in the second week in August and I fear that the house will not be habitable while the

works are proceeding … I cannot look forward to passing another winter in the House, without serious danger to those who inhabit it.[22]

By now Robert Boyce must have thought that his doubts about the physical shortcomings of the Palais Strousberg had been fully vindicated. Rather than merely improving the deficient drainage, he recommended that 'the existing arrangements should be entirely changed' with the reduction of the number of 'closets, sinks and lavatories; to alter, with few exceptions, those that remain, so that they may discharge externally and not through the body of the house as at present, and to divert the underground sewers so that they may pass through the courtyard of the building'. The overall cost was some £700, but 'There is no doubt that it is absolutely necessary that the sanitary state of the building should be at once placed on a proper footing.'[23]

***

Thankfully, there were more glamorous matters to take the Malets' minds off the inadequacies of the house's sanitation arrangements. With its bustling commercial and political activity and growing moneyed population, Berlin was fast becoming a new European centre for the fine arts, attracting British artists. One of these was Sir Frederic Leighton, a favourite of the Crown Prince and a friend of the late Odo Russell (whom he had portrayed in 1863).[24] Leighton had studied at the Berlin Academy of Art, and at the end of his career the distinguished artist and President of the Royal Academy of Arts served on the selection jury of the 1891 Berlin Art Exhibition. Earlier, in 1886, William Blake Richmond had exhibited four portraits and his painting *Sarpedon* at the Berlin Royal Academy of Art Jubilee Exhibition, receiving a gold medal from the Emperor. Just as their modern counterparts support British culture abroad, the Malets visited the exhibition. They were evidently impressed by Richmond's work, for they commissioned him to come to Berlin to paint their portraits.

Writing to his family from the Embassy on 8 November 1887, Richmond recounted how he had been assigned a footman and a fine large room to use as a studio located on the attic floor. His daily routine, he later recounted, was to paint both of the Malets at the same time. He found them both 'charming and welcoming, he full of wisdom and dignity and she small and not pretty but pleasing and ladylike.'[25] Richmond especially enjoyed seeing Rodd again: he had taught Rodd at the Slade School of Art, when, encouraged by Sir Edward Burne-Jones, the multi-talented Rodd had entertained the prospect of becoming an artist before deciding to join the diplomatic service.

Richmond had completed the Malets' portraits* by the end of November 1887. In elaborate frames, they were exhibited at the New Gallery in London in 1888, Malet depicted in full diplomatic uniform. The critics were not kind. The *Athenaeum* reported that 'By far the most masculine and energetic portrait here by Mr. Richmond is the life-size, nearly whole-length *Sir E. Malet* (153) in his official

---

* The portraits are still in the ownership of the Malet family and located at Dillington House, Somerset. Unusually, Richmond depicted both sitters facing to the right rather than, as was the tradition for pairs of male and female portraits, one facing left and the other right.

21. & 22. Sir Edward Malet and Lady Ermyntrude Malet in a pair of portraits by William Blake Richmond painted at the Embassy in 1887.

costume which, as treated here, does not lend itself to art.'[26] *The Illustrated London News* was even less complimentary: 'The hideous diplomatic costume worn by [Sir Edward Malet] seems to be too heavy for his Excellency's legs to support, whilst the expression on his face is shy rather than reserved, saturnine rather than determined'. Lady Malet's portrait depicted her in a cream satin dress holding an ostrich feather, standing in a conservatory full of flowers. 'Lady Malet, on her part, seems to carry in her face the effects of over-dressing, mental and physical. The former protests against the latter – but "noblesse oblige" and she wears as the outward witness of her martyrdom a vapid face and a white satin dress trimmed with the richest lace.'[27]

Rodd was tactful about his friend Richmond's portrait of the Ambassador. 'If this formal portrait was not one of Richmond's successes, he was a great success himself.'[28] Indeed, while he was in Berlin, Richmond asked if he might be able to portray the famous Chancellor Bismarck. Perhaps feeling that he did not wish to be outdone by another of Richmond's sitters, W.E. Gladstone – whom Bismarck did not admire – the German Chancellor granted the request, and, accompanied by Rodd, Richmond arrived at Bismarck's private country residence at Friedrichsruh* near Hamburg in November 1887. During his stay he made four drawings and a (now lost) portrait in oils. Perhaps sensing that he was off-duty and could relax, Bismarck treated Richmond to some surprisingly candid opinions and confidences.[29]

***

The winter season of 1888 brought more excitement. Passing through Berlin on their way to St Petersburg, Lord and Lady Randolph Churchill were invited to stay

---

* The Emperor Wilhelm I had granted Bismarck this residence in 1871.

with the Malets on their return from the Russian capital. The second son of the 7th Duke of Marlborough, Churchill had married the American beauty Jeanette Jerome at the British Embassy in Paris in April 1874. Appointed Secretary of State for the India Office in 1885 and Leader of the House of Commons and Chancellor of the Exchequer in 1886, Lord Randolph was a close personal friend of Count Hatzfeldt, the German Ambassador to London. His personal conviction that Great Britain and Germany were natural allies spilled over into the proffering of unasked-for advice in this area to his political colleagues in the Foreign Office, much to their irritation – and, in Berlin, Malet's. In December 1886 Churchill had controversially resigned as Chancellor of the Exchequer.

Queen Victoria was alarmed at Lord Randolph's international travels, believing him 'devoid of all principle, who holds the most insular and dangerous doctrines on foreign affairs, who is very impulsive and utterly unreliable'.[30] During his first brief visit to Berlin, Lord Randolph met Herbert Bismarck at a dinner, but he reassured the Prince of Wales that nothing serious had been discussed concerning politics or diplomacy.[31] The British Government issued official denials that the ex-Cabinet member was travelling on government business, but nevertheless the unsanctioned diplomacy (of whatever form) and ambassadorial largesse was to continue in St Petersburg, where the stylish couple were entertained by Head of Mission Sir Robert Morier and Churchill granted a private audience with Tsar Alexander III. On 23 January 1888 the couple arrived back in Berlin for a ten-day stay at the Embassy, Malet meeting them on their arrival at the railway station and accompanying them to 70 Wilhelmstrasse. Ermyntrude, a friend of the Churchill family, apologised, diplomatically, for the smallness in scale of her dinner party that night in their honour, compared to the kind of events they would have been treated to in St Petersburg; nevertheless the party was a success. Invited to a gala performance at the opera attended by the German Emperor, even the stylish Lady Randolph (accompanied by Lady Malet) found she had to make a visit to the Court Mistress of the Robes to ensure that she was dressed correctly.[32] Further meetings with the imperial family were to follow when they were invited to Potsdam. The Crown Prince's eldest son, nineteen-year-old Prince Wilhelm, took tea with the Churchills at the Embassy, treating the guests to an increasingly heated monologue on what was always to be a pet subject, the importance of discipline at court balls.[33]

Using embassy stationery Lord Randolph wrote to his mother, evidently pleased with the way his trip had gone (apart from the interest shown by the press):

> Here we are very comfortable. I never travelled with so much circumstance before. The Malets are most kind and anxious to make everything very pleasant …. To-night Malet has an immense feast – thirty-six persons. I went this morning to Potsdam to write my name on Prince William, who called on us yesterday and saw Jennie while I was out. Then luncheon with Herbert Bismarck – very pleasant …. We talked very freely for a long time, and drank a great deal of beer, champagne, claret, sherry and brandy! H.B. is delightful – so frank and honest …. Some correspondents have been to see me, but I have been very snubby to them.[34]

***

It was at this time that Malet became involved in the progressively bitter relations between Crown Princess Victoria and the German imperial family (as well as German public opinion) over the medical treatment of her husband the Crown Prince. In January 1887 Friedrich developed a chronic hoarseness, the Crown Princess worryingly describing his symptoms to the Malets during her many visits to the Embassy. Later that year a growth on Fritz's larynx was surgically removed, only to reappear. The affliction was later diagnosed as terminal cancer. Fritz and Vicky secured the opinion of the British specialist Sir Morell Mackenzie, who recommended certain treatments that ran counter to the opinions of German doctors, even though evidence would suggest that it was the German doctors who had actually recommended the British specialist to the Crown Prince in the first place.[35] The oppressive atmosphere was exacerbated by the Crown Prince and Princess's eldest son Wilhelm's ever more acrimonious relationship with his parents, especially with his mother. Influenced by his grandfather the Emperor, Chancellor Bismarck, Herbert Bismarck and reactionary opinion in certain German political circles, Wilhelm's attitude towards the country of his mother's birth was to become increasingly vehement.

On 9 March 1888 the ancient Emperor Wilhelm finally died. Berlin was a "City in mourning": the streets all draped in black, with long pieces of black cloth hanging from the windows, black flags overhead and black drapery in the shops of various kinds; the people in mourning attire, and many persons selling to the passers-by the funereal garlands, wreaths and bouquets of appropriate flowers, intended to denote sympathy with the public regret.'[36] The close family relationships between British and German royalty naturally made this an important diplomatic event for the Embassy, and the roof of the building was draped in black. The Prince and Princess of Wales and their son Prince Albert Victor* arrived in Berlin from England on 14 March for the state funeral, Rodd for the next few days kept very busy hosting the royal mourners. The Emperor's funeral procession passed westwards from the Royal Schloss along Unter den Linden, through the Brandenburg Gate and the Tiergarten, for the burial at the Royal Palace of Charlottenburg, the route lined with burning torches upon pillars festooned with black crêpe and evergreens.[37]

Rodd later admitted to finding his duties at this time very onerous, as the staff struggled to find room in the Embassy for all the royal visitors' attendants as well as the protocol associated with the visit, both expected and unexpected: one morning Rodd's attention was drawn by loud cheering outside in the street, to find that Chancellor Bismarck had suddenly

23. The Embassy 'in mourning' for the death of the Emperor Wilhelm I, as reported by *The Illustrated London News*, 24 March 1888.

* Prince Albert Victor, Duke of Clarence (1864–92), known as 'Eddy'.

arrived at the Embassy to pay a call upon the Prince of Wales. Rodd's ingenuity – not to mention that of the household staff – was surely tested to the limit by Bertie on Sunday, 18 March, when, on the last day of the royal visit Rodd was suddenly asked to arrange a 'small impromptu' dinner party for what turned out to be thirty-two guests that very evening. Nevertheless he rose to the occasion, as, perhaps more importantly for the Prince, did the Embassy's chef, Mr Xavier, and the event passed off as though it had been in the diary for weeks.[38]

Armed with the knowledge that the Emperor's successor, Fritz – now Friedrich III – was by now living on borrowed time, Bismarck could effectively afford to ignore the new Emperor and Empress and concentrate on the succession of their son, whose behaviour was becoming increasingly overbearing. Friedrich's physical capacity as the Head of State was deteriorating fast: following a tracheotomy in February 1888, he was no longer even able to speak. To offer her support at such a critical moment for her daughter and son-in-law, in late April 1888 Queen Victoria herself visited Berlin on her return from holiday in southern Europe. Arriving at Charlottenburg railway station, she was met by Malet and other members of the embassy staff, and on 25 April, amid cheering crowds,

> went first to the British Embassy in the Wilhelm Strasse, which is a pretty house. Sir Edward Malet, & Ly Ermyntrude received me at the door, & he led me into the drawing-room, where we found Pss Bismarck, an elderly, rather masculine & not very 'sympathique' lady, & her son Ct Herbert, both very civil. Pce Radolin & his daughter, were also there. We took tea, & I was afterwards shown the Ball Room, a fine room, & the Dining Room. Then we took our departure, & drove to Mon Bijou, a Schlösschen of the Emperor's, in the grounds of which stands the very pretty English Church Vicky helped to get built…. The crowd was still great when we left, & the people were very friendly.[39]

That evening, the Malets dined at the Neues Palais with the Queen and other German dignitaries. The following day Queen Victoria left Berlin, her daughter Vicky's increasing emotional strain taking its toll, breaking down as her mother departed.[40] The atmosphere was grim: Queen Victoria and her daughter shared the terrible memory of their beloved husband and father's Albert's own premature death in 1861.

As well as providing comfort and moral support to her family in Berlin, the Queen's visit had poured some oil on to troubled waters over recent rumours and speculation over a possible marriage between the new Empress's daughter (another Victoria) and Prince Alexander of Battenberg, a marriage which was never to take place. The prospective match had been vetoed by the Emperor Wilhelm on the grounds of inequality of rank, while Bismarck feared Russian influence were it to take place, suspecting that the British were behind the idea. Manipulating the German press against the marriage, Bismarck instructed his Ambassador in London to warn the British Foreign Secretary of its likely adverse consequences, while Malet counselled Queen Victoria against the wisdom of her visit to Berlin.[41] Victoria herself was becoming increasingly concerned about her grandson Wilhelm's negative attitudes towards the land of his mother and grandmother. Indeed, the previous November Malet had been directed by Lord Salisbury to visit the German Foreign Office and ensure that 'Prince William's prejudices against

England, if they exist, may be dispelled.'[42] A month later, Queen Victoria had told the Embassy to clarify the point that 'there was no intentional ill will or controversy btn Pce. Wm. & his English Relations but that they had been shocked & pained at his behaviour towards his Parents for some time past…'[43]

Sir Frederick Ponsonby related the story that it was during the Crown Prince and Princess's stay the previous year in the sunnier climes of San Remo for Fritz's health that Fritz's diary was surreptitiously smuggled to England for fear of it falling into the hands of the Crown Prince or Chancellor Bismarck and being destroyed. The diary dated from the Franco-Prussian War and showed that Fritz, as well as Bismarck, had played a key role in the unification of Germany. According to Ponsonby, the English doctor Hovell (Mackenzie's assistant) was deputed to take the diary, not straight to England, but instead into the eye of the storm, to Berlin, where he managed to rouse the Ambassador from his bed late one evening. The diary was safely sent to London via the diplomatic bag.[44] In reality, preparations for safeguarding Fritz and Vicky's papers had been underway for some time: while staying at Windsor during Queen Victoria's Golden Jubilee celebrations during the summer of 1887, they had ensured that three chests of confidential papers were safely stored at Windsor Castle.[45] The papers were later returned to Berlin on Vicky's instructions.

When the diaries were published in Germany, Rodd recounted how Bismarck's reaction was characteristically explosive. Calling at the British Embassy to pay his respects on the occasion of Queen Victoria's birthday, the Chancellor turned his wrath on Lady Malet, the Ambassador having left the building. Rodd, who witnessed what took place, recorded the substance of Bismarck's candid harangue to the unfortunate Ambassadress. Bismarck told her he wanted Malet 'to know and I want your country to know that it was I and only I who alone made this German empire. It was my sole work. And how do you think I accomplished this? How did I succeed in triumphing over every obstacle and in crushing every man who stood in my way? … I will tell you. All this I achieved through … *cunning*. I set one man against another, and again and again I broke them.'[46]

***

Berlin was plunged into royal mourning for the second time in three months when, after only ninety-nine days on the throne, Fritz died a painful death at Charlottenburg on 15 June 1888. In a fruitless attempt to prevent his mother from removing private papers, Wilhelm had given orders that the building was to be surrounded the moment news broke of his father's death, and that no one – without exception – was to be permitted to leave.[47]

It was time for the Prince and Princess of Wales to make their way to Berlin once more, this time to pay their respects to their late brother-in-law. Rodd had to give up his rooms in favour of an 'improvised camp' for attendant staff in the Secretary of the Embassy's office.[48] Accompanied by their son Eddy, the Prince and Princess lunched at Potsdam with the new Emperor, Bertie's nephew – now the Emperor Wilhelm II – together with the new Empress and on Sunday, 24 June attended a ceremony at the English Church, where the Chaplain preached a special funeral sermon. Another dinner with the Malets at the Embassy followed,

24. Queen Victoria, the 'Grandmother of Europe' in a family group including her grandson the Emperor Wilhelm II, her eldest daughter the Empress Frederick and her son Edward Prince of Wales in a photograph taken at the Palais Edinburgh, Coburg in 1894 by J. Russell.

after which, accompanied by the Ambassador and Ambassadress, they drove in an open carriage to Friedrichstrasse railway station to start back for England, cheered all the way.[49] Despite appearances relations between England and Germany had, however, hit a new low during the visit: Malet reported to Lord Salisbury that Herbert Bismarck had blithely informed the Prince of Wales of his belief that the late Emperor Friedrich had been unfit to rule on account of his illness, and that the country had in effect been governed by his wife,[50] comments that Bertie and Alexandra understandably found rather less than amusing. Later that year, at Vicky's request, Rodd published Fritz's biography. Its uncritical and hagiographical contents[51] infuriated her son.

In Germany, a new era had dawned with the new, young Emperor Wilhelm II, who came to know the Embassy building as intimately as his uncle the Prince of Wales. Malet cheerfully reported to Lord Salisbury: 'Our dinner to the Emperor went off exceedingly well. His Majesty was more than in a good humour; he seemed to be quite light-hearted, and to enjoy the dinner and all the company invited to meet him. He talked to me after it was over until the time came for him to go away. He spoke with the greatest respect of the Queen.'[52] Even so,

25. A banquet in the Embassy ballroom during the Prince of Wales' visit to the German Emperor, as reported in *The Graphic* on 5 April 1890.

Wilhelm's attitude towards his many British royal relations was always ambivalent. His relationship with his uncle the Prince of Wales was to become increasingly complex, a mixture of envy, rivalry, resentment and jealousy of Edward's court, of his personal style and effortless leadership of society. For his part, Bertie disliked his nephew's air of superiority – Wilhelm had now become an Emperor while Bertie was to remain a Crown Prince for another twelve years – together with his seriousness and his military obsessions. The Princess of Wales never disguised her festering personal hatred for Berlin and all things German following the Prussians' conquest of Schleswig-Holstein in 1864. It was a loathing that came to be directed against her nephew Wilhelm in particular. Naturally, the British Embassy was sometimes the theatre in which these animosities were played out: at that same dinner on 30 March Wilhelm told Malet that, like his mother, he had 'that good stubborn English blood which will not give way', refusing to apologise for the slight he had given his uncle Bertie the previous October, when he had refused to meet him in Vienna.[53]

Chancellor Bismarck survived working with his erstwhile royal protégé only until the middle of March 1890 when he resigned from his post as Wilhelm sought to gain authority over the man who had dominated German political life and foreign policy for over three decades. Once again Bismarck suspected British influence behind the scenes; on the contrary, the British Government feared the instability that that the loss of so powerful a figure might well cause. Just a few days after Bismarck's fall Bertie and his son Prince George made a week-long official visit to Berlin, during which they were treated to military pageants and 'gorgeous' gala banquets, one of which was held in the British Embassy.[54] The two

Princes paid a visit to the recently-fallen Chancellor, but despite the irritation this may have caused Wilhelm, 'Nothing could have gone off better than the Prince of Wales' visit. There were no contretemps of any kind. The Emperor and H.R.H. appeared to be equally satisfied and pleased,' Malet sanguinely reported back to London.[55] Bismarck himself had made a theatrical final departure from his home on Wilhelmstrasse, driving with his son in a carriage past the Embassy, along streets thronged with people to the railway station where his successor as Chancellor, Leo von Caprivi, together with the assembled diplomatic corps, bade him farewell.

***

Journalists have always been fascinated by diplomatic lifestyles, and in late 1893 Malet gave an interview to *The Illustrated London News* as the first of a weekly series entitled 'Our Ambassadors'.[56] The writer effusively reported his experience in arriving at 70 Wilhelmstrasse and walking into the

> private study and business room of the Ambassador himself… whom, on entering, you are sure to find engaged in reading or writing. But he will at once leave off and receive you with the most exquisite courtesy – no matter what your errand – and place you completely at your ease. Dapper and delicate in person, of soft and insinuating voice, with a shrewd and penetrating eye, dashed, perhaps, with just a little distrustfulness and with a flattering preference for listening rather than expanding to his visitors, his Excellency is a perfect type of the trained and wary diplomatist.

Lady Ermyntrude was also praised. '… an Ambassadress worthier in all respects than Lady Ermyntrude could not well have been found, and though at Berlin there is not much society in the English sense of the term, it is admitted by all that, whether entertaining in her palace of the Wilhelmstrasse or in her summer *villegiatura* at Potsdam,[*] Sir Edward's social coadjutor is the perfection of a hostess.' Others, however, found her shy. Charles Hardinge remembered that she hardly spoke at all at dinners. Malet used to ask his staff to dine with them 'so as to draw her out, and we attempted to do so by addressing our conversation to her, but it was hard work, and whether it was that we succeeded too well, I am told that in her old age she never stopped talking. It should, however, be stated that when she did speak she showed an intimate knowledge of internal home politics.'[57]

26. Lady Ermyntrude Malet portrayed in a feature article on the British Embassy in Berlin in *The Illustrated London News*, 25 November 1893.

[*] Like many members of the British diplomatic corps in Berlin before and after, the Malets had a private summer house in Potsdam.

Despite her shyness, many praised Lady Ermyntrude as a kind and thoughtful hostess. Charles Lowe recalled how he and his wife were always invited to the Embassy at Christmas,

> when with the other guests we were invited to dip our hands in lucky bags – one for each sex. Lady Ermyntrude always made a point of going over specially to London herself to select those expensive Christmas presents for her guests. Thus my wife was fortunate enough to draw a gold bracelet set with diamonds, while to me fell a silver sovereign-purse which could equally accommodate gold pieces of twenty-mark, and I only wish I could now be blessed with an accumulated value of its contents.[58]

Generously, every New Year's Day Malet gave a party for apprentice Berlin chimneysweeps in a public hall. He was also an amateur poet and playwright, *The Illustrated London News* recounting that 'Some of his dramas – "Caterina Corio, Queen of Cyprus", for example, and "The Ordeal" – have been privately acted at Cairo, Rome and elsewhere, the author himself, like Shakespeare, taking part in their stage interpretation.' It seems likely that such private performances were given in the Embassy, using the sectioned-off stage in the red room.

Hardinge remembered that in the twelve months or so he spent in Berlin as Third Secretary in the middle of the 1880s, Sir Edward had been '*persona gratissima* at the German Court and in society', but that by the end of his posting the young Emperor was treating him with 'great discourtesy'. Hardinge ascribed this to the fact that Malet 'had behaved like a gentleman and had done his duty to his country in connection with the tragedy surrounding the illness and death of the Emperor Frederick'.[59] After eleven years' service in Berlin, in the summer of 1895 Malet wrote to the Queen to tell her that he wished to retire. His relations with Wilhelm continued to decline as hostile German sympathies responded to Britain's activities and perceived geopolitical ambitions in South Africa, where the Boers could count on instinctive support from Germany. That October, following talk of Germany taking the Transvaal under its protection, shortly before the Ambassador's departure from Berlin, Malet told the German Foreign Minister von Bieberstein that there might be 'serious consequences' if Germany continued to support the Boers.[60] Wilhelm decided to regard such remarks as a threat, a British ultimatum to Germany to desist from such support. It was an inference Malet strongly denied.[61]

Cecil Spring-Rice arrived to take up the post of Embassy Second Secretary in October 1895 and described a typical evening in the last few weeks of the Malets' posting to Berlin. Although generous with their hospitality towards the embassy staff, after enduring eleven years of representational duties the couple's entertaining routines had evidently become stuck in a rut:

> We dine with the Ambassador nearly every night and play whist afterwards. It is all regulated carefully. At eight exactly we enter the drawing-room in proper precedence, that is by seniority; we are received by the Ambassadress in turn; also in precedence. Then at eight o'clock and five minutes, dinner is announced and we go in. As the same party meets every night and has met every night for more than a year, the conversation is not greatly varied. At nine-thirty we leave the table, stay

ten minutes in the drawing-room with the ambassadress and then file into the smoking-room where we stay till ten. At ten precisely we rejoin the ambassadress and drink tea till ten-thirty, when we play whist till twelve, when we all go to bed. This is repeated every day with absolute uniformity so that there is never any doubt as to when to go and when not to go .... Unfortunately my knowledge of whist is defective, so I generally sit by and read.[62]

In another letter to his brother, Spring-Rice described the Malets' official departure from Berlin: 'The ceremony at the station was a curious one; full of formality tempered by kissing. I admire the reserve of both of them; all sorts of interesting things were going on but neither of them showed it. They were both absolutely impassive ...'[63] According to Rodd (who had left Berlin for another posting in October 1888), as a sign of deteriorating relations and an ominous pointer to the future, the Emperor had shown Malet his displeasure at the Ambassador's apparent 'threat' regarding the future of South Africa by not sending an official from the Palace to represent him at the station for the Malets' departure.[64]

Hardinge remembered that 'without being a brilliant man, Sir Edward was a man of tact, of sound common sense and judgment, and imbued with all the best traditions of diplomacy and of our Diplomatic Service.'[65] For Rodd, he was 'the kindest of men and the best of friends, who was like a father and a brother to his staff.'[66] On his return to England Malet maintained his literary interests, writing two volumes of memoirs, and undertaking some less onerous duties on the fringes of the political and diplomatic worlds. He and Ermyntrude remained childless. He died in June 1908 and, having married into the Russell family, his ashes joined those of Lord Ampthill in the Bedford family chapel at Chenies in Buckinghamshire.

Ermyntrude survived her husband by nineteen years. She died at her house in Eaton Square in London in March 1927, a month after Lady Ampthill's death at Ampthill House in Bedfordshire. After her return to England from Berlin in 1884 Emily had been made a Lady of the Bedchamber by Queen Victoria, a position she held for the remainder of the Queen's reign. Left with her memories of Berlin from the 1870s and 1880s, Emily never remarried and outlived her husband by forty-two years. Like Ermyntrude she had lived on into the Jazz Age, a new post-World War era of abstract art, scientific advancement, female emancipation and revolution.

CHAPTER 6
1895–1908: 'FAMILY EMBASSY'

> What, indeed, is to be made of a Sovereign, who, arriving with his Imperial Consort to a dinner of State at the Embassy, ushered himself in with the following tirade: – "This is abominable, Lascelles. Here I am in the uniform of your King's Navy come to dine with you, and at this moment your ships are bombarding my Consulate at Samoa". Things once went so far that Lascelles, with a courtly bow, replied: – "In that case, Your Majesty, I can do nothing but beg my Sovereign to replace me by someone who will be better able to maintain those good relations between the two countries which I am sure Your Majesty desires." "Don't talk damned nonsense, Lascelles! Of course I want you, and no other Ambassador here."[1]

The Emperor Wilhelm II's behaviour could be eccentric, unpredictable and dramatic, as Malet's successor Sir Frank Lascelles came to know only too well. Even so he was able to develop a good working and personal relationship with him, certainly the best of the three British Ambassadors to Wilhelm's Court.

Once Sir Edward Malet had informed Queen Victoria that he wished to leave Berlin, the question necessarily arose over who should succeed him. After discussing the matter with her new Prime Minister Lord Salisbury on 6 August 1895 the Queen spoke personally on the matter to her grandson Wilhelm, her guest at Osborne House at the time. Hinting at the possibility of appointing a special military ambassador rather than a career diplomat, this was a prospect Wilhelm apparently 'jumped at'[2] fitting in with his ambitions for Berlin's importance and status to be given better international recognition, as well as appealing to his military proclivities. As Lord Salisbury was to describe it, the Emperor wanted 'a soldier or a *grand seigneur*'.[3] Secretary of State for War the Marquess of Lansdowne duly asked the distinguished Field-Marshal Lord Wolseley if he wished to take the post of British Ambassador to Berlin. Unfortunately for Wolseley, that meant sacrificing the post of Commander-in-Chief of the British Army, in his sights once Queen Victoria's cousin George, Duke of Cambridge relinquished it. Wilhelm was anxious for Wolseley to assume the ambassadorship and Queen Victoria informed Lansdowne that her nephew would be disappointed if this did not become reality. Wolesley was naturally flattered at the offer, but he told Lansdowne that he much preferred an appointment which would after all be the pinnacle of his military career – the head of the British Army.

It was an awkward situation, Queen Victoria realising that offering Wolseley both opportunities at the same time had not been a sensible tactic, as he was bound to choose the army over the diplomatic service. Wilhelm, she knew, 'would be grievously disappointed', and she broke the news to him from Balmoral in late

August. She explained that Wolseley had made his own choice, and that she and Lord Salisbury had decided to offer the post to Sir Frank Lascelles, the current British Ambassador to St Petersburg. Attempting to reassure Wilhelm over his anxieties about Berlin's importance in international diplomatic rankings she explained that Lascelles was 'one of our best diplomatists'. 'In this choice I have been most anxious to find someone who would be agreeable to you and would do all he could to maintain the best relations between the two countries; and I am sure Sir F. Lascelles will do that.'[4] And so Lascelles left the Russian capital, his period as Ambassador there much curtailed.

Victoria was also able to reassure her grandson, who had a deep regard for such matters, of Lascelles' aristocratic credentials: his grandfather was the 2nd Earl of Harewood;* his mother was the daughter of George Howard, 6th Earl of Carlisle; and he was the first cousin of the Duke of Devonshire. Entering the diplomatic service in 1861 at the age of twenty, he served as an attaché in Madrid and then Paris, where he married Mary Oliffe, the daughter of the official physician to the British Embassy. He briefly served in Berlin under Loftus, who found Lascelles and his wife 'very popular in society and agreeable additions to our small circle'.[5] He was then in Paris again before appointments, on the usual diplomatic merry-go-round, to Copenhagen, Rome, Washington, DC, Athens, Cairo and Sofia, rising up through the ranks to become Minister to Romania in 1887, to Persia and then to St Petersburg in 1894.

27. Sir Frank Lascelles caricatured by 'Spy' [Sir Leslie Ward] for *Vanity Fair*, 27 March 1902.

* * *

Within a comparatively short time of his arrival in Berlin in January 1896 Lascelles experienced a foretaste of the gradual deterioration in Anglo-German diplomatic relations that was to characterise the next two decades. Tensions were continuing to mount over the two countries' colonial rivalries in Africa, particularly in the south of the continent. In December 1895 Dr Leander Starr Jameson made a raid on the Transvaal, the Emperor's Government sending a supportive telegram to Paul Kruger, its President, the following January. It proved a diplomatic disaster in Germany's relations with Great Britain.

Nevertheless and in complete contrast with what was to be his relationship with the new Ambassador's successor, Wilhelm was to develop a personal rapport with Lascelles and often visited the Embassy on an informal basis during his

* The family seat is Harewood House, near Leeds.

ambassadorship. Spring-Rice recounted one such imperial visit in March 1896. At about ten in the evening

> … there was a crowd before the Embassy. Three carriages drove rapidly up. Policemen started up from the ground in every direction. The first carriage stopped and a uniformed gentleman stepped out, followed by another, whom I recognised as the Emperor. He was met on the steps by Sir Frank, who escorted him up the stairs, laughing and talking. The crowd observed in stolid silence.

Spring-Rice then set off for a party. At half past midnight he returned to check on events, only to find that the Emperor was still in the Embassy, talking with the ladies in the front drawing room. 'He talked continually, giving hardly any time to answer – about 'grand-mamma' and Cowes, and Lord Dunraven and his journey to Cumberland'. The Emperor then stood up, but instead of leaving, asked for a whisky and soda and cigar, and, crossing the entrance hall, went into the Ambassador's office, 'where he talked, walking about rather excitedly, with gesticulations – not waiting for an answer'. By this time everyone was exhausted but etiquette forbade them from leaving before the royal guest. 'We waited and waited. No move. At last, at 1.30 am he got up and went.'[6] Spring-Rice had no illusions about the reasons for such overtly friendly behaviour: it was intended to nullify bad feelings about the Emperor's ostensibly anti-British conduct a few weeks earlier in the wake of the Jameson Raid affair.[†]

A major feature of the winter social scene in Berlin was the regular Wednesday afternoon receptions at the Embassy for the British community in Berlin,[7] and a flavour of the social atmosphere of Lascelles' period as Ambassador was given by Lady Susan Townley in her memoirs. Lady Susan married the diplomat Sir Walter Townley in 1896 and they were posted to Berlin in 1898. She remembered that during the winter season of 1900 the Emperor Wilhelm was in mourning for his mother-in-law,[‡] 'and we on our side were also in Court mourning, so that neither the Court nor the Embassy could entertain or see anything of society. But it was possible for the Emperor to come alone to a "family" Embassy, even though he was in mourning, so it happened that he often dined quite informally with his dear friend, Sir Frank Lascelles, our delightful Chief.'[8]

The Emperor's birth had been a difficult, breech one, during which his mother the Crown Princess had nearly died. Despite painful and fruitless attempts at improvement in childhood, one of his arms was infirm. This has been interpreted as one of the reasons behind Wilhelm's friction with his parents, especially with his mother; for, rather than supporting her son in successfully mastering and disguising his disability, she saw it as a weakness.[9] Her habit of unfavourably comparing Wilhelm with the sainted reputations of his two younger dead brothers[§]

[†] As well as being a frequent personal visitor to the building, Wilhelm had a personal reason to be deeply grateful for his close association with the Embassy and its personnel. In 1880 he had accidentally capsized a skiff belonging to the Embassy on one of the lakes around Potsdam, tipping him and Lady Ampthill into deep water. She managed to support him for five minutes before help arrived and so prevent him from drowning (as told by Lady Ampthill to Lord Frederick Hamilton, reported in his *The Vanished Pomps of Yesterday: Being Some Random Reminiscences of a British Diplomat*, pp. 74–5).

[‡] Adelheid of Hohenlohe-Langenburg (1835–1900).

[§] Sigismund (1864–66) and Waldemar (1868–79).

hardly improved the relationship. At meals Wilhelm had to use special cutlery, which on one occasion, when dining at the Embassy, had been forgotten and so had to be sent for from the Imperial Palace. It was hardly surprising that Wilhelm disliked bringing attention to his infirmity in this manner, particularly in such august surroundings. His characteristic short temper took over the occasion and '… to the dismay of all present, he let the sparks fly, upbraiding his equerry for his forgetfulness.'[10] On the other hand Lady Susan remembered that 'At dinner on these informal occasions at the Embassy he was at his best, gay, debonair, informal, and witty. After dinner I often had a chance of a *tête à tête* with him, for there were no ladies present, except old Lady Edward Cavendish, Sir Frank Lascelles' sister, who entertained for him, and his then unmarried daughter, Florence.'[11] Lascelles had been devoted to his wife, but in 1897, not long after their arrival in Berlin, she had died. Lascelles much mourned her.

Lady Susan recounted that she and her husband 'were once present at a dinner given to the Kaiser at our Embassy in 1899 when Cecil Rhodes, who was the guest of honour, asked to meet him'. This was on 14 March of that year, following a private interview between Rhodes and the Emperor: despite Wilhelm's jealousies of British colonial activities in Africa, he came to admire Rhodes' strident self-confidence in furthering Great Britain's ambitions in that continent. Fittingly in the railway king Strousberg's former home, before going into dinner Rhodes spoke of his grand conception of a British-built Cape to Cairo railway. Following the ladies' customary withdrawal after dinner, Rhodes tried to divert Wilhelm's attention regarding railways in Africa towards the possibility of building them in Mesopotamia. For the rest of the evening Wilhelm was thoughtful and reserved: with hindsight, Lady Susan believed it was at that moment that he thought up the idea of the Berlin to Baghdad Railway.[12]

***

Court functions in Berlin revolved around an annual winter 'season' that lasted from the New Year until Easter. During the season the well-to-do flocked to the city from all over Germany and many entertainments were organised. The Emperor was anxious that his court should shine – it was another example of his jealousy of England, with its long-established fashions and traditions he felt contrasted unfavourably with those in the recently established parvenu capital of Germany. Wilhelm very much wanted to increase the glamour and ceremony of his court, and to attract the rich and famous to the capital. Even though Lady Susan generally disliked 'dull, heavy Berlin', the magnificence of Emperor Wilhelm II's court deeply impressed her, describing the Royal Schloss with its 'great white-painted rooms with their crystal and gold, and their countless mirrors, the throne-room with its throne, worthy of Solomon, under its magnificently ornamented dais…'[13] The magnificence was accompanied by great formality for those attending the functions.

Under Wilhelm II court culture blossomed and featured extraordinarily archaic ceremonial and extravagant pomp and circumstance, all detailed in the official Prussian Court handbook that classified the different members of the royal household and various connected families, plus over 2,300 court officials with their various rankings. These ranged from the high-ranking members of the Principal

Chamberlain's office (located at 73 Wilhelmstrasse), to administrators, musicians and artists at the royal theatres, and rifle loaders, silverware superintendents and equerries. Court precedence was regulated to no fewer than sixty-two individual rankings, a uniquely high number in European court history. Complicated protocols dictated who could and who could not take part in an enormous number of ceremonial occasions, and there were detailed instructions as to how guests were to behave, how they were to dress, and the order in which they could be presented to the different members of the imperial family.[14] Playing their rigidly defined parts in all of this formality were more diplomats in Berlin than at any other capital, many German states continuing to send a separate legation to Berlin.

Following the annual *Graturlirungscour* and *Militärcour** of 1 January for diplomats and military personnel, the first event of the Berlin winter season was the *Schleppencour*† at which guests and diplomats would ascend a long staircase at the Royal Schloss, where, at the top, a guard of honour waited and presented arms to all the ambassadors. Progressing through the rooms the guests finally came to the famous White Room, described *in Baedeker's Berlin and its Environs* for 1912 with some concern for exactitude as 'a large hall 105 ft in length, 52 ft in width and 43 ft high'. Although the room dated from 1728, in the mid-1890s Wilhelm typically had it refurbished in a more ostentatious style:

> The ceiling has been raised and has received a rich plastic decoration, the four central spaces being adorned with the arms of the Hohenzollern as Burgraves, Electors, Kings and Emperors. The reliefs on the vaulting between the walls and the ceiling are by O. Lessing and represent victorious war as the fosterer of art, science, trade, and industry. The walls are decorated in coloured marble and gilded bronze. Between the coupled pilasters on the long side are 9 marble statues of Prussian rulers as they appeared at the time of their accession to the throne …[15]

In this vast and overblown room the Emperor and Empress would be waiting on thrones, surrounded by other members of the imperial family, the German princes and other members of the Court. Ambassadors' wives, in the order dictated by diplomatic protocol – Great Britain was still first – entered the room and arriving opposite the throne would make a low curtsey, and then went to stand at the foot of the throne. The senior Ambassadress, the Doyenne, then called out the names of each lady to be presented to the Court. When the last had passed the Doyenne followed her out of the room, without turning her back on the Emperor and Empress. Then it was the turn of the ambassadors who underwent much the same process, and then other diplomats and members of the Court. Finally a buffet supper was served.[16]

At court balls the guests were required to assemble in the ballroom before a certain time. At one side of the room were the thrones for the Emperor and Empress and to the right chairs for the ambassadors' wives; their husbands stood, all in the correct diplomatic order. To the left of the thrones were the German princes. As the Emperor and Empress entered the room, they usually split up in order to walk round each side of the room, or 'make the circle', briefly speaking

---

* 'Congratulatory' and 'Military' courts, for New Year's Day.
† Named after the long trains – *Schleppen* – worn by the ladies.

28. The glamour of the Berlin season as captured by the artist Adolph Menzel in his 'Supper at the Ball' ['Das Balsouper'] in 1878.

to all of the guests. The dancing, when it began, was to be undertaken only by young men and women who were suitably practised in the art, all under the rigid oversight of *Vortänzer*, or superintending young officers aiming to see that the dancing was strictly conducted according to etiquette. Predictably, this rigid approach might well have had the opposite effect from the one intended: 'the best thing for the new-comer who arrived with ideas of amusing him or herself was not to try and dance at all,' remembered a British military attaché.[17] Supper was at 10.30, followed by more formal dancing, the event finishing before midnight as guests passed slowly through the long gilded halls to their waiting carriages.[18]

Up to 2,000 people attended court balls at the Palace.[19] 'Never have I known anything so stiff and formal as Berlin "official" receptions,' Susan Townley later recounted:

> Nobody spoke above a whisper, and the room was sibilant with hissed consonants. I frequently had to attend these gatherings, and they were something of an ordeal to one unaccustomed to an etiquette so rigid and so complicated. For instance, there was a distinct code of etiquette concerned with the sofa. Unfortunately, I committed a serious breach of this sofa etiquette at a party which we attended at our Embassy on the very day of our arrival in Berlin, when I ventured for a moment to sit down at one end of a huge settee, in the distant corner of which, talking together, sat two ladies whom I afterwards discovered were Countess Bülow, the wife of the Minister for Foreign Affairs, and Countess Brockdorff, the Grande Dame de la Cour' … The two women remarked pointedly, 'Ah! Now we are three Excellencies on this sofa!'[20]

Lady Susan immediately jumped up, later learning that as a member of the Embassy she was expected always to pay very formal respects to Countess Bülow, the wife of the Foreign Secretary (in 1900 he was to become German Chancellor).

New Year's Day was a particularly important and splendid occasion: 'All the Ambassadors go in state coaches to see the Emperor, and all the generals and many of the Princes to up to Berlin to pay respects: the place is full of splendid uniforms and gold coaches. In the afternoon the Emperor calls on the Princes and Ambassadors, leaving cards in person; his coach is bigger and finer than the others,' as Spring-Rice recounted in a letter of 2 January 1897. Stable hands and coachmen prepared the Ambassador's coach and horses at the off-site stabling and brought it to the Embassy for Sir Frank to undertake his formal diplomatic duties. Perhaps he was biased, but Spring-Rice thought the British Ambassador looked the best.[21]

The annual New Year's custom of receiving hundreds of cards from acquaintances, noting who had left them, and then returning the compliment by paying return visits and leaving cards was always a trying exercise for embassy staff and the Ambassador and his wife, as Lady Emily Russell had found. James Rennell Rodd had noticed that Field Marshal von Moltke, who attended a dinner at the Embassy in the winter season of 1888, had perfected a timesaving yet polite method of dealing with these tedious necessities of protocol: when visitors called on his residence to offer their card, a porter stood ready with a supply of cards immediately ready to offer them in return.[22]

But, despite all the ceremony, glamour and close family dealings with the Emperor, Spring-Rice was not alone in sensing the gradual deterioration in German–British diplomatic relations, writing at the end of 1895 concerning hostile articles in the German press: 'It is curious how detested we are and especially odd to find that in Germany we are hardly ever mentioned without some term of abuse or reproach.' But he was enjoying himself in the capital, where there were many sources of entertainment, theatres and concerts. Most diplomatic staff until the Second World War were expected to find their own accommodation at whichever mission to which they were posted and the unmarried Spring-Rice had set up lodgings with fellow bachelor Colonel James Grierson, the Military Attaché to the Embassy. The duties of a military attaché were 'primarily to keep the military authorities in his own country abreast of the development of military matters in the country in which he was resident,' Grierson's biographer carefully explained.[23] The Colonel had spent time liaising with the German Government in the late 1880s while working in the Russian section of the army intelligence division and was liked by the military-minded Emperor.[24]

As Odo Russell's fourth son, Lt. Colonel the Hon. Alexander Russell (Fritz's godson, and who was to serve as Military Attaché in Berlin before the Great War), described, the position in the German capital was 'a more brilliant one on account of the special attention which the Emperor … invariably paid to the military representatives of foreign powers. The number of parades, military functions, gala operas, etc to which we were invited was larger, I am convinced than at any other Court, and on nearly all these occasions the foreign Military Attachés … were "made a fuss of" by the Emperor.'[25] Wilhelm was quite capable, however, of manipulating the friendships he made with British military attachés to obtain and pass on sensitive information to his own Government. Intelligence gleaned from Colonel Leopold Swaine, for example, about British battleships and troops was passed on to the German Government and even to the Tsar of Russia.[26] The unfortunate Swaine was used as a go-between on several occasions between Wilhelm and the Prince of Wales and between Wilhelm and the British Ambassador and sometimes became the temporary focus of Wilhelm's fury. Wilhelm was also to turn several of

Swaine's successors into the hapless recipients of his personal displeasure against British policy.

Attended by a manservant and in typical bachelor fashion, Spring-Rice tended to use his lodgings, where he had his pictures and books, as little more than a dormitory. He found Colonel Grierson 'as tough as nails'. Grierson took full part in a hectic social life amongst the embassy staff and with the German Court, recording balls and other entertainments in his diary.[27] However, from the point of view of sharing lodgings one must wonder how much the cultured Spring-Rice and the military-minded Grierson had in common with each other. The Colonel's furniture consisted of 'military pictures of the proceedings of his Scotch regiment in various parts of the world, and of his brother officers; various arms, trophies of war, which he won in battle from people who tried to use them against the Scotch regiment; and one armchair. In a stable below, he keeps a mare and six dogs.'[28]

**

Major British state occasions such as coronations, jubilees and royal birthdays and weddings are great opportunities to promote the country abroad, and in July 1897 the Embassy celebrated the Diamond Jubilee of Queen Victoria in the German capital with an 'English dinner' and children's entertainment 'which was a pretty sight – all the little English boys and girls marching along with enormous British flags.'[29] More exhausting for the embassy staff was the six-hour rail journey to Kiel on the Baltic coast for a festivity given by the Emperor on board his yacht. Wilhelm's behaviour continued to test their patience (and stamina) as well as those of the British and German Foreign Offices, but there was at least some reward for anyone with a sense of humour. The Emperor's close relationship with the Embassy and its staff 'affords us endless amusement with his goings-on,'[30] Spring-Rice recounted in letters to his family and friends, these 'goings-on' including his habit of catching people psychologically off-guard by calling on them early in the mornings before they had risen. It was all part of Wilhelm's political modus operandi; he treated Chancellor Bismarck to this conduct,[31] and on more than one occasion he adopted the same tactics towards the British Ambassador in the Embassy itself.

One morning in December 1896 Spring-Rice was sitting at his desk in the Chancery perusing some all-too-typical anti-British sentiment in the German press when 'a pale servant raced in' and told him that the Emperor was in the building but the Ambassador was still in bed. Spring-Rice got up to speak to Wilhelm, only to find him in the Ambassador's office 'rampaging about with a clattering sword – confidential print lying everywhere about'.* Wilhelm told Spring-Rice he was determined to see the Ambassador. Spring-Rice rushed upstairs to raise him, finding him 'in pink pyjamas, two horror-stricken servants rushing about his room'. Lascelles instructed Spring-Rice to keep the Emperor occupied while he would go downstairs as soon as he could. Spring-Rice did his best to entertain an impatient Emperor; fortunately five minutes later 'an unwashed and strangely apparelled Ambassador shot down the stairs'. The Ambassador then asked Spring-Rice to produce a particular telegram for the Emperor, but, highly embarrassingly,

---

* The Emperor had presumably gained entrance into the Ambassador's study to the right of the entrance hall.

29. The Emperor Wilhelm II strikes a modest pose in Ferdinand Keller's portrait of 1893.

he was unable to lay his hands on it. He was mortified; but for his part, Wilhelm was greatly amused, asking Lascelles if his secretaries were 'as bad as his own aides-de-camp. Such were the Imperial words which will naturally live for ever in my mind', Spring-Rice mournfully recorded.[32]

While Lady Susan Townley had good memories of Berlin in the early months of her husband's posting, this changed after the start of the Boer War in 1899, members of the Court splitting into pro-Boer/anti-British and pro-British groups. The Emperor was fixated by the war, giving him as it did a practical opportunity to test out pet military theories – from the safe distance of Berlin. When dining at the Embassy he often took the opportunity to lecture his fellow guests on the mistakes he believed the British generals were making, and to suggest possible improvements. 'He would stride up and down the room, explaining what _he_ would have done had _he_ been an English general.'[33] Lascelles was personally treated to the Emperor's Boer War obsession at extremely close quarters. The Ambassador recounted to Lady Susan another example of the Emperor's unannounced early morning visits:[34]

One day, one of the Embassy maidservants was busy washing the doorstep at eight o' clock in the morning, when a car drove up out of which sprang two German officers in uniform. One of them asked to see the British Ambassador, who at that early hour was still asleep. 'Never mind,' he said, 'tell him the Emperor is here and desires to see him instantly'. The surprised housemaid summoned the butler, who rushed upstairs to raise Sir Frank. 'What is it?' he enquired sleepily, for his habit was to work long past midnight, and the general order was not to call him until he rang the bell. 'What is it?' he growled. 'It is the Emperor', said a voice at the door, and a figure pushed past the horrified servant. It was indeed His Majesty, who in his impatience had followed the servant up to Sir Frank's bedroom.[†]

Our Ambassador's embarrassment can be more easily imagined than described. 'Here was I,' he said to me afterwards in describing the scene, 'still half-asleep, unwashed, unshaved and unfed. I had not even had my breakfast. My bedroom slippers and my dressing-gown were both out of reach. My frantic desire was to find an excuse to open my window, for I

[†] The door to the master bedroom of the house was located on the first floor above the dining room, at the top of the staircase, the door opening on to the landing above the entrance hall.

became acutely conscious that my room was stuffy. A bright idea! I offered His Majesty a cigarette. If he accepted I would get the chance of getting out of bed to find one – a man is at such a terrible disadvantage when an Emperor sits on his bed! But the Kaiser did not want to smoke. He had come to see me on very important business. He pushed me back on the pillows and advanced nearer, unfurling and placing before me a roll of documents and maps which he had brought with him. Then I realized that it was a question of yet another campaign which he had worked out. I seized the excuse of insufficient light for the study of the plans to plead for permission to get out of bed for a moment. I secured gown and slippers, pulled back the curtains and threw open the window.* But the Emperor declared that I would catch cold, and insisted on my getting back into bed before he would expose his plan of campaign'. Half an hour passed and the key to British victory was placed in Sir Frank's hands, with an earnest request that it might be instantly dispatched to London. Then His Majesty prepared to leave. As he turned towards the door Sir Frank sprang out of bed and again possessed himself of his slippers. Standing in his pyjamas, he bowed as the Emperor passed out, but was still further discomfited to see through the open doorway a magnificent *Garde du Corps* officer in uniform, who had been waiting for his master outside. Pointing to Sir Frank in his undiplomatic attire, the Emperor called out, '*Hier is eine Erscheinung!*' ('Here's a vision!'), and shaking hands with the Ambassador he ran down the stairs and out of the house, laughing heartily.[35]

Meanwhile Florence Lascelles 'had mobilised the servants in the hall to try to make a better effect'.[36]

The Emperor's antics of this sort became an international joke. 'More Revelations! The Kaiser and Sir Frank Lascelles: An Ambassador in his Shirt.' screamed the front page of the *Daily Graphic* on 13 October 1906, in a short article appearing to refer to the same incident, coinciding with the publication of the gossipy Court memoirs of the Prince of Hohenlohe-Schillingfürst. There had been chatter in the Continental press that the Emperor had entered the bedroom of the French Ambassador to Berlin while he was asleep, but the latter was able to put the story straight and record that the incident had in fact taken place in the British Embassy.

***

On 31 December 1899 Grierson noted in his diary that he had

Dined at the Embassy and with Sir Frank at the Schloss. We had, first, service in the chapel … Then as the service ended at 12 o'clock the guns began to fire thirty-three rounds that it was the *1st January* 1900 … The Germans call this the new century tho' we do not, and the mutual congratulations were numerous. Then we had a 'Defilir Cour' before the Emperor and Empress, and then I drove back with Sir Frank to the Embassy where we all wished one another a Happy New Year.[37]

* The master bedroom windows overlooked the Embassy's internal courtyard.

30. The Embassy's spectacular staircase hall (from *The Illustrated London News*, 25 November 1893).

At a dance held by the Townleys on 24 January Grierson told Lascelles that Lord Roberts had asked him to go to South Africa to be in charge of the foreign military attachés there, and by the end of that month he had left Berlin. The Townleys left themselves a few months later, having been posted to Rome, a post they were initially unable to accept owing to the high associated costs: 'To settle up accounts in Berlin, transport our household to Rome, and furnish a home there, meant an expenditure of hundreds of pounds – which we had not got.' The problem was remedied in a highly unorthodox manner, by placing a bet on the winning horse at the Lincoln Handicap at 72/1.[38]

January 1901 marked the bicentenary of the Kingdom of Prussia. As representatives from European courts arrived in the capital the streets of Berlin were gay with decorations. But a few days later the festivities were interrupted by some disturbing news from England: the elderly Queen Victoria was ill. The Embassy received worried enquiries from well-wishers, *The Times* reporting that 'All the festivities for which the Ambassador, Sir Frank Lascelles, had issued invitations, have been abandoned.'[39] As news of the Queen's condition worsened, deserting the celebrations the Emperor made his way to England to be with his grandmother at Osborne House. Dining with Lascelles while waiting for news from England, at about half past seven on 22 January embassy staff received the dreaded bulletin carrying the news that the Queen had died; the Emperor himself had been at her bedside when she breathed her last. This communication transmitted to the Imperial Court, later that evening Master of Ceremonies, Count zu Eulenberg, and the Empress's Mistress of the Robes, Countess Brockdorff, paid their calls upon Lascelles and Lady Edward Cavendish. News quickly spread in Berlin through a special edition of a newspaper.

In a black-lined edition *The Times* correspondent wrote that 'It is impossible on the first receipt of the intelligence, although it had not been unexpected, to realize the change – the blank – created by the removal of the unparalleled personality of the Queen with particular reference to the relations of Germany and England,'[40] although it was recognised that the close dynastic ties binding together the two countries were 'a matter for congratulation'. On 31 January Lascelles himself left for England to attend the state funeral in London. In his absence, the Emperor had ordered that the ships of the German navy, and all public buildings, were to fly their flags at half-mast with the British flag at the mainmast on the day of Queen Victoria's funeral, Saturday, 3 February 1901. That same day two memorial services were held in St George's Church in Berlin. The first, 'official' one stood in for the funeral service itself; as Lascelles was attending the 'real' service in England, it was hosted by the Embassy's First Secretary, the 3rd Viscount Gough. A number

31. The new English Church in Berlin not long after its construction shown in an engraving published in *The Graphic* on 10 July 1886.

of distinguished German guests were present, amongst them several members of the German imperial family, other German royal families and members of the diplomatic corps, '[t]he greater part of the Church was filled with brilliant military uniforms.'[41] At two o'clock the same day the British community in Berlin attended a second service, the numbers so great that many were unable to enter the church.

While the Prince of Wales succeeded to his mother's throne as King Edward VII immediately upon her death, diplomatic and royal protocol demanded the official announcement of his accession worldwide by representatives of the royal family. On 7 April 1901 the Special Mission for this arrived in Berlin from its previous port of call, St Petersburg, Lascelles entertaining members of the Mission to lunch and dinner at the Embassy the following day. The formal announcement of the accession took place on 9 April at the Schloss, followed that evening by a State banquet and the re-presentation of Lascelles' diplomatic credentials to the Emperor (as was required following a change of Monarch). Wilhelm II remained with the English guests until nearly midnight, presenting gifts to the members of the Special Mission.[42]

Just four months later, on 5 August, after a long and painful battle with breast cancer, Wilhelm's mother died. Never having achieved a happy relationship with her eldest son, for many years Vicky, the 'Empress Frederick', had lived in widowhood at Friedrichshof, a vast schloss near Kronberg she built in memory of her much-mourned beloved husband. Bertie made yet another melancholy visit to Berlin for the funeral of his favourite sister: she was buried with full honours next to her beloved Fritz in the family vault in Potsdam.

Close British and German royal family ties soon created further opportunities for the Emperor Wilhelm to revel in pomp and circumstance in Berlin. King Edward and Queen Alexandra's eldest son, Prince Albert Victor ('Eddy'), had died in 1892, so it was their second son, George, who became Prince of Wales upon Bertie's accession to the throne in 1901. Plans were made for him to make a visit of a 'family character'[43] to Berlin in January 1902 to congratulate the Emperor on his forty-third birthday, but after Prince Bülow had publicly spoken against Great Britain in response to speeches by Colonial Secretary Joseph Chamberlain, the King had decided to cancel the visit. But he later changed his mind, and so the Prince of Wales arrived in Berlin by special train on 26 January 1902, to be met by the Emperor, attended by other members of his close family and Court, as well as Lascelles. The Prince, wearing the uniform of the First Prussian Dragoon Guards, was cheered as he and the Emperor left the Lehrter Station* and made their way eastwards through the Brandenburg Gate, along Unter den Linden and to the Royal Schloss.

* Now Hauptbahnhof.

***

Cecil Spring-Rice had left Berlin in October 1898 for further diplomatic postings in Constantinople, Tehran and Cairo. But he kept in touch with Lascelles in Berlin, and in 1903 Florence Lascelles invited him back to stay at the Embassy on his way to his new posting at St Petersburg. That Christmas, he returned to stay in Berlin. Despite their seventeen-year age difference, romance blossomed, and in January 1904 Spring-Rice proudly reported their engagement in a letter to his great friend Eleanor

32. Cecil Spring-Rice, his wife Florence and their two children photographed in December 1915.

Roosevelt.[44] When the German press contacted him requesting a portrait photograph to publish in connection with the marriage, Spring-Rice (who had evidently not lost his sense of humour) instead supplied one of fellow St Petersburg diplomat Ronald Lindsay,[†] 'a very good-looking Secretary of the Embassy, which was duly published over his name.'[45] Florence's reaction to this practical joke is unrecorded. The couple were married at the English Church in Berlin and held their wedding breakfast at the Embassy.[46]

According to German court etiquette, Florence Lascelles had not been considered sufficiently experienced to act as her father's hostess in Berlin after the death of her mother.[47] Indeed, the prudery and rigidity of the protocol demanded in the court of Wilhelm II had intruded even into her leisure hours. On one occasion, riding a bicycle in the Tiergarten, Florence suddenly encountered the Emperor. Later, the Embassy received his instruction that she was to desist from cycling in the future, as Wilhelm did not approve of ladies riding bicycles. 'You can imagine the lady's fury!' remembered Gleichen, the Military Attaché,[48] who also recalled that at the time, when being driven in carriages in Berlin ladies were expected demurely to look down at all times, lest they inadvertently caught the eye of swaggering members of the opposite sex.

Lady Edward Cavendish continued the role of the Ambassador's hostess after Florence's departure from Berlin upon her marriage. In a series of letters she and Sir Frank kept Florence and her new husband (affectionately known in the family as 'Springy') informed of goings-on in the Embassy. Enlivening the usual round of receptions, balls and bridge parties was in March 1905 the sudden arrival of an ostrich destined for London Zoo, which a member of the Embassy's household staff was deputed to collect from the railway station. The bird was given a temporary home in the former stables in the cellar near some hot water pipes, keeping the children amused during a party, strutting up and down in the small courtyard beneath the dining room windows. Lady Cavendish thought she had now seen everything as a diplomatic hostess: '… never among all the changes and chances of this mortal life had I expected to have an ostrich committed to my care.'[49]

† Coincidentally, a later Ambassador to Berlin (see Chapter 12).

Florence was able to assume the duties of a fully fledged diplomatic wife when Spring-Rice was made British Minister in Tehran in 1906 and afterwards Minister to Stockholm, in 1913 reaching the summit of his career when appointed Ambassador to Washington. The posting was not altogether successful, Spring-Rice's apparent reticence in persuading the United States to enter the Great War provoking political disapproval at home. He was to die unexpectedly in Ottawa early in 1918 on his way home to England, not long after having been replaced as Ambassador at the American capital. A few weeks earlier he had penned the verse 'I vow to thee, my country'. Florence was left a widow with two children, reliant upon the charity of her late husband's American friends.

**

Although in 1903 there was some talk of transferring him to Paris,[50] Lascelles stayed in post in Berlin until 1908. In February of that year in a letter to his daughter written at half past three in the morning he described a packed day at the height of the Berlin winter season. On the previous night there been a dance at the Embassy for the diplomatic corps which had gone on until late. Rising late the following morning, Lascelles had enjoyed a good game of golf (one of his favourite pastimes) with the visiting Bishop of London in melting snow. Then he had an hour's conversation with von Bülow; attended a ball at the Austrian Embassy where he had to stay for supper as he had been placed next to the Crown Princess; wrote a very long letter to Foreign Secretary Sir Edward Grey; and then, at last, a letter to his 'dear daughter'. The Embassy was full of guests and the following day he could look forward to a masked ball given by Prince and Princess Friedrich Leopold 'which is likely to be dull although it is believed that the Emperor is preparing to play pranks under his mask'. The Embassy would hold its own ball on the coming Monday, and on Tuesday there would be the final court ball of the season.[51]

Lascelles had managed to cultivate good working relations with the Emperor, who on many occasions used his royal family connections to gain privileged and occasionally indiscreet access into the Ambassador's confidence – as well as his Berlin home. But some believed, particularly towards the end of his ambassadorship, that these amusing confidences had gone too far and that Lascelles had failed fully to appreciate Wilhelm's real and growing hostility towards the powerful country of the other half of his family and his consequent efforts to strengthen German military power. A toxic mix of distrust, resentment and jealousy characterised Wilhelm's attitudes to his uncle's diplomatic triumphs of the Entente Cordiale of 1904 and the Anglo-Russian Agreement of 1907, which were to create the British, French and Russian alliances that would be in place at the outbreak of the Great War.

'Your letter of the 2nd breathes distrust in Germany and you are right. She has never done anything for us but bleed us. She is false and grasping and our real enemy commercially and politically.'[52] Thus wrote Sir Francis Bertie in 1904, as a mood of Germanophobia and distrust of Germany, her motives and intentions began to grip a group of influential diplomats and the Foreign Office. The attitude was articulated in a memorandum produced by Sir Eyre Crowe,

33. The British Embassy photographed from the south east in 1896.

head of the Foreign Office's Western Department, on *The Present State of British Relations with France and Germany* (1 January 1907), in which he opined that the preceding two decades had witnessed German foreign policy characterised by 'a disregard of the elementary rules of straightforward and honourable dealing.'[53] Crowe came to distrust Lascelles' close relationship with the German Emperor and sanguine reports back from Berlin which, it was felt, underestimated Germany's military ambitions.[54]

After leaving Berlin, Lascelles continued to make efforts to promote Anglo-German friendship and cooperation. The writer of his obituary remarked that the former Ambassador, who died in London on 2 January 1920, gave some impression of laziness, especially in putting pen to paper (certainly, and frustratingly, unlike most his predecessors and successors in Berlin he left no memoirs or diaries), but that 'he will hold a lasting place as one of the kindest, most courteous and most temperamentally steadiest of Englishmen of his day.'[55]

CHAPTER 7
1908–1914: 'The Most
Important Post in Europe'

King Edward VII told Sir Edward Goschen, Ambassador to Vienna since 1905, of his appointment to the ambassadorship in Berlin in person on a train in Austria on 13 August 1908. 'I am going to give you a bit of news about yourself – which I am afraid will not be very agreeable to you – but it is one of those things with wh.[ich] diplomats have to put up!' he told Goschen. 'We are going to take you from Vienna – and send you to Berlin! I know you won't like this – but you must forget all that is disagreeable in it in the thought – that being sent to the most important post in Europe is a great honour and compliment!'[1] Goschen was horrified.

He recorded that 'H.M. was kindness himself all through the interview and did what he could to gild the blackest and most nauseous of pills. I am fearfully depressed and unhappy about it and shudder when I think what Boss* will…'[2] As the train pulled into the spa town of Bad Ischl, Goschen met Wickham Steed, *The Times* correspondent in Vienna. '[A]lmost in tears' he mournfully (and prophetically) told Steed of his impending transfer:

> I shall have to go. I cannot refuse the King. But I have felt at home in Vienna, and I am certain that my mission to Berlin will end in failure, for there can be no means of avoiding catastrophe. The German Emperor will not listen to our proposals for a naval arrangement, and he pretends that we, not the Germans, are forcing the pace. Germany is the innocent lamb of whom we are accusing of troubling our waters. If he goes on in that way, a conflict between us and Germany is only a question of time.[3]

Goschen had no illusions about the seriousness of the international situation of which his new job was the very focus. Worried that he would not be able to establish a working relationship with the Emperor based on mutual confidence, he dreaded the prospect of the responsibility of dealing with growing German military expansion that he believed must end badly, despite any efforts he might make to try to prevent it. Moreover, he would not be able to avoid close personal and professional association with that outcome. Even before Goschen's commenced his ambassadorship there were ominous developments in the gradual breakdown of peace in Europe, as the Hapsburg monarchy formally annexed Bosnia and Herzegovina – those provinces Austria had administered and occupied according to the 1878 Treaty of Berlin – and the German Emperor pledged to support Austria's actions.

In Vienna, Goschen and his wife prepared for the transfer to Berlin, writing to Lascelles to ask about the carriages, horses and stores Lascelles intended to leave behind on his departure and proposing to visit Berlin to talk matters over in person in early September. Every new ambassador had to decide whom from

---

* One of Goschen's pet names for his wife.

his predecessor's domestic staff to retain, and while Lascelles had recommended Goschen retain the embassy housekeeper Marie, he also wondered whether his daughter Florence might like to take her on, as Lady Goschen apparently preferred to manage the housekeeping herself.[4]

The Goschens' last day in the Austrian capital was 7 November, which Goschen recorded was a 'Black Saturday…. We had tears in our hearts at leaving dear old Vienna* where we have had the best 3 years of our Dip. Life.'[5] Arriving in Berlin the following day, they were met by the embassy staff who consisted of 'De Salis, very nice tho' rather deaf, Mounsey, Clark, and to my surprise an Honorary Att. of the name of Monck – by whom – or at whose request app'td I know not'[6] (Goschen had brought his own private secretary, H.J. Bruce, with him from Vienna). That evening the new Ambassador glumly remarked in his diary, 'Very cold at Embassy. Hosta† went to the Adlon Hotel, where she is very comfortable. I stay here, where I am not comfortable. Both Boss and I much depressed – we don't like the House – and we miss our Vienna. Lunched and dined at the Adlon – pretty good – and fussed about the House …'[7]

The new Adlon Hotel had recently been built overlooking Pariser Platz on the corner of Wilhelmstrasse and Unter den Linden, next door to the British Embassy. The site had been occupied by the Palais Redern, designed by Karl Friedrich Schinkel in 1828–29 and itself partly a conversion of the Palais Kamecke (1729–36).[8] By the end of the nineteenth century the Palais Redern was regarded as an important Berlin historical monument, but the hotelier Lorenz Adlon had been looking for just such a key geographical location to build a huge luxury hotel of the kind found in other great European cities, to rival the Kaiserhof as the favoured destination for the international great and good.‡ Always keen to increase the global prestige of Berlin and to improve its facilities to rival other capital cities, the Emperor Wilhelm agreed to the demolition of the historic Palais and the construction of Adlon's grand hotel on its site.

After building work had commenced Adlon realised he needed space for more guest rooms to improve the chances of recouping his massive investment.[9] Accordingly, he managed to purchase an adjoining plot of land to the south on Wilhelmstrasse to build an extension. The Wilhelmstrasse wing of the hotel became its 'rear' entrance, the 'couriers'' wing where the 'outdoor servants' (i.e. coachmen, grooms and, increasingly by this time, chauffeurs) were housed. The hotel constructed a courtyard garden/terrace using some open space§ located to the rear of the Embassy and, as a result, its rear service facilities (including the

---

* The Embassy/Residence in Vienna was located near to the Belvedere Palace at 6 Metternichgasse and was completed in 1875, its architect the Austrian Viktor Rumpelmayer (1830–85). The design and appearance of the state rooms are the closest surviving approximation on the British diplomatic estate to those of the vanished Embassy in Berlin. The building is still in use, now exclusively as the Ambassador's Residence, a separate embassy building having been built in the grounds in the late 1980s.
† Goschen's wife.
‡ Two other top-rank hotels in Berlin in the early twentieth century were the Esplanade (Bellvuestrasse 16–18a, near Potsdamer Platz (400 rooms), some elements of which survived the Second World War, and the Hotel Bristol, Unter den Linden 5–6, next to the Russian Embassy (320 rooms), the site of which was swallowed up by the rebuilt Soviet Embassy during the Cold War.
§ The same garden that in 1884 Lord Ampthill described could be appreciated from the windows at the rear of the Embassy (see Chapter 3).

kitchens) overlooked the Embassy. 'The wall at the back of the house is dreadful. When I stand close to the window in my room and crane my neck I can just see the sky, and all the rooms on that floor are in consequence of the height of the wall much darkened,' Lady Edward Cavendish remarked in January 1907 on first experiencing the new hotel's physical effect on the Embassy,[10] and understandably this was to be a source of increasing irritation to subsequent Ambassadors.

The Adlon opened to great fanfare on 23 October 1907 and became one of the most famous luxury hotels in Europe, the destination of choice for celebrities and international VIPs. Its prime location – in the heart of the government quarter and midway between the French, British (and later) the American Embassies and a short distance from the Chancellery and government ministries – gave it considerable cachet as a place for journalists, politicians and diplomats to meet in comfort and style. The 1912 edition of *Baedeker's Berlin and its Environs* described the Adlon as having 325 rooms (180 with bathrooms), and the building also housed a travel and tourist office. Despite British Ambassadors' gripes about the location of its rear services, the hotel became an extremely convenient facility for the Embassy, occasionally providing accommodation to supplement the Embassy's guest rooms when required and an additional upmarket location for entertaining.

***

Although it was Goschen who succeeded Lascelles, several candidates were in the frame for the job. In late 1907 King Edward VII had briefly toyed with the idea of moving the Secretary of State for War Lord Haldane from the War Office to the position, but this came to nothing.[11] Another possible candidate was Sir Arthur Nicolson, who, as we have seen, had begun his career as a junior diplomat in Berlin under Russell in the 1870s. His son Harold believed him to have been preferred by the Emperor himself, but again, this did not come to fruition.[12] Others included two young diplomats who had served in Berlin under Malet: Fairfax Cartwright,[13] then Minister in Madrid, and Sir James Rennell Rodd, by then Head of the British Legation in Stockholm. Serving as an Embassy Secretary in Berlin, Cartwright had known Wilhelm II personally and had some German blood in his family. On 16 June 1908 King Edward VII wrote to his nephew proposing him as Ambassador, but, just as had been the case in 1895, Wilhelm was fixated on the idea that any replacement for Lascelles should not be a career diplomat, but instead someone 'who plays a prominent part in your country',[14] by which he meant an Establishment figure such as Lord Curzon, Lord Rosebery or Lord Cromer, the former Consul-General to Egypt.

Rodd claimed that shortly after he had attended his former Chief Sir Edward Malet's funeral in June 1908 he was offered the post of Ambassador to Rome but subsequently learned that the King had ideally wished to send him to Berlin instead. What stopped the King and members of the Foreign Office from even proposing him was Wilhelm's probable reaction: to add to his habit of waking people up early, another trait was the possession of a long memory for perceived diplomatic slights, in this case Rodd's sympathetic biography of the Emperor's father, published twenty years before. However (at least in retrospect[15]) Rodd claimed he had understood the likely difficulties and had no desire for the job.

King Edward VII preferred personal meetings that enabled him to meet and discuss matters face to face rather than relying on arid and potentially misleading official correspondence. Accordingly, with the termination of Lascelles' ambassadorship due that October, he suggested a meeting with Wilhelm in August 1908 to sort the matter out. The meeting would also provide an opportunity for Edward to discuss other matters with his nephew, including the pressing and worrying issue of German naval expansion, a prominent feature of the massive industrial growth and modernisation of Germany that characterised Wilhelm's reign. In fact, the issue of Lascelles' successor had previously been raised during the Emperor's state visit to Great Britain in November 1907: the Ambassador's term of office had actually expired in October 1906, but had been extended for two years; the Foreign Office had wanted to ensure the Emperor was forewarned that this would not recur.[16]

Accompanied by his friend Sir Charles Hardinge (by now Permanent Secretary of the Foreign Office), Lord Ponsonby and Stanley Clark, his personal physician, King Edward set out for the spa town of Bad Ischl, a favourite of the Austrian Emperor Franz Josef, where the King was to be present at the Emperor's Diamond Jubilee celebrations. Agreeing to meet the German Emperor at his late sister's home of Schloss Friedrichshof on 11 August 1908, King Edward informed his nephew that the intention was not to appoint Cartwright. He later reported this conversation to Hardinge, recounting how the Emperor had appeared relieved that Cartwright had been withdrawn as a candidate for the post. Hardinge wondered whether this was due to the fact that Cartwright faced the same kind of potential difficulties in dealing with the Emperor as did Rodd. Two decades before he had published a satirical novel caricaturing certain members of Berlin society, a deed not calculated to endear him to Wilhelm.[17]

Edward told his nephew that although Cartwright was now out of the frame, there was no question of a 'big name' from outside the diplomatic service being appointed to Berlin. Sir Edward Goschen's name was raised, perhaps under the influence of Hardinge, who seems to have worked with the King to advance the prospects of those who shared his robust attitude towards Germany.[18] He was not alone in this sentiment. Later, Foreign Secretary Sir Edward Grey thought Goschen had 'mature experience and a somewhat phlegmatic temperament' and 'robust common sense' that might be good proof against 'Imperial blandishments', and was known to be aware of Germany's increasingly likely hostile intentions.[19] This was in contrast to Lascelles, who, it had increasingly been felt, had become too close to and incapable of standing up to the Emperor.

Born in 1847, Goschen's ancestry was German; he was the grandson of a Leizpzig publisher whose son Wilhelm Göschen, like Strousberg, had migrated to London. Here he made a successful career in merchant banking, anglicising the family name by dropping its *umlaut*. The family became extremely successful in their adopted country, making their mark in the highest echelons of political and diplomatic circles, an example of how, very slowly, the ranks of these elites were beginning to be opened on the basis on merit and not simply of birth. Edward's elder brother George's political ambitions eventually reached exceptionally dizzy heights when, following Lord Randolph Churchill's brief tenure, he served as Chancellor of the Exchequer from 1887 to 1892. Edward entered the diplomatic service in 1869 and served in Belgrade and Copenhagen and became Ambassador to Vienna in 1905. In 1874 he married Harriet ('Hosta') Clarke in the United States.

The slightly less important subject of the ambassadorship to Berlin successfully resolved, Hardinge discussed the naval issue with the Emperor, who later boasted to a dismayed von Bülow of his bullish and hardly reassuring response to the Briton's comments about the current pace of German armament: 'Then we shall fight, for it is a question of national honour and dignity.'[20] On the positive side, however, Edward agreed to make a state visit to Berlin the following February, a visit that had originally been planned for the spring of 1908 but had been cancelled early that year. It was not an event that King Edward anticipated with pleasure; his nephew's energetic and humourless company was always at odds with his own personality. From a diplomatic point of view meetings between the two Monarchs were of course unavoidable, but Edward and Alexandra hardly relished them: in November 1902, as the Emperor left King Edward at the end of a visit characterised by a particularly strained atmosphere, the King was overheard saying, 'Thank God he's gone.'[21]

One of Goschen's first political duties as Ambassador was that of reporting the fallout created by the '*Daily Telegraph* affair' of October 1908, a delayed consequence of the Emperor's state visit to England in November of the previous year, after which he had decided to remain in the country for another month in a private capacity. Staying as the private guest of Colonel The Hon. Edward Montagu-Stuart-Wortley at Highcliffe Castle in Dorset, and never known for circumspection in his pronouncements, Wilhelm made some unfortunately judged remarks on the relationship between England and Germany, including self-proclaimed 'advice' given to the British over the course of the Boer War. A year later, on 28 October 1908, the remarks were published in the *Daily Telegraph*, despite Wilhelm's having 'cleared' them with members of his Government.[*] The Emperor's reported opinions did not go down well with the German public.

***

By February 1909 the Goschens had evidently settled sufficiently into the Embassy to be able to welcome King Edward VII and Queen Alexandra on the postponed state visit. Accompanying the King again was Sir Charles Hardinge, visiting the capital and the Embassy in which he had worked a quarter of a century earlier. The visit was certainly not without mishap. The Queen arrived at the Embassy earlier than expected, at the same time as a new carpet, which, consequently, the embassy staff had no time to lay down.[22] Then, driving to the Palace, the horses pulling the carriage carrying her and the Empress reared dangerously several times.[23]

Despite all the elaborate protocols of Berlin court etiquette and the calculated finery of the surroundings, the Emperor still regarded the Royal Court at Windsor as the definitive example for Berlin and Potsdam to follow, and before the King's visit he had warned the British Ambassador that 'It won't be like Windsor, but we shall do the best we can in any case.'[24] The visiting royal couple's programme – from 10 to 12 February – was intense. It included a 'family luncheon' at the Royal

---

[*] The material contained within the article was unfortunately circulated in Berlin at a time when the Chancellor, von Bülow, was on leave and it fell between several stools.

Schloss; a reception by the civic authorities at the Brandenburg Gate; a gala dinner at the Schloss; a visit to the Rathaus; luncheon at the British Embassy; a court ball at the Schloss; a motor-drive to Potsdam to visit the Royal Mausoleum; luncheon with the 1st Prussian Dragoon Guards; a family dinner with the Crown Prince; a gala performance at the opera; sightseeing in Berlin; and luncheon in the Schloss. As this was a state visit, the King and Queen and their entourage stayed with their official hosts, the imperial family, and not at the Embassy.

'The entry into Berlin was a really magnificent sight. The sun shone intermittently and lit up the waving line of bayonets,' as Field-Marshal Lord Grenfell, who accompanied the King on the visit to represent the British army, described the scene as the British royal family arrived at the capital. 'The streets were lined by the cavalry and infantry of the Guard, in all twenty thousand men, and at one part, on the Unter den Linden, the veteran soldiers of the 1870 War, their breasts covered with medals, kept the street.'[25] The Emperor's love of Prussian military show and splendour was being given full rein. Such pomp and circumstance did not, however, impress Princess Marie Radziwill, who described the scene:

> They've built a whole crowd of stands which make the Pariserplatz look horribly narrow, and they've decorated all the Unter den Linden with frightful little flags and horrible paper garlands … The King has just passed by beneath my windows … in an open carriage drawn by six horses. The Queen covered by a cloak of ermine was in a great closed glass coach with the Empress, so that the public were scarcely able to see her.[26]

After their visit to the Rathaus, the King and Queen were the honoured guests at a diplomatic luncheon for sixty-five guests[27] at the British Embassy, attended by all the foreign ambassadors in Germany, their wives and a number of German aristocrats. Discussing his late sister the Empress Friedrich, Princess Radziwill was much taken by King Edward's personal charm, and having hardly been able to see Queen Alexandra in her coach, she now in person found her 'very elegant … dressed in mauve velvet [and] astonishing for her age, she is so slight and well preserved.'[28] After lunch, the King, dressed in a tight Prussian uniform, sat on a sofa chatting to the British-born Princess of Pless,* a personal friend. According to her, the sofa was a rather low one, and their conversation went on for an hour, because (she wrote with hindsight) the King was not feeling well, and did not want to have to make 'forced conversation.'[29] Indeed, all was not well. Hardinge later related 'I noticed that [the King] suddenly fell backwards with his eyes closed and I thought he had had a stroke.' Lord Grenfell described it as 'A violent fit of coughing [which] ended in a sort of a collapse.'[30] The British contingent and Goschen were petrified, Hardinge rushing to the King to unfasten his collar and then running to fetch his doctor, Sir James Reid, who was in the next room.[31] The guests were directed to withdraw into an adjoining room while the King received attention – 'His pallor terrified us all', according to Princess Radziwill[32] – but he seemed to recover almost at once, and a quarter of an hour later the guests were invited to return. Grenfell later remarked that 'it was characteristic of him when he came round that he refused to go home, lighted another large cigar, and remained for some time talking to the Ambassador and his guests.'[33]

* Now Pszczyna in Poland.

Hardinge thought Reid treated the matter very casually, ascribing the brief incident to a 'form of bronchial attack and in no sense dangerous'. But Hardinge was not convinced and immediately reported the matter and his doubts and fears to Lord Knollys in London.[34] The King's Principal Secretary later reassured the British Embassy that the King tended to suffer from giddy spells, particularly after luncheon.[35] But Hardinge was right to be so worried: the affliction was in fact a severe case of bronchitis. Indeed, Edward was already experiencing some bronchial difficulty when he left London, and the harsh winter climate of Berlin was hardly likely to improve his symptoms. Other people had noticed the King's poorly appearance during the state visit: Princess Radziwill related that the Emperor had confided in her – perhaps with some degree of *Schadenfreude* – that he was shocked to see his uncle so changed, only a year since he had seen him last.[36] Understandably, Hardinge and Goschen spent the rest of the luncheon and state visit dreading that the King might have another mysterious attack and actually die while in Berlin, and as a result of the incident the packed programme was modified, the visit fortunately progressing without further mishap. The royal party left Berlin for England at 10 p.m. on 12 February, aboard the special carriages the King used for travel on Continental railway systems with luxurious and comfortable furniture, carpets and bathrooms. Hardinge later related how Princess Pless had unsuccessfully tried to get the King to see a 'quack doctor', and then attempted to see him again as the royal train slowly passed westwards through Spandau, Edward refusing permission to stop the train.[37] It was to be the last visit that Edward made to Berlin. As a state visit, it was largely deemed to have been a success in the city itself, but so far as Sir Frederick Ponsonby was concerned, 'To my mind the effect of this visit was nil.' He believed that the majority of Germans hated the King and the British, blaming Edward for creating his own network of alliances which had left Germany effectively isolated. The King's relations with his nephew the Emperor were ominous, he thought: 'the whole atmosphere when the two were together seemed charged with dangerous electricity.'[38] '[T]he result of the King's visit to Berlin may mean an "armistice" but that is quite another state of things from an alliance,' thought the Berlin correspondent of *The Graphic*, while a scarcely more optimistic view expressed in the same publication opined that

> To pretend that the visit was a mere act of international courtesy is obviously idle. It may be true that it will not succeed in eliminating the profound causes of disagreement between Great Britain and Germany, but that it was intended to make the effort no candid observer can doubt. For years past, the estrangement between the two Powers has been growing. Since 1908 they have been in a state of veiled war.[39]

Princess Radziwill noticed the King's apparent personal unhappiness while in Berlin, quite apart from his medical afflictions, believing him to have been 'very put out and annoyed here. He wanted to be amiable and yet his nephew is personally displeasing to him'. On the same day of his 'fainting-fit' at the British Embassy he was expected to make an appearance at a ball:

> Our Majesties made him turn up at half-past-eight, whereas in England they don't dance before eleven. It was directly after dinner and he hadn't had time to smoke. At the Ball he was thirsty and asked for a whiskey [*sic*] and water; he was informed that this wasn't available. He asked

for a game of cards and he was told that this was not the custom at the Prussian Court. Finally he demanded a cigar and they replied that people didn't smoke in the Palace. After that the King went off to bed! How incredibly tactless we are! I shall always have the feeling the King will remember these pin-pricks which increased the grievances he already had. Here they're very satisfied and repeat that perpetual ineptitude, that England is jealous of Germany![40]

Despite a gradual deterioration in relations between the two countries, it naturally continued to be the Ambassador's duty to host events for the closely related British and German royal families. Amongst the successes of a large embassy ball in February 1910 for over 350 guests including four of the Emperor's sons was a memorable tableau: suddenly the doors were opened for flowers to be dragged in on sledges by four embassy dogs: Daisy, Jones, Raffles, plus 'Mrs. Trench's toy bulldog'.[41]

***

Meanwhile back in England the Royal Household was becoming increasingly concerned by the King's state of health: falling asleep suddenly during meals was a not uncommon occurrence, and he seemed ill and worn out. On Saturday, 7 May 1910 Goschen received the news he and Hardinge had been dreading ever since witnessing the King's brief collapse at the Embassy. The bronchitis that had beset the King on that occasion had returned while he was on holiday in Biarritz that spring. Returning early in May to Sandringham, the illness had worsened and, without much warning, Edward died just before midnight the previous evening. Goschen was extremely saddened. It was 'a great national calamity … a man respected and loved and admired throughout Europe', and he felt his loss 'privately as well as nationally.'[42] The following day the German Chancellor and Foreign Secretary Schön paid sympathy calls on the Ambassador, followed by a 'stream' of foreign ambassadors and other visitors. The Embassy went into full diplomatic mourning mode as Goschen recorded the receipt of 'heaps of telegrams and a great deal to do.'[43] Nearly all the Embassy attended a service at the English Church, draped in black, to mourn the King. Afterwards, and in sharp contrast to his relaxed relationship with Lascelles, the Emperor paid the one and only visit he ever made to the Embassy during Goschen's ambassadorship, staying for about ninety minutes. Just as his predecessor had done in 1901 following Queen Victoria's death, Goschen left for England shortly afterwards in order to attend the King's state funeral, held at Windsor on 20 May in the presence of many of the closely related crowned heads of Europe. 'The Emperor's suite is worrying us at this moment, as he is taking over nearly a hundred people, including friseurs, major-domos, innumerable valets, etc., besides, of course, the official suite. The number of people it takes to dress him in his uniforms!'[44] marvelled the newly arrived member of the Embassy Harold Beresford Hope as he was set to work helping to organise the Emperor's attendance at the event.

Attending his first court ball in February the following year, Beresford Hope related to his family that as the Ambassador could not be present at the event because he was ill, according to Berlin diplomatic court etiquette the British

Embassy guests, instead of being presented first, had to wait until all the other members of the diplomatic corps had had their turn, which meant a wait of over two hours. Amusingly, he recounted, those at such receptions who were familiar with the exigencies of protocol at Court knew how get a seat at supper:

> The ladies picked up their trains and skirts, and the very minute the Emperor and Empress were safely passed ran with the men as hard as they could over miles of slippery parquet down corridors and through endless rooms to the series of rooms where supper is served, so as to be sure of getting places at the round tables where a regular sit-down affair like dinner is served. Those who arrive late may have to wait and wander about for a quarter of an hour, looking for vacant places. Only the very highest dignitaries are placed at the Emperor's table; all the rest scramble for seats.[45]

Meanwhile, vainly attempting to keep the modern world at bay, the Emperor's continued obsessive interest in the rigours of correct court protocol and tradition meant that he was 'furious about the tango. He has approached some of the Ambassadors and hoped that they will not allow it at Embassy balls, and has issued orders that no officers in uniform are to dance it under pain of dismissal, which banishes it from all the purely German balls. As everyone has been learning it most diligently I expect there will be a great deal of discontent.'[46]

Goschen himself loved music, playing the violin and taking music lessons in Berlin during his ambassadorship. To celebrate New Year's Day of 1912 Goschen recorded that he and his wife had had a dinner 'at home' to which all the embassy staff came, followed by a 'musical rag.'[47] Like ambassadorial couples before and since, the Goschens seem to have had (or, at least, gave the impression that they had) an insatiable energy for entertaining and being entertained. This was and still is very much a prerequisite of the job, where daily duty requires an endless enthusiasm (or rather, perhaps, self-discipline) and facility, either at one's own embassy or at events in foreign embassies, for being sociable and polite to VIPs and opposite numbers in the diplomatic corps. But keeping up appearances and a relentless social life sometimes became difficult for the more junior members of the Berlin embassy staff. Goschen's private secretary, Henry James Bruce, whom he had brought with him from Vienna, glumly recorded in his memoirs written four decades later that 'There was the same round of frock-coated *jours*[*] in our Embassy as in others.'[48] Disappointingly, even when interesting guests made an appearance they did not always live up to the staff's expectations. An example was Sir Arthur Conan Doyle: despite prompting from the other guests, the only subject the internationally famous creator of Sherlock Holmes wanted to talk about was social legislation.[49]

Another trying dinner guest was the elderly Prince Christian of Schleswig-Holstein, a member of the British royal family who had lost an eye in a shooting accident decades earlier. Beresford Hope remembered a small and frustrating dinner party (at which no ladies were present) where Prince Christian was 'a severe physical effort for everybody, as one eye is gone and the other fixes you with a glassy stare, and when anything is said to him he takes five minutes to

---

[*] 'At-homes'.

understand it.'[50] The Prince had 'dined out' on his affliction for years, exhibiting his collection of different colour glass eyes to his fellow guests by taking them out and changing them between courses.[51] Bruce found it very demanding having to be on duty at these seemingly endless embassy dinners, as well as dining *en famille* with the Ambassador, as the food (prepared by two French chefs) and wine were evidently very rich. Nor could he easily get time off, Goschen apparently finding his services indispensable. This all took its toll and, writing in the 1940s, Bruce freely admitted that he had suffered a nervous breakdown at the time.[52] He did eventually manage to break free from Berlin in August 1913, when he became the Head of Chancery at the British Embassy in St Petersburg.

Despite worsening international relations during the Agadir Crisis in 1911–12 (Germany had sent a gunboat to the port in response to the French occupation of Fez and north Morocco), there were some small signs of a thawing of the cold diplomatic atmosphere between Germany and Great Britain, both in the Foreign Office and the press. During a visit to Berlin the influential financier and socialite Sir Ernest Cassel was informed by the Emperor of his desire to try to smooth over growing tensions by having talks with a high-level member of the British Cabinet. In February 1912 former War Secretary and newly created Lord Chancellor Richard, Viscount Haldane was accordingly despatched to Berlin over Goschen's head. It was a direct snub to the Ambassador's authority and experience, and unpopular with the Foreign Office. Viewed in retrospect, it was a portent of the Government's approach towards the Foreign Office and professional diplomats that was to characterise the years immediately after the Great War. On the positive side, Haldane could speak German and was familiar with his opposite numbers in Berlin. 'Goschen was an excellent man, but had hardly sufficient imagination to be capable of getting on to more than agreeable terms with the Germans,'[53] he patronisingly later wrote of the Ambassador who was his host in Berlin during his brief visit of 8 to 10 February 1912.

Haldane and his physiologist brother (acting as his private secretary) were met at Friedrichstrasse Station by the Ambassador's motor car (which by now had supplanted the smelly horses) and embassy porter.[54] Meeting the German Chancellor Bethmann-Hollweg for lunch at the Embassy, he enjoyed further discussions and the following day lunched with the Emperor and Admiral Tirpitz at the Schloss, all arranged by Goschen, followed by a further meeting with the Chancellor.[55] Haldane's negotiations in fact produced few concessions on the German side and no definite reassurances concerning the naval issue but instead some disturbing proposals for the British to remain neutral in the event of Germany's future military involvement: the Ambassador and the Foreign Office were not impressed. In any case, Goschen's mind must have been otherwise occupied. Alone in Berlin, his wife Hosta convalescing at Arco (a health resort in the Tyrol), he received the devastating news of her death on 15 February. She had not been well for some time but even so this was a terrible shock. Goschen buried her at Flimwell, Sussex (where he was to join her a dozen years later) and made no further entries in his diary for almost six months.

***

On 1 January 1913 Goschen admitted that he had come 'a little out of my shell' and he had held a dinner party for some of the embassy staff, entertaining them with his violin.[56] Whatever inner turmoil he may have been feeling due to his bereavement, duty came first and diplomatic life had to go on, including another royal visit in May, when King George V and Queen Mary were guests at the Emperor's daughter Princess Victoria's wedding to Ernest Augustus, Duke of Brunswick. They were amongst many European royal families in Berlin for the event; while some of them lodged at the Adlon Hotel, the Emperor's cousin and his Queen were accommodated at the Royal Schloss. It was classed as a 'private' visit rather than a state one, so that only members of the Royal Household attended, rather than members of the British Government. Beresford Hope was not impressed by the efforts made to welcome the King and Queen at the railway station. 'We all went down in uniform to the station and found it decorated with a few ferns and palms, a strip of red carpet, and dozens of Union Jacks bought at a toy-shop, as the blue was far too light and the crosses all wrong.' Standing attentively in a line, the embassy staff were all presented to the King and Queen.[57]

On 23 May the royal couple attended a luncheon at the Embassy. Ponsonby, again part of the royal party, did not attend, but he 'heard it was all very well done, and the King made a capital speech to the British community'. On the whole this time he was 'inclined to think that the visit helped towards establishing good feeling towards the two countries, but, of course, one can never get over the fact that we were practically rivals and that the German navy league had done all it could to poison the minds of the people against us.'[58] The wedding and other glamorous events took place on 24 May. Overlaid by the experience of what was to come, the Embassy's Commercial Attaché Sir Francis Oppenheimer's memories of these events were vivid and poetic: 'In retrospect the splendour of massed royalty, as I saw it on that gala night, before the lights went out, recalls to me the final flare up in a fireworks display when masses of multi-splendoured rockets and bengal lights illuminate the sky and then slowly, one after the other, burn themselves out and drop silently into the night.'[59]

The King and Queen left Berlin for England on 27 May, and Oppenheimer remembered how he and the other embassy staff had to wait in the Chancery until the royal couple left, only to learn at the very last minute that they would have to change into 'diplomatic mufti' rather than formal diplomatic dress for their farewells at the railway station.[60] Continuing the royal family's long association with Berlin the royal couple's son the Prince of Wales (later King Edward VIII) made a brief visit to the city on 30 August that year.[61] Godfrey Thomas, a young embassy attaché, took the Prince to funfairs, *a palais de danse* and various nightclubs.

Two new members of the Embassy's staff arrived in December 1913. One of them was Second Secretary Frank Rattigan, who arrived on New Year's Eve. He and his wife intended to live in style in Berlin, arranging for all of their antique furniture to be sent from England for their apartment in the Bendlerstrasse* in the

---

* Now Stauffenbergerstrasse, named after the leader of the July 1944 plot against Hitler who was executed in the 'Bendlerblock' on Bendlerstrasse.

34. Detail of an 1893 map of Berlin, showing the government district and location of the British Embassy.

Tiergarten the following March.[62] The other was Sir Horace Rumbold,* the new Counsellor and Goschen's deputy. Hoping that by this stage of his career his next posting would be as the head of an important mission, Rumbold instead found himself posted as the second-in-command in Berlin, in what was, however, to prove a momentous period of his life. Presented with his wife to the Emperor at the first court ball of the new season in January 1914, the event did not run as smoothly as might have been hoped. Told Rumbold's surname, Wilhelm's long memory for diplomatic slights surfaced once more. Suddenly, recalling that Rumbold's late father (himself a distinguished diplomat and British Ambassador to Vienna) had been an outspoken critic of Prussia and what he believed to be its long-term and sinister geopolitical ambitions, Wilhelm rudely turned away.[63]

The Rumbolds and Rattigans were present at one of the last big embassy events of the vanished world of imperial Berlin, when Goschen held a large dinner party and ball for more than two hundred guests on 3 February. The Crown Prince and Princess and other members of the imperial family were there, together with embassy members and many foreign ambassadors and ambassadresses, representatives from other German princely families, and members of the German Foreign Office. 'The dances were waltzes, the Française, and the Lancers, and there was a "flower-waltz" after supper, which was served at midnight'.[64]

It was at the end of that month Goschen recorded in his diary an example of one of the less-than-glamorous duties of an ambassador (and his wife) and still very much part of the job: that of operating a luxury hotel for British VIPs visiting the host country on official business, organising their meals and arranging their programme during their visit. An ambassador's residence can provide better security and business convenience than hotel accommodation, and, in general, it remains more economical to make use of a residence's guest rooms in this way than to purchase hotel rooms. The VIP in question on this occasion was the Postmaster-General Sir Charles Hobhouse, Goschen's guest from 26 February to 3 March. The Emperor had invited Hobhouse to lunch on Sunday, 1 March, but when the day arrived the Postmaster-General discovered that, because the Ambassador was indisposed, he was expected to find his own way to the Schloss.

The Emperor Wilhelm's long-standing concerns that Berlin and the Imperial Court were inferior to London and Windsor and that the British looked down on them both, were not, perhaps, totally unjustified. Berlin was

* See Chapter 12 for biographical information on Rumbold.

by no means the most attractive of European cities. Its palaces, monuments, streets, public edifices, and parks or gardens, in spite of a stately spaciousness, fail to impress the mind with a sentiment of characteristic national grandeur. Berlin society likewise, though including many eminent persons besides those connected with the Court and Government, is scarcely the most refined and intellectual in Germany,

The Illustrated London News had patronisingly pronounced in 1888.[65] Wilhelm had over the years attempted to remedy these kinds of criticisms, but a man like Hobhouse was not easily won over. The Postmaster-General made his way through the imperial city from the Embassy to the Royal Schloss for his appointment with the Emperor, only to find that its imposing interior was 'like a glorified Clapham villa, neither taste nor space being shown, the pictures being very indifferent, and the decorations gorgeous without beauty.'[66] After lunch he was treated to a wide-ranging ninety-minute discussion with the Emperor, 'rather to the astonishment of his suite, aeroplanes, Zeppelins, the Hamburg-Amerika and Herr Ballin, his brother Prince Henry, Mexico, were all in turn our topics. He was vivacious, restless, buttonholed me, well informed, uncertain, a remarkable individuality, but not a commanding personage. I was very glad to have had the interview, but he seemed to be only dangerous because he was unstable.'[67] When Hobhouse left for the return journey to England, Goschen recorded in his diary that 'I saw him in my bedroom to say goodbye. He is not a bad chap – but I rather resent having been asked to put him up,'[68] expressing a feeling common to members of the diplomatic service at the time that visiting politicians were more of a nuisance than anything else.[69] Goschen was to agree with the opinion voiced by his Commercial Attaché that visiting official delegations in particular were badly behaved abroad.[70]

In late June 1914 Goschen and his Counsellor Rumbold travelled to Kiel to attend the annual regatta. On the east of the Jutland peninsular to the north of Hamburg and captured from Denmark in 1864, Kiel had been developed as the principal naval centre of Germany. Ever trying to emulate the British, Wilhelm had encouraged the establishment of a 'Kiel Week' to rival Cowes Week. Millionaires were encouraged to attend in their yachts as the Emperor held a series of events at sea and on shore. For their part, the Royal Navy put through their paces several state-of-the-art 'Dreadnoughts', built during the naval arms race between Great Britain and Germany that had characterised the previous two decades.

It was then time for Goschen to take some summer leave. Leaving for London directly from Kiel, he left Rumbold to return alone to the Embassy in Berlin to take over as Chargé. Rumbold arrived back in Berlin in the long midsummer evening of 28 June, to hear the news that the Archduke Franz Ferdinand had been assassinated at Sarajevo by Serbian nationalists.[71] He now found himself responsible for British government representation in the German capital during what were to be the weeks leading up to the outbreak of the Great War.

CHAPTER 8
AUGUST 1914: 'ONE CONTINUOUS ROAR AND HOWL OF RAGE'

'When I think of Kiel and now! It seems almost incredible,' Sir Horace Rumbold wrote home to his wife on 30 July 1914. [1] During the past month his diplomatic skills and experience had been tested to the limit as the European powers' network of diplomatic and political alliances and rivalries coalesced and edged the continent closer and closer to war. All those grand, glittering Berlin parties, banquets and balls, elaborate court etiquette, the crowned heads of Europe gathering in palaces and embassies for yet another inter-dynastic marriage or state visit, must suddenly have seemed no more than a dream.

The day after his return to Berlin from Kiel Rumbold paid a call on the Austro-Hungarian Ambassador and, the following day, discussed the international situation with Alfred Zimmerman, the German Under-Secretary for Foreign Affairs. [2] For the first three weeks of July the Austrians made no official response to the assassination of the heir to the throne of Austro-Hungary in the Balkan country they had recently annexed. Rumbold's superiors in London – Foreign Secretary Sir Edward Grey, and Goschen himself – assured Rumbold that the matter was not really as serious as might be thought, and would calm down. Rumbold, sitting in the Chancery offices in the British Embassy in Berlin located in the eye of the potential storm, begged to differ. During the course of July he had gained intelligence that Germany would definitely stand by her ally, Austria, and it seemed to him that Germany was in fact goading Austria to make a move and so provoke European conflict.

That move finally came on 23 July, when the Austrians delivered a note to Serbia, published in the German press the following day. This accused Serbian officials of planning the assassination. Rumbold interpreted the development as one that would lead to a European war [3] as it virtually amounted to a deliberate ultimatum in order almost to 'pick a fight' with Serbia. The sad diplomatic truth was that if Austria were to take military action against Serbia, then Russia, owing to its alliance with the latter, would be bound to intervene. Arriving at work on 25 July, Rumbold found on his desk a telegram from Grey instructing him to go to the German Foreign Ministry to endeavour to persuade the Germans to use their influence with Austria to give Serbia more time to respond to the ultimatum. The awful reality of the implications of current events was beginning to dawn. If Russia did go to war with Austria over Serbia, then Germany, owing to her own alliances with Austria, would be bound to attack Russia. Then, any war between Russia's ally France and Germany would involve Great Britain, particularly if the Germans passed through Belgium on their way to France, a consequence of the 1839 Treaty of London in which the European powers had recognised and guaranteed Belgian neutrality and independence.

War between the European powers had for many years been regarded by many qualified to judge as likely, or even inevitable, especially given the developing military rivalry and suspicions between Britain and Germany. Even so (for the British at least) in one sense the emerging situation must have appeared unimaginable, if only because of the close monarchical, family and diplomatic ties Britain and Germany had enjoyed from the beginning of the eighteenth century. These ties had intensified since Queen Victoria's marriage to Prince Albert of Saxe-Coburg in 1840, and by the early twentieth century the international dynastic consequences of that union spread as far as Russia. Many members of this extended family had spent time in the British Embassy in Berlin, including the current Emperor himself. The Embassy, which over the past forty years had played a leading role in the manifestation and celebration of these close alliances, and which the British had acquired partly to satisfy the German imperial family's desire for Great Britain to represent itself in Germany in a suitably grand building, was now, ironically, to be at the centre of events in which the two countries rapidly became mortal enemies.

'[H]ere I am having <u>the</u> time of my life in the sense that I am doing the most exciting and responsible of work. Since yesterday morning Europe is in the midst of the most dangerous crisis of modern times …. Yesterday the whole staff & I were working at the Embassy until 8 p.m.,'[4] Rumbold wrote on 25 July to his wife, who was in England expecting the birth of their third child. He and the Chancery staff were working frenetically in the Embassy as the diplomatic situation worsened around them. On the 27th Goschen returned from his month's leave. 'Telegrams now began pouring in', Rumbold recounted, 'and our Staff was literally worked off its head. Three of our Secretaries and the Archivist were away, and the whole of the burden of ciphering and deciphering telegrams fell on the four of us who remained.'[5] The crisis had indeed come at an unfortunate time in the course of the year when many of the embassy staff (not to mention members of the British Government) were on summer leave: Frank Rattigan, Hope-Vere (Third Secretary), J. B. Monck and G. F. Sampson (Archivist) were absent, but on 28 July Odo Russell's son, Military Attaché Lt. Col. Alexander Russell, returned to work.

Under normal circumstances Rumbold himself would have taken some holiday at this juncture, but he recognised that his duties as second in command to Goschen during the worsening crisis did not make this a practical or responsible possibility. With some degree of understatement, while he was 'taking it easy as the responsibility is off my shoulders' now Goschen was back at work, Rumbold feared the way events might lead, realising that there might well be a 'general bust-up in which we may be involved.'[6] Just as it was to be a quarter of a century later, the embassy staff's responsibility to represent Great Britain at the very centre of German power during a seemingly inevitable slide to European war, powerless to do anything practical to prevent it, must have been exceptionally nerve-racking, and the pressures continued to worsen. 'The work at the Embassy is so great that one or two of the Staff showed signs of collapsing and one or two of the Attachés did for a while,'[7] Rumbold recounted. Given the stress and responsibilities, Rumbold thought Goschen was coping well, but even so the strain and long hours were beginning to tell: 'I was with him till past midnight last night. The Chancery is in the dining-room* and yesterday we played 2 rubbers of bridge whilst awaiting tels

* As no entertaining was taking place at this juncture, and the Chancery's work was increasing exponentially given the circumstances, the Chancery had presumably taken over the dining room next door.

35. At the end of the Great War Sir Edward Goschen's care-worn features are all too apparent in a photograph by Walter Stoneman, 1918.

in and out,[8] no doubt to calm frayed nerves. With the news that Germany was reportedly mobilising its land and sea forces, the British Government in London required the Embassy to find out whether, if Germany were indeed intending to attack France, they would send their army through neutral Belgium.

To add to the high-level and momentous diplomatic pressures, there were the Embassy's consular responsibilities in looking after the interests of British nationals based in Germany, many of whom were understandably increasingly becoming alarmed and uncertain as to what action they should take were they to find themselves in a country suddenly at war with Great Britain. Telegrams flooded into the Embassy from British subjects requesting advice: 'We were in great difficulty, not being able to advise them, as we could not assume that we were going to war with Germany.'[9] On 1 August, with train services across Europe beginning to be curtailed, Rumbold himself thought it sensible, in view of the way events seemed to be leading, to make personal practical arrangements to leave Berlin. Writing to his wife in a letter which he hoped would reach her in the personal baggage of a British officer returning to England (since the regular bag service was not running) Rumbold told her that 'This afternoon I packed most of the plate-chest and propose to finish all that, first thing tomorrow morning. Packing won't take me long — if it comes to that. Last night Gurney, Russell & I were cyphering until 1.30 am having sent the 2 Attachés to bed. The latter were dead beat.'[†] He was full of praise for Goschen, who had thanked Rumbold for the way he was helping him. 'I feel rather short of sleep besides being very depressed by the criminal folly of it all... Our Amban [sic] stands out from the rest of his colleagues. As a matter of fact he is in one of the most responsible positions in Europe. Rattigan has proved a "rotter". He is not yet back. He, Hope-Vere, Monck & Sampson are away, but Rattigan and Monck are now starting back. Perhaps they will be too late for the fun.'[10] He recalled that 'we were practically living on our nerves and we are so hard pressed that we had to have night shifts. We could not have gone on very much longer.'[11]

Cutting his month's leave short, Rattigan managed to get back to Berlin on 1 August. Goschen told him that the Germans believed England would remain

---

† The two attachés in question were Richard John Vereker Astell and Godfrey Thomas. In August 1913 Thomas had hosted the Prince of Wales' visit to Berlin (see Chapter 7) and later became his Private Secretary (see Chapter 13).

neutral and that the previous evening a crowd had gathered outside the Embassy singing 'God Save the King'.[12] Indeed, six days earlier crowds outside the Embassy had occasionally been heard to cry out 'Hoch England!' in the hope that England was 'putting a restraining pressure' on Russia.[13] But these apparently benevolent attitudes towards the British were deceptive. On 2 August Rumbold again wrote to his wife:

> We are prepared for the worst. Every body here assumes as a matter of course that we are going to join in and we are besieged all day long by British subjects asking for advice. The whole thing is, to me, a gigantic nightmare and I keep on wondering whether I am in a sane world … every hour brings some new developments … It has been, and still is exciting to the uttermost degree but it is too awful to think what the next few months have in store.[14]

By midday that day Russia and Germany were at war. The Russian Ambassador left his Embassy on Unter den Linden in front of a hostile and violent crowd. His car (lent by James Gerard, the American Ambassador) was attacked[15] and the atmosphere darkened still further.

The following day the Embassy's Commercial Attaché in Frankfurt, Sir Francis Oppenheimer, arrived to obtain advice from the Ambassador and lunched in the Embassy, along with the Military Attaché Lt. Col. Russell and Godfrey Thomas; Goschen had to leave the meal when the Foreign Secretary telephoned him from London warning that he had heard that Germany was about to declare a state of 'national emergency'. Goschen told Oppenheimer that he was convinced that if Germany was made to realise that it was a certainty that Great Britain would declare war if necessary, then war could be averted, but he demurred from obtaining instructions from London to that effect, wearily telling him that 'I am too old a hand at this game to ask for instructions; I am here to receive them and carry them out.'[16]

On Tuesday, 4 August the British Government instructed the Ambassador to request Germany to refrain from taking any steps 'to infringe Belgian neutrality', with a reply requested by midnight.* Goschen forwarded the request, only to be informed that Germany had already entered Belgium on its way to France, a fact which he duly reported to London. At the Embassy later that day, Rumbold and Godfrey Thomas received a new telegram from London which they promptly deciphered. It was an instruction from the British Government to Goschen to request that Germany withdraw from Belgium, a satisfactory answer to be received, again, by midnight. 'You and I will, I am sure, never forget deciphering the Ultimatum to Germany,' Rumbold reminisced with Thomas a dozen years later.[17]

As Goschen left the Embassy for the German Foreign Ministry further down the street to pass on this message, did he reflect to himself that his fears when King Edward VII had offered him the post of British Ambassador to Germany during that train journey in Austria in August 1908 had been more than justified? Gerard, the American Ambassador, remembered how he had arrived at the German Foreign Office to find Goschen sitting there. Goschen told him – in English – that

---

* 11.00 p.m. in Britain.

he was there to ask for his passports.[†] The American was sure that that what looked to him like a German journalist, sitting in the same room, overheard this conversation.[18] The British Ambassador informed the German Foreign Secretary, Gottlieb von Jagow,

> that unless the Imperial Government could give the assurance by 12 o'clock that night that they would proceed no further with their violation of the Belgian frontier and stop their advance, I had been instructed to demand my passports and inform the Imperial Government that His Majesty's Government would have to take all steps in their power to uphold the neutrality of Belgium and the observance of a treaty to which Germany was as much a party as themselves.[19]

Von Jagow told Goschen that the German Government could not comply, but it was agreed that the Ambassador would go and talk to the German Chancellor, Bethmann-Hollweg. The latter was furious and shouted at Goschen for twenty minutes. Famously, he blamed Great Britain for going to war for the sake of 'a piece of paper', a treaty promise with Belgium which Goschen patiently explained his country was honour-bound to uphold. But Bethmann-Hollweg 'held Great Britain responsible for all the terrible events that might happen.'[20]

Key staff were by now taking their meals with the Ambassador at the Embassy.[21] During dinner that night, the butler brought in an 'extra'[‡] issued by the *Berliner Tageblatt* announcing in enormous letters that England had declared war on Germany and that the British Ambassador had requested his passport: it would appear that Gerard had been correct in his suspicions that his conversation with Goschen had been eavesdropped. Worse still, the Ambassador and his staff learned from the butler that this front page – effectively a poster – had been distributed all over Berlin, and as Rumbold recounted, its effect was immediate. Gerard, too, noted that 'at this news the rage of the population of Berlin was indescribable'.[22] If there had been any goodwill towards the British over the previous few weeks, it had now suddenly turned into outright hostility.

A large crowd quickly gathered in the street outside, and its howling could easily be heard even though the Ambassador and his dining companions were seated in the dining room, separated by two large rooms from the street. The meal continued. So that they could smoke, at about 9.30 p.m. Goschen and his colleagues 'unwisely'[23] moved from the dining room to the drawing room at the front of the house, its windows overlooking the street. The crowd was alerted to their presence the moment they switched on the lights: suddenly stones were smashing through the windows. The embassy staff came to the horrifying realisation that the building was under attack.

Foreign embassies are always an easy and obvious target for local dissatisfaction, sometimes violent, against the regimes they represent. Dangerously, in this particular case the grudge against the British was also directed at the very representative of Great Britain's Government – the Ambassador, at that moment inside the Embassy

---

[†] The standard practice when a foreign ambassador left post, enabling him to leave the country to which he was posted.
[‡] Goschen describes it as a 'flying sheet' (*Dispatch from the British Ambassador to Berlin*, Parliamentary Paper Cd 7445, 8 August 1914).

36. A full-page spread in *The Illustrated London News* of 15 August 1914 and headlined 'Not As We Treated Germany: Our Berlin Embassy Mobbed' recorded the dramatic events of a week and a half earlier. The illustration was based on the journalist F.W. Wile's account of the occasion.

– who had issued Germany with the hated ultimatum which had brought about a declaration of war between the two countries. The building was being guarded by three mounted policemen, but, peering through the front windows Rumbold quickly came to the conclusion that they – and indeed the embassy staff marooned in the building – were greatly outnumbered by the surging and dangerous crowd outside. He[24] telephoned the German Foreign Office further down Wilhelmstrasse – the government department responsible for foreign embassy security – and von Jagow sent police reinforcements. Simultaneously, other members of staff ensured that the Embassy's front door was securely locked, before retreating into an inner room for safety.

By now under heavy attack from the crowd, completely enclosed on three sides by other buildings, the former Palais Strousberg was proving unexpected value as a fortress. '[T]wo or three mounted policemen were vainly trying to prevent the demonstrators from climbing up on to the window-sills. The crowd seemed mad with rage and was howling 'Down with England! Death to the English peddler nation! Race treachery! Murderers!' etc.'[25] Using stones, keys, knives, sticks[26] they smashed all the front windows – those of the drawing room to the left of the building, and the Ambassador's office to the right, as well as the bedrooms upstairs overlooking the street. Members of the crowd who managed to climb up on to the raised ground-floor windowsills started breaking what was left of the windows with sticks and anything they had to hand as a weapon, including an umbrella, which fell into one of the rooms. The embassy staff retained it as a souvenir of the occasion, eventually presenting it to *The Times* correspondent in Berlin as a trophy for the newspaper's London office.[27]

After bidding farewell to the departing French Ambassador at the Lehrter railway station, James Gerard had gone for a walk through the Berlin streets. Arriving at the junction of Wilhelmstrasse and Unter den Linden, he came upon the great crowd and witnessed people throwing stones at the Embassy's windows. The story subsequently went round in Berlin that the embassy staff leaned through the broken windows, mocked the crowd and threw pennies at them, but Gerard did not see this, and Rumbold certainly denied that such behaviour had occurred.[28] Gerard surmised that since the streets around the Embassy were covered in tarmac rather than cobblestones, members of the crowd must have brought their missiles with them with the express intention of doing damage. More worryingly, Gerard then turned back through the crowd into Unter den Linden where he found a throng outside the Adlon Hotel. A man on the edge of the crowd 'begged' Gerard not to enter, as apparently 'the people were looking for British newspaper correspondents'.[29]

The attack and the shouting of insults against England – 'one continuous roar and howl of rage'[30] – continued for half an hour. Rumbold later recalled that, peering through the windows, the crowd he could see outside on Wilhelmstrasse was 'crammed from kerb to kerb with a crowd consisting of quite well-dressed individuals, including a number of women'. He hoped never to see such a 'mob' again.[31] For its edition of 15 August *The Illustrated London News* published an artist's impression of the Embassy siege, based on the accounts provided by an eyewitness, Frederic William Wile, the Berlin correspondent of the *Daily Mail*, who was twice arrested that night. Wile recounted the behaviour of the crowd:

'The realisation of what was now upon them turned the Germans into infuriated barbarians …. Arrived before the Embassy, the mob set up thunderous yells, intermingled with 'Treacherous England', 'Death to the traitors' and other cries'. *The Illustrated London News* entitled the picture and Wile's account as 'Not As We Treated Germany: Our Berlin Embassy Mobbed',[32] contrasting the violence with the civilised and quiet manner in which Goschen's opposite number in London had been left in peace in the German Residence at 9 Carlton House Terrace that same evening.* The Berlin crowd was after blood, particularly that of British journalists.

Gerard was so concerned that the British Embassy may have been damaged to the extent that the British Ambassador might not wish to remain there that evening that he thoughtfully ordered a car and, with Roland Harvey, British Embassy Second Secretary, forced his way through the menacing crowd still blocking Wilhelmstrasse outside the Embassy and was let inside, greeted by 'hooting and hisses'.[33] British sangfroid was, however, very much in evidence: 'Sir Edward and his secretaries were perfectly calm and politely declined the refuge which I offered them in our Embassy.'[34] Gerard also offered to help British subjects now finding themselves stranded in extremely hostile territory. Next, one of the embassy servants informed Gerard that there were even more people gathering out on the street outside, 'watching [Gerard's] automobile', a convertible. Gerard instructed the servant to go outside (which by this stage must have taken quite a bit of courage on the servant's part) and instruct Gerard's chauffeur to drive off very slowly once he was inside. Even so, the crowd hissed as the car slowly drove away, and one man jumped on to the vehicle's running board, hitting Harvey, who was still with the American Ambassador, in the face. Gerard was having none of that: he immediately got out of the car and chased the perpetrator down the street, managing to catch up with him. Gerard's German footman 'came running up and explained that I was the American Ambassador and not a Britisher. The man who struck Harvey thereupon apologised and gave his card. He was a Berlin lawyer, who came to the Embassy next morning and apologised again for his "mistake".'[35]†

By about 11.30 p.m. the police had managed to disperse most of the crowd.[36] Goschen reported in his official dispatch that von Jagow came to see him and expressed 'his most heartfelt regrets' for what had happened. 'He said that the behaviour of his countrymen had made him feel more ashamed than he had words to express. It was an indelible stain on the reputation of Berlin.' The 'flying sheet' had not been authorised by the Government, hence their lack of preparedness for guarding the Embassy'. Goschen was satisfied that 'no apology could have been more full and complete'.[37] The British Embassy staff apart from Goschen (who, of course, lived there) were now able to leave the building in relative safety, and apart from some members of the public who were still loitering in the area attempting to attack one group of staff leaving in a car, nothing further untoward occurred. Rumbold made his way to his flat to prepare in earnest to leave Berlin, leaving instructions for his wife's maid[38] (who had just returned from leave) concerning

* See below.
† American ambassadorial appointments to major diplomatic posts were (and remain to this day) usually political in nature, made by the incumbent US President and not filled by the American professional diplomatic service; hence Gerard was not necessarily able to speak German. Before his appointment to Berlin he had been Justice of the Supreme Court of the State of New York.

his belongings, and then left for what was to be for good. Like many diplomats who in hostile circumstances have to leave in a great hurry the countries to which they are posted, Rumbold was understandably worried about what would become of his and his wife's possessions after his departure – 'On August 5, 1914, I had left everything behind – wine, linen, knick-knacks on the table, etc', he was later to write,[39] although he arranged for some of his papers and belongings to be sent for safekeeping at the Embassy.‡ His colleagues made similar arrangements: the Ambassador would have had no choice given the short notice but to leave his possessions in the Embassy, in any case, protected within the confines of diplomatic protocol,§ deemed to be the safest place to store them. Afterwards Rumbold and some of the other staff made their way back to the relative sanctuary and security of the Embassy to spend what was left of the night as best they could.

That night, in London, a vast crowd had gathered in Whitehall and in front of Buckingham Palace waiting for news from Germany. When news came through that war had been declared, the response was upbeat: 'an enormous shout went up', while 'The German Ambassador, who looked haggard, was in no way molested as he motored home.'[40] Haggard he might have been, but on retiring to bed that evening at 9 Carlton House Terrace, there was to be no rest. After the 11 o'clock deadline had passed, Harold Nicolson,¶ a junior member of staff at the Foreign Office, knocked on the German Embassy's door. He was carrying the correct text of the official British Government response to the German Government's failure to meet the deadline, declaring war and enclosing the Ambassador's passports. Unfortunately, amid the stresses of the moment and due to a misunderstanding at the Foreign Office an incorrect text had been sent to the Ambassador earlier that evening, before the deadline had even expired. Nicolson was directed to the Ambassador's bedroom and gave him the correct text, noticing that he had already partly opened and seen the content of the earlier message.[41]

Back in Berlin, the following morning (5 August) the Emperor Wilhelm's aide-de-camp paid a call to the Embassy to express regret for the events that had occurred the previous night. Rumbold thought the 'regret' disingenuous,[42] the ADC pompously explaining that 'you will gather from those occurrences an idea of the feelings of [the Emperor's] people respecting the action of Great Britain

‡On his return to England Rumbold discovered that the chest containing these articles had been seized by the police and impounded on their way from his residence to the Embassy. Learning that Kühlmann, Counsellor at the German Embassy in London, 'had had to leave behind some valuable pictures when the Embassy was withdrawn … I let the Germans know that Kühlmann's pictures would not be released until the German police handed over my papers and plate. They promptly did so.' (Rumbold, *The War Crisis in Berlin, July–August 1914*, 1944 edn, pp. 326–7).

§ For centuries, diplomatic premises have been classed as immune from the attentions of the local populace, police and security services unless entry has been authorised by the Head of Mission, a custom later codified in the 1961 Vienna Convention on Diplomatic Relations. In view of this, the embassy/high commission/ residence is usually the safest place to store valuables when diplomatic staff evacuate a mission. Traditionally, it has been rare for the premises of a British embassy/residence to be illegally entered, even during periods of great local unrest. There have, nevertheless, been instances of such violation and consequent damage of contents, including Baghdad in 1958, and Tripoli and Tehran in 2011. In these cases, just as in Berlin on 4 August 1914, mobs besieged and attacked the buildings concerned, but this time successfully gained entry and managed to destroy, loot or damage much of the contents.

¶ The son and biographer of Arthur Nicolson, Lord Carnock (see Chapter 2); see Chapter 12 for his subsequent career in Berlin.

in joining with other nations against her old allies of Waterloo'. The ADC added that although the Emperor had been 'proud' of the honorary titles of British Field-Marshal and British Admiral, 'in consequence of what had occurred he must now at once divest himself of those titles.'[43] Goschen reported in his dispatch that this message 'lost none of its acerbity by the manner of its delivery.'[44] Goschen received his passports later that morning.

Throughout the day paper ashes floated up and down the Embassy's internal courtyard as files and books of correspondence were burned in the central heating boiler.[45] Embassy staff were performing another of the standard diplomatic protocols for sudden departure from host countries in hostile conditions: the burning of ciphers and other sensitive documents, lest they fall into the hands of the enemy power. It had been agreed that the American Embassy (which until 1917 was to act as the 'protecting power' overseeing the interests of many Western powers in Berlin) would look after the Embassy building while the British were absent. That afternoon the American Embassy First Secretary Joseph Grew visited the Embassy to arrange for this, and help and witness the sealing of those embassy archives not earmarked for destruction. 'These archives dated back many years and were of historical value. They were bound in volumes which were contained in glass-fronted bookcases ranged around the gallery of the library. We attached a label on each bookcase and sealed the label with our respective seals. This work took nearly three hours. The heat was stifling,' Rumbold remembered.[46]

Rumbold stayed at the Embassy that night, and all seemed relatively calm, although the American Military Attaché George Langhorne arrived with the disconcerting news that he had heard people on the street saying they intended to burn the building down.[47] What would have been a miserable and tense dinner was served to the Ambassador and his staff, and with some difficulty: as part of the anti-British public hostility which had suddenly erupted in Berlin many tradesmen who had long done business with the Embassy now refused to supply it with anything at all, even food. But Goschen managed to circumvent this difficulty by sending an Italian temporary sous-chef out to go shopping incognito.[48] Indeed, it was becoming impossible for anyone British to remain in Berlin: according to Joseph Grew they were 'spat on in the street' and, if found, arrested by the police.[49]

Realising they could no longer remain in what was now very hostile territory, that evening British press correspondents based in Germany entered the relative safety of the Embassy, camping for the night in the Chancery. Amongst them was Wile. An American citizen, he had begged the British to help him get out of Germany[50] on the grounds that he had been a correspondent of a British newspaper: Gerard had some difficulty in obtaining Wile's passport from the German Foreign Office.[51] The press correspondents were joined by members of the British Legation from Dresden, and slept in one of the drawing rooms. It must have been a tense and uncomfortable night for everybody. But Rumbold, at least, retained a sense of humour, accidentally witnessing the journalists' 'toilette', 'really a most comical sight'[52] early the next morning, 6 August 1914. Their makeshift ablutions finished, the press correspondents left at about six o' clock, and the British Embassy staff at about seven.

By now very few native German staff remained on duty in the Embassy, most of them having been mobilised. Rumbold left a trusted Chancery servant[*] who had worked at the Embassy for the past thirty-five years in day-to-day charge of the building. But three locally engaged members of staff were not to be so friendly. As the British gathered together in the front drawing room ready to leave, these German employees were given a month's wages, but once they had the money they dramatically tore off their liveries, spat on them and refused to carry any trunks or luggage to the taxi cabs waiting in the street outside.[53] No doubt shaken and angered by this spectacle, the British staff walked out of the front door, dragging their luggage on to Wilhelmstrasse and into waiting taxis, leaving the Embassy behind them.

Police had been posted along the usual route from the Embassy to the Lehrter railway station, but as a diversionary tactic, the taxis carrying the British took more circuitous routes along back streets in order to avoid more crowd trouble. Once at the station, Count Wedel, acting on behalf of von Jagow, gave his official farewell to the Ambassador and his staff, who caught the 8.16 a.m. train westwards towards the German border with Holland and the ferry for England. At each station in Germany through which the train passed, the Ambassador later reported that 'great crowds' thronged the platforms to hurl insults, but that a retired colonel of the Guards, who accompanied the party to the Dutch border, tried to stop them.[54] The journey was delayed, taking twenty-four hours to reach the coast. After its arrival at Harwich the departing German Ambassador embarked on the same ferry back to Holland.[55] Once on the train from Harwich to Liverpool Street Station in London, the party dined together for the last time and drank to each other's health. Goschen recorded in his later dispatch to the British Government how impressed he was by the conduct of his staff:

> One and all, they worked night and day, with scarcely any rest, and I cannot praise too highly the cheerful zeal with which counsellor, naval and military attachés, secretaries, and the two young attachés buckled to their work and kept their nerve with often a yelling mob outside and inside hundreds of British subjects clamouring for advice and assistance. I was proud to have such a staff to work with, and feel most grateful to them all for the invaluable assistance and support, often exposing them to considerable personal risk, which they so readily and cheerfully gave to me.[56]

It was not to be the last time that a British Ambassador and his staff were to evacuate 70 Wilhelmstrasse at the beginning of hostilities with Germany.

---

[*] This was probably Schönemann (see Chapter 9).

CHAPTER 9
1918–1920: 'SOLID AND UNCHANGED'

The dramatic breakdown of diplomatic relations between Great Britain and Germany that the British Embassy in Berlin had witnessed in July and August 1914 was followed by the most terrible war that mankind had yet seen. Sixteen million people were killed in a conflict that wiped out much of the generation that fought it, but on 11 November 1918 the guns stopped. As Philipp Scheidemann declared a new German Republic at the Reichstag on 9 November, Karl Liebknecht proclaimed from the Royal Schloss an alternative, socialist republic. The day before the Armistice was signed the Emperor Wilhelm II abdicated, humiliatingly fleeing to Holland where he spent the rest of his life in exile.[*] In 1917, in response to British dislike of all things German, King George V, no stranger to Berlin or to the Embassy, had tactically changed the British royal family's German surname from Saxe-Coburg-Gotha to 'Windsor' to distance it from its close German family connections. Other members of the royal family were encouraged to give up all German dignities and titles. Although he had not shared his parents' own animosity towards Wilhelm, for the rest of his life King George refused any further personal contact with his cousin, looking upon him 'as the greatest criminal known for having plunged the world into this ghastly war … with all its misery.'[1]

'When Sir Edward Goschen and I left the Embassy house early on the morning of August 6th, 1914, the ground floor was in disorder and looked almost as if it had been wrecked, for most of the double windows had been smashed by the crowd on the night of August 4th,'[2] Rumbold was later to tell the King. Important documents had been deliberately destroyed and embassy and personal valuables stored in the cellars and rooms. Throughout the Great War the Embassy had remained in the care of the locally engaged Chancery servant[†] Goschen and Rumbold had entrusted with the task, who lived with his family in the building. Diplomatic relations had been broken off and there was no ambassador in either London or Berlin. The United States acted as the 'protecting power', keeping a watchful eye on the building and its caretaker, until it entered the war itself in 1917, succeeded as the 'protecting power' by Holland.

Soon after the official end of hostilities, the British sent representatives from several military and civilian organisations to Berlin. These included the Red Cross and Prisoners of War Commissions, and the most obvious and convenient place for their offices was the former British Embassy. But although the Great War was over, Berlin itself was far from peaceful. Popular disquiet over Germany's having effectively been 'stabbed in the back', widespread conspiracy theories over the

---

[*] Wilhelm spent the rest of his life at Huis Doorn, dying on 4 June 1941.
[†] Probably Schönemann, who had worked in the Embassy since Lascelles' time.

'real' reasons behind the sudden German surrender, the Emperor's abdication and increasing Communist agitation spurred on by the 1917 Russian Revolution were at the root of major riots by 'Spartacists'* in central Berlin that began in December 1918. They were only the latest in a series of riots and strikes that the city had witnessed during the Great War. In the heart of the government district, the Embassy and the Adlon Hotel now found themselves at the very centre of a battlefield as mobs fought in the surrounding streets in a war for supremacy of the capital and of Germany itself.

'[T]he situation was very critical,'[3] the Red Cross representative in Berlin based at the Embassy reported to London on 9 January 1919. During the course of that day there was severe fighting just outside on Wilhelmstrasse and at the Brandenburg Gate, which had begun the day in the hands of government troops, had then fallen to the rebels, only to be retaken by government forces that same evening. The Freikorps – led by members of the former German officer class – set up machine-gun positions on the roof of the Adlon Hotel and fired at agitators in the Pariser Platz below. Raking machine-gun fire on the streets made it dangerous for the Red Cross staff to remain in the vicinity, and at one stage they were advised to shut the office as soon as possible and retire to their hotel. 'This we did about noon and I am glad to say that hitherto everything has gone well with all of us', however they were later asked not to return to Wilhelmstrasse.[4] The rebels attacked the Chancellery further south down the street and were repulsed with heavy losses.

Walking around the streets of Berlin that January of 1919, Count Henry Kessler recorded vivid impressions of sudden outbreaks of extreme violence while simultaneously and only a short distance away, normal Berlin life miraculously continued. On 7 January 'The Wilhelmstrasse was again choked with people … Hundreds of people rushed in the direction of Tiergarten. I remained where I was and could see that Spartacus was trying to push forward from Unter den Linden to Wilhelmstrasse …. About half past five Pariser Platz and Wilhelmstrasse were in the hands of Government troops.'[5] As he was walking south down Friedrichstrasse the following day

> Suddenly gunfire broke out at the Unter den Linden end … I went down the Linden which was blocked off and darkened. Posts in combat helmets stood by the house entrances. Wilhelmstrasse was blocked but illuminated. The sentries on the Wilhelmplatz say the houses on the Mohrenstrasse are occupied by Spartacists. In the Hotel Kaiserhof, which is closed and dark, lie government troops. The Leipziger Strasse looks like normal, except for the closed shops.

In contrast, 'On the Potsdamer Platz the great conditoreis† [sic] – Josty, Fürstenhof, Palastcafé, Vaterland – are open, brightly lit, and overflowing.'[6]

In an attempt to control the streets, the entire government quarter was for periods of time shut off to everyone without special permits, and for months Berlin teetered on the brink of complete anarchy. On 8 April 1919 Kessler recorded that 'The Wilhelmstrasse is jammed with artillery and machine-guns. On the Wilhelmplatz two machine-guns are mounted on lorries to dominate the street

---

* Named after the 1st century BC leader of the slave rebellion against the Roman Republic.
† Confectionery shops.

right and left. Noske‡ guards everywhere, steel-helmeted and loaded with hand-grenades.'[7] To escape the unrest, the German Government decamped to Weimar, the new German constitution drafted there giving the city's name to the new republic even after the Government's return to Berlin. Becoming law in August 1919, the new constitution replaced the former hereditary monarchy with an elected President as Head of State, working with a national Parliament (Reichstag), a Chancellor and Cabinet of Ministers.

The terms of the 1919 Treaty of Versailles that resulted from the Paris Peace Conference were deeply unpopular when they became public knowledge in Germany that summer. In order to contain Germany's ability to wage war in the future the treaty terms limited the size of her military capability and the extent of her territories. Germany's army was to be limited to 100,000 men; the Rhineland was to be occupied by Allied troops; Alsace-Lorraine was transferred back to France; Poland was reconstructed, with access to the Baltic coast through a 'corridor' created by the transfer of West Prussia, Posen and Silesia; Danzig§ was to be a free city under the League of Nations; Memel¶ was to be administered by the Allied states; and Germany's colonies were confiscated.

To help stabilise the political situation, in July 1919 the Allied Governments requested that the new German Government establish full diplomatic relations with them as soon as possible, with it being agreed to send ambassadors to Germany as from 1 July 1920. That January Victor Hay, Lord Kilmarnock had been appointed as Chargé d'Affaires in advance of the appointment of a full British ambassador. In the absence of specialist diplomatic staff the British Government had had to rely on the resident military for detailed information about German politics, economics and social matters, and there was still some concern that the Chargé lacked the necessary authority over the British Military Mission and other military control commissions based in Berlin.[8] Sydney Waterlow of the Foreign Office's Central European Department admitted:

> Our Berlin Embassy is very much in the limelight and is likely to be more so in the early future. If it does not shew [sic] up well – if the Prime Minister continues to feel that it cannot be depended upon for intelligent information, he is likely to turn more and more to the soldiers. The position and prestige of the Foreign Office itself are closely involved in the success of the British Embassy.[9]

With a degree of understatement (in view of the circumstances) Kilmarnock recommended that it remained 'undesirable' for any diplomats to bring their wives and families to Berlin.[10] The political situation remained unstable in the extreme: in March 1920, in an attempt to overthrow the German Government, Wolfgang Kapp and General Walthar von Lüttwitz marched on the city with Freikorps soldiers. The Government was again forced to flee the capital, this time to Stuttgart. The putsch was quickly defeated, but during its course Allied diplomats and Commission personnel based in Berlin were cut off for nearly a week from any contact with the outside world. By June none of the British-based staff working in

‡ Named after Gustav Noske, Minister of Defence.
§ Now Gdansk in Poland.
¶ Now Klaipėda in Lithuania.

Berlin had yet been able to take on accommodation or set up long-term housekeeping arrangements and were living in hotels, which was of course very expensive. Kilmarnock wrote to the Foreign Office in London about the high costs the Mission's staff in Berlin were forced to endure there compared to other capitals, suggesting the posting be described as 'expensive rather than normal' from the point of view of staff allowances, while food shortages were a real problem.[11]

***

The issue of who would become the next full British Ambassador to Berlin was highly contentious. Once Goschen had served his 'natural' time in Berlin, Lady Susan Townley had understood that her husband was lined up for the job. The Great War, of course, intervened, but she claimed[12] that one of the main reasons he was not appointed was that she was continually dogged by controversy. When the Townleys were posted to Washington, she was hounded by the American press keen to publish sensational stories about her, the issue becoming so serious that it damaged the couple's diplomatic standing in the city. Sir Walter's final posting, in 1917, was as British Minister to Holland, where his wife's former friendship with Wilhelm II came back to haunt her: a parliamentary question was asked as to whether she had formed part of 'the committee which received the ex-Kaiser on his arrival in Holland' in late 1918, the official answer being that she 'happened to be motoring in the neighbourhood … and happened to be one of the spectators who witnessed' the arrival of the Emperor, but was not part of any special reception committee.[13] That was indeed how she accounted for her presence in the vicinity in her memoirs, but the apparent 'indiscretions of Lady Susan' were, according to her, cited as the main reason why her husband felt forced to resign from the diplomatic service in July 1919.[14] By 1922, when Lady Susan published her memoirs, the couple were living in the country, busy breeding 'Large Black pigs which, if not quite so interesting, is at least more remunerative and less exacting than diplomacy!'[15]

Another diplomat tipped for the job was someone with rather more extensive and recent practical experience of the posting, Sir Horace Rumbold, who by this time was serving in Warsaw as the first British Minister in the new British Legation, established after the Treaty of Versailles.* In 1919 there were rumours in the Foreign Office and the press to this effect.[16] It was, however, not to be. Instead of an experienced career diplomat, Prime Minister Lloyd George gave the job to Edgar Vincent, Baron D'Abernon. It was one of a series of diplomatic appointments Lloyd George and his successor Bonar Law made that favoured specialist 'experts' for ambassadorial positions† over career diplomats. Such a policy had to some extent been advocated by the MacDonnell Commission of 1914, which concluded, *inter alia*, that the professional diplomatic service needed to be transformed from its traditional makeup of generalists of 'elite' aristocratic, Establishment backgrounds in favour of external specialists in fields such as finance, politics and economics. The

* The Legation occupied rented accommodation in the Branicki Palace in Warsaw, at the corner of Aleje Jerozolimskie and Nowy Świat.
† The politician Lord Derby's appointment to Paris in April 1918, the businessman Sir Auckland Geddes to Washington in March 1920, and Lord Crewe to Paris in December 1922 are other examples. The British Government occasionally continues the practice of making political appointments to diplomatic posts.

37. The elegant Edgar Vincent, Lord D'Abernon caricatured by 'Spy' [Sir Leslie Ward] for *Vanity Fair* on 20 April 1899 with the title 'Eastern Finance'.

old 'elite' career diplomacy, conducted behind closed doors, was popularly seen as having partly been responsible for the tortuous international politics that had helped lead to the Great War; in contrast, a 'new' diplomacy would be much more open in character, taking the form of pragmatic discussions of international difficulties. Indeed, Lloyd George's own preference, to be echoed in the following decade by his later successor Neville Chamberlain, was to undertake diplomacy himself through international summits and face-to-face meetings. It was not the only major change in the Foreign Office and diplomatic service at this time: in 1919 the two organisations were merged and a number of reforms introduced in an attempt to make the amalgamated service, in twenty-first century terms, more 'accessible', 'relevant' and 'fit for purpose'.‡

D'Abernon's field of expertise was in international finance, regarded as a fundamental requirement for the job of British Ambassador in Berlin during the post-war years in order to restore the damaged German economy. In this way, it was reasoned, the country could achieve political stability and so not be a target for the spread of the dreaded Bolshevism. On a more cynical level it would also more quickly be able to repay the war reparations to other European powers as agreed in the Treaty of Versailles. D'Abernon was, however, very much part of that same British Establishment from which the MacDonnell Commission recommended the diplomatic service distance itself. Born in 1857, the son of the 11th Baron D'Abernon, he had previously worked in a variety of specialist quasi-government positions. Ottoman Turkey had declared bankruptcy in 1875 and its finances were placed under European supervision. Appointed British, Belgian and Dutch representative on the Council of the Ottoman Public Debt Administration at Constantinople, D'Abernon became its President and, shortly afterwards, financial advisor to the Egyptian Government, an endeavour in which he was extremely successful. In 1889 he

‡ For example, the Foreign Office and Diplomatic Service were made into one with a new Selection Board, the entry examinations were changed and there were new pay scales, all designed to open up the organisation to a wider range of candidates. A century on, the notion that the Foreign Office and its staff are part of the problem and not the solution in European diplomacy refuses to go away. See Tim Ambler's blog 'Is the Foreign Office Fit for Purpose?', 29 November 2012 (www.adamsmith.org/blog/politics.../is-the-foreign-office-fit-for-purpose/) and Tim Ambler and Keith Boyfield, *EUTopia: What EU would be best and how do we achieve it?* (Adam Smith Institute, 2006).

became Governor of the Imperial Ottoman Bank in the Turkish capital, but found himself in great difficulty in 1895–96 when he became *de facto* responsible for a financial panic that led to a collapse in share values – shares in which D'Abernon had himself been speculating. When the Bank was besieged by angry investors, D'Abernon was forced to make a hasty, undignified exit out of a rear window and over the rooftops. These activities were not calculated to endear him to the French Government, who themselves had heavy financial involvement in the affairs of the Ottoman Bank, and suffered consequent losses. As Sir Charles Hardinge drily recounted, 'His actions as president of the Ottoman Bank in Constantinople had been such as to have become a byword in financial circles.'[17]

D'Abernon became MP for Exeter in 1899. He never achieved ministerial office, but in 1912 became Chairman of the Royal Commission on Imperial Trade and Natural Resources of the British Dominions and then, in 1915, Chairman of the Central Control Board (Liquor Traffic). In this latter post he became closely involved with the Government's initiative to increase manufacturing output during the Great War and improve public health through the control of alcohol consumption, strongly advocating the introduction of what was to be a long-surviving piece of legislation: controlled licensing hours for public houses.

D'Abernon recalled in his memoirs that the Foreign Secretary, Lord Curzon, offered him the job of 'Ambassador Extraordinary and Minister Plenipotentiary' and that his mission 'was in character somewhat different from the usual diplomatic appointment.'[18] He was certainly not alone in describing his posting as unusual, particularly as (although D'Abernon was an accomplished linguist) Lloyd George assured him that being able to speak German was not a prerequisite for the job. Hardinge later described the appointment as 'highly criticised': as Permanent Under-Secretary of State, it would have been normal for the Foreign Secretary to consult him first about such a move, but this did not occur, probably, Hardinge surmised, because he would have tried to block it. He later learned, however, that Foreign Secretary Lord Curzon had been placed under some pressure by Lloyd George to make the appointment.[19] D'Abernon certainly believed that Lloyd George had been greatly influential in his appointment, and thus that his ambassadorship had a particularly high political status.[20] The appointment attracted much criticism, particularly in *The Times*, whose editor, Sir Wickham Steed, was habitually critical of Lloyd George's diplomatic endeavours.[21] Once D'Abernon's appointment had been announced, a series of articles appeared in the newspaper criticising his suitability for the post, with an unequivocal leader on 29 June 1920:

> We confess we should have preferred the choice of the Prime Minister to have fallen upon a public man whose career had been free from any connexion, no matter how honourable, with international finance; and we hold that the Prime Minister would have been well-advised had he paid heed to the representations upon the appointment of Lord D'Abernon which we believe to have been made to him by the Foreign Secretary, Lord Curzon, and other responsible counsellors.[22]

On the other hand, some establishment figures congratulated D'Abernon. Lord Londonderry was 'more than delighted to think that at the most difficult point, there is someone who has full grasp of the situation'; Berlin was 'one of the most difficult posts imaginable'. While commiserating with the disappointment of professional diplomats, he had a dim view of their specialist training and experience which 'can have no other effect than to make them mere machines, and the more the high jobs are given to outsiders the better for diplomacy.'[23] In the House of Commons on 1 July the Prime Minister was asked 'what qualifications Lord D'Abernon possessed superior to those of trained diplomats which postulated his appointment as Ambassador to Germany; and whether it was the considered policy of the Government to offer the more responsible posts of the diplomatic service to persons without diplomatic training, seeing that this policy was not calculated to attract talent to the Diplomatic Service'. In a written reply, Bonar Law stated 'that the appointment of Lord D'Abernon had been made with special reference to the economic and financial problems of the international situation, in which matters Lord D'Abernon possessed particular experience and qualifications. The appointment was of a temporary character. The answer to the second part of the question was in the negative.'[24] The following day D'Abernon was in Berlin.

From Warsaw, Sir Horace Rumbold wrote despondently to Hardinge:

I have done hard and exacting work here for 11 months, not in anticipation of any reward or advancement – incidentally, the recent appointments in our service show clearly enough that we cannot expect advancement ....
To sum up, what I feel is that no matter how hard one works and how much satisfaction one may give one's own department, nothing counts. Nothing could be more discouraging than this reflection.[25]

Writing in 1922, Lady Susan Townley was, predictably, blunter. Lloyd George, she remarked, had the habit of 'popping the plums of our service into the mouths of ex-Cabinet Ministers and others, although in most cases they had no claim to them, being devoid of that expert training which is necessary for the proper fulfilment of the functions appertaining to so highly specialized a profession'. She made a not particularly subtle swipe at D'Abernon himself, describing for example how the Prime Minister had professed ignorance of a particular Russo-German agreement negotiated in Berlin: 'How could such an Agreement have escaped the vigilance of "the man on the spot"?'[26] Indeed, some were to criticise D'Abernon's seeming lack of understanding of those areas of the job that were not economic in character.

***

D'Abernon was tall, handsome and cultured, with a personal expert knowledge of and interest in fine art, using his large personal fortune and eye for good pieces to build up an important collection.* His other great lifelong interests were horseracing and golf; reputedly he played the game almost daily in Berlin and took much interest in the establishment of new golf course near the Wannsee.[27] His appeal and sophistication only intensified when in 1890 he married the glamorous Lady Helen Venetia Duncombe, the younger daughter of the Earl of Feversham, who, like her elder sister, was a great society beauty: the French art dealer René Gimpel remarked in his diary that she 'must be the prettiest woman in England.'[28] She kept an apartment in the Palazzo Giustiniani on the Grand Canal in Venice where the fashionable society portraitist John Singer Sargent painted her in 1904,[29] exhibiting

---

* See Chapter 11.

the portrait at the Royal Academy of Arts in London in 1905. The following year, Sargent portrayed Lord D'Abernon himself as a commission from D'Abernon's Exeter constituents to mark his retirement as their MP.[30]

Lady Gladwyn[*] described Lord and Lady D'Abernon as 'an astoundingly handsome couple.'[31] But, despite having secured one of the great beauties of the age as his wife, D'Abernon seems to have remained only too aware of the attractions of other members of the opposite sex, and the early years of the D'Abernons' marriage, which was to be childless, were evidently difficult. 'He had been a great *coureur des femmes* and was dubbed "the Piccadilly Stallion"', as Lady Gladwyn later put it.[32] At one stage, 'not able to stand it any more',[33] Lady D'Abernon left her husband, fleeing to Cairo. There, Lady Cromer, who was familiar with D'Abernon from his time in Egypt, persuaded her not to abandon the marriage but to return to her husband. Years later, like many women of her class, Lady D'Abernon was to find a new purpose in life in training as a nurse during the Great War and qualifying as an anaesthetist. Lady Gladwyn was later of the opinion that the D'Abernons had effectively led separate lives until the appointment to Berlin in 1920, but then 'she greatly admired his brilliance and made a superb hostess for him.'[34]

Despite D'Abernon's wealth, handsomeness and cultural sophistication, at least in Berlin he presented a ramshackle demeanour: 'His bulky, gigantic figure, topped by a small but fine head, with thick white hair and a somewhat rough, equally white beard, his astonishing neglect of all the conventions of Saville [*sic*] Row, his gaping collars and his almost incredible frankness, were unforgettable,'[35] and something of this appearance was to be captured by Augustus John in his 1925 portrait of D'Abernon. The fact that the new Ambassador did not come from a Foreign Office or diplomatic service background apparently soon became obvious: 'It was clearly impossible to distrust for long a man who simply asked you point-blank the question he had on his mind, without a trace of that diplomatic finesse which one expected in an Ambassador.'[36] René Gimpel described him as 'tall and well proportioned, with a broad, short, pointed beard, a mild gaze, and blue eyes. He is really a magnificent old man.'[37] On his arrival in Berlin on 2 July 1920 D'Abernon immediately paid calls on the German Foreign Minister, Dr Simons, and the Head of State, now a President – Friedrich Ebert, to whom he formally announced that the British Government had given him the duty of establishing full diplomatic relations with the new German Republic. Given his economic background, some of the more reactionary German press feared D'Abernon's real plans for their country, wondering whether he would 'certainly squeeze Germany to the utmost.'[38] *The Illustrated London News* photographed D'Abernon at his desk in the Embassy, 'having left for his post within a few hours' of his appointment.[39] But he did not remain in Berlin for long that summer, leaving to take part in a war reparations conference at Spa in Belgium.

***

The Embassy itself was in a state of some disorder. This was not surprising: in the weeks leading up to the outbreak of the Great War it had been the scene of intense,

---

* The wife of the diplomat Sir Gladwyn Jebb.

stressful activity, its staff departing from it in some haste, after using the building, with a number of outsiders, as an emergency hotel. It had been attacked and its windows broken. The only people who lived in the building after early August 1914 was 'the caretaker', Schönemann, and, until a British-based head of mission took over, a representative of the Dutch Embassy, the protecting power since 1917.[40] No British-based staff had used the building until late in 1919 when it became the offices of various Commission personnel and on occasion a refuge from violence on the streets outside. As in many similar circumstances before and since, a building's occupation by a nomadic set of staff operating in stressful and difficult circumstances is not usually conducive to its welfare. On 6 December 1919, shortly after nine in the evening, fire suddenly broke out: 'flames burst from the Embassy roof, and blazing high into the air, were visible for a great distance from the Wilhelmstrasse.'[41] Unfortunately, the firemen found that 'their hose leaked, since it was made of war-made material and so contained no rubber'. Even so, the fire was contained, and most of the Embassy's rooms, apart from the staircase hall and its roof, escaped damage, but Schönemann was unable to account for how the fire had started. With diplomatic relations with Germany about to be resumed, the Ministry of Works undertook necessary repairs,[†] but to maximise its use for representational work by the Ambassador and Ambassadress, the Embassy needed to be open for business in the way it had been before 4 August 1914, and to that end in late July 1920 Lady D'Abernon travelled to Berlin.

The purpose of her trip, she explained, was that

> [T]he disorder and inevitable neglect of War and post-War years made it expedient and indeed urgent that I should go to see what was required at the Embassy the the way of a household staff and of re-decorations and furniture. After five years of neglect, followed by a serious fire and the installation in the Embassy of the British Military Mission, it was perhaps unavoidable that everything (with the exception of a few rooms occupied and cleaned for the Kilmarnocks) should be in a state of indescribable filth and disorder.[42]

She travelled to Berlin on the overnight train service, arriving at six in the morning on 31 July, Lord Kilmarnock and his staff dutifully turning up at the station to greet her, rather to her dismay, as she was feeling dishevelled after the long journey. She got to work immediately, 'endeavouring to straighten out some of the confusion that prevails on the domestic *Hausfrau* side of the Embassy.'[43] At least some of the building was in chaos, especially the complex of cellar rooms, full of 'filth and rubbish … that no servants could cope with.'[44] The situation was indeed so bad that it was proposed to engage soldiers to help. But the efforts were not without their rewards: Lady D'Abernon was later to report that in the basement rooms she found stored 'gorgeous buff and scarlet liveries … by the score'[45] dating from Lascelles' time, and a cache of good wine, together with the embassy silver.

Lady D'Abernon arranged the furniture and made the rooms look as though some thought had been put into their appearance. For the most part content with the reception rooms, she thought the bedroom floor above would 'never be satisfactory' because of the building's location in the busy centre of Berlin: the bedrooms

† See Chapter 11.

38. The beautiful Lady D'Abernon as portrayed by John Singer Sargent in Venice in about 1904.

located at the front of the house faced on to the busy and noisy Wilhelmstrasse, while the ones to the rear were 'overhung by the vast and gloomy Adlon Hotel.'[46] During this fleeting visit she would have preferred to occupy one of the quieter bedrooms at the back of the house, but the Kilmarnocks had allotted her one at the front. This she found so noisy that she was prevented from sleeping, so to pass the time away during these periods of insomnia she would sit and stare out of the window on to the street below, 'watching the lumbering conveyances and the unusual pedestrians that pass to and fro'. Some of these pedestrians were indeed unusual, early signs of the licentiousness (or rather perhaps behaviour inspired by economic desperation) that would come to characterise some of the culture of Weimar Berlin. One night she noticed a figure wearing a skirt, hat and veil standing for a long time in a doorway on the other side of Wilhelmstrasse. This individual was eventually joined by a man, and when the couple strolled northwards towards Unter den Linden and became visible under the street lamps, it was apparent that the 'woman' was in fact a man in drag wearing a scabbard hanging from a military belt: 'It was not the first time that from my window I have seen men street-walkers dressed up as women, but never before one with a cavalry belt and sabre superadded.'[47]

> Lady D'Abernon had a no-nonsense approach towards her host, Lord Kilmarnock:
> Physically he is an insignificant little man, but I fancy he may be endowed with shrewdness and sang-froid. His favourite occupation is acting and playwriting. He is not particularly interested in passing events which perhaps accounts for apparent lack of fore-sight and initiative. An amiable trait is his kindness and compassion for 'down and outs'. He begs me to take on all the people he now employs but as these are mostly cripples and derelicts, I skate lightly away from the subject whenever it is raised, being resolved to engage an entirely new and efficient staff when we come to the Embassy.[48]

It was agreed that the Kilmarnocks would continue to reside in the building until D'Abernon arrived properly to take over as Ambassador, when they would move out into nearby accommodation.

**

While Lady D'Abernon was busy making the building ready for use as an embassy again, Lloyd George sent her husband on another special diplomatic assignment, this time to Warsaw to head an Allied Mission to help the Polish Government with a pressing danger: the advancing Bolshevik army. Sir Horace Rumbold understandably felt that his authority was undermined by this Prime Ministerial-sanctioned presence – especially given D'Abernon's recent appointment to Berlin. Hardinge described the situation: 'Lloyd George was not quite satisfied with the position in Poland and sent Lord D'Abernon from Berlin on a special mission to supervise Rumbold.'[49] The latter was wearily sardonic in his views on events as the Red Army continued to advance towards Warsaw, writing to his wife on 5 August 1920:

> We may all be in flight in 2 or 3 days from now. I wonder what will happen to all the nice furniture and good beds etc which I could not

pack up. The Bolos, if and when they get here, will make hay of these. It is very depressing but there it is. Some fate pursues me. Just 6 years ago I was burning archives at Berlin before our departure and we are doing the same thing now.[50]

The following day the Red Army was just twenty-five miles from Warsaw when D'Abernon telegraphed to Curzon advising the British to despatch a Franco-British Expeditionary Force of at least 20,000 men. On 13 August the special mission evacuated Warsaw, along with Rumbold. On 18 August, after a battle outside the city, the Russians began to retreat, Rumbold returning to Warsaw the following day. D'Abernon's estimation had rocketed in the eyes of Lloyd George, but D'Abernon himself had a high regard for Rumbold. Hardinge was later to state that after a month's stay in Warsaw D'Abernon reported back to London that 'it was quite useless for him to stay there since Rumbold was "King of Warsaw".'[51] But Rumbold's luck did not improve. Appointed shortly afterwards to be Head of Mission in Constantinople, most of his treasured possessions were stolen when the carriage carrying them was detached from the rest of the train while in a siding in Vienna. Later on the same journey he lost his cases of claret when they were accidentally destroyed by a train engine at Trieste.[52]

Lord and Lady D'Abernon officially arrived in Berlin as Ambassador and Ambassadress on Monday, 25 October 1920.[53] The following Saturday Dr Wirth, the German Minister of Finance, came to lunch. Evidently, Schönemann, the Chancery servant entrusted by Goschen and Rumbold to look after the building, had performed his duties well: 'a great character and absolutely to be trusted. Throughout the war he had sole charge of the Embassy, and handed it all over when the war was finished, without a tablecloth or a bottle of wine being found to be missing,' a Foreign Office official reported.[54] Thus, the D'Abernons were able to serve Wirth 'from the depths of an unviolated pre-war cellar some excellent old vintage, left by Sir Edward Goschen' which had 'a genial, mellowing effect' upon him.[55] That evening[56] they held a diplomatic reception constituting D'Abernon's official – and compulsory – entrée as British Ambassador to Berlin. His official appointment had been in July, but the entrée had had to be delayed owing to his duties in Poland and elsewhere. The D'Abernons wanted to do things differently, and so the event was held at 9.30 in the evening in contrast to the normal custom of holding it during the afternoon, and, unusually, women were invited in their own right, as guests of Lady D'Abernon.[57] Lady D'Abernon wrote the satisfied comment on the invitation to the event: 'This break away from the traditional receptions held by new Ambassadors was a success.'[58] The chiefs of the Inter-Allied Commissions of Control attended, as well as the entire diplomatic corps and the German Foreign Office, bringing the total number of guests to around three hundred, easily accommodated in the Embassy's capacious reception rooms. It was the first major official party in the building since the first half of 1914, and Lady D'Abernon evidently took pains in her preparations to ensure that, despite the events of the last six years, the Embassy should look its best.

It was also the first reception in the British Embassy to be held in the new German Republic. While the glamour of the imperial pre-Great War years could not be recreated in terms of the guests – Lady D'Abernon drily noting that amongst them, 'beauty was not conspicuous'[59] – they did at least wear colourful uniforms and ribbons. The ballroom was decorated in white and yellow, and Lady D'Abernon arranged flowers throughout the reception rooms. Adding to the colour were the 'buff and scarlet liveries' worn by the embassy servants and, in the dining room, piled high on the sideboards was the embassy gold plate salvaged from the cellars.[60] '[T]wo of the old German retainers, Fritz and Elf,* enjoying the recovery of their cocked hats and egregiously long, gold-laced coats', stood to attention, their main duty seemingly consisting of 'holding, with outstretched arms, long gilt staves surmounted (in this Embassy) by the British Royal Arms. Then, but only when special *Wichtige*† guests arrive, they strike their staves three times on the ground .... All of this was carried out exactly as it used to be before 1914.'[61] Lady D'Abernon 'wished the Embassy to appear no less luxurious and dignified than it had been in the years before the war, because the first time people visit a place they notice what it looks like. The German officials must have thought that England remained – at least to all appearances – solid and unchanged.'[62]

Lady D'Abernon was an experienced and consummate hostess and wanted to ensure that her husband's 'coming out' into Berlin diplomatic life went off as well as it possibly could. She was not the first and certainly not the last diplomat or diplomatic spouse to realise that one of an embassy's many roles is to act as a stage upon which a country can subtly influence and impress visitors by its overall appearance, well-chosen display and entertainment. Now, rather than acting as a stage for the reception of the German imperial family and a demonstration of close British–German monarchical ties as had been the case before August 1914, the Embassy was be used to represent Great Britain in the new German Republic. It had entered a new and challenging era.

---

* It seems unlikely that these were the same German employees who had stamped and spat on their liveries on 5 August 1914 (see Chapter 8).
† Important.

CHAPTER 10
1920–1926: 'DIPLOMACY ASSISTED BY ART'

'Superb and vital [D'Abernon] would stride up and down his study in the Embassy, pumping hope, energy and ideas into the defeatist ministers of the Weimar Republic. It was in that study, with its three gaunt windows gaping upon the Wilhelmstrasse, with its ugly panelling and its grim leather chairs, that was born, not Locarno only, but also the rentenmark,' wrote Harold Nicolson in 1939.[1] He was under no illusions about who was responsible for enabling Germany to take control of its finances and overcome the continuing major threats to its authority and stability in the early 1920s. D'Abernon did indeed manage to overcome the initial distrust that so much of the British Establishment had felt towards his appointment, as the Embassy's commodious and grand entertaining spaces were used to stage events both large and small and became a convenient meeting place for the major players in politics and economics at this pivotal moment in Germany's history.

In the early 1920s the issue of the level of reparations that Germany should pay to the victors of the Great War dominated European diplomacy. Meanwhile an unprecedented economic crisis began to spiral out of control as the Weimar Government resorted to printing money to pay its debts. By 1923 trillions of marks were needed to purchase even everyday items, ruining livelihoods and naturally affecting the everyday lives of members of the Embassy's staff. Lord D'Abernon sent regular updates to the Foreign Office in London explaining the continued rise in the cost of living and the resultant problems, regularly requesting increases in his staff wages and allowances, to the predictable reluctance of the Foreign Office and Treasury. Somewhat to the surprise of these departments whose staff felt, not unreasonably, that D'Abernon's appointment had after all been foisted on them precisely because of his hailed economic expertise, in the early months of his ambassadorship D'Abernon also attempted to increase the number of embassy staff to cope with a growing amount of work and took on an additional property.

D'Abernon asked Foreign Secretary Lord Curzon's agreement to the engagement of Fritz Stenzel[*] as a Chancery servant. 'Chancery servants' were engaged to undertake much of the routine 'back office' work in the Embassy, including purchasing rail tickets and reserving seats and sleeping compartments for the regular accompanied courier or diplomatic bag service of documents between London and Berlin. Like many of the Embassy's domestic staff, they were 'locally engaged'; that is, they were German, not British, and hence their local knowledge and contacts were invaluable. There are, and remain to this day, two further advantages in employing locally engaged staff. One is an invaluable

---

[*] 'Stengel' in D'Abernon's letters and minutes.

stock of continuity of knowledge, as, not subject to being moved around different posts they tend to stay in their jobs for many years. The second reason is more cynical: providing their own accommodation and not entitled to the same foreign allowances as British-based colleagues, they are cheaper to employ.

In early 1922 Foreign Secretary Lord Curzon sent a circular to all heads of mission pinpointing the perennial disadvantage in employing locally engaged staff: security concerns, issues that were to become increasingly pressing in the following two decades:

> While it is many cases no doubt convenient and economical to employ native servants, it is a matter of great importance that they should not have any opportunity of obtaining confidential information or have access to confidential documents of any kind. There is, for instance, danger in foreign Chancery Servants being entrusted with confidential despatch bags which it is necessary to fetch from or send to any point outside the Legation, or being allowed to open or close such bags. At Posts at which no British Chancery Servant is employed, these duties should always be discharged by some member of the staff who is of British nationality ....[2]

Stenzel had first started work in the Embassy for the British Military Mission in 1918 or 1919, and was evidently efficient and trustworthy. Over the following months D'Abernon was to argue for Stenzel, the ever-loyal Schönemann and another locally engaged member of staff, Schneider, to be paid in incremental amounts to keep up with the increasing cost of living. D'Abernon argued that all three men were able to speak some English, thus possibly making the employment of a British-based Chancery servant 'an unnecessary luxury.'[3] In April 1922 he reported that the cost of living had risen so rapidly in Germany that it was now more than four times what it had been in 1921. After paying his daily tram fares to and from the Embassy and for rent, heating and lighting, Stenzel for example now had only 1,150 marks per month left over to pay for food and clothing for himself, his wife and child: 'Their diet consists almost entirely of bread and margarine and potatoes, with a little milk for the child', the Ambassador reported to the Foreign Secretary. The purchase of new uniforms was out of the question, 'yet the Chancery Servants at His Majesty's Embassy obviously cannot appear in rags when receiving callers.'[4] Although Schneider was a younger man and single, he had to support his widowed mother. 'This position is obviously not without danger to honesty and reliability', and D'Abernon reported that corresponding wages in other foreign missions in Berlin were higher than those paid at the British Embassy. For all these reasons, D'Abernon proposed increasing Schönemann's wages to 7,000 marks per month; Stenzel's to 4,500 and Schneider's to 3,500; figures which the Foreign Office in London adjusted downwards to 6,000, 3,500 and 3,000 respectively.[5]

On his way to England following a visit to Berlin in December 1923 Sir Lionel Earle, Office of Works Permanent Secretary, came across Schönemann as he was leaving the Embassy building. The servant accompanied Earle to the station to help him with his luggage, and on the way told Earle that, having lost all of his savings through the devaluation of the currency, he was now ruined. Aware of the man's loyalty to the Embassy during the war, Earle gave him 'all the notes I had, not of great value, I fear, amounting to hundreds of millions of marks, and he knelt down on the platform with tears in his eyes and kissed my hand.'[6]

***

As far back as 1904 Lascelles had pressed for an improvement in the amount of Chancery accommodation in the Embassy for the commercial, naval and military attachés as well as for the Chancery servants, asking for offices to be extended into unused stables in the cellars.[7] Despite London's perennial concern for economy, such was the growth in number of the embassy staff in the early 1920s that in 1921 the British Government purchased a house at 17 Tiergartenstrasse, an attractive leafy road running along the south-eastern fringe of the Tiergarten about a kilometre and a half from the Embassy. With its stock of spacious villas and relative proximity to the government district, this fashionable and upmarket residential area was during this period becoming a major diplomatic quarter of Berlin. Indeed, since the 1880s the expanding area had been under discussion as a suitable one in which the British might either build a new embassy or move into an existing building. The villa housed the British Consulate-General (which dealt with local issues and the general interests of British subjects and businesses in Germany), the Commercial Secretariat, the military attachés,* and the British Passport Office.

Although perfectly legitimate, the job of Passport Control Officer served as cover for the British Secret Service operating in the German capital. By the mid-1920s the Officer was Frank Foley, also head of Military Intelligence based in Berlin. After the Soviets set up an embassy in the German capital, the British Government started funding the establishment of a German 'station' for the Secret Intelligence Service as a counter to Bolshevist activities in the city. The first British Secret Service agent in Berlin had been Henry Landau, who had operated successfully in the Low Countries obtaining enemy information during the Great War. Arriving in Berlin in October 1919, he too had used the office of Passport Control Officer as cover, but left the service in 1920 after getting into financial difficulties, eventually being replaced by Frank Foley.[8] Foley was to liaise with a number of British and foreign double agents working against the Russians (and later the Nazis), but his long Berlin posting – he was to remain there until the eve of the Second World War – was visited by tragedy: his young daughter Ursula fell down the steps of the Embassy building, an injury that triggered chronic epilepsy; he and his wife decided to have no further children.[9†]

As well as offices, the building also housed three flats for embassy staff, including Major Timothy Breen, also of the Passport Control Office, whose role doubled up as Embassy Press Officer. Breen's had been a far-sighted appointment by D'Abernon – at least seen in retrospect. The Foreign Office had established a News Department during the Great War and, writing in 1939,[10] Harold Nicolson described how important it was for specialist press officers to work at the same

---

* Although it seems that the military attachés may not actually have moved there at this time, for by 1926–27 they were housed in an additional office on Pariser Platz (see Chapter 12).
† It is unclear whether she fell down the staircase inside the Embassy, or the steps outside the building. As there was no downstairs guest toilet at 70 Wilhelmstrasse (see Chapter 16), the incident may have taken place in the staircase hall.

post for a number of years in order to gain a deep knowledge of the host country's politics, personalities and general issues in more informal ways than would be possible for an itinerant ambassador. According to Nicolson, the functions of a press attaché were to 'read, digest, and translate articles in the local journals. He interviews British and other Press correspondents and tries to secure that the views of his government obtain adequate publicity. And he is to establish contacts with local journalists who provide valuable information.'[11] Awarded the Military Cross, Breen had been a prisoner of war in the Great War, and worked at the British Military Mission at the Embassy in Berlin from 1919 to 1921.[12] He was held in great esteem by D'Abernon, who 'considered him to be man of rare ability. He found his insight into men and affairs in Germany prophetic and unerring.'[13] He was to remain in post until 1937.

By this period, some of the British-based embassy and consular posts were taken by women, at first performing the tasks of shorthand and typing, but later, for example, filling consular positions in the Passport Office. At the time these posts were 'unestablished'; that is with no attached pension, and could be terminated at one month's notice, with an annual allowance of twenty-one days' leave (including public holidays) on full pay. Berlin was evidently not an easy posting for anyone during this period: as well as continued challenges in coping with the fast rising cost of living the embassy and consular staff faced problems finding suitable and inexpensive accommodation in a city where many inhabitants remained hostile to the victors of the Great War. In 1921 it was reported to London that the embassy typists 'could not be expected to put up with impossible conditions among undesirable Germans ... decent pensions being very difficult to find and many not being prepared to take English people'. The Embassy and Foreign Office enumerated the various problems the staff had to face in Berlin in 1925: 'a bath costs at least one shilling and sixpence and an extra charge is made if more than two baths are demanded in one week; laundry charges are heavy; fresh fruit is almost prohibitive, an orange costing sixpence and a banana fourpence .... It is considered that twenty-five shillings a week is insufficient for [the reasonable amenities of life] and to meet the cost of clothing, leave, medical, dental and other incidental expenses.' Indeed, two shorthand writers had recently had to leave post owing to financial difficulties. The Foreign Office pressed for, and achieved, an increase of 40 per cent on their current £250 per annum.[14]

As the cost of living continued to rise, the secretaries' wages were increased yet again in the late summer of 1925. The shorthand typists lived in furnished bed-and-breakfast accommodation and detailed their weekly expenditure to the Foreign Office in London, expenditure which included one 'show' or entertainment per week: 'one finds that one must spend more on entertainments and incidental expenses here than one would if living at home or in England: otherwise life in Berlin would be very miserable indeed,' wrote embassy typist May Wilson.[15]

***

Echoing Emperor Wilhelm II's concerns about the status of his capital city, Lady D'Abernon was not, in general, impressed by Berlin. For her it lacked

the charm and romance of cities that have matured slowly with succeeding centuries. There are no narrow streets, no changes of level, no crooked passages, no unexpected courts and corners .... Architecture is devoid of any marked tendency or character .... The squares, unlike those in London, are not enclosed and are usually destitute of trees. The majority of public buildings are not very large and lack distinction.

But she did like the nearby Tiergarten: 'It has straight avenues alternating with meandering green glades and is larger and more countrified than Hyde Park, and therefore pleasanter and more varied for riding.'[16] Her dim view of the capital was worsened by the increasing privations the city underwent during the very difficult economic circumstances that coincided with the early years of D'Abernon's ambassadorship. On 6 November 1920 she recorded in her diary that to celebrate the anniversary of the Russian Revolution there had been a strike in Berlin that included electrical workers: 'Every street in Berlin is plunged in Cimmerian darkness.'[17] When the level of Germany's war reparations were finally agreed in Paris the following January, Lady D'Abernon noticed a distinct worsening of atmosphere and growing German resentment of the demands that were to be put on the country. 'Socially things are more unpleasant than at any time since we came. We had laid the foundation of normal human relations, but the flood of bad feeling stirred by the decision of the Supreme Council has swept all these bridges away.'[18] Two large dinners and a dance had to be made up exclusively of diplomatic guests rather than German ones as she decided it was 'inexpedient' to invite Germans at that point and make things even worse by giving them an opportunity pointedly to decline the invitation.[19] A reception held shortly afterwards that she attended she found 'glacial', leaving her afterwards feeling 'estranged, discouraged, resentful and filled with an increasing distaste for my social duties here.'[20] It was all beginning to get her down and, following an unexpected eighteen guests for tea one evening, she confessed that 'I find this life of endless representation complicated by packing and travelling, and a complete dearth of leisure not merely antipathetic but terribly exhausting.'[21] She was neither the first nor the last diplomatic wife to feel that way, but nevertheless made use of the Embassy's capacious rooms to full effect during her time in Berlin. At the King's birthday celebration on 4 June 1921, the embassy gold plate was again put on show in the dining room, filled with perfumed red roses, 'and in the white and yellow ballroom every available space was garlanded with pink "American Pillar"'. The dinner was followed by a 'lively little dance.'[22] Writing thirty years later about diplomatic entertaining in general, William Strang explained that 'Almost all diplomats, British and foreign, deplore the tyranny of the cocktail party as a diplomatic institution, yet almost all of them feel obliged to give and to attend such parties'. Such events had a practical purpose: rehearsing Lord Beaconsfield's views during the 1878 Congress of Berlin, Strang explained that parties could act as 'a clearing-house or exchange and mart for political rumours ... and the means of dealing quickly and informally with a lot of minor business for which the day would otherwise be too short',[23] and (despite occasional exhortations* for long-distance, digital technology to replace personal contact in diplomatic activity) this remains the case to this day.

* For example, 'Diplomats need dragging into the modern era', Roger Boyes, *The Times*, 1 June 2016.

39. Lady D'Abernon seated in the Embassy's ballroom amongst the state portraits of Monarchs.

'Darling Helen, you were so wonderfully dear and kind to me, and it was an absolutely perfect time. How happy and comfortable you made me and how very dear your welcome,' wrote Grace, Marchioness Curzon, the Foreign Secretary's American-born second wife to Lady D'Abernon after attending several such parties while staying in the 'perfect' Embassy in late 1921.[24] During her stay she inconveniently went down with a bad cold and was confined to bed, 'in all this magnificent luxury and wonderful comfort.'[25] Despite the doubts and challenges Lady D'Abernon was experiencing in Berlin, Lady Curzon evidently thought that she made 'the most perfect Ambassadress … They seem to entertain a great deal … Everything is quite beautifully done. Helen says she likes the Germans to feel that <u>we have won the war</u>!'[26] Quite how openly Lady D'Abernon expressed this rather undiplomatic sentiment to her German guests – given the extreme financial privations the country was experiencing at the time – can only be guessed at. The relatively higher spending power of foreigners in Germany, whose enhanced purchasing ability, buoyed up by favourable currency exchange rates and consequent higher standard of living, understandably provoked some hostility. But from Lady Curzon's point of view, 'All I can say is that [the Embassy] is a thousand times better in every way than the Embassy in Paris, in the Derbys' time or at the present time.'[27]

Before she went down with her cold, Lady Curzon had attended an embassy dinner party, her fellow guests including the French, Spanish and Belgian Ambassadors and Lord Kilmarnock and his handsome eldest son, the twenty-year-old Josslyn Hay, who had recently passed the Foreign Office examinations. His first official posting was to Berlin in January 1920 as an attaché with his father, and after Kilmarnock moved to the Rhineland to become High Commissioner he remained in Berlin as the Ambassador's private secretary. Hay became close to the D'Abernons but, despite showing much promise as a diplomat, was to resign in March 1922, nine months before the official end of his posting.[*] The many other embassy guests during this period included a successful Berlin wine and spirit merchant named Joachim Ribbentrop[†] and his wife, who engineered invitations to embassy functions through the clever use of personal contacts.[28] His business supplied many German and foreign diplomats in Berlin with wines and spirits, including D'Abernon and his successors.[‡]

***

Frustrated that Germany was not honouring her Treaty of Versailles and reparation obligations (on which they had defaulted) in January 1923 French troops marched in and occupied the industrial Ruhr area of Germany. This was followed by mass

[*] Much to the horror of his parents, in September the following year he became the third husband of Lady Idina Gordon, eight years his senior, and in 1924 moved with her to Kenya. On the death of Lord Kilmarnock in 1928, Hay became the 22nd Earl of Erroll and 5th Baron Kilmarnock. In early 1941 he was found murdered in his car outside Nairobi. The most likely suspect, Sir Jock Delves Broughton, with whose wife Hay had been having an affair, was acquitted; the identity of the murderer and the possible 'real' reason for it has become the subject of considerable speculation and conspiracy theorising.
[†] Ribbentrop later adopted the German 'nobiliary particle' *von* in 1925 after being 'adopted' by Gertrud von Ribbentrop. He had acquired the wine and spirit business partly through his marriage to Annalies Henkell in 1920; her family company were the principal producers of the German sparkling wine *Sekt*.
[‡] See Chapter 12.

demonstrations and protests in Berlin, the population fearing that coal shortages would inevitably follow. Many became convinced that France was determined to 'divide and rule' its old enemy's territory by encouraging separatist movements to break Germany up; yet more food shortages followed and inflation again worsened as the German Government continued to pay the wages of those employees in the Ruhr who, in protest against the French occupation, refused to work. Anti-French sentiment reached frenzied proportions and badly affected diplomatic gatherings. Although a 'triumphant' fancy-dress ball had been held in the Embassy on 1 February 1922,[29] the D'Abernons felt that it would be sadly impolitic to attempt to repeat the event the following year owing to so much ill-feeling in Berlin towards Germany's historic enemy.

During his brief parliamentary career Lord D'Abernon had struck up a close friendship with the Liberal Prime Minister Herbert Asquith, and, in particular, with two of his children, Raymond (who was killed in the Great War) and Violet (Bonham-Carter), whom he invited to Berlin in early March 1923. Setting out from Liverpool Street Station, at the German frontier Violet encountered the Weimar Republic's trademark rampant inflation for the first time: exchanging the sum of two pounds, she received 200,000 marks, 'great bundles of paperchase money which I cld [sic] hardly carry.'[30] She and her maid Rose arrived in Berlin at 10.30 p.m. on 2 March. Reaching the Embassy, Violet recorded in her memoirs an experience that still holds true today: the reassuring feeling of arriving as a residential guest at a British diplomatic residence in a foreign city after a long and tiring journey.

> It was divine to arrive dirty & exhausted at the cleanliness and comfort of the Embassy …. Dear Tyler* opened the door & I was told Helen had gone to bed after the ball last night but that Edgar was up and alone. It was the greatest fun finding him in a big delightful room. He & Helen have managed to miraculously introduce into this house some of the charm and beauty of Esher† … I had dinner & then, after a short & amusing talk with Edgar, bed ….[31]

Violet was amongst the eighty or ninety guests, including representatives from 'social, professional, literary and official circles',[32] at Lady D'Abernon's last Saturday evening 'jour' of the 1922–23 'season', which continued the imperial tradition of taking place in the winter months. It was another personal experience for her of the 'sharp end' of Weimar politics and economics: Lady D'Abernon had invited no French guests, for she had witnessed that at other diplomatic events Germans tended to take their leave the moment any French arrived, with the atmosphere quickly descending into mutual loathing. In gushing 1920s style, after her stay in Berlin, Violet wrote to Lady D'Abernon thanking her for her 'thrilling' visit, like many others heaping praise upon her hostess's diplomatic skills in what were, as she herself had witnessed, trying circumstances. 'I can't tell you what admiration I felt for your masterly performance on that most difficult stage. But you must have heard it all a thousand times already.'[33]

---

* The embassy house-steward of the time; his daughter Marjorie worked as a typist in the Embassy (*Red Cross and Berlin Embassy…*. p. 116).
† Esher Place, Surrey, the D'Abernons' British home.

The Ambassadress spent much of the following few months away from Berlin, returning in mid-October 1923, the economic situation worsening still further. The diplomatic corps in Berlin was giving less ostentatious entertainments, while 'over everything and everyone there hangs a dull fog of uncertainty and apprehension.'[34] Sleeping that winter in a bedroom overlooking the Wilhelmstrasse, Lady D'Abernon noticed that even the street outside was quieter than normal – it used to be 'insufferably noisy' due to the traffic, but it was now, with an absence of motor cars, 'quite silent and still.'[35] But all the same on 2 November she was awakened by a small military band passing outside, 'the first time since we came in 1920 that any military music has been heard in Berlin.'[36]

***

'The extent to which the Auswärtiges Amt[‡] turn to D'Abernon in all their difficulties'[37] (as Lady D'Abernon put it) was demonstrated the following week at 2.00 a.m. on Saturday 10 November when the ambassadorial couple were woken by an urgent knocking at the Embassy's door. Taking advantage of German resentment over the French occupation of the Ruhr, a violent, anti-government national revolution had been declared in Munich which, it was feared, would spread to the rest of the country, and D'Abernon's help and advice was needed. 'The chief agitator and organizer, a man of low origin' (as Lady D'Abernon described him[38]) was Adolf Hitler. In a demonstration of force, German government troops were directed to march in Berlin, but the revolt was quickly extinguished – permanently, the Ambassador believed. The threat to the Weimar Republic had been serious, a real danger of separatism and of right-wing forces from Bavaria marching on Berlin in an attempt to take political control. Hitler and his co-conspirators were arrested and tried for treason, Hitler sentenced to a derisorily short prison term, a period of time which was however sufficient to give him the opportunity to plan for the future and write *Mein Kampf*.

The economic and political situation worsened, and a few days after the attempted Hitler putsch D'Abernon had to begin considering whether to send his female staff back to the UK for safety. Communist agitators erected barricades in the Lustgarten[§] in front of the former Imperial Schloss and surrounding streets. In response, endeavouring to prevent another pitched battle in the government district of the sort that Berlin had witnessed in 1918, 1919 and 1920, on 27 November the police cordoned off Wilhelmstrasse. That evening the D'Abernons went ahead as planned and held an embassy dinner. The Dutch Ambassador, one of the guests, was apparently oblivious to the deteriorating situation in the capital. Lady D'Abernon ascribed this to the fact that the British Embassy was close to the government offices, unlike the Dutch counterpart which was located in the suburbs. Its central geographical location might present its own set of practical problems, as she well knew, but at least it meant, as a result, that the British knew what was going on in the city: 'It should never be moved or exchanged for a countrified suburban residence.'[39]

‡ The German Foreign Office.
§ 'Pleasure Garden', located in front of the Altesmuseum, an area that once formed part of the Royal Schloss and later served as a military drill ground.

An enormous 'French and Entente' dinner was held on 10 December 1923, which, given the toxic political situation, inevitably involved 'excluding all but official Germans'. But as a sign that the mood was beginning to change, on 12 January the D'Abernons secured a diplomatic coup when the German President and Mrs Ebert came to dinner and music, staying until late. 'Berlin regards this as a great event because it is the first time they have dined in an alien Embassy or indeed any Embassy at all,' Lady D'Abernon recorded, in an echo of the first visit the Emperor and Empress had made to the British Embassy fifty years before. The event passed off well, supplemented with 'large tumblers of Lager beer'[40] and was reported in the British press as 'one of the most brilliant of the season.'[41] Indeed, by the end of 1923 D'Abernon had been able to breathe a little easier and to record with some satisfaction that Germany had successfully walked a tightrope and come through the following dangers in the previous twelve months: 'The Ruhr Invasion; The Communist Rising in Saxony and Thuringia; The Hitler *Putsch* in Bavaria; An unprecedented financial crisis; The Separatist Movement in the Rhineland.'[42] By then he had been Ambassador in Berlin for a year longer than an originally intended 'temporary' period of two years, but there was no appetite in London to move him on and replace him, particularly on the part of the recently elected Government of Ramsay MacDonald, which relied heavily on the experience of diplomats already in post.[43]

The United States had reopened full diplomatic relations with Germany in 1922, and over the course of 1923 and 1924 the country gradually returned to a firmer economic and political footing. The American Dawes Plan provided economic assistance to Germany and other European governments and the French withdrew from the Ruhr. In 1923 Chancellor Gustav Stresemann's appointment of Dr Hjalmar Schacht as President of the Reichsbank helped bring more stability to the currency, as did the introduction of the new, more dependable, Rentenmark on 15 November. D'Abernon became heavily involved in negotiations for an Anglo-German Commercial Agreement, the discussions for which took place not only at the Chancellor of the Exchequer's residence at 11 Downing Street in London, but also at the British Embassy in Berlin.

***

In early March 1925 D'Abernon invited the internationally acclaimed Welsh-born artist Augustus John to stay at the Embassy. John took advantage of his 'artist in residence' status to see as much of Berlin as he could, facilitated by the fact that the Ambassador gave him a key to a side door to the 'tradesman's entrance' to the right of the house so that he could come and go as he pleased.[44] On one night's foray into Weimar Berlin's nightlife John entered a door marked 'bodega', innocently assuming the establishment to be a kind of wine bar. Flattered by the unexpected attentions of a number of young women, he suddenly noticed that his watch had been stolen. 'Thereupon I rose and in my sparse German, referred to the "Englische Bodschaft" [*sic*] and the "Polizei"! General consternation!' However, the young woman who had taken the watch was intercepted and everything calmed down. John recounted how, despite these excitements, he returned to the Embassy 'pleased with [his] evening.'[45]

While in Berlin the artist began several portraits, including one of Gustav Stresemann. D'Abernon had first met the German Foreign Minister at the Embassy in 1921, and they had struck up a particular friendship, D'Abernon priding himself on enjoying his special confidence. Augustus John had asked if he might portray him, and the Ambassador had made the necessary arrangements. D'Abernon had the sudden thought that he could use the portrait sittings to discuss various important matters, the problem normally being that he found it difficult to get a word in edgeways when conversing with Stresemann:

> Augustus John knew no German, so the conversations could be carried on between Stresemann and myself as if we were alone …. Things fell out according to plan. After a sentence or two on the subject of international conciliation, Stresemann naturally wished to interject considerations of his own, considerations which, developed without restraint, would have been neither consenting nor concise. But Augustus John protested and imposed artistic authority; I was therefore able to labour on with my own views without interruption. Being by nature a poor expositor, and having only a limited command of technical German phrases, the assistance given by the inhibitive gag of the artist was of extreme value. Without Augustus John, armed with his palette and his paint-brushes, the chances of profitable interchange of thought would have been considerably diminished.[46]

As for the portrait itself, D'Abernon described it as 'a clever piece of work – not at all flattering; it makes Stresemann devilish sly – but extremely intelligent. The sitter is indeed most intelligent, but not sly.'[47] Augustus John felt that his portrait 'was not in the least flattering but Stresemann faced it bravely: his wife was taken aback, I could see.'[48]

D'Abernon had been involved in producing a note proposing a security agreement between Britain, France and Germany, and found that much further progress towards European security had been made during the one-sided discussions at the portrait sittings. For example, according to him he had managed to persuade Stresemann to persevere with discussions concerning a pact of reciprocal guarantee. Stresemann was able to take on board D'Abernon's suggestion of the possibility of an 'iron curtain', a neutralised zone between France and Germany.[49] These discussions were to culminate in the Treaty of Locarno in October, in which

40. 'Gustav Stresemann: The Moving Spirit for Germany at Locarno': Augustus John's portrait of the German statesman was reproduced on the cover of *The Illustrated London News* of 12 December 1925.

France, Germany and Belgium signed an agreement confirming the German frontier with France and Belgium and arranged for the demilitarisation of the Rhineland (formerly established under the terms of the Treaty of Versailles).* The settlement was guaranteed by Great Britain and Italy. British Foreign Secretary Austen Chamberlain, American Vice-President Charles Dawes, French Foreign Minister Aristide Briand and Stresemann all received the Nobel Peace Prize for the Treaty. The month it was signed at the Foreign Office in London D'Abernon welcomed Prime Minister Ramsay MacDonald to the Embassy with a formal luncheon and dinner. MacDonald's various official engagements included meetings with Stresemann and Chancellor Dr Luther[50] but he also found time to enjoy a round of golf with the Ambassador, as revealed in a newsreel of the time.[51] D'Abernon congratulated himself that the discussions he had enjoyed with Stresemann during the portrait sittings might be described as 'Diplomacy assisted by Art,'[52] and John's portrait of 'The Moving Spirit for Germany at Locarno' was reproduced on the cover of *The Illustrated London News* for 12 December 1925.

Meanwhile, as the sybaritic delights of the 'roaring twenties' began to take hold in Berlin as the economic situation continued to improve, Count Henry Kessler, a regular embassy guest, recounted that a social whirl that was beginning to echo the busy social 'season' in the imperial Germany of the not-so-distant past:

> You have no conception of the social whirlpool into which I have been drawn; and I confess to being rather overwhelmed by it. Hardly a day without a lunch, a reception, a dinner and one or two balls, or routs. I never get to bed before 3 or 4 in the morning and am simply dried up …. Never has there been such a season here, everybody is dead beat.[53]

***

In recognition of his achievements in Berlin D'Abernon was made a Viscount in the 1926 New Year's Honours. 'I never forgot that it was through you that I first became connected with the Berlin Embassy and that the early years were under your auspices and guidance,' D'Abernon told the former Prime Minister Lloyd George,[54] as the congratulations flooded in. Despite his having been 'parachuted' into the role of Ambassador over the heads of so many experienced diplomats (and consequently the focus of much distrust and resentment), in 1925 and 1926 many of D'Abernon's embassy and consular staff wrote to him praising his ambassadorship. A letter from Ralph Stevenson was typical:

> In 1921 when I joined your staff the realisation of your projects seemed so far away as to be almost mythical – and yet in four short years you have succeeded. I find it difficult to set down all I think without being fulsome… all I can say is that I am proud to have served under you.[55]

He also missed playing golf with his former Chief.

In July 1926 D'Abernon's successor – Sir Ronald Lindsay – was announced, slated to start work in Berlin when D'Abernon departed, probably that autumn, by which time it was expected that Germany would have entered the League of Nations.[56] In September 1926 that historic event duly occurred, the highlight of

---

* French forces left German territory in the Rhineland in 1930.

41. Augustus John's portrait of Lord D'Abernon, painted at the Embassy in 1925, shows the Ambassador's reportedly somewhat dishevelled appearance.

D'Abernon's ambassadorship, in his opinion creating a new foundation upon which strong and secure relations between Germany and the Allied countries could continue to be negotiated.[57] Amid flurries of official leave-taking events and orgies of praise and backslapping, D'Abernon and his wife made preparations to leave the Embassy that had been their official home for six years. On 6 October they gave a dinner to the President himself, Paul von Hindenburg, at which, amongst the guests, were the Stresemanns, and Herbert's son Prince von Bismarck. On 7 October a farewell reception took place for the diplomatic corps, members of the Embassy and members of the British community in Berlin.

There was a very busy programme on Friday 8 October. George Lyall, the British Consul, gave a speech for the departing couple in which he thanked D'Abernon for his solicitude for the interests of the British community in Berlin and other areas of Germany. D'Abernon in turn thanked the British community for their efforts in rebuilding relations between the two countries.[58] The embassy and consular staff clubbed together to present an inkstand to the departing couple. Later on 8 October the Ambassador took part in the formal ceremony of presenting his letters of recall to Hindenburg, who gave him fulsome thanks:

> … The close of your mission coincides with that of an important epoch in post-war European history. With the coming into force of the Locarno treaties and with Germany's entry into the League of Nations, the policy of permanent European peace has made an important step forward. In this evolution, you have taken a paramount share which will not be forgotten.[59]

Unusually, the German President also paid tribute to Lady D'Abernon for her contribution to her husband's diplomatic work. The official German thanks for D'Abernon's efforts in getting Germany back on track took a more concrete form than eulogistic speeches in the shape of a gift of a large silver *épergne* dating from 1750[60] and four silver candlesticks, all from the State Museum in Dresden, gifts of such great financial value that D'Abernon had to obtain British government consent before he could accept them.[61] This was followed by a lunch at the German Foreign Ministry and a gala dinner given by Hindenburg in the evening. On Saturday, 9 October it was Stresemann's turn to fête the couple at another gala dinner.[62] By now quite possibly exhausted, the couple finally left Berlin on 10 October 1926.[63]

As the economic situation had improved, so had the national mood, and as they drove through the streets to Friedrichstrasse Station and the train for England they received a 'wonderful ovation both from unknown people and from hundreds of acquaintances and friends. During the last weeks of our embassy we were surprised and touched by many and various manifestations of esteem and goodwill for which previous contacts had not altogether prepared us. These were not confined to the circle of Official and society people but came from all sorts and conditions of men – indeed many came from complete strangers.' Lady D'Abernon confessed in her memoirs that this warmth of a farewell contrasted with the sometimes harsh view she had taken of the German people during her time in Berlin.[64] The state reception room at the station were opened for the couple's formal leave-taking, attended by Stresemann as Foreign Minister and the diplomatic corps, together with the British Embassy staff, the Consul, the Chaplain and many other members of the British community in the city. 'Masses' of flowers had been arranged in 'the special saloon attached to the train'. Taking his leave of Stresemann for the last time, the D'Abernons said their goodbyes to the British Embassy staff and, leaning out of their carriage window as the engine puffed and the train slowly moved off, 'waved a last farewell.'[65] The D'Abernons' triumphant departure from Berlin was featured in the British press. In sharp contrast to its criticism of D'Abernon's appointment in 1920, *The Times* now opined that the demonstrations of 'public and private regret' in Berlin over his departure 'has been an eloquent tribute to the general appreciation of the success which has attended Lord D'Abernon's work in the service of European peace, and the part played by the British Embassy, both politically and as a social meeting-ground, in the cause of improved understanding between Great Britain and Germany.'[66] Writing of Lady D'Abernon, *The Illustrated London News* remarked that

> Full marks are always given by public opinion to the wives of our Ambassadors and our Governors overseas when they have helped their husbands in difficult and subtle tasks. Lady D'Abernon has by common consent been awarded in addition a sort of gold medal of public praise for the tact, charm and good sense with which she handled social problems of quite unusual difficulty .... The personal success of the British Ambassador and Ambassadress in Berlin is once more proof of the fact that every great constructive human scheme depends for its success or failure on the individual.[67]

Equally obsequiously, another commentator pronounced that Lady D'Abernon 'conducted the social side of the Embassy life with a skill which won respect and affection on all sides. Many stories are told of the matchless tact and unassuming grace with which she smoothed the path of ladies of the diplomatic circle less born to their position than herself.'[68]

Writing in 1947, Cynthia Gladwyn remembered the D'Abernons in Berlin when she visited in the winter of 1925, painting a striking picture of Lady D'Abernon 'beautiful, but remote and rather frightening', with an elegant and memorable dress sense: 'Queen Alexandra had just died, and I remember thinking her mourning dress was a work of art in itself – she disliked pure black, and at one evening party wore a black tulle dress relieved by a scarf of pale grey tulle, and she had one black pearl ear-ring and one grey one …'[69]

On his retirement from Berlin, D'Abernon became more deeply involved in the art world, having become a Trustee of the National Gallery in 1907 and later of the Tate. Spending an increasing amount of his time at the couple's rented apartments in *palazzi* in Rome, he died in 1941. Lady D'Abernon survived him by another thirteen years, dying in May 1954 at the age of eighty-eight. Not long before, she had given the British Government nine Italian Old Master paintings from the D'Abernons' collection in Rome for display in the British Embassy there,[70] where they remain to this day.

CHAPTER 11
INTERLUDE: 'THE PERFECTION OF ENGLISH TASTE'

'On quitting Prince Bismarck I walked down the street some two hundred yards, past the Foreign Office, past the Ministry of the Interior, and arrived at my own residence, the British Embassy, a handsome building, with Greek columns on the façade. It is a good house, with many points to recommend it … The size of the rooms … is their redeeming point. They have no pretension to good taste,' Sir Edward Malet remembered.[1] It is worth pausing to consider the interior appearance of the building in which this story has so far taken place.

Furnishings

The British Government found no reason for its taxpayers to purchase furniture for buildings the Government did not own, so, at least initially, a convenient solution was for an incoming ambassador to purchase the Embassy's furniture from his predecessor, Odo Russell spending an equivalent of £6,050.8s.6d. in this manner for the apartment he rented from Count Arnim.[2] However, the large and capacious rooms of the former Palais Strousberg posed more of a challenge. In 1878 Russell reported that the furniture from the Leipzigerstrasse property 'was found to be insufficient and had to be increased, completed and renewed', adding up to an additional £4,360.16s., increasing his total expenditure to £10,411.4s.6d.[3] (It is unclear whether any of Strousberg's own furniture was available for purchase).

Following Russell's death, Boyce reported to HM Treasury that his executors were prepared to sell the furniture for the state rooms and Chancery to the British Government for some 65,462 marks (at the time about £3,273), an 'extremely moderate' valuation, in his opinion.[4] Its purchase removed the necessity for Russell's successors to furnish the place themselves – at least for the next few years. The fixtures included three large gas burner lights (two in the ballroom and one in the library), other gas fittings, kitchen fittings and three fireplaces (two in the principal bedroom and one in the second bedroom). Boyce also advised that there would be additional costs – £1,500 to £2,000 – required to replace items removed by Lady Ampthill upon her departure from Berlin, as well as repairs to some furniture. Indeed, the furniture had evidently seen heavy use since Odo Russell had acquired it for the Embassy, much of it 'considerably worn, and the covers on chairs, sofas etc. require immediate renewal.'[5]

The black-and-white photographs and prints of Victorian interiors naturally cannot give any idea of how colourful they actually were, and Boyce's list of furniture at 70 Wilhelmstrasse[6] conjures up the bright colours of the mid-1880s. The drawing room overlooking Wilhelmstrasse, for example, called the 'Green Room', contained furniture upholstered in pale-green silk with curtains to match, and had four floor-to-ceiling mirrors. The walls of the 'Red Room' next to it were

lined with red silk. In contrast, the
room beyond that (called in a plan of
1876 a 'boudoir') was blue in theme,
with furniture covered in blue satin
damask. Beyond the dining room was
the 'Oriental Room' with a large centre
ottoman covered in yellow silk, red
festoon blinds at the windows, five
mirrors and, to provide a suitable 'exotic'
theme, two wooden blackamoor figures.
The vast ballroom at the rear contained
twelve settees.

42. The 'gorgeous' ballroom recorded in a feature
on the Embassy during Sir Edward's Malet's
ambassadorship in *The Illustrated London News*
of 25 November 1893.

Fine Art, 1870s–1880s

While by this stage furniture was beginning to be the subject of government
intervention in British embassies, the same did not apply as regards fine art in any
of the buildings. In some respects this was surprising. The very important function
of art in government buildings remains to this day one of creating a suitably
dignified and cultured ambience, of enhancing the surroundings and promoting
the image that the United Kingdom wishes to project to foreign visitors. But at this
period little thought seems to have been given to this particular issue, the
assumption remaining that ambassadors would fill the gaps on the walls with their
own possessions. The international image of Britain was at stake however, and it
gradually became clear that this arrangement was not only haphazard, but
worryingly unpredictable in its outcome. There was naturally no central control
over the quality of the art in question, and in any case it would in the normal
course of events be removed on the departure of each ambassador from post.

Most of the art at 70 Wilhelmstrasse in Russell's time would have been
supplied by himself, some of it appearing in an illustration in *The Graphic* of
29 June 1878, accompanying a short account of one of the Russells' receptions
during the Congress of Berlin.[*] This shows at least fifteen pictures densely hung
on the drawing room walls in the typical 'salon' style of the era, including a female
portrait and a seascape above one of the doors. Successive Dukes of Bedford had
collected a wealth of high-quality fine art over many generations for display at
Woburn Abbey and their London homes, and, in view of Odo Russell's problems
with money and the generosity of his elder brother the 9th Duke, it is likely that at
least some of these works were borrowed from that collection.

Fifteen years later, the feature on Sir Edward Malet in *The Illustrated London
News* edition of 25 November 1893 provided detailed illustrations and descriptions
of some of the reception rooms including 'the gorgeous ball-room, which is used as a
banqueting room on State occasions.'[7] The size and height of the ballroom demanded
large full-length portraits, and in the middle of the room was displayed a huge one
of Queen Victoria after Franz Xaver Winterhalter, featuring a view of Buckingham
Palace in the left background. This portrait is also visible in a photograph from the

---

[*] See illustration 11 and endpapers.

43. Sir Edward Malet portrayed in his study in a feature in *The Illustrated London News*, 25 November 1893.

1880s, at that stage hanging the far end of the ballroom. It would have been the only piece of 'official' art supplied at the time, provided by the Lord Chamberlain for the use of the Ambassador in his capacity as the British Monarch's representative to the Prussian Court. State portraits of this type were officially sanctioned copies of paintings (in this case one dating from 1843) on display in royal residences in Great Britain, the size provided to each mission dependent upon its relative importance; the Berlin portrait was naturally a very large example. It was most likely displayed in the Berlin properties previously occupied by the British Embassy before the acquisition of 70 Wilhelmstrasse: on 20 October 1860 Walpurga Hohenthal, one of the Crown Princess's ladies-in-waiting, married British diplomat Augustus Paget in front of (presumably this) portrait of Queen Victoria at what was then the British Legation.[8]

The Illustrated London News reporter described how the portrait of Queen Victoria was flanked 'by one of her Georgian predecessors to the throne' (its identity as yet unknown) on one side, and on the other, a full-length portrait of the King of the Belgians, 'presented to Sir Edward when he left his previous post in Brussels'[9] and which Malet had evidently taken with him to Berlin. At the far end of the room, hanging where the portrait of Queen Victoria had been located in the 1880s, can be seen in the illustration the famous full-length portrait by Sir Joshua Reynolds of Elizabeth Keppel, Marchioness of Tavistock, a painting commissioned in the previous century by the Bedford family and still on display at Woburn Abbey.[10] Its display in Berlin† enabled the Malets to show off some of their illustrious family history to their German guests, the Embassy after all having become 'a kind of appanage of the Bedford family'.[11] Some of Malet's personal collection of art was also on view (and described) in his office. Many heads of mission like to display personal possessions collected over the years and mementoes from their diplomatic careers, and Malet was no exception. His collection included portrait prints of British politicians, including one of the 1844 double-portrait of Sir Robert Peel and the 1st Duke of Wellington by Winterhalter painted for Queen Victoria and one of Charles James Fox after Sir Joshua Reynolds' original. Both of these are visible in the background of a picture of Malet standing in his office, while a general view of the room shows a typically nineteenth-century dense hang of pictures on the wall and displayed on a dado shelf.

† The portrait returned to Woburn Abbey presumably when the Malets left Berlin in 1895. For a number of decades it has been displayed in the Reynolds Room at Woburn Abbey, framed in a much simpler frame, to match other Reynolds portraits in the same room.

44.-46. Sir Edward Malet's study, the cluttered red room and the green drawing room as seen *The Illustrated London News*'s feature of 25 November 1893.

According to this article, other pictures in the room included a series of 'fine Seringipatam battle pieces' and an engraving of the *Signing of the 1796 Treaty of Poonah* by Daniel (taken from the original at the Malet family seat at Wilbury in Wiltshire). This reportedly held particular significance for Malet, as his grandfather Sir Charles Warre Malet had been involved in this treaty, in which all the Maharatta Kingdom was signed over to the 'John Company'. Amongst several prized objects was a miniature in silver of Cleopatra's Needle, which the Prince of Wales had presented to Malet as thanks for accompanying his sons up the Nile when Malet was agent and Consul-General in Egypt, and a saddle presented to Malet by the Khedive of Egypt. Finally, a perennial favourite of diplomats, there were lots of framed photographs. Many of these featured Malet with various heads of state, including one taken with Wilhelm II at Lord Salisbury's family seat at Hatfield House during the Emperor's state visit to Britain in 1891, and a signed portrait of Chancellor Bismarck.

The Embassy's succession of reception rooms were described in the article as 'sumptuous', 'all furnished in the perfection of English taste', with 'perhaps the most luxurious of these being the octagonal one' (in 1884 known as the 'Red Drawing Room' – it was the room with the concealed stage). In an accompanying illustration this room is shown, in typical Victorian style, choked with furniture including upholstered sofas and chairs, a large set of shelves fitted beneath an elaborate plaster relief, and a wide rug on the ornate parquet floor. An image of the main reception room in the house on the right of the entrance hall (the 'green' drawing room) is shown similarly furnished with comfortable upholstered furniture, much of which dated from Russell's time.

Refurbishments

By the time that Sir Lionel Earle was serving as Permanent Secretary of the Office of Works (1912–33), the Office of Works Supplies Division in London was responsible for the procurement and supply of furniture for embassies[12] (ambassadors were however still at liberty to provide their own furniture in areas of the house, if they wished – and this is still the case today*). To this was added the Office of Works' overall responsibility for the provision, care and maintenance of embassy buildings. Over the course of the seven decades 70 Wilhelmstrasse was in use as the British Embassy the Office of Works would have replaced and refurbished the furnishings and redecorated the representational rooms several times over. For example, as we have seen, as Malet had requested in 1885 the front drawing room was subdivided at some stage, and for the financial year 1891–92 he requested reimbursement for some structural repairs, internal repainting, alteration to the floor of the porter's room in the entrance hall, and repairs and cleaning of furniture. This included re-covering various sofas and armchairs, cleaning and beating carpets, and repairing three red silk blinds in the 'Oriental Room'.[13] At some stage, probably in the 1890s, the gas lighting was converted to electricity. Unfortunately, most of the documentary evidence for the changes to the building's interior over the passage of time has disappeared. The precise reason for this is unknown, but it seems likely that after the events of the Second World War the Ministry of Works (as it was by then) regarded at least most of these files as obsolete.

It is clear from the letters Lascelles' sister Lady Edward Cavendish wrote to her niece Florence after she left Berlin on her marriage that the Embassy underwent some refurbishment in 1905–7. Florence's aunt exhibited a not uncommon trait of diplomats and their families in quibbling with the decisions made by distant London-based staff: 'Upstairs is unfinished as the baths will not come, and that since July; as if there were no baths in Berlin …'[14]; 'The bath near my room is finished and it is nice having one, but I should not have chosen the one that has been sent. It is very big, high and we certainly could have chosen a better one here, at less expense I should think.'[15] The refurbishment was complete by early 1907. 'The front drawing room is clothed in all its abundant greens and I hope it does not jar on everyone as it does on me.' The decoration of the red (octagonal) room had been 'very much improved', with pilasters and other plaster decorations: 'why four ugly heads in profile medallions hanging from wreaths are considered pretty decorations I do not know, but as they are all white they are not aggressive. In each recess is a great gold applique with electric light which gives none in the room, but the lighting behind the cornice is pretty and effective…' However, expenditure on refurbishment had evidently not extended to the furniture, which was 'unchanged and looks very shabby'.[16]

No stranger to luxurious interiors, Lord D'Abernon was fulsome in his praise of the Embassy building: '… one of the best houses for reception I have ever seen … the sweep of five salons leading to a large and lofty ball-room at the end of the vista gives an impression of size and dignity.'[17] In 1922 he was photographed sitting in the lofty red room, dwarfed by its size. Taken from the same angle as the photograph on which the engraving in *The Illustrated London News* was based thirty years before, with the passage of time and changing decorative tastes the room was now shown with far less furniture than before. The photograph shows the Edwardian

* Although this tends to be only for the 'private' areas of the house used solely by the head of mission and his/her family, not the representational areas.

47. Lord D'Abernon, seated in a niche in the red room in 1922, seems dwarfed by his surroundings.

alterations, with pilasters framing each of the four niches, an ornate surround fixed for the relief sculpture high up on the wall, and sculptured medallions in the arches above the south, west (and presumably east and north) sides of the room. Additional sculptural features have been placed in the apses above each niche, now featuring ornate light sconces. An early photograph of the dining room shows a very dark, heavy interior while a later one, after the 1919 fire, shows it much lighter in style, with the dominating heavy Corinthian pilasters mostly removed, the room lit by light sconces, for Lady D'Abernon the whole effect displaying that 'hybrid Georgian style peculiar to the Office of Works.'[18]

48. A 1930s photograph of part of the Embassy's large collection of silver.

Embassy Silver

During her searches through the basement in August 1920, Lady D'Abernon found a fine silver-gilt dinner service and some large Empire pieces of gold plate,[19] all of which, as we have seen, she made good use of in her arrangements. The decision to provide certain British missions abroad with a service of plate was made in the early nineteenth century, according to rules and regulations governed by the Treasury and the Lord Chamberlain's Department, rules which included the requirement for the head of mission to check the plate on a regular basis. Several British embassies retain their nineteenth-century silver services, inscribed with the name of the diplomatic mission. The large quantity of table silver sent to Berlin was not new but 'recycled', purchased *en masse* from a Mr Arbuthnott at £4,000 in August 1816, and sent to Berlin later that year, Arbuthnott's coat of arms having been beaten out and replaced by the royal one and inscribed as belonging to 'His Majesty's Mission at the Court of Berlin'. It packed into nine chests and included several early nineteenth-century Empire-style pieces – for example two large candelabra and six ice buckets – that incorporated fashionable (for 1816) Ancient Egyptian motifs. There was also a large mirrored centrepiece and eighty-four silver plates. In the course of its usage in Berlin the silver had to be repaired at least twice (1842 and 1863) and, supplemented by some later pieces, was listed in a separate inventory.[20]

Fine Art during D'Abernon's Ambassadorship

In August 1920 Lady D'Abernon claimed that there was 'no good furniture in the house, no tapestry and no pictures,'[21] but by June of the following year she could report that the Embassy, now decorated with their own pictures, tapestries, and Oriental carpets 'looks really rather well,'[22] a remark that contradicts her husband's recollection of the situation at that time. While he was pleased with the building, for him there was one thing missing: art. This was a pity, he felt, for otherwise the Embassy would have been 'really beautiful.' The building's central problem, he pinpointed, was the fact that it suffered, 'like all official habitations … in comparison with a private residence, from an absence of works of artistic merit';[23] ironic, considering that Strousberg had a purpose-built art gallery in the building for the display of his own large collection. As we have seen the building did, however, contain a few notable 'permanent fixtures', the painted frieze by Schaller and relief sculpture (in the former music room/ballroom/stage room/red drawing room); a ceiling painting in the library by Peters; and a sculpted frieze or friezes by Otto Lessing in the ballroom.

The British way of doing things was in contrast to that in some of the other embassies in Berlin. French embassies were furnished to great propaganda effect by the Mobilier National, originally created to furnish royal palaces and nationalised by the French Republic together with the vast collections of fine and decorative arts amassed over the centuries by French Monarchs and Napoleon Bonaparte. In October 1933 the newly arrived American Ambassador, William Dodd, recounted his impressions of the French Embassy on Pariser Platz in Berlin:

> In the reception room there was a marvellous rug with a huge letter N in the middle to remind one, especially Germans, of the conquests of Napoleon …. The walls were covered with beautiful Gobelin tapestries. The chairs were Louis XIV style. When the party of thirty went into the dining-room …. I noticed Gobelins on the walls, also portraits of French generals of the Louis XIV period, a peculiarly good painting of the young Louis XV, and a lavish table with decorations in the best of form and taste…. Such was the show of democratic France to autocratic Germany.[24]

It was not until 1898–99 that there was anything approaching an overall strategy for the provision of works of art in government buildings in the UK, when the Treasury granted the Office of Works the sum of £150 per annum to acquire suitable items for government buildings in London. However, although it was admitted that some kind of proper strategy was necessary to provide 'official' art appropriate for the grandeur of British government buildings, it was perhaps not surprising, given that Department's ever-practical attitude, that the Treasury particularly encouraged the purchase of large pieces, in order to 'save a good sum in decoration.'[25] This was the genesis of what was to become the UK Government Art Collection.

The new policy still did not extend to the acquisition of works of art for British government buildings abroad. As time went on, however, fewer and fewer diplomats had the means to emulate Russell and Malet by filling the gaps with items from their own collections. And even if they had, for personal reasons they might hesitate to do so: given the volatile political situation during much of his ambassadorship, D'Abernon was understandably concerned about bringing his own possessions to Berlin. Thus, it came to be that usually there was little or no art on display at all in embassies and legations, or reliance had to be made on gifts or loans, often of uneven quality. As Monarchs came and went, missions gradually built up collections of state portraits, and by the time of D'Abernon's ambassadorship there were additions to the portrait of Queen Victoria in the ballroom, in front of which Lady D'Abernon was photographed in the early 1920s.* Reflected in a mirror in this photograph can be seen the state portrait of Queen Alexandra, the pair to the one of King Edward VII, both sent to Berlin in 1903. As time went on these were supplemented by state portraits of King George V, Queen Mary and their successors.[26]

The D'Abernons took many opportunities to look at private art collections in Berlin and Germany during their ambassadorship. On Monday, 8 February 1926, for example, they attended a dinner party given in their honour by Count Henry Kessler and admired his works by Aristide Maillol and Georges Seurat.[27] Lady D'Abernon's memoirs record visits to museums and collections during her travels in Germany, and she paid particular attention to art and artefacts when visiting German political figures or staying as their guests. While he was apparently unwilling to bring his own works of art to Berlin from England, it is clear that from very early in his ambassadorship D'Abernon continued to spend large amounts of money acquiring and selling art in Berlin through the city's growing art trade which was by now beginning to rival London and Paris.[28] He was of course doing this during the volatile inflationary period of the early 1920s, and enjoyed regular correspondence over the purchase and sale of works of art with Berlin dealers including Galerie Van Diemen Co. (Unter den Linden) and Herren Leo Blumenrich (Dahlem), and Paul Cassirer. In the 1890s Paul Cassirer and his cousin Bruno had helped support the development of the 'Berlin Secession', that group of artists who dissented from the prevailing state-sponsored and traditional-leaning art and architecture endorsed by the Emperor Wilhelm II. Cassirer's gallery on Viktoriastrasse exhibited modern and avant-garde French and German art including work by Paul Cézanne, Max Liebermann, Aubrey Beardsley and Henri de Toulouse-Lautrec in a modern gallery designed by Kessler's friend Henry van de Velde.

Despite the fact that D'Abernon's ambassadorship coincided with an extraordinary flowering of avant-garde artistic endeavour in the very city to which he was posted, many if not most of the works of art he purchased at this time seem to have been traditional rather than contemporary pieces. He was also collecting silver, writing to Crichton Brothers of Old Bond Street in London on 23 October 1924 to direct them to send two of the four casserole dishes he had purchased there to Berlin (despite his worries about security), and reminding them that he was always on the lookout for silver 'of a very bold and peculiar pattern at not too high a price', in particular a Queen Anne or George I tea urn 'not too large and really practical.'[29] In October 1923 he purchased a portrait of a woman in a blue dress by Manet from Cassirer, a few years later unsuccessfully trying to sell it in London, and there were extensive negotiations over the authenticity of *St Francis in Ecstasy* by El Greco, which Cassirer was offering to sell him.[30] It is unclear as to whether he displayed these valuable works in the Embassy itself at any time during his ambassadorship; he directed a number of his purchases in Berlin to be sent to the D'Abernons' homes in London, Surrey and Rome.

Feeling that the Embassy badly needed pictures, within a few weeks of his official arrival in Berlin D'Abernon purchased a landscape painting ascribed to Salomon Ruysdael which he hung in the dining room. The purchase was made from

* See illustration 39.

'Wertheim's, Berlin' [sic][31] for the equivalent of £94. D'Abernon routinely collected Dutch and Flemish paintings, including paintings by Jacob Ruysdael, Rembrandt and Franz Hals. Only two weeks before their arrival in Berlin in October 1920, the D'Abernons paid a call on René Gimpel's gallery in Paris to see a painting by Cuyp, *The Flight into Egypt*, and Gimpel remarked that D'Abernon himself owned a Rembrandt that had been shown at the Grafton Gallery in London the previous year.[32] In March 1921 the Ambassador purchased a painting[33] in Berlin for 10,000 marks by the sixteenth-century German artist Lucas Cranach, but he evidently changed his mind about this shortly afterwards, selling it back to the dealer as part payment for another painting – perhaps deemed to be more suitable for display in the Embassy, for whatever reason, perhaps one of size – a 'picture' by Sebastian 'Francks.'[34†] The total sum for this transaction came to 25,700 marks. The pound sterling to German mark ratio that D'Abernon gave (in December 1923) was 240 marks to the pound.

D'Abernon did not entirely confine his Berlin collecting habits to Old Masters. In April 1922 he had purchased a pastel sketch by the contemporary German avant-garde artist Max Liebermann, at 30,000 marks, from Cassirer. By then D'Abernon calculated that the exchange rate was 1,110 marks to the pound, a dramatic illustration of the rampant inflation of the period. On a less avant-garde level, D'Abernon also recorded that he had purchased a number of historic topographical engravings of Berlin and a classical bust of the *Diadumenos*.

As well as portraying Gustav Stresemann, during his stay at the Embassy in 1925 Augustus John painted an informal portrait of D'Abernon which captures something of the Ambassador's reportedly untidy appearance.[‡] It is possible that D'Abernon hung this somewhere in the Embassy, although if he did so it may have been on the basis of a temporary loan from the artist; the portrait was in John's studio at his death in 1961.[§] After D'Abernon's return to England at the end of his ambassadorship, John painted a second, much more formal, full-length portrait of the former Ambassador in diplomatic dress, quite different in mood to the first portrait. The artist was to be surprised when D'Abernon unsuccessfully attempted to persuade his fellow Trustees of the Tate Gallery in London to purchase it from him, rather accepting it as his gift;[35] Lady D'Abernon was later to donate it to the Gallery.

That portrait was not the first work of art D'Abernon had purchased for which he later sought reimbursement from the British taxpayer. In late 1923[36] Sir Lionel Earle stayed with the D'Abernons in Berlin. The reason for this visit is unclear[37] and is not mentioned in Earle's autobiography. It may have been a simple duty visit: Earle records similar visits to Cairo in 1919 and to Athens, in connection with embassy buildings and their associated problems. During his stay D'Abernon accompanied him on a private visit to the Palace of Sanssouci in Potsdam to see the collections of drawings and paintings.[38]

On 4 December 1923 D'Abernon wrote to Earle summarising a conversation they had had during his stay, Earle reportedly having admired at least some of

† Sebastian Vrancx.
‡ See illustration 41.
§ The portrait was sold at Christie's on 21 June 1963 (Lot 151) and was eventually purchased by the UK Government Art Collection in 1985.

D'Abernon's works of art on display in the Embassy. His visit turned out to be serendipitous, for Earle had already been giving some thought to the unsatisfactory issue of works of art for embassies, 'anxious to obtain legislation to let the National Gallery hand surplus pictures to him for hanging in embassies abroad, instead of wasting in cellars'.[39]* D'Abernon was apparently prepared to sell his Ruysdael, 'Franks' and 'Liebermann' to the British Government as permanent decorations for the Embassy, together with a billiard table he had purchased, all adding up to a sum of some £278. The billiard table was of 'French pattern' and stood in Strousberg's former library, in use as an office since the 1880s; it was where the Embassy's historic archives, sealed up by Sir Horace Rumbold on 5 August 1914, were located. Patently there was some need for such a 'recreational facility': Russell's billiard table had been amongst the pieces of furniture the British Government had declined to purchase after his death. But D'Abernon's had a double use, for he informed London that a special wooden top had been made for it to convert it into a table 'which has been found useful for conferences etc.' He had also funded some 'special lighting.'[40] D'Abernon was also happy to donate the topographical prints of Berlin and the classical bust. Earle wrote to Sir George Barstow of the Treasury in London shortly afterwards that the idea was 'a new departure, but … provided the sums were not too heavy, it might be good policy'. He drew the line at the billiard table, however, 'as we do not provide such things.'[41]

Enquiries were made of Sir Charles Holmes, Director of the National Gallery, as to the artistic and financial value of the pictures D'Abernon was offering for sale. Holmes imagined that the Ruysdael and 'Franks' were no more than 'large furniture pictures.'[42] (This is certainly borne out by the prices D'Abernon paid for them in comparison to the works he purchased for himself: for example, in December 1919 he paid a dealer in Paris £9,000 for *Madonna and Child with Two Saints* by Cima[43] and in 1925 he bought *The Mob Cap* by Reynolds for £2,800.) Holmes' views on the type of art required at that time for embassy walls were unsentimental. Rehearsing the views expressed in the 1890s that one of the practical benefits of art in British government buildings was covering as much wall as possible, D'Abernon's 'large furniture pictures', he advised, could usefully be 'regarded as part of the fixed decorations of the building', 'large decorative panels' so that hopefully the transaction would not encourage other diplomats to copy his example and start purchasing works of art at their posts which they could count on selling on to the British Government later. But the Liebermann was a different matter: 'Might not awkward questions be asked in Parliament if it was discovered that the British Government was buying works by living German artists?'[44] His advice was taken, and the two historical paintings (but not the Liebermann) were purchased from D'Abernon for the sum of £201, the same sum as he had paid for them. The Office of Works assured the Treasury that their purchase was 'very desirable as their removal would diminish considerably the attractiveness of the Embassy from the point of view of furnishing.'[45] This was indeed, as Earle pointed out, 'a new departure' and the first known example of the British government purchasing fine art for permanent use in British embassies. Something similar

* The notion that national collections are packed with unseen stored masterpieces is not new, seemingly always articulated using the clichés 'wasting away', 'dusty', 'cellars', 'vaults' and 'attics'.

was to happen shortly afterwards in 1926 when the Thun Palace in Prague was acquired from Count Thun for use as the British Embassy and Residence, when a large proportion of the Count's art collection, comprising works by Central European artists, was purchased at the same time; they remain in the building to this day. These activities were followed in the 1930s by more strategic initiatives to provide suitable art for such buildings in order to enhance their appearance, and in subsequent years the emphasis was to change from the acquisition of large 'decorative' pictures by foreign artists to works by British ones to support the British diplomatic effort abroad.[†]

When D'Abernon left Berlin in October 1926 he sold the Liebermann pastel sketch (entitled *Gabriel Schillings Flucht* according to Cassirer[‡]) back to Cassirer, offering it for the equivalent of £30 or £40, telling them that 'It has been a great resource during my stay here to visit your varying collection and to discuss art matters with you.'[46] Most of D'Abernon's correspondence with Cassirer had been with the gallery's employee Fraulein Ring; tragically, Paul Cassirer himself committed suicide in January 1926 after his marriage failed.

Heads of mission were required to sign an annual certificate for official furnishings, and where possible fittings and fixtures were officially inspected when heads of mission left post. Earle was particularly pleased (if not downright sycophantic) with the D'Abernons in this regard:

> My dear Helen, Among the many glories of your and the late Ambassador's reign at Berlin, one of the most notable, in my opinion, is the admirable way in which you have cared for the Embassy and the Government property therein installed. I have lately received a report from my technical officers who have inspected the house and furniture before the entry of the new occupants, and, with the exception of one or two quite minor things which are missing, they report that the whole establishment has been most admirably looked after. It is such a comfort, and so rare in these official residences, to get such a glowing report as this that I cannot refrain from writing to express not only the grateful thanks of the Department and the First Commissioner [of Works], but even of H.M. Government, for the scrupulous care which you and Edgar have taken in these matters.[47]

Although the Ruysdael painting was in 1923 described as hanging in the Embassy dining room, the display locations of the other works of art D'Abernon left behind in the Embassy is not known. The author has found no photographs either of the two paintings themselves or as featuring in the background of the few photographs that survive of the Embassy's interior. Nor were they ever recorded by the Office of Works or its successor in London in any inventory that has survived to the present day.[48] Not even the title of the Sebastian Vrancx is known. Witnessing the Embassy's visitors and drama over the next decade and a half, after 3 September 1939 these works of art were to take their chances with fate.

---

† See Chapter 16.
‡ *Gabriel Schillings Flucht* [*Gabriel Schilling's Flight*] was a 1912 play by Gerhart Hauptmann (1862–1946).

CHAPTER 12
1926–1929: 'SO ENGLISH & SOLID & DECENT'

Vita Sackville-West hated Berlin, in particular her husband Harold Nicolson's posting there as Counsellor at the British Embassy:

> I really do get into despair about it; you would too, my sweet, if I went and lived in a place you loathed in pursuit of a profession you really deprecated because it took me away from what you considered to be my legitimate pursuits; and profession moreover which ... entailed a great many obligations which you thought utterly infra dig.* No, Hadji† would not like it either. No, he wouldn't.[1]

An eccentric diplomatic wife in what was an unconventional, but ultimately successful marriage that combined long and fruitful independent literary careers, Vita (shortened from Victoria) did not accompany her husband to Berlin. The couple both experienced homosexual relationships, and one of Vita's – with the novelist Violet Trufusis (née Keppel) – famously included an attempted 'elopement' abroad, pursued by Nicolson. Vita certainly did not approve of her husband's choice of career. 'I do so hate diplomats,' she told her close confidante Virginia Woolf in a series of letters written during Harold's posting to the German capital, '... I feel an awful fish out of water.'[2] She particularly loathed the service's social mores and expectations, especially for wives, the need put on a show for receptions and lunch and dinner parties for people with whom she would not otherwise have chosen to spend any time: 'I feel that the next person who kisses my hand will get his face smacked.'[3]

She was actually no stranger to this small world: her aristocratic family, the owners of Knole in Kent, one of the largest houses in England, had a long association with the diplomatic service that she so despised. John Frederick Sackville, 3rd Duke of Dorset, had been the last British Ambassador to the French Court before the Revolution, while in 1802 his widow's second husband, Charles Whitworth, became the first to the French Republic. Another member of the family had married Odo Russell's eldest brother, Hastings, in 1844, and their daughter Ermyntrude, as we have seen, caught the eye of Sir Edward Malet. Later Lionel, 2nd Lord Sackville served in posts that included Berlin,[4] and became British Minister to Buenos Aires in 1873 and Ambassador to Washington in 1881. Coincidentally, amongst the many suitors Vita's striking mother, Victoria, received while acting as her father's hostess in Washington had been Charles Hardinge and Cecil Spring-Rice.

The ambassadorship in Berlin had not remained a political appointment after the departure of Lord D'Abernon: the new Conservative Foreign Secretary Austen

---

* Humiliating.
† Vita's pet name for her husband.

49. Sir Ronald Lindsay in diplomatic dress photographed leaving the Embassy to present his credentials in 1926.

Chamberlain (and former Embassy visitor) appointed career diplomat Sir Ronald Lindsay to the position. Born in 1877, Lindsay was from yet another long-established aristocratic family. Joining the diplomatic service in 1899 he was posted to St Petersburg (where, as we have seen, his handsome looks were temporarily 'appropriated' by his colleague Cecil Spring-Rice), followed by Tehran, Washington and Paris. Appointed assistant Private Secretary to Foreign Secretary Sir Edward Grey, Lindsay later served at The Hague before being seconded to the Egyptian Government's Ministry of Finance. In 1919 he returned to the diplomatic service as Counsellor in Washington, becoming Head of Mission in Turkey in 1924. Lindsay's first wife died in 1918; in 1924 he married the American Elizabeth Hoyt.

Lindsay arrived in Berlin in late 1926. By this time the number of embassy staff was expanding again, and, following a visit to Berlin in early January 1927, Sir Lionel Earle reported that in addition to the property at 17 Tiergartenstrasse additional offices for the commercial and service attachés had been taken on at 3 Pariser Platz. Since this was 'quite the most expensive position in the whole of Berlin', he recommended that they should look for somewhere more economical in the longer-term. The best solution was to convert one of the flats at 17 Tiergartenstrasse (which he very optimistically estimated was 'about seven minutes' walk' from 70 Wilhelmstrasse) into office accommodation.[5] It was not a popular suggestion amongst those affected. The commercial, military and naval attachés wrote to London stating that 'The chief objection to 17 Tiergartenstrasse is the great difficulty of access. It is not on or near a bus, tram or underground route and from whatever side it is approached a walk of some distance is necessary or a cab must be taken.' The business centre of Berlin could not be reached in less than thirty minutes' walk (they were right), and the location of the building in relation to the Embassy and the other government offices in and around Wilhelmstrasse, particularly the German Foreign Office, was 'extremely unfavourable.'[6] If an international or economic crisis were suddenly to develop that required their constant presence at the Embassy, they would be unable to perform their duties effectively.

The advocates of economy in HM Government were once again triumphant, however, and in May 1927 Lindsay agreed to the conversion of a staff flat at 17 Tiergartenstrasse into the necessary office space. This building would henceforth continue to accommodate the Consulate and Passport Control offices, plus the Commercial Secretary and the three military attachés. Major Breen's flat would be moved to the mansard floor of the building; quarters occupied by the building's porter would be moved within the basement to allow some of the space to be used for file storage. This was without doubt a sensible financial solution, but given the geographical separation of the two buildings it would also have had the inevitable effect of further exacerbating the 'them and us' attitude of the consular and attaché staff in the leafy Tiergarten and the 'real' diplomats in the Chancery in the busy heart of the Berlin government area, a mentality with a long tradition in the Foreign Office even when the two groups of staff are working within the same building. Frank Foley's deputy, Leslie Mitchell, was an example: according to a colleague 'He was always kowtowing with people in the Embassy. I think he thought the consulate was a bit below him.'[7] '[C]ommercial attachés were decidedly looked down upon by the regular diplomats', remembered one commentator[8] and the Commercial Attaché at Bucharest, for example, was never even invited for dinner at the Embassy there. As later Ambassadors to Berlin were to experience, the attachés' prediction that the separation would pose practical problems for the Embassy proved to be correct.

***

Harold Nicolson's father was Sir Arthur Nicolson, Lord Carnock, who served at the British Embassy in Berlin in the 1870s and rose through the ranks to become Permanent Secretary at the Foreign Office in 1910. Harold was born at the British Legation in Tehran in 1886 and entered the diplomatic service in 1909, serving in Madrid and Constantinople before being drafted, during his home leave in London in August 1914, to deliver the 'correct' declaration of war on Germany to the German Ambassador in London. After the end of the Great War he was present at the Paris peace negotiations in 1919 and then became private secretary to the Secretary-General of the League of Nations. In 1925 he was sent to be Counsellor in Tehran, a posting for which he and his wife had a shared hatred: Vita did not accompany Harold there on a permanent basis. It was not a happy time. Nicolson was demoted to First Secretary after criticising British policy towards Persia, and it was only when he was posted to Berlin in 1927 that he returned to the rank of Counsellor.

In Vita's absence, Nicolson's time in Berlin was spent in a relatively unconventional manner for a diplomat of his seniority, unable most of the time to receive and entertain guests in the traditional manner with his wife by his side, either at home or at the Embassy. Instead, he entertained alone, hosting an eclectic succession of urbane visitors who took the opportunity of his presence in Berlin (and his considerable generosity) at the very height of the city's cultural golden age to lodge with him, sometimes for extended periods. Noël Coward was one such visitor in November 1927: Nicolson lunched with him and accompanied him to a review at a large music hall.[9] (Coward was trying to gain some inspiration for *This Year of Grace*, a review he was currently working on in London.) In February 1928 Nicolson entertained the American novelist Sinclair Lewis for drinks and dinner,[10] and in April visited the State Opera House with Ivor Novello to hear some Puccini, noting that Novello 'suffers dreadfully from the worship of "flappers".'[11] A few weeks later the literary critic Cyril Connolly was another visitor.[12]

50. Vita Sackville-West at home at Long Barn, Kent during Harold Nicolson's summer leave in 1929, with their sons Ben and Nigel, in a photograph probably taken by Harold.

Although she did not live with her husband in Berlin, Vita did occasionally travel out to visit him, accompanied by their children, Ben and Nigel, during school holidays; the two boys enjoyed playing badminton in the Embassy's ballroom.[13] The long railway journeys across Europe did at least offer Vita an opportunity for writing: she started the first chapter of her novel *The Edwardians*, set in her ancestral home of Knole,* in the restaurant at Cologne railway station while waiting to change trains.[14] But, despite all its cultural manifestations she hated Berlin, describing it as 'pure loathsomeness,'[15] and Harold too was unhappy about her absence and their inevitable farewells.

Lindsay served as Ambassador in Berlin for less than two years: in the summer of 1928 he was recalled, promoted to be the Head of the Foreign Office. Nicolson was a guest at the farewell lunch for the departing Ambassador and Lady Lindsay at the President's Palace further south down Wilhelmstrasse, recording his impressions of the long-vanished 'lovely garden – huge trees running in an avenue down to the Tiergarten, with lawns and fountains filling up the space between them.'[16] The eighty-one-year-old Hindenburg was very friendly towards Nicolson, recalling his memories of 70 Wilhelmstrasse in the 1860s and 1870s before it became the British Embassy. He remembered Nicolson's father, of whom Harold was using what spare time he had during his Berlin posting to write a biography, using the Embassy's archives.[17] Nicolson now became Chargé d'Affaires until the arrival of Lindsay's successor, who had finally achieved the ambassadorship – Sir Horace Rumbold.

Like so many of his fellow diplomats, 'Sir Horace was born into diplomacy,' as the journalist Bella Fromm put it.[18] His father (also Sir Horace) enjoyed a distinguished career in the service, and Rumbold began his career working alongside him as an honorary attaché at The Hague. His subsequent career took him to Cairo (twice),

* Named 'Chevron' in the novel.

Tehran, Vienna, Madrid and Tokyo. In 1905 he married Ethelred Constantia Fane, the daughter of yet another diplomat. Rumbold succeeded his father to a baronetcy in 1913, and was at that stage of his career hoping, as we have seen, to become a head of mission; instead, he was appointed number two in Berlin. Returning from Germany after the dramatic events of July and August 1914 he worked in the Foreign Office in London and in 1916 became Minister in Berne. Sadly, the third child Lady Rumbold had been expecting during Rumbold's difficulties in Berlin in July and August 1914 – a daughter – died in July 1918.

After the 1919 Treaty of Versailles Rumbold became Britain's first Minister to Poland rather than, as had been rumoured, returning to Berlin as Ambassador. Later serving as High Commissioner and Ambassador in Constantinople, he attended the Lausanne Peace Conference and then served again in Madrid before his appointment as Ambassador to Berlin in 1928. 'At last. It was long overdue and a rectification of what should have been already done in the past,' Sir Robert Vansittart told Rumbold when the news was announced.[19] Rumbold had thought that his luck had deserted him yet again so far as Berlin was concerned. He had been given to understand that he would succeed D'Abernon, but yet again was thwarted and instead sent to Madrid, which although 'very pleasant ... is rather a backwater'. He had previously 'wiped Berlin off the slate.'[20]

Lindsay wrote to Rumbold in March about some of the administrative details regarding the running of 70 Wilhelmstrasse, although his familiarity with it would naturally have made taking the house on an easier task for Rumbold than for others. Lindsay reckoned that some of the servants were worth continuing in service, and, on a practical level, wondered if Rumbold wanted to purchase any of Lindsay's wines, but Rumbold reported that his own 'cellar is fairly well stocked for the moment and I propose to take what I have to Berlin with me, but I should be very glad to take over all your claret, fin champagne and various oddments such as sherry and liqueurs, etc ... I also get my champagne direct from Moet and Chandon.'[21] He was to supplement his holdings with purchases from Ribbentrop's wine business, while the wine merchant was to cultivate Rumbold's friendship by inviting him to tennis at his home in Dahlem.[22]

Rumbold arrived at Friedrichstrasse Station on the overnight train on 3 August 1928 for a week's stay to present his credentials and get the measure of Berlin again before returning properly as Ambassador the following month. Together with representatives of the Berlin diplomatic corps Nicolson had to be on duty to receive his new chief at his arrival in Berlin, on what, as he recounted to Vita, turned out to be a memorable occasion:

> At seven I had to get up in order to meet old Rumbold. I put on my top hat and tails, and motored in on a lovely clear morning feeling rather stiff and cross in my stiff clothes. There is no doubt moreover that I do not like Ambassadors arriving when I am in charge. They had opened up the special waiting-rooms at the Friedrichstrasse [station][†] – and there was the whole staff there looking very lovely, and two representatives of the German Government. The train came in and old Rumby bundled out rather embarrassed with an attaché case in one hand and in the other a

---

† The same rooms used for the D'Abernons' official departure.

novel by Mr. Galsworthy. I introduced him to the German representatives and to the staff, while the crowd gaped and gaped and the policemen stood at the salute. Photographs were taken, and then very slowly we passed through the waiting rooms preceded by the Oberbahnfhofführer* to the waiting cars. I carried the attaché case. We drove round to the Adlon where he is staying until the Embassy is in order. We were greeted by the whole Adlon family. Rumby was confused. 'Never,' he said, 'have I felt so odd.'[23]

Rumbold's memories of those July and August days of 1914 must have come flooding back, when, as Nicolson put it to Vita, 'he was Counsellor and crept out of Berlin under cavalry escort and amid the booings of a crowd. It is odd thus to return. He is a nice old bumble bee – and I am quite happy with him. But he is not Lindsay – no, no.'[24] His return to the Embassy from which he and his colleagues had departed so suddenly exactly fourteen years before must have felt very strange – perhaps especially when he found the archives in the library gallery apparently sealed just as he had left them.† At the official ceremony at which Rumbold presented his letters of credence to the German Head of State, Hindenburg made particular mention of that time, referring in his speech 'to the prominent posts held by Sir Horace Rumbold in his country's service and to his previous knowledge of conditions in Germany, which would seem to render him particularly well suited to his new task.'[25] Rumbold would have needed no reminding.

The new Ambassador left Berlin a week later and Nicolson was temporarily left in charge again. On 16 August Vita and their sons arrived, this time staying at the summer house Nicolson had acquired – in that long diplomatic tradition – in Potsdam. But the time was no holiday for Nicolson as he had to deputise for the new Ambassador, his duties including entertaining the sixty members of the British delegation to the Inter-Parliamentary Conference that was touring Europe, involving a series of dinners, one of which took place at the Adlon. This was exactly the kind of event Vita loathed in her role as Harold's wife. '"His Britannic Majesty's Chargé d'Affaires and Mrs Harold Nicolson request the honour …" Will you, please, Virginia, consecrate a kindly though sarcastic thought to me at 8.30 on Saturday evening?'[26]

On 10 September Rumbold returned to Berlin to take up the post of Ambassador, Lady Rumbold finding '[t]wo smart little house-maids dressed in blue cotton frocks and white caps in the morning, and black alpaca frocks and caps and aprons in afternoon' and a new porter 'who sits in the hall always and looks like a footman. But he has to be glued to his little cup-board over-looking the entrance, as people come at odd moments to see H. or me.'[27] There were, however, routine staffing problems. The French chef and sous-chef Rumbold had engaged as from the first of that month were suddenly demanding to be paid for working during August. 'I left your mother to grapple with him this morning but have not heard the result of the struggle,' Rumbold wrote to his daughter. 'These French cooks require watching and if they are worsted in the first round they acquire a respect for one.'[28]

---

* Station master.
† Precisely when Harold Nicolson opened up the sealed cupboards to start using the Embassy's historic archives to research the career of his father is uncertain.

51. Sir Horace Rumbold arrives at Friedrichstrasse Station on 3 August 1928; Harold Nicolson stands behind him, to the right.

Exactly a year later Rumbold's robust attitude towards his domestic staff was to be needed again when three German embassy footmen and two German housemaids tried to pressurise him into raising their wages by threatening a walkout. Rumbold called their bluff and 'told them to go to a warm place'. Not at all concerned about their departure, he was in any case 'very glad to get rid of the footmen who are a weedy lot of different sizes. We are now getting three robust men of 6 feet or over. But we might just as well have saved the wages etc. of 5 servants whilst we were on leave.'[29]

Earlier in the summer of Rumbold's arrival, Vita had become desperate about her husband's career, sending him a plaintive letter on 12 July 1928: 'I was plunged into despair this morning by your letter saying you might have to stay in Berlin till 1930. I had come to count really on you getting away in the spring of next year. I see the point about staying with Rumbold till he has settled down, but it can't take him two years to settle down!'[30] What she really wanted was for her husband to change career. Later during her stay in Berlin with Harold during August 1928, articulating feelings that many a diplomatic spouse will have experienced down the years, she wrote plaintively to Virginia Woolf: 'Am I forever … to spend my life walking the streets of Potsdam, Belgrade, Bucharest, Washington? … I remembered also that the Foreign Office had refused to pay for the dinner to the MPs,* which had cost us something over £100.'[31]

* * *

Rumbold's appearance and demeanour were a source of perplexed amusement to embassy staff and outsiders alike. Daniel Binchy, head of the new Irish Legation in Berlin, described in his *General Report* of 1930 how he 'remains somewhat of a mystery to me. He makes the impression of an exceptionally stupid man, but this is belied by his very good career in the diplomatic service …. Since his arrival here he has not been a prominent figure in either the political or social world.' Perhaps with a political axe to grind, Binchy opined that the British Embassy had 'fallen considerably from its former high estate, and is nothing like as powerful as it used to be under D'Abernon, when German politics were dictated and German Governments made and unmade in his reception rooms.' Binchy put this down to several reasons, including differences in personality between the two Ambassadors, and Germany's growth in self-confidence after its economic and political recovery since the difficult early 1920s. Personally, he found Rumbold remote, possibly he thought due to traditional English hostility towards Ireland, and Binchy reported how over the past season as a diplomat he had been invited to the bare minimum of social functions at the Embassy: one luncheon, one dinner and one reception. But he was on friendlier terms with other members of the Embassy, the academic finding Harold Nicolson 'the most remarkable man I have met since I came: utterly unlike the conventional British Diplomat, careless in dress, unconventional in language and behaviour and – graver still – interested in Literature!'[32]

Harold Nicolson himself thought Rumbold and his wife pleasant enough, but 'They are really so appallingly English that it is almost funny … as English as eggs and bacon.'[33] As an example of the self-deprecating, 'not wanting to make a fuss' behaviour that has come to be regarded as a typically British characteristic, he recounted to Vita an anecdote about a lunch Lady Rumbold gave in the Embassy, when a guest, Frau Weissmann:

> broke a yellow Chinese bowl. She was taking out her little bag … only it wasn't a little bag; it was a large black bag heavily bound in steel. The handle of the bag stuck somewhere in her bodice. She tugged. It then sprang into the air, turned several somersaults, and descended rapidly upon a yellow Ming bowl,† biting a huge piece out of it. Frau Weissmann turned the colour of one of those purple strawberries. Lady Rumbold said, 'Oh, it was <u>entirely</u> my fault; one should not leave such things lying about.'[34]

The Rumbolds may have been concerned that either Harold or Vita might parody them in one of their publications. They were right to be wary: in 1927 while posted to Tehran Nicolson had published *Some People*, a book about an apparently imaginary group of characters he had encountered over the course of his diplomatic career.

---

* The Foreign Office's refusal to pay this bill, at least immediately, seems surprising; the fact that the event was held at the upmarket Adlon Hotel (perhaps necessary during the 'dead' month of August while there were staffing problems) may have been the reason.
† Possibly a survival from the decorative schemes of the 1870s/1880s, perhaps from the 'Oriental Room'.

One of these was 'Titty', Nevile Titmarsh, an amusing but hopeless diplomat whose lengthy career of short postings in Europe and South America 'read like a timetable'.

But as Binchy rightly surmised, appearances were deceptive, and Rumbold had already had proved his mettle as Head of Mission in Warsaw, Constantinople and Madrid. His German knowledge and expertise were finely honed through his previous experience in the capital and he had had every expectation of being appointed Ambassador to Berlin earlier in the decade. One diplomatic observer described him as 'stiff, ruddy, tall and phlegmatic', but also 'loyal, dependable in [his] relationships, perfectly upright and honest …'[35] Lord Hardinge admitted that 'Although on casual acquaintance [Rumbold] might appear to be an ordinary person, he was in my opinion one of the shrewdest and cleverest persons in the Diplomatic Service.'[36] Now Rumbold was to face new challenges. With Stresemann and Hindenburg still in power (as Foreign Secretary and President respectively) the dynamics of the Weimar Republic were still just about in place, but Rumbold – like Nicolson – was fully aware of what was going on in the background: rearmament, increasing anti-Semitism and a rise in popularity of the National Socialist Party under Adolf Hitler, whose ambitions for political power, it was becoming all too clear, had only temporarily been extinguished.

Rumbold's social duties as Ambassador began in earnest that autumn of 1928 with a visit from Prime Minister Ramsay MacDonald on 14 October. On the following day, MacDonald became the first ever foreign statesman to address the Reichstag, afterwards dining at the Embassy.[37] Amongst the guests invited to the dinner were Gustav Stresemann and his wife Käte, together with the unlikely combination of Albert Einstein and Oswald Mosley and his wife Cynthia ('Cimmie'‡), accompanying MacDonald on a driving trip to Vienna, Prague and the German capital. Someone suggested that Mosley, Cimmie and Nicolson invite Frau Stresemann out for dinner during the visit, with the recommendation that they go with her to see something of Berlin's famed night life, as Käte Stresemann 'was very young for her age and very gay.'[38] The appeal of the Berlin cabaret, with its androgyny, transvestism and homosexuality was extremely attractive to the young poet W. H. Auden (who described Berlin as 'the buggers daydream. There are 170 male brothels under police control … I am a mass of bruises'[39]) and his friend the novelist Christopher Isherwood. But, despite their own reputation for high living, it was lost on the Mosleys:

> Cimmie and I had never seen anything like that night in our lives. In several of the many resorts to which we were taken, the sexes had simply exchanged clothes, makeup and the habits of Nature in crudest form. Scenes of decadence and depravity suggested a nation sunk so deep that it could never rise again …. My last memory of that night in Berlin is of poor Harold dropping to sleep at six o'clock in the morning while vigorous ladies waltzed with red roses behind their ears and roses drooping from their mouths – and not only ladies – until one of those terrible paper balls in use in German night clubs hit our Counsellor a blow in the eye severe enough to wake him up, and with fresh excess of official zeal he swept us off to bed.[40]

‡ The second daughter of Lord Curzon, former Viceroy of India and Foreign Secretary.

Ramsay MacDonald did not accompany them that evening,[41] but, according to Mosley's son Nicholas, he was not without his own sensual pleasures during the trip through the Continent: while in Vienna he had become involved again with an old flame. Oswald Mosley ungallantly later described her as 'an old Viennese tart: faded blond, very sophisticated, very agreeable.'[42]

The nightclubs and cabaret acts were an international draw. At the age of nineteen, travelling to see her brother (a law student in Germany) in 1929 the society beauty Diana Mitford visited the city with her new husband, Bryan Guinness. There, they met Nicolson at the Embassy. Diana had been told by a friend before she left England, 'You will love Berlin, my dear. It is the gayest town in Europe; in fact, my dear, you'll never have seen anything like it.' They went to 'all the famous night-clubs where men pretended to be women and vice-versa. At one of them there was a telephone on each table, but we could not see a soul worth ringing up'. She thought the nightclubs 'not in the least amusing; grim would have been a more appropriate word.'[43] It was a view which the Ambassador, however, did not seem to share, or rather, perhaps, he preferred to remain diplomatically aloof from it all. Confiding in his stepmother in March 1929 he related that

> We have had one or two very fashionable ladies as guests lately who,
> I believe, came to Berlin to sample the night life of the place which
> is unequalled anywhere. I confined myself to taking one at a time to
> a delightful night restaurant called the Tcharkass where a Roumanian
> Tzigane orchestra plays. They were delighted. At 1 a.m. I handed them
> over to a younger man who took them round the town.[44]

Amongst Rumbold's other standard duties as a new ambassador in the first months of his posting was the need to make official calls on forty-two envoys from different countries. The Rumbolds held their introductory diplomatic reception on 6 November 1928, with over six hundred guests, Lady Rumbold recording 'Lots of gold plate and bright pink carnations, and <u>delicious</u> buffet of elegant cakes and canapés'. Just as in 1920, the guests were met by 'an impressive being in cocked-hat, black and silver livery, great silver chain and huge 'baton', who stood facing the entrance and striking the floor loudly whenever someone arrived.'[45] The following month saw the Embassy's Christmas dinner for twenty-two embassy staff and 120 children from the British community, but under ambassadorial strictures: 'Only mothers of children under 6 are allowed to come. Otherwise we should be swamped.'[46]

Vita stayed with Harold in Berlin that Christmas, and early in the New Year they welcomed the Bloomsbury Set: Leonard and Virginia Woolf, Virginia's sister Vanessa Bell and Duncan Grant. Vita had looked forward to the visit for weeks, particularly to seeing Virginia again, and had booked the group into five rooms at the Prinz Albrecht Hotel* (at nine marks per day per room)[47]; she excitedly met them all at Friedrichstrasse Station on 17 January. But although Vita much enjoyed

---

* At 9 Prinz Albrecht Strasse, near the corner with Wilhelmstrasse. Originally built in 1887–88 as the Hotel Römerbad, by the 1920s the hotel was also being used for meetings by the National Socialist Party and from 1934 became part of a complex of buildings used by the state security system, next to Gestapo headquarters, with Heinrich Himmler at its head; it was known as the 'SS House'. The buildings were badly damaged by Allied bombing in the Second World War and demolished in the early 1960s. The Topography of Terror museum now occupies part of the archaeological site.

Virginia's company, the group all seem to get on one another's nerves: Vanessa Bell described the week's visit together as 'very rackety'[48] and there were several arguments and awkward moments.[49] On 22 January Count Henry Kessler, who remained on the embassy contact list, invited them all for tea. Having spent some time with Nicolson, Kessler was to come to the conclusion that he was 'an entertaining personality, but somehow I do not like him, without quite being able to make out why.'[50] On the other hand, his admiration of Vita and her social manner would have perhaps surprised her, given her horror of diplomatic events and small talk: 'the great lady, of slender build and great elegance, with ease of manner and style in every movement, a person who has never experienced a moment's embarrassment or a feeling of social barriers.'[51] Vita was less generous in her description of Kessler: she first met him while he was supervising her translation of work by the German poet Rilke and had reported to Virginia Woolf that 'He is very rich, owns a copper mine in Mexico, and is a bugger. I thought as much.'[52]

Vita's horror of diplomatic events continued that winter 'season' of 1929. On 30 January she and Harold attended

> a great huge dinner at the Embassy – footmen in knee breeches; a sort of Suisse holding a silver-topped pole which he banged on the floor every time the door opened; stars and ribbons; a lady who had had five husbands, including a Persian prince, and a final husband who is the nephew of the first one – she changes her wig, too, according to her mood, so that it is sometimes grey, sometimes black, sometimes red -; gold plate in rivers down the table; and the Papal Nuncio in rose-red silk with a great gold cross on his breast. (He'll probably be the next Pope.)[53]

That intensely cold winter they also attended 'The British Colony Ball' and another party at the Embassy.[54]

Nicolson's circle included the author Somerset Maugham and David Herbert, the second son of the Earl of Pembroke. Herbert had started a directionless career in Berlin finding young ladies for the impresario Otto Kahn to spend evenings with in his suite at the Adlon, followed by employment as an English 'artistic consultant' at a Berlin film studio, and then a short-lived job teaching German film actors and actresses to speak English.[55] Sharing an apartment with the future author Christopher Sykes (a newly arrived honorary attaché) he met Nicolson and, through him, Cyril Connolly, who

> amused himself by writing extraordinary plays which were acted by Christopher Sykes, Cyril and myself. These playlets were always on the same theme, with the same characters, and inevitably took place in the Orient. Cyril was the pimp, Christopher was the carpet-seller and I was the slave-girl. These plays were regularly acted in Harold's apartment in front of a most austere and distinguished audience, including the British Ambassador and his wife. The entertainments did not create a scandal but then Berlin in those days was, to say the least of it, a very odd place.[56]

* * *

Despite its perceived aesthetic ugliness, Herbert loved life in Berlin ('an orgy of fun'[57]), its theatres, opera, restaurants, nightclubs, bars, brothels and uninhibited

52. Sir Horace Rumbold accompanies the Duke and Duchess of York to Potsdam on 15 March 1929. The group is pictured in front of the garden façade of the Palace of Sanssouci.

creative and intellectual life.* It was a world which Nicolson's many cultured visitors clearly also loved, making full use of his generous hospitality for weeks on end. Cyril Connolly documented one of his visits, arriving in Berlin early in the morning and breakfasting at the Adlon. During his stay he went sightseeing, lunched with Ivor Novello, went to the zoo, the theatre and cabaret, had tea with the Ambassador, went to a 'palais de danse' and thoroughly enjoyed 'appreciation, good living, friends and bachelor society.'[58] Writing on British Embassy notepaper he reported back to a friend on 3 June 1928: 'It is very pleasant here, only Bobbie, me, Harold and Raymond Mortimer leading a luxurious reading party life at Potsdam, on a lake. We have a boat and bathe, when bored we go into Berlin to a cabaret crawl.'[59]

Visitors to Berlin during this period also included the Duke and Duchess of York.† Arriving in Berlin with an entourage of seven staff on 15 March 1929 on their way to Oslo to attend a royal wedding, it naturally fell to the British Ambassador to act as their host. The couple breakfasted at the Embassy before spending twelve hours in the city, their sightseeing (pursued by members of the press) including the former Royal Schloss, by then a vast echoey museum occasionally used for

* Walter Ruttmann's film *Berlin: Die Sinfonie der Grossstadt* (1927) hauntingly evokes the appearance and atmosphere of Berlin during this period.
†Later HM King George VI (1895–1952) and HM Queen Elizabeth, The Queen Mother (1900–2002).

official receptions, its colourful former imperial denizens long since departed. The visit to the former grand residence of the couple's royal – and still very much alive – German relatives must have been unnerving, while Lady Rumbold, who remembered the by now psychologically distant world of the Imperial Court of 1913 and 1914, must have found it equally so.

> We were shown the private rooms of the Emperor – even his tiny bed-room, so pathetic. Quite small & dark, with a little dressing-room next to it. It impressed the Duke of York much to see the whole of the vast palace turned into a museum, so cold-blooded he thought. We saw the table on which the Emperor signed the order of mobilisation of the Army in 1914.

Afterwards the Ambassador took the royal couple to that other former centre of Hohenzollern power, Potsdam, before attending a tea dance and leaving that evening. 'We have all fallen in love with the little Duchess, a perfect <u>pet</u>, so pretty, such a lovely smile. How lucky he is!'[60]

Rumbold clearly enjoyed the 'Buccaneers'[‡] dance a few nights later, a fancy-dress party for embassy staff:

> My costume was a success and fairly 'knocked the females in the Old Kent Road'. We had the most delicious sausages and cold beer at about 2.15 am and didn't get to bed until 3 am. Many of the dresses were very becoming. MacFadyen as a French boulevardier of the 1860's was priceless while Preenley [?] – alias Col. Thompson – was got up regardless of cost in a Louis XV costume.[61]

But eight days after their visit to Berlin, Rumbold unexpectedly had to be on official duty again when the Yorks made an emergency stay at 70 Wilhelmstrasse on their way back from Oslo after missing their connection in Berlin. His initiative as a host was put to the test, as he related to his daughter:

> So here they are, and we must amuse them as best we can to-day. This isn't easy on a Sunday. We are taking the party out to Wann See [sic] to lunch and, then, perhaps, to the Tempelhofer Field. Perhaps they will go to the cinema a little later on. Then they will dine here and go off after dinner. I haven't seen them this morning and think that they are best left in peace.[62]

That April the former diplomat, British agent and author Sir Robert Bruce Lockhart visited Berlin, and was entertained in Nicolson's apartment so that he could meet another visitor, Lord Londonderry.[63] Two days later Nicolson had dinner with H. G. Wells and his companion, Moura Budberg. Posted to the city in 1912 with her first husband, a Secretary at the Russian Embassy, like the Rumbolds Moura had experienced what turned out to be the last months of pre-Great War imperial Berlin; during the Russian Revolution she had become Lockhart's close companion in Moscow. Wells was in Berlin to give a lecture at the Reichstag a few days later, an event which turned out to be a bit of an embarrassment: 'One simply could not hear a word, not a single word. It was rather a disaster,' Nicolson told Vita.[64] The event was followed by dinner at the Adlon, attended also by Albert Einstein.

‡ A club for embassy staff.

Not all visitors were as socially engaging. In June, when Sir Charles Hardinge (by now Lord Hardinge) made a visit to Berlin, Nicolson found that he was expected to entertain the senior civil servant alone at the Embassy, the Rumbolds having a prior engagement that evening. It was a strained occasion, the haughty and formal Hardinge 'sitting very upright in a chair in the drawing-room' before they ate solemnly together at a small round table[65] in the building Hardinge had known as a young man in the 1880s.

***

To the mystery of the German Government, in the middle of a new crisis over changed Great War German reparation payments, the British Government temporarily recalled Rumbold from Berlin in July and August 1929 to act as British representative at the Red Cross Conference in Geneva. Nicolson was once again in charge of the Embassy, a duty forced upon him while in the middle of his own leave in England. But now he had a little more to think about on the career front. Following his visit to Berlin in April, Robert Bruce Lockhart had taken on board Nicolson's professed wish to make more of a promising literary career for himself. In the meantime Lockhart had talked with his own boss Lord Beaverbrook, with the result that he was now able to offer Nicolson a job on the *Evening Standard* writing the gossip column 'Londoner's Diary'. After all, Lockhart reminded him, 'you hinted that you might not stay indefinitely in the diplomatic service,'[66] a view no doubt at least partly influenced by Vita's dislike of the service and later exacerbated by Nicolson's forced return to his Berlin duties that summer.

In 1928 Vita had confided in Virginia her dread of the future with Harold should his diplomatic ambitions come to fruition:

> … Harold now says he wants to be an Ambassador – but can you see poor Vita as an ambassadress? I can't – and the prospect fills me with dismay. Really fate does play queer tricks on one, when all one wants to do is to garden and write and talk to Potto* – and instead of that one will go to pay calls in a motor with an ambassadorial footman on the box and a cockade in his hat.[67]

Without Harold's knowledge, she had been 'pulling strings' with Lady Lindsay, with whom the Nicolsons were great friends, asking her to make her husband aware that Harold was looking to return to London to work in the Foreign Office. Harold was furious: 'I won't have my career arranged by women.'[68] But with the prospect of 'three years interlarded with large slabs of Berlin', Vita felt 'as though the top of my head were coming off, – a wild, helpless feeling.'[69] 'Oh God, how I hate the Foreign Office! How I hate it, with a personal hatred for all that it makes me suffer! Damn it, damn it, damn it – that vile impersonal juggernaut that sweeps you away from me,' she wrote to Harold in November 1928.[70]

Nicolson was very much in two minds about the *Evening Standard* job offer and the prospect of leaving the diplomatic service just when he could have hoped for a future posting to a more agreeable capital and even (as Vita feared) to be a head of mission himself. 'I heard from the Ambassador that there are five Legations

---

* Vita's nickname for Virginia Woolf.

to be filled – Mexico, Athens, Belgrade, Bucharest and Oslo', and he felt very attracted by the prospect of Athens: 'Five years in Athens, and then an Embassy,' he wrote to Vita in August.[71] On the other hand, he had written to Lockhart in late July about the 'flattering' offer: 'I long to get back to London and into the whirl of real life again. Being Counsellor in Berlin is very like being First Secretary at Stockholm. I am a stepney wheel of a car that is seldom taken out of the garage.'[72] In September he finally made up his mind and accepted the job offer and agreed to start at the *Evening Standard* on 1 January 1930 at a salary of £3,000.[73]

***

Nicolson was by this stage feeling better disposed towards his chief, describing Rumbold's return to Berlin from Switzerland on 1 September 1929: 'Rumbie, Mrs. Rumbie, Miss Rumbie & Master Rumbie nebst Valet Rumbie all got out of the train in a row, & each one clasping a novel by John Galsworthy. I never saw anything look so English & solid & decent.'[74] This Gilbertian ensemble featured another character: Cumbridge, Rumbold's personal valet. Cumbridge liked to impersonate the Ambassador, on one occasion going so far as to attend a party dressed as Rumbold and wearing his decorations; Rumbold sacked him soon afterwards.[75]

His forced attendance at the Geneva Conference had deprived Rumbold of a summer holiday, and he found the looming prospect of the heavy entertaining duties for the winter of 1929–30 distinctly unappealing. Now beginning in early November, the Berlin winter season had expanded since imperial days, but Rumbold had come up with a crafty strategy to avoid some of it: he and his family would go to Sicily,

> as I still have 3 weeks leave due to me. This is a dodge for curtailing the winter and its entertainments which I find awfully trying …. By going away about November 15 I calculate that we shall escape all dinners etc until January. But we shall, ourselves, give a dinner of 50 before we leave and try to work off all the 'duds' at one go.[76]

Leaving for Sicily as he had planned on 15 November, Rumbold left Nicolson in charge for the last time, before returning to Berlin in the middle of December. In anticipation of his departure from the Foreign Office, Nicolson had by now given up his apartment and was lodging at the Prinz Albrecht Hotel. The Embassy gave a Buccaneers Club farewell dinner for him at which there were nearly forty guests, and where a 'speech by Rumbie … gave me a lump in my throat. Speech by me – very restrained but gulpy. Musical honours. All went off very well. It is quite extraordinary how nice people are to me here. They really are sorry I am going.'[77] There followed another farewell dinner at the Embassy itself the following night, and then Harold Nicolson, to Vita's delight, left Berlin, his job as Counsellor at the Embassy, and the Foreign Office. 'How glad I shall be when the train moves out of the Friedrichstrasse!' he had told Vita,[78] while on 19 December he confided in his diary, 'I am presented with a cactus. The end of my diplomatic career.'[79]

CHAPTER 13
1930–1933: 'As If We Were Living in a Lunatic Asylum'

Early one freezing morning in January 1931 Lady Rumbold travelled to Berlin's Tempelhof Aerodrome.[*] Finally, after an excited crowd had waited in the cold for several hours, Amy Johnson's plane could be heard in the distance. The plane landed and taxied to the terminal where Johnson was rushed at by photographers and journalists. In an age of aeronautical experimentation and endeavour, the famous female pilot (the first woman to fly solo from England to Australia the previous year) was attempting to fly from England to China, via Berlin, Warsaw and Moscow. Atrocious winter weather had forced her to make unexpected landings at Liège and Cologne, and then driving snowstorms had delayed her scheduled arrival in Berlin by several hours. Johnson spent the night at the British Embassy as the Rumbolds' guest, Lady Rumbold finding her "a dear little thing, looks anything but strong, [with] a soft gentle voice and manner ... dreadfully cold and tired on arrival'. They 'hated seeing her off at 8.30' the following morning for Warsaw[1] (her trip finally had to be aborted when her plane came down in Poland, but she later managed to complete the adventure). It was a British aeronautical success story in contrast to the tragedy of the previous autumn, when the airship R101 had crashed at Beauvais on 5 October on its maiden voyage to Karachi, killing forty-eight of the fifty-five passengers and crew. Five days later a special memorial service for the dead was held at the English Church in Berlin attended by the Ambassador and Lady Rumbold, the embassy and consular staff. The presence of many Germans in the congregation was a testament to what *The Times* described as a deep sympathy that was felt in Germany for the tragedy, as recently there had been 'increasingly close contact between aeronautical circles in the two countries'[2] (Germany, too, was experimenting with this form of air travel, in the form of Zeppelin airships). Many people left written and telephone messages of condolence and sympathy at the Embassy and Consulate.

Amy Johnson was just one of several of the Rumbolds' celebrity guests in 1930 and 1931. 'Every conceivable person came to the ball, including bankers, journalists, actresses, tennis stars, etc. etc.' Rumbold wrote to Harold Nicolson in London about a large embassy party held on 17 January 1930 just a few weeks after Nicolson's departure from Berlin.[3] Four or five hundred people were there, so many that the Rumbolds had to extend the run of state rooms into the former billiard room. One guest was the author and playwright Edgar Wallace, one of the best-selling authors in Germany at the time.[4] Wallace visited Berlin, his 'pet city',

---

[*] Designated as an aerodrome in 1923, the D'Abernons had visited Tempelhof in August 1925; the first terminal building had been built in 1927. The aerodrome was to be vastly enlarged and reconstructed between 1936 and 1941 by the architect Ernst Sagebiel. It is no longer used for air traffic.

53. Sir Horace Rumbold arrives at the Metropol Theatre, Berlin with Charlie Chaplin on 10 March 1931.

frequently, preferring it 'to any other city in the world, outside London,[5] receiving journalists and theatrical producers at the Adlon. He did not, however, impress Rumbold who, along with his staff, had wondered at the ball whether Wallace was 'getting copy for a new story which might be entitled "The Embassy Mystery" or something of the kind. He struck me as very common,' he confided to Nicolson.[6] In contrast, in June that year Rumbold was able to tell his son that his own literary hero, John Galsworthy, had paid them a visit while in Berlin to give a broadcast, describing him as 'a nice man with no frills on him.'[7]

In stark contrast to his visit to the city a decade earlier when virtually no one had recognised him, on 9 March 1931 enormous crowds waited for Charlie Chaplin at Friedrichstrasse Station when he arrived in Berlin for the premiere of his latest film, *City Lights*. 'A large force of police was present both at the station, in the Unter den Linden and in front of the Adlon to protect him from his admirers. Even so he could hardly reach his hotel,' Rumbold told his son Tony.[8*] There were so many of Chaplin's fans outside the Adlon that Hedda Adlon remembered how, in an episode worthy of one of the 'Little Tramp's' films, because the buttons had been ripped off by souvenir hunters, Chaplin's trousers inadvertently began to descend once he was safely inside.[9] 'Your mother wouldn't rest until she got hold of him and he is coming to dine and do a play with us to-night. We shall attract a lot of attention,'[10] Rumbold continued. As he left after dinner, Chaplin treated the embassy staff assembled on the main staircase to a trademark twirl of an imaginary cane, and the Rumbolds' daughter, Constantia, gained his signature and a quick sketch of the 'Little Tramp' for her autograph book.[11] Amid large crowds,

* Tony followed his grandfather and father and entered the Foreign Office in 1935, eventually emulating his grandfather by becoming Ambassador to Austria from 1967 to 1970.

the Rumbolds accompanied Chaplin to the Metropol Theatre where Emmerich Kalman's operetta *Das Veilchen von Monmartre*† was playing. After the performance the Rumbolds went backstage to meet – and be photographed with – all the actors. Chaplin, who was staying in one of the VIP suites at the Adlon while in Berlin (to study German and film production methods), also met Albert Einstein and Marlene Dietrich, who had recently starred in the Berlin-made film *The Blue Angel*.

Rumbold and his staff had to cope with another prime ministerial visit in July 1931, Rumbold jadedly recording that although the visit had originally been scheduled for a fortnight earlier and had had to be changed at the last minute he 'never had a line of thanks either from the PM or from [Foreign Secretary Sir Arthur] Henderson for all my trouble and hospitality.'[12] Rumbold had met Ramsay MacDonald on his arrival at the railway station, worked with him in the Chancery and then gave a dinner party in his honour. Lady Rumbold was not in Berlin at the time to act as hostess, and the Ambassador recounted the proceedings to her in some detail:

> For the first time I had the big dining-room table bare of a cloth and the silver-gilt candelabra etc. with the flowers looked very well. We had, of course, to have a round table in the window. I put the Prime Minister opposite me and made his side the important side. He took in Frau Curtius and had Frau Stresemann on the other side.[13]

After dinner many more guests arrived, Rumbold introducing them to MacDonald, 'who really laid himself out to talk to all of them at considerable length. The result was there was always a queue of anxious colleagues waiting to be introduced.'[14] 'Everybody seemed delighted to have an opportunity of seeing each other again, and I was congratulated by innumerable people on the success of the party,'[15] which did not end until one in the morning. Unusually, the Prime Minister left for England by plane, from Tempelhof Aerodrome, escorted by three British aeroplanes which 'took off perfectly and disappeared into the distance in a V shaped formation, to the admiration of the Germans.'[16]

***

Away from these diplomatic duties and entertainments, the political atmosphere in Germany was rapidly changing for the worst. The relatively peaceful boom years of the late 1920s had dissolved into new economic and political misery for Germany on the back of the October 1929 stock market crash in the United States, the same month that Gustav Stresemann died suddenly from a stroke. In 1931 five major German banks crashed and thousands of German businesses folded, resulting in mass unemployment: of the world economies, Germany suffered the most in the Great Depression. Memorably described by Christopher Isherwood in his 1935 novel *Mr Norris Changes Trains*, extreme violence between rival political factions erupted on the streets and public places of the capital. One of those factions was the National Socialist Party under Adolf Hitler, who skilfully manipulated the dire economic and political situation to present himself as the solution to Germany's problems. In 1930 the ever-fragile Weimar Government collapsed, to be followed by

† *The Violet of Montmartre.*

a series of short-lived minority administrations. Rumbold strongly encouraged the support of the minority Government under Chancellor Heinrich Brüning against the enticing prospect of the National Socialists, about whom he had no illusions.

On 9 September 1930 Rumbold wrote to D'Abernon thanking him for sending him the third volume of his published diaries. Anticipating the results of the elections that coming Sunday, he reported that 'The National Socialists are certain to increase their representation (some people think they will get 50 or 60 seats): They are daily perpetrating outrages which must tend, in the long run, to disgust the moderate and order-loving German.'[17] His optimism was misplaced: the Nazis increased their seats in the Reichstag from twelve to one hundred and seven. Meanwhile, evidence was mounting that the measures set out in the Treaty of Versailles a dozen years before were being deliberately worn down. While the Embassy's Military Attaché Colonel Marshall-Cornwall reported breaches of agreements over rearmament that he was actually able to witness, there were growing German demands for an end to war reparation payments, for Germany's former colonies to be returned and for the issue of the 'Polish Corridor' be resolved in Germany's favour.

From the heart of the government district in Berlin, Rumbold reported to London the gradual electoral gains in Germany on the part of the National Socialists as they used the Weimar Republic's democratic process to gain power. To increase his influence, Hitler was already trying to make personal contact with the British, his close associate 'Putzi' Hanfstaengel approaching the British Military Attaché to find out whether he might bring the Nazi leader to lunch at the Embassy to meet the Ambassador. This Rumbold absolutely forbade: 'I won't see Hitler, and I won't let any member of my staff see Hitler.'[18] But he also understood and drew the British Government's attention to what it was about Hitler and the Nazis' abhorrent violent and anti-Semitic policies and propaganda that appealed to much of the German electorate: the Nazis' vitality, modernity and energy in contrast to the dullness and steadiness of the Weimar Republic; their calculated appeal to youth and discipline and to the very basic patriotic and local issues that had all been neglected by established political parties.[19]

Hitler's opponents came to believe that if he and the National Socialists were actually to come to power, events could have only one outcome: a second world war. Having witnessed mounting German nationalism before, Rumbold was fearful of the consequences. He glumly told his stepmother in December 1931:

> We have the regulation Xmas dinner for staff and shall be about 24
> – including one or two homeless individuals. I am giving the male
> members of staff who have establishments either a bottle of vintage port
> or a bottle of whisky and this ought to cheer them up. One needs a bit
> of cheering up these days as the economic outlook for Europe and the
> world in general is very depressing …. The world, indeed, seems to have
> gone mad. I except our own country and Italy.[20]

***

Rumbold kept in contact with Harold Nicolson after his departure from Berlin, and in January 1932 Nicolson returned to the capital on a private visit, staying again at the Prinz Albrecht Hotel and attending a large dinner at the Embassy on the 23rd, reporting to Vita that the traditional embassy formal dining protocol was unchanged: 'A vast banquet. Rows of state liveries, and the porter going flump with his mace when one came in. The Papal Legate in scarlet, the new French Ambassador with a conceited swing to his head. And all the usual appurtenances of a diplomatic dinner. I wore my little flag.'* But he noticed that something <u>had</u> changed: the atmosphere, which now felt sinister. 'Old Friedländer Fuld was there. She was dressed in a dowdy little shift – none of the emeralds and diamanté of the past. This is because she is afraid of Hitler who has said that if he comes into power he will get rid of all the Jews. Which includes Jewesses. Most disturbing.'[21]

Even so, Nicolson at least momentarily regretted his decision to leave the Embassy:

54. Crowds gathering outside the Presidential Palace on Wilhelmstrasse on 15 May 1932, looking northwards towards Pariser Platz; the Embassy's façade can be seen in the middle distance.

> I was warmly welcomed by my ex-colleagues. I sat there looking up the table through the gold candelabra upon those shirt fronts and ribbons. Well, well … I keep on reminding myself that if I had stayed in Diplomacy I should now be Minister at Montevideo and not pleased at all. Yet I cannot hide the fact that when I last sat at that table I was a person of consequence … [22]

He had found writing the gossip column 'Londoner's Diary' for the *Evening Standard* an unappealing task unworthy of his literary abilities. After their meeting in Berlin in 1929 Nicolson had kept up a friendship with Oswald Mosley, even joining his 'New Party'. Changing career again, for a time he diverted his literary talents into editing the Party's weekly journal *Action*, but when support for the New Party collapsed and Mosley's political inclinations began to embrace the fascist leanings[†] that Nicolson and Rumbold despised in Germany, Nicolson broke off with him.

Over the next few months the Nazi Party increased its grip on Germany while their supporters terrorised opponents on the streets of Berlin. Hitler's propaganda chief Joseph Goebbels' inflammatory speeches reverberated through the

* Nicolson's CMG.
† The British Union of Fascists was established on 1 October 1932.

government district as the National Socialists gradually achieved a majority in the Reichstag. As part of a coalition government, Hitler was finally made Chancellor of Germany on 30 January 1933; the public reception for him outside the Chancellery on Wilhelmstrasse that evening was rapturous. The French Ambassador André François-Ponçet watched the infamous, carefully stage-managed torchlight procession through Berlin to celebrate the Nazis' success 'with heavy heart and filled with foreboding.'[23] Emerging from the Tiergarten through the Brandenburg Gate, the procession passed the French Embassy on Pariser Platz and then turned right past the Adlon Hotel down Wilhelmstrasse. From the windows of number seventy the Rumbolds were also watching:

> From 8 pm till past midnight a continuous procession went past the Embassy, of Nazis in uniform and their admirers, bands, flags, torches, over 4 hours of it! The old President watched from his window, and a little further down the street the new Chancellor Hitler and his supporters stood on a balcony and had a stupendous ovation. On <u>our</u> steps, and perched high up on the ledge with the columns stood wild enthusiasts, singing all the old German hymns! Every now and then there were shouts of 'Germany awake', 'Down with the Jews', 'Heil Hitler!' It seemed as tho' the whole of Berlin was processing along the Wilhelm Str.[24]

Rumbold could hardly have forgotten watching another immense crowd outside the Embassy on a night eighteen years before, and, after watching for a time from the same windows he retreated, in disgust, to an inner room.[25]

* * *

Hitler did not wait long before taking action to bring about the new society he wished to see in Germany by consolidating the Nazis' grip on power: in the March elections, the party won forty-four per cent of the national vote. Rumbold recounted to London the round-up of Jews and communists, the closure of bars and nightclubs, how control was being gained over the police and how the very democratic process that had brought the new Chancellor to power was systematically being extinguished in favour of a merciless dictatorship. The journalists, writers, artists, conductors, scientists and performers who had made Germany – and Berlin in particular – such a centre of creativity over the past decade, began to flee the country. Many of them had enjoyed hospitality at the Embassy, the cultivated and urbane Count Kessler amongst them. The economic crash had badly affected his personal fortune, forcing him to sell his precious art collection. In March 1933 he fled to Paris where, in November 1937, he died, never to return to Germany.

Rumbold had refused to meet Adolf Hitler before he came to power. But as British Ambassador to Germany he now had no choice but to meet the new Chancellor, and did so at the presidential dinner for heads of foreign missions in Berlin hosted by Hindenburg on 8 February; they met again at the opening of the International Motor Show in Berlin, when Rumbold introduced Hitler to his daughter.[26] It must have been a peculiar sensation for Rumbold: at imperial balls and regattas he had witnessed the last few months of the pre-Great War Hohenzollern order and been introduced to the Emperor. Now he was forced to pay his respects to a German Chancellor 'of low origin',[27] little formal education, and of a character he could never have previously imagined.

On 27 February visitors on the upper floors of the Adlon overlooking the Pariser Platz and guests at a reception at the French Embassy opposite suddenly noticed a red glow to the north: the Reichstag was on fire. Rumbold witnessed it from close at hand: 'The cupola was glowing like a live coal and was a wonderful sight.'[28] The cause was apparently arson, on the part of a simple-minded Dutch communist sympathiser. But even if he had not been 'framed' for the crime (as many suspected), the event was a gift to the Nazi Government, allowing it to justify the declaration of a national emergency and clamp down on political opponents (rule by emergency decree having been permitted in certain circumstances by the Weimar Constitution). With the building in ruins, the new Government's Reichstag was opened at the Garrison Church in Potsdam on 21 March, a location replete with Prussian historical and military symbolism and the burial place of Hitler's hero, Frederick the Great of Prussia. The event was attended by the diplomatic corps, including Rumbold. The following day the displaced Reichstag met at the Kroll Opera House in Berlin and passed the enabling bill abrogating the Weimar Constitution; Hitler subsequently extended his power over all local authorities and states in Germany. The previous federal state was now unified and centralised, something that not even Bismarck had managed to achieve.

As all the trappings of the Nazis' dictatorship intensified around him – suppression of the free press, free speech and avant-garde artistic endeavour; persecution of those who did not, could not, or might not agree or fit in with the new state; random arrests and concentration camps – Rumbold reported that it was now the case in Berlin that 'nobody feels himself safe or able to talk or walk freely.'[29] 'The aspect of the streets during the last ten days certainly reminded me of the crisis preceding the war in 1914, the same crowds in Unter den Linden, the singing of 'Deutschland über Alles', alternating with the Nazi song, and the marching and counter-marching of Nazis and Stahlhelm with bands and flags,' he told Godfrey Thomas,[30] his colleague from the Embassy in the summer of 1914, now Private Secretary to the Prince of Wales.

The first major organised anti-Jewish demonstration in Berlin after the Nazis came to power took place in early April 1933 in the shape of an official boycott of Jewish shops, businesses, lawyers and doctors. Lady Ovey, the wife of Sir Esmond Ovey, Ambassador to Moscow, was staying with the Rumbolds at the time and she, Lady Rumbold and the Rumbolds' son Tony went to see for themselves what was happening on the Berlin streets. They were unable to gain entrance to Wertheim's department store, finding a huge crowd outside and Nazi soldiers blocking the doors. There were similar scenes along the other shopping streets, and Lady Rumbold was outraged.[31] Christopher Isherwood also witnessed these events, even unnervingly finding that one of the members of the Hitler Youth who was boycotting a Jewish shop was a former lover; the following month, a few days after watching the mass burning of 'decadent' books on the Opernplatz, he returned to England. The change of mood and behaviour in the course of a few months on the part of some of the population of Berlin was profoundly disturbing. Oswald Mosley and his wife Cimmie had been shocked by scenes of 'decadence and depravity' during their visit to nightclubs in Berlin in 1928. 'Yet', Mosley observed in retrospect and (as his son pointed out[32]) apparently without irony, 'within two or three years men in brown shirts were goose-stepping down these same streets around the Kurfürstendamm.'[33]

Rumbold again met Hitler on 11 May, the same day that Sir Robert Vansittart, the Permanent Secretary of the Foreign Office, had a meeting with the German Ambassador in London. Rumbold told Hitler to his face that the British Government strongly objected to his Government's treatment of Jews, but it was to no avail. Writing to Sir Clive Wigram, Private Secretary to King George V shortly before his departure from Berlin, Rumbold confessed that 'Many of us here feel as if we were living in a lunatic asylum.'[34] His candid report to the Foreign Office in London of 26 April 1933 summarising the evils of Nazism became known as the 'Mein Kampf Despatch'.[35] By now Rumbold had spent nearly five years in Germany; his successor was announced in early May 1933. In traditional fashion, there were a number of leave-taking ceremonies. At a farewell dinner at the Embassy on 26 June the embassy staff presented Rumbold with a Berlin porcelain statuette of King Frederick the Great of Prussia. The twenty-eighth of June saw a farewell visit to Hitler, and a lunch given by the Anglo-German Society.[36] But Rumbold's formal farewell to the German Head of State, President von Hindenburg, could not take place at the Presidential Palace on Wilhelmstrasse as the President was at his country residence at Neudeck* in East Prussia. Unusually, therefore, the Rumbolds travelled there to take their leave, accompanied by the Embassy's Counsellor Basil Newton, who had succeeded Harold Nicolson in 1930. The Rumbolds lunched with Hindenburg, who presented the departing Ambassador with the insignia of the first class of the German Red Cross and a signed photograph of himself in a large silver frame.[37]

'[W]e have lived through the most epoch-making times here', Lady Rumbold reported to her mother in March 1933.[38] She, her husband and daughter left Berlin on 1 July. Given the political circumstances in Germany, it was neither an auspicious nor a satisfying time for Rumbold to depart: he confessed to his successor that 'I leave Berlin with a sense of depression or rather deception, due … to the reflection that the work on which I have been engaged for the last four or five years is, so to speak, on the scrapheap.'[39]

***

Harold Nicolson, who had long ago set aside his initial bemused opinions of the Ambassador, described Rumbold in the dedication to his book *Diplomacy* as 'an ideal diplomatist.'[40] Separately he opined that 'The Governments to which [Rumbold] was accredited became aware that here was a man without prejudice or vanity, a man of complete integrity, a man whom they could trust to understand and report their point of view, a man whose every word was riveted in concrete.'[41] Writing specifically of his time in Berlin, Nicolson described Rumbold as

> perhaps too domestic to enjoy society to the extent which his father had enjoyed it, but he was a very hospitable man. It was a pleasure to him, in a vulgar world such as the Berlin of 1929, to maintain the old patrician

* Now Ogrodzieniec, Poland.

standards and to show the profiteers of the Weimar Republic that it was possible to have grandeur without extravagance and elegance without ostentation. The influence which he exercised in Germany was due in no small part to the atmosphere of effortless distinction which he and Lady Rumbold created at the Berlin Embassy. The politicians, bankers and journalists who attended his receptions would feel that they passed from a world of strife and falsity into something which, in its age-long authenticity, was absolutely certain of itself.[42]

In semi-retirement, Rumbold was to enjoy two further non-ambassadorial diplomatic appointments and wrote a vivid memoir of the Berlin summer of 1914, *The War Crisis in Berlin*, first published in 1940. He died in May 1941. He had lived long enough to witness the German bombing of London in the months following the Battle of Britain, sincerely hoping that the RAF would reciprocate and flatten the centre of Berlin.[43] After his death Foreign Secretary Anthony Eden confided that he had deplored the Government's decision to move Rumbold from Berlin at such a critical juncture in 1933, 'when he was doing such wonderful service. No-one ever had a clearer perspective of the dangers …'[44]

But even if Rumbold's two successors as British Ambassador to Germany had enjoyed his same perspective on events, in the end they were unable to have much influence over what was to come.

CHAPTER 14
1933–1936: 'SHINING EMBASSY'

55. Sir Eric Phipps photographed in diplomatic dress in the Embassy's staircase hall on 18 October 1933, the day he presented his credentials to President Hindenburg.

Dapper in his diplomatic uniform, on 18 October 1933 Sir Eric Phipps was photographed in the Embassy's staircase hall next to the splashing fountain. 'This morning I presented to President Hindenburg the letter whereby the King has been graciously pleased to accredit me to him as His Majesty's Ambassador,'[1] he proudly recorded in his diary for that day. He had arrived in Berlin on 2 August, a month after Rumbold's departure. Another member of a diplomatic family, Phipps was almost fifty-eight; having entered the diplomatic service in 1899, he had spent much of his career in Paris.

The early period of Hitler's chancellorship was a time of great diplomatic turmoil, exemplified by events just four days before Phipps presented his credentials. During a routine luncheon in the Embassy for British consular officers based in Germany, the disturbing news came through that Germany had withdrawn its delegates from the Disarmament Conference in Geneva and from the League of Nations: D'Abernon's acclaimed diplomatic achievements were being reversed. Lunch was abandoned as all were put to work translating Hitler's proclamation and radio broadcast, and reporting the news to London.[2] Phipps had his first personal interview with Hitler at the Reich Chancellery on 24 October,[3] encountering for the first time the torrential and more than occasionally frenzied monologues that were to punctuate their relationship.

In retrospect, it is clear that Adolf Hitler set out from the beginning to take whatever means were necessary to scrap the terms of the Treaty of Versailles and obtain Germany's economic, military and political rehabilitation and future growth and expansion (*Lebensraum*). That this enterprise would include concerted efforts to exterminate an entire race of people and others classified as undesirables, together with the attempted German domination of firstly Eastern Europe, then

Western Europe – if not the world – is also clear. But those involved in the 1930s were not possessed of a crystal ball. While many (including Sir Horace Rumbold) were distrustful of Hitler's motives from the start – and they were, of course, right – others agreed that the Treaty of Versailles had treated Germany unfairly and believed that Hitler's will might somehow be contained, particularly if pernicious influences from what were perceived to be the less 'moderate' members of his entourage could be removed. For the generation that had fought in and/or had lost friends and relatives in the carnage of the Great War, the idea of another confrontation with Germany, another war only twenty years on, this time with more sophisticated weapons and almost certainly extensively deployed on civilian populations from the air, was unthinkable.

Phipps was presented with a challenging task for a British Ambassador to Germany: the necessity, as the UK's representative on the spot, to manage these varying attitudes and to deal directly with an increasingly unpalatable totalitarian regime in a traditional ambassadorial way. In so doing he naturally had to undertake the same type of entertaining and representational work that Harold Nicolson was to later describe in his book on diplomacy[4] with an administration whose deeds soon confirmed all Phipps' worst fears about its dangerous character. Traditional-style diplomatic cocktail parties in Berlin during the increasingly oppressive atmosphere and coarsening of cultural life in the Nazi era must undeniably have been difficult to endure, 'with their accompanying conversations, restricted to enquiries about health, travel, other parties and petty gossip,'[5] while diplomatic dinners, according to the American Ambassador (a university academic), were devoid of intellect, as 'no one ever feels free to say anything about the fields of history and literary criticism, because nobody knows history and literature and because no one trusts anyone else.'[6]

Nazi Germany brought another set of challenges for Phipps and his colleagues in the Embassy and Consulate-General and consular staff in Hamburg, Munich and elsewhere: the perpetual need for consular assistance for British citizens. In this new political world many foreigners inadvertently fell foul of the increasingly authoritarian conduct of the Nazi Government and its numerous acolytes on the streets, uniformed or not, operating as thugs on its behalf on an amateur as well as professional basis. Anyone could get into serious trouble simply for failing to acknowledge a passing member of the military; on one occasion a member of the embassy staff was attacked on Unter den Linden for failing to salute a column of SA 'Brownshirts.'[7]* Even foreign journalists were at risk: in October 1933 Phipps became involved in the case of *The Daily Telegraph*'s correspondent in Munich, Noël Panter, who was arrested and charged with treason merely for reporting a parade before Hitler of 20,000 SA members at Kelheim in Bavaria.[8] Nor, increasingly, can the embassy staff have been unaware of growing rumours about the horrors daily being perpetrated on the very doorstep of Berlin in the concentration camps at Oranienburg and Sachsenhausen, and, just a kilometre to the south of the Embassy, in the state security offices on Prinz Albrecht Strasse. Added to this was the increasingly pervasive, violent and sinister anti-Jewish propaganda being pasted up in the streets.

* The *Sturmabteilung*, a uniformed paramilitary army protecting the National Socialist Party.

Germany's withdrawal from the International Disarmament Conference called for a major international diplomatic response, and on 19 February 1934 Viscount Cranborne of the Foreign Office and Anthony Eden, Lord Privy Seal, arrived in Berlin from Paris for talks. On 21 February Phipps and his wife gave a 'small luncheon' at the Embassy;[9] amongst the guests was the German Chancellor himself. Others included Foreign Minister von Neurath, the Propaganda Minister Joseph Goebbels, Reich Minister Rudolf Hess, Sir William Strang (then Head of the League of Nations Section at the Foreign Office in London), long-serving Press Attaché Timothy Breen, and Embassy Counsellor Basil Newton. Eden recalled that

> This was, I believe, the first occasion on which Hitler had been to a meal
> in a foreign embassy. I can still recall the scene as Cranborne and I stood
> watching the German leaders file into the Embassy drawing room. They
> made an incongruous pattern. 'Athos, Porthos and Aramis', murmured
> Cranborne to me, looking at the Chancellor, von Neurath and Goebbels.
> Hess was quieter and less conspicuous behind his black brows.[10]

First Secretary Ivone Kirkpatrick had been deputed by Phipps to find out what Hitler would like to eat for lunch; challengingly for hosts in the 1930s the Chancellor was both a vegetarian and a teetotaller. Hitler's meal was served completely separately from the other guests and comprised 'a vegetarian soup, a dish of mixed vegetables and a vanilla soufflé.'[11] The frigid atmosphere between Hitler and Eden – who were seated next to each other – was broken when they found a subject they had in common: the Great War, and Hitler invited Eden to come to stay with him at 'his cottage on the Austrian frontier'.[12][†] Eden also talked with Goebbels, and after lunch he had another long conversation with Hitler. Eden remembered that

> There had been large crowds outside the Embassy during the greater part
> of the day, especially while Hitler was there. As he left they gave him a
> vociferous greeting. Clearly, this man had a hold upon their imagination
> far exceeding that of any of his predecessors. For the first time I had a
> glimpse of what the fanatical devotion of a German crowd could be.
> Hess and Goebbels had left after luncheon and I had been amused to
> notice that Goebbels had watched closely from the window to see what
> kind of reception Hess was given, before venturing out himself to get
> his acclaim.[13]

One person irritated at not having been invited to this event was Joachim von Ribbentrop, who, having joined the National Socialist Party soon after it had come to power, had moved up in the world from being a mere Berlin wine and spirit merchant by appointment to various embassies. His self-proclaimed specialist British knowledge and connections had impressed Hitler to the extent that he had been used for some pseudo-diplomatic missions, including a recent exploratory visit to London to meet Prime Minister Stanley Baldwin. Eden had refused his invitation to dinner at his home in Dahlem, and Ribbentrop's pride had evidently been dented:

> I hear the Chancellor is lunching with Mr. Eden at the British
> Ambassador's. Might I suggest that he mention conversationally to Mr.
> Eden that I have the Chancellor's complete confidence in questions of

---

† The Berghof, near Berchtesgaden in Bavaria, close to the Austrian frontier.

foreign policy …? Otherwise I should be in a false position vis à vis Eden, and indeed Baldwin and my other English friends, especially as I have the feeling that Phipps, with the friendly agreement of our own officials, wants as far as possible to exclude me ….[14]

That feeling was correct, but considering that Ribbentrop and his wife had been guests at British Embassy functions in a private capacity long before Hitler had come to power, the latter's exclusion of Ribbentrop must, understandably, have been frustrating. Ribbentrop was, however, placated by being allowed to attend another of Hitler's meetings with Eden but he was not permitted to take part in the discussion.[15] Von Neurath visited the Embassy again the following day for a further session with Eden, and Phipps felt that the meetings had generally gone well. Eden made the most of his remaining time in Berlin to visit museums and then, with Phipps, paid a call on the German President, von Hindenburg. For Eden, this was a very strange experience indeed: 'Every single male member of the family, with whom [he] had spent [his] life before the war, was dead, wounded or captured', and yet here he was paying a call on 'the man who had overshadowed the enemy scene.'[16]

One of the ambassadorial duties Nicolson described in his book on diplomacy was that of getting to know the government in the country to which ambassadors were posted. Accordingly, as evidenced in his diaries and despatches to London, Phipps attended to this duty with the members of the progressively unpleasant and frightening Nazi regime. Amongst his hosts was former Great War flying ace Hermann, now General, Goering, President of the Reichstag and Commander-in-Chief of the German air force. The description of the once handsome but now obese Goering recorded by Martha Dodd, daughter of the American Ambassador, was characteristically full of cold hatred. He looked

podgy and ridiculous from afar, but close up he is more than that. Of medium height, his once slender body has been transformed into a huge paunchy blob of flesh, lumpy and protruding in places. The once finely-cut face is now lost in rolls of fat; the cheeks like swollen growths under wide-set blue eyes, which are as cold as snakes; the chin a curious protuberance; all line, beauty or bone structure vanished in a coarse and florid cushion euphemistically called a face.[17]

Phipps' own opinion of Goering, his tastes and interests, was sardonic, particularly after being forced to endure one of Goering's 'Germanic' events that were often on his favourite theme: hunting. On 10 June 1934, at his country residence, Carinhall,* Goering proudly showed off to his guests his new bison enclosure and plans for re-establishing a kind of German primeval forest suitable for native 'German' animals. Phipps described this particular occasion to his colleagues in London with such sarcasm and biting wit that it became known as the 'Bison Despatch', one of many first-hand accounts Phipps provided of the behaviour of the upper echelons of the Nazi regime at the events he attended. The following day, in a report to Foreign Secretary Sir John Simon, Phipps summed up his feelings:

The chief impression was that of the most pathetic naïveté of General Göring who showed us his toys like a big, fat, spoilt child: his primeval woods, his bison and birds, his shooting-box and lake and bathing beach,

---

* Named after his late first wife.

his blond 'private secretary',[†] his wife's mausoleum and swans and sarsen stones, all mere toys to satisfy his varying moods, and all, or so nearly all, as he was careful to explain, Germanic. And then I remembered there were other toys, less innocent though winged, and these might some day be launched on their murderous mission in the same childlike spirit and with the same childlike glee.[18]

A few days later, the journalist Bella Fromm was one of Phipps' embassy luncheon guests when Goering arrived late, his self-importance characteristically coming to the fore:

Beginning at the door, he moved his paunch gaily across the room, medals and decorations tinkling and clattering, he shouted to the hostess, 'Personal call from Venice. … Had to wait till the Führer was on the wire … I was all set to follow him to Venice, in case he needed me. You know what he said? 'For God's sake, stay where you are. I am coming back earlier than I had planned' … Phipps' monocle glittered in his frozen mask. François-Poncet clenched his teeth in a broad grin. The servants tiptoed around the table.[19]

Amusing all this might have seemed to those with a keen sense of the absurd, the true murderous nature of the regime was horrifyingly demonstrated just a fortnight later when Hitler ordered the immediate assassination of a number of senior members of the SA on charges of their plotting against the Government — amongst them the SA Chief of Staff himself, Ernst Röhm — during what became known as the 'Night of the Long Knives'; an event that gave Hitler an excuse to settle old scores with a variety of perceived enemies, the final death tally was at least eighty-five.

In Nazi Germany the task of keeping embassy contact lists up to date must have been something of a challenge. Preserved amongst Phipps' archives is an embassy 'Register of Cards' for 1933 which routinely lists VIPs of the time, including Hess, Goering and von Ribbentrop, together with their addresses. Entries for several other contacts are crossed through and annotated with the words 'dead' [from natural causes or not?], 'suicided' [sic] and 'hiding abroad'. Included in the lists are details for Ernst Röhm and Gruppenführer [Karl] Ernst, both entries crossed through and annotated with the single word 'SHOT'.[20]

At a private dinner in mid-July Phipps complained to von Blomberg, Minister of Defence, about the murder of former Chancellor Kurt von Schleicher and his wife during the bloodletting, but Blomberg's rejoinder to Phipps was that, in contrast to Germany, 'defeated and crushed' and 'suffering from fifteen years of "Socialist" government', England 'was a happy island, far from external strife'. That night Phipps angrily recorded in his diary that 'I persist in believing … that our high standard of civilization is not solely due to the salt water surrounding us.'[21] He also noted that there had been a recent change in atmosphere in the city, Hitler and von Neurath motoring along a deserted Wilhelmstrasse outside the Embassy as they arrived at the Adlon Hotel for their final visit to the Siamese royal family (on a state visit to Berlin).[22] The crowd was held back and the local population forbidden to open any windows.

† Actually his mistress, the actress Emmy Sonnemann.

On 2 August 1934 eighty-six-year-old President Paul von Hindenburg died, and as a mark of respect the Embassy flew the Union Jack above the building's portico at half-mast. The last link with the Prussia of the nineteenth century and the imperial world the Embassy, its former residents and staff had witnessed before the Great War was buried on 7 August. That September Hitler's grip on power became absolute as he proclaimed himself both President and Chancellor of Germany.

56. Sir John Simon, Sir Eric Phipps and Anthony Eden on the Embassy's steps on 25 March 1935 on their way to meet Adolf Hitler.

* * *

'Germany does not want war and is prepared to renounce it absolutely as a method of settling her disputes with her neighbours, provided she is given real equality ….'[23] the Liberal Peer Lord Lothian confidently stated in an article in *The Times* on 1 February 1935 following a brief visit to Berlin and a discussion with Hitler (apparently at the instigation of Ribbentrop) that lasted more than two hours. Phipps was wearily sardonic about this amateur diplomacy: 'The fact is British missionaries of peace of varying shades of political thought seem to come here in growing numbers, and, after conversations with various personages, return to England with some plan of their own whereby peace is to be ensured for a given number of years.'[24] In Berlin for a dinner of the Association of Rhodes Scholars,* Lothian was able to report to Phipps the worrying claim Hitler had made that the German navy was now one-third the size of Great Britain's.[25] Relaying Hitler's professed desire to speak directly with a leading British politician, he suggested that Sir John Simon discuss the possibility of a British–French–German air pact, and so a future meeting was arranged. 'Berlin is agog at the prospect of the approaching visit of Sir John Simon and Mr. Eden,'[26] Phipps reported. The visit was fixed for 7 March, but Hitler postponed it, angered by a British Government White Paper on increasing public expenditure on rearmament. Effectively tearing up the Treaty of Versailles, on 16 March Hitler suddenly announced the reintroduction of conscription in Germany and the creation of a large national army of thirty-six divisions. In these inauspicious circumstances, after some debate on the British side, the ministerial visit finally went ahead for 24 March, with Simon, Eden (who stayed at the Adlon Hotel), Lord Cranborne, William Strang and Ralph Wigram forming the British delegation. Dining at the Embassy the night they arrived, the party held meetings at the Reich Chancellery over 25 and 26 March.

The talks began at 10.30 in the morning of 25 March, and went on until 7.30 that evening, with a break for lunch at von Neurath's villa in the grounds

* Lothian had been General Secretary of the Rhodes Trust since 1925 and, as a close friend of Lady Astor, a member of the amorphous 'Cliveden Set'.

57. Crowds witness Hitler's arrival at the British Embassy on 26 March 1935.

of the Foreign Ministry. On the German side were Hitler, Baron von Neurath, Ribbentrop (Hitler's 'Special Commissioner for Disarmament Affairs') and Paul Schmidt, Hitler's interpreter. Phipps attended with the British delegation. At 6.30 p.m. some two hundred expectant representatives of the international press corps who had waited for an hour in the British Embassy ballroom were given an insipid statement about progress so far.[27] That night, at a state dinner at the Reich President's Residence on Wilhelmstrasse, during renewed dinner party talk about their shared Great War experiences, Eden and Hitler intriguingly discovered that they were opposite each other in the German and British trenches on the same day, 21 March 1918. The French Ambassador, who had also served on the Western Front, was saddened to hear this: 'You missed him? You should have shot him,' he later told Eden.[28]

The talks continued the following day, this time the British taking their turn to host some fifty guests for lunch.[29] This was Hitler's second visit to the Embassy, and was photographed entering the building and standing on the Embassy's steps, while crowds of spectators once again lined Wilhelmstrasse. His entire cabinet were there, including von Ribbentrop, Goering and his fiancée, the actress Frau Sonnemann, Herr and Frau Hess, von Neurath, the economist Hjalmar Schacht, and Dr and Frau Goebbels. The seating plan records one large table in the centre, surrounded by four smaller ones. Naturally, Hitler had pride of place at the large table, between Frau Hess and Lady Phipps, with Phipps, von Neurath and Sir John Simon opposite.[30]

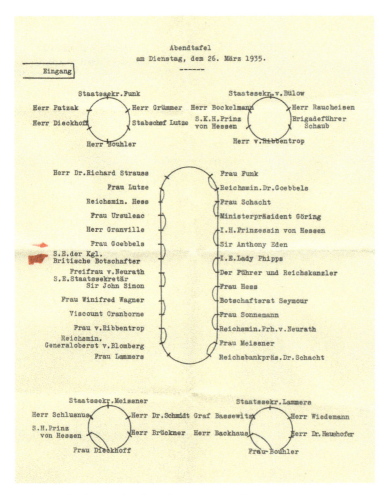

Abendtafel
am Dienstag, dem 26. März 1935.

Eingang

Staatssekr.Funk

Herr Patzak   Herr Grümmer   Herr Bockelmann   Herr Raucheisen
Herr Dieckhoff   Stabschef Lutze   S.K.H.Prinz   Brigadeführer
                    von Hessen   Schaub

Herr Bouhler   Herr v.Ribbentrop

Staatssekr.v.Bülow

Herr Dr.Richard Strauss   Frau Funk
Frau Lutze   Reichsmin.Dr.Goebbels
Reichsmin. Hess   Frau Schacht
Frau Ursuleac   Ministerpräsident Göring
Herr Granville   I.H.Prinzessin von Hessen
Frau Goebbels   Sir Anthony Eden
S.E.der Kgl.
Britische Botschafter   I.E.Lady Phipps
Freifrau v.Neurath
S.E.Staatssekretär
Sir John Simon   Der Führer und Reichskanzler
Frau Winifred Wagner   Frau Hess
Viscount Cranborne   Botschaftsrat Seymour
Frau v.Ribbentrop   Frau Sonnemann
Reichsmin.
Generaloberst v.Blomberg   Reichsmin.Frh.v.Neurath
Frau Lammers   Frau Meissner
                 Reichsbankpräs.Dr.Schacht

Staatssekr.Meissner   Staatssekr.Lammers

Herr Schlusnus   Herr Dr.Schmidt Graf Bassewitz   Herr Wiedemann
S.H.Prinz
von Hessen   Herr Brückner   Herr Backhaus   Herr Dr.Haushofer

Frau Dieckhoff   Frau Bouhler

58. Seating plan for a meal at the Embassy on 26 March 1935.

As *The Times* reported, there was no agreement reached between the two parties, but this had not apparently been the intention. 'The conversations have been carried on in the frankest and friendliest spirit and have resulted in a complete clarification of the respective points of view. It was established that the aim of the policy of both governments is to secure and strengthen the peace of Europe by promoting international cooperation.'[31] At the time Sir John Simon stated that his intention was to hear what Hitler himself had to say from his own lips so that he could present these views to the British Cabinet,[32] an approach optimistically reliant upon Hitler's honesty. That night Hitler gave a smaller dinner and reception at the Reich Chancellery before Eden and Cranborne left for talks in Moscow, with Simon returning to London the following day.[33] Writing on 28 March, Phipps reported that throughout the visit Hitler was 'charming and even seductive' and 'most friendly, civilized and reasonable'; he did not show the visitors the other side to him, 'the tiger side.'[34] The Germans seemed to be impressed that the British Foreign Secretary had come to Berlin, but Eden thought that, from the British point of view, the visit as a whole had been disappointing. In retrospect Simon

felt 'no doubt that we were right to go, but I am equally clear that Hitler never intended to agree to any limitation on Germany's totals and designs. The main advantage of the meeting was that we received more information as to the extent to which German rearmament had gone.'[35]

***

59. Hitler leaves the British Embassy on 26 March 1935 as seen in a press cutting from a German newspaper.

As a matter of course the Nazi Government and its members organised official entertainments to which foreign diplomats were invited, events that were of a very different character from the elegant imperial balls at the Royal Schloss. Phipps and the French Ambassador were guests at a dinner celebrating Goering's impending marriage to Emmy Sonnemann at which their host boastfully displayed his characteristic unwillingness to distinguish between his personal property and that of the German state, particularly where art treasures were concerned. Goering

> showed us a series of magnificent pictures by old masters which, he told us with pride, he had requisitioned from the Kaiser Friedrich Museum.[*] The Director had, it seems, objected to this raid on public treasures of which he is the guardian, but General Goering said that he had been implacable and had threatened to take away twice as many pictures if those he had chosen were not brought round to his 'palace' the next morning.[36†]

On 9 April Phipps attended an opera performance on the eve of Goering's marriage, the happy couple unselfconsciously occupying the box at the State Opera House formerly reserved for the Emperor and Empress. Indeed, Phipps drily remarked in his diary that in Berlin

> a visitor … might well have thought that the monarchy had been restored and that he had stumbled upon preparations for a royal wedding. The streets were decorated; all traffic in the interior of the city was suspended for about seven hours; over thirty-thousand members of the par-military formations lined the streets, whilst two hundred military aircraft circled the sky.[37]

Phipps went to the marriage ceremony and reception at what had become one of the Nazis' favourite Berlin watering holes, the Kaiserhof. Conveniently located

---

[*] Now the Bode Museum, Berlin.
[†] Goering's rapacious attitude towards art collecting was to be given full rein following the Anschluss with Austria and Germany's subsequent invasion of much of the rest of Continental Europe; his siphoning up of art treasures, many of them from Jewish collectors, came to be conducted on an industrial scale.

opposite the Chancellery, Hitler had adopted the famous 'padded, sombre, luxurious'[38] nineteenth-century hotel as his main headquarters before coming to power.

The streets outside the Embassy were thronged with eager crowds – as they always were – for Hitler's birthday, 20 April: the American Ambassador recorded how, on his way like other ambassadors to sign the customary book of congratulations in the Presidential Palace on Wilhelmstrasse, he came across 'tens of thousands of Germans, men, women and children, [standing] behind ropes on both sides of the street for two whole blocks, waiting for a glimpse of the Fuhrer ...'[39] But that

60. Sir Eric and Lady Phipps greet guests at the Embassy's Silver Jubilee party on 13 May 1935.

May the Silver Jubilee of King George V enabled the British to hold a series of national celebrations of their own. The English Church was packed on the 12th for a thanksgiving service at which Phipps read the lesson in a repeat of the same service held at St Paul's Cathedral in London earlier that week.[40] Out of 1,200 invitations to members of the British community in Berlin, some seven hundred guests attended a large party in the Embassy for the Jubilee. Some photographs survive from this event, showing Sir Eric and Lady Phipps (wearing a boldly patterned full-length dress) waiting to greet arriving guests, probably in the front drawing room.

With the title 'Shining Embassy', the diary section 'London Day by Day' of the *Daily Telegraph* for 29 August 1935 reported that 'The Embassy in Berlin has taken the lead in a campaign for a brighter Wilhelmstrasse. The Embassy has just been repainted,* and [the] picture today shows it in striking contrast to a rather drab series of official buildings. Its pillars are a dazzling white, and its window boxes – probably the only ones in the street – are green.'† The appearance of the building in the 1930s can very briefly be seen in an amateur colour home movie taken by American impresario Hall Clovis,[41] looking south along Wilhelmstrasse from the junction with Unter den Linden, a lone unadorned building amidst a sea of swastika banners. What is ominously clear from photographs and films from the Nazi period is how conspicuous the British Embassy (and other foreign embassies) must have seemed in the Berlin cityscape, when most other buildings in the capital – especially those in the government quarter and along Wilhelmstrasse – were festooned with the stark red-black-and-white emblems of the Third Reich. The city was undergoing many architectural changes, including the demolition or modernisation of a number of government buildings on Wilhelmstrasse. One of the most noticeable changes was the felling of all the trees along the Unter

---

* As requested by Phipps in late 1934 (see Chapter 15).
† This seems inaccurate: no window boxes appear in any extant photographs from this time.

den Linden that had given the avenue its name, to be replaced by columns and appropriately German Biedermeier-style street lamps, rendering the avenue more suitable for wide military parades. The columns would be put to full practical use during the Berlin Olympic Games in 1936.

***

Much to the derision of the British press, Unity Mitford, one of the daughters of Lord Redesdale, had fallen hook line and sinker for the trappings and ideology of the Nazi regime. In the autumn of 1933, under the initial influence of Hitler's close associate 'Putzi' Hanfstaengel, she had visited the 'new' Germany of the Nazis with her elder sister Diana. Spending much time in Munich, she had contrived to meet Hitler himself, whom she hero-worshipped, as well as a number of senior members of the Nazi hierarchy. Beginning to spend more time in Germany than in England, she was occasionally invited to the British Embassy. Lady Phipps remembered her appearing at a luncheon party there as a

> Deutsches Mädchen battleship of a woman, walking upstairs into the drawing room, and gave a Nazi salute. Eric was a small man, he stood on tiptoe and reached up to shake her hand which made it a bit ridiculous. Eric refused to let it influence the lunch party. She wanted urgently to talk about it all, she made it sound incredible, her story of sitting next to [Hitler's] table, determined to meet him. It was unlikely to work, Hitler was prudish, afraid of girls. I remember her telling me that her favourite among Nazis was Streicher. She brushed aside my protests, and said Jews were traitors.[42]

At first, Unity's parents were coldly angry about their daughters' visit to Germany (they attended the 1933 Nazi Party Congress at Nuremberg, the first since the Nazis had come to power). 'I suppose you know without being told how absolutely horrified Muv[‡] and I were to think of you and Bobo[§] accepting any form of hospitality from people we regard as a murderous gang of pests. That you should associate yourself with such people is a source of utter misery to both of us ...,'[43] Lord Redesdale told Diana. But the two sisters were not alone in Britain in their sympathy for the new regime. To add to the numerous historic royal connections between Germany and the United Kingdom, many aristocratic families had a strong affinity with Germany stretching over several generations, with a long tradition of sending children to Germany to be 'finished' while learning the language and absorbing German culture in one of the country's great historical cities. Violet Bonham-Carter, for example, had been 'finished' in Dresden and Paris, and Unity and Diana's brother Tom studied in Germany and Austria. As well as sympathy for Germany's perceived unfair treatment by the Treaty of Versailles and subsequent overbearing attitude of the French, in the early years of the Nazi regime Hitler's policies were not universally regarded with total negativity but with interest in the way he seemed to be leading his country out of the economic doldrums, and with some degree of success.

‡ The Mitfords' nickname for Sydney, Lady Redesdale.
§ The Mitfords' nickname for Unity.

At the small school in Munich at which Unity was learning German, several of her fellow well-bred English student colleagues had fallen for 'storms',* the British Consul in Munich's widow later recalling that 'Lots of English girls got tied up with SS men, you know, the boots, the red leather of their cars. We had a lot of trouble,'[44] a point echoed by Lady Phipps: '… these sloppy English girls were always having affairs with dreadful SS types, and Eric had the trouble of clearing it up. If you were at all snobbish you asked the Ambassador for help' (rather than his more lowly consular staff).[45] That was exactly what the Redesdales did in January 1935, travelling to Berlin and checking in at the Adlon. Lady Phipps remembered them as 'distraught parents,'[46] but it was to no avail. Both Unity and her father were guests at a lunch given by the Phipps on 26 October 1935, Unity seated next to Ivone Kirkpatrick, her father a safe distance away at the other end of the table.[47] At another dinner in Munich the same month, with the excuse that she had to meet Hitler's arriving train, Unity suddenly rose and left. Sorrowfully, Lord Redesdale turned to a fellow guest: 'I'm normal, my wife is normal, but my daughters are each more foolish than the other. What do you say about my daughter, isn't it very sad?'[48] His patience was wearing thin. Meeting the British Consul in Munich, St Clair Gainer, he pleaded, 'Can't you persuade Unity to go away?'[49]

After falling headlong in love with the British Union of Fascists leader Oswald Mosley, Unity's elder sister the society beauty Diana Mitford had notoriously divorced the husband with whom she had visited Berlin in 1929. Mosley's wife Cimmie (née Curzon), with whom he had visited Berlin and the Embassy in 1928, died of peritonitis in May 1933, but his passionate affair with Diana continued (even though Mosley was also unfaithful to her). Diana visited Germany several times following her trip with Unity in 1933, and she claimed gradually to have become a close confidante of Adolf Hitler himself. She had also become friendly with Magda Goebbels, the wife of Hitler's Propaganda Minister. Mosley and Diana decided to marry, but did not want the fact to become known to the British press, whose demand for stories about the Mitfords, Mosley and their apparent fascist inclinations was voracious. Performing the ceremony at the English Church in Berlin would hardly have been practical in this regard and might well have proved difficult, since Diana was a divorcée. According to Diana herself,[50] the couple had wished to get married in Paris, but advance notice of this would have been posted up by the Consulate there, thereby publicising the forthcoming event. But then the British Consul in Munich told her that there was a reciprocal arrangement in Germany whereby British and German subjects could be married by the other country's registrars.

Magda Goebbels offered the use of her own home for the marriage, which took place on 6 October 1936 at the Goebbels' official ministerial residence on the recently renamed 20 Hermann Goering Strasse, a short distance from Wilhelmstrasse, on the Tiergarten side of the Chancellery gardens, and not far from the British Embassy.† Diana remembered standing with Unity in an upstairs room

* Stormtroopers.
† Successive changes to the name of the street that lay between the Tiergarten and the rear of what were once the gardens leading from the government buildings on the western side of Wilhelmstrasse reflect political changes. From the 1860s it was named Königgrätzerstrasse, after the Great War Budapesterstrasse, then Friedrich Ebert Strasse. The Nazis changed it to Hermann Goering Strasse, and later it reverted to Ebertstrasse.

looking down into the Chancellery gardens seeing Hitler walking towards the house: 'the leaves were turning yellow and there was bright sunshine. Behind him came an adjutant carrying a box and some flowers. M‡ was already downstairs.'[51] As well as Hitler, the few people present included Joseph and Magda Goebbels. The wedding breakfast was held at the Goebbels' villa at Schwanenwerder, and then, after hearing Hitler address the crowds at the Sportspalast there followed an intimate dinner with the Chancellor, rounded off by a stormy wedding night at the Kaiserhof Hotel. Hitler gave Diana a silver-framed photograph of himself as a wedding present.

61. Hermann Goering and his wife Emmy leave the English Church in Berlin after a Memorial Ceremony for King George V on 28 January 1936, from *The Illustrated London News.*

***

In January 1936 the happy Silver Jubilee celebrations of the previous May gave way to mourning for King George V's death; on hearing of his estranged cousin's last illness, the seventy-six-year-old exiled former Emperor Wilhelm II had telegraphed Queen Mary to express his sympathies. Attended by Hitler, on 28 January the Embassy held the King's 'funeral' service for the diplomatic corps and the German Government at the English Church, which the previous November had celebrated its fiftieth anniversary. Despite occasional financial problems, by this stage the church had become 'one of the most flourishing congregations in the jurisdiction of Northern and Central Europe,'[52] to the extent that a new Lady Chapel had been erected earlier that year. There was an additional service for members of the British community, and the church was packed. In the time-honoured custom, members of the German Establishment paid calls on the Ambassador to express their condolences. The visitors included General Goering, who, standing in Phipps' office in the Embassy overlooking the street noticed a large crowd gathered outside. Suddenly (as Phipps drily noted) Goering remarked, 'It is curious, but wherever I go it is always the same thing!'[53]

Two months later Hitler gave orders for the German army to reoccupy the Rhineland as the first move in a deadly game of international brinkmanship that would culminate in the German invasion of Poland in September 1939 and the Second World War.

‡ Mosley.

CHAPTER 15
1936–1937: 'Mayfair Rushing Hitlerwards'

'One of the best places in Berlin from which to watch the many processions on Saturday was … the British Embassy …. As a private spectator [Phipps] spent the early part of the afternoon on the Embassy balcony with Sir Robert and Lady Vansittart, watching Herr Hitler's triumphant progress to the Stadium,' the *Daily Telegraph* reported[1] at the beginning of the Olympic Games in Berlin in August 1936. The International Olympic Committee had awarded Berlin the Games in 1932, before Hitler had come to power, but they turned out to be a gift to a regime that was highly skilled in the arts of viscerally impressive display. Hitler used the Berlin Olympics to present the German Reich in a positive light and demonstrate to the world the economic, social, architectural and engineering advances the regime had made since gaining power. There was a spanking new Olympic Stadium to the west of Berlin, and a tidied-up capital that was beginning to be aggrandised under Hitler's plans for an international city fit for the 'Thousand Year Reich'. Berlin was redecorated and spruced up, with care taken to remove from visitors' sight the more overt signs of the anti-Jewish propaganda and brutality that were by now ubiquitous.

The Games began on Saturday, 1 August 1936 with the Olympic torch run in Berlin along streets lined with cheering crowds. In a new ceremony dreamed up by the German Games administrators and imbued with pseudo-Classical symbolism, the torch had been carried in a series of relays from the location of the initial lighting ceremony on 20 July 1936 at Olympia in Greece. Reaching Berlin, the torch runner made his way northwards along Wilhelmstrasse past the British Embassy, turning east on to Unter den Linden for a ceremony at the Lustgarten, the Linden's serried ranks of street lamps that replaced the former stately avenue of lime trees by now draped with rank upon rank of swastika banners. Later, as an airship dramatically hovered above the massed crowds filling the government district, Hitler drove in a cavalcade from the Chancellery along Wilhelmstrasse and west through the Brandenburg Gate and the Tiergarten towards the site of the new stadium built by his favourite young architect, Albert Speer. Another torchbearer followed the same route for the opening ceremony in an Olympic Stadium draped with huge swastika banners. The French Ambassador later sardonically remarked:

> Crowned heads, princes and illustrious guests thronged to Berlin, eager to meet this prophetic being who apparently held the fate of Europe in his hand and to observe the Germany which he had transformed and galvanized in his irresistible grip. Beholding a flawless organization, an impeccable order, a perfect discipline, and a limitless prodigality, everyone went into ecstasy.[2]

Berlin welcomed a huge number of international visitors during the Games, the Adlon Hotel hosting the International Olympic Committee itself. As is the case today, the Embassy arranged a series of social events during the Olympics to promote British interests as a means of furthering the general 'soft' diplomatic effort. Phipps was unfortunately, however, unable to host them with his wife, Frances, who had had to return home owing to illness. Her role was assumed by her sister Sarita,* the wife of Sir Robert Vansittart, Head of the Foreign Office in London and a convinced Nazi sceptic; he – like many other members of the British Establishment – had been specially invited to the Games by Ribbentrop.[3] The couple lodged at the Embassy as Phipps' guests, Goebbels sending a bowl of orchids for Lady Vansittart's arrival. The German political class were curious to meet Sir Robert, whose reputation for anti-Nazi views had preceded him: on 5 August he had a private interview with Hitler in the Reich Chancellery.

Saturday, 8 August saw one of the largest events ever held in the Embassy – a reception for nearly one thousand guests. These included the entire British Olympic Team with accompanying officials and British VIPs – there were almost one hundred members of both Houses of Parliament in Berlin for the Games, including the millionaire MP Henry 'Chips' Channon and his wife Honor. On the German side were a number of prominent members of the Nazi Government, including Goebbels, Ribbentrop, von Neurath and Interior Minister Frick. Guests mounted the steps from the street into the entrance hall, presented their invitations and then were directed to turn left through the ante-room into the front drawing room where Phipps and Lady Vansittart stood ready to greet them. Amidst the bustling throng, footmen carried trays laden with drinks for guests. The windows in the front drawing room were open that summer's evening, and suddenly Lady Vansittart was distracted by a loud altercation taking place in the street just outside. Guests peered out of the windows to see what was happening: it was the sinister Chief of the SS, Heinrich Himmler, one of the guests, loudly dressing down a policeman for having stopped his car in the wrong place.[4]

The huge event was not without logistical problems. The Indian hockey team arrived half an hour late and left not long afterwards, finding the party overcrowded.[5] According to the press, another problem was a shortage of staff on the domestic front. 'A friend who flew back from a weekend in Berlin told me that he heard English visitors commenting on the fact that no names were announced at the big British Embassy reception. The explanation is that it was almost impossible to find a suitably qualified footman,' the *Daily Telegraph* gossiped[6] (it was the holiday season and there were many social events in Berlin, but even so this is a surprising claim, given the amount of notice the Embassy would have had for the occasion and its diplomatic importance). According to this report, the chief attraction for British visitors at the party was Dr Goebbels, whose 'small figure in evening dress was surrounded by a throng of guests, and the embassy staff was kept busy with a stream of introductions'. The British guests were to be disappointed in their hopes of conversation, however, as Goebbels could not speak a word of English. Meanwhile, peering at the arriving

* The sisters' father was the sculptor Sir Herbert Ward (1863–1919).

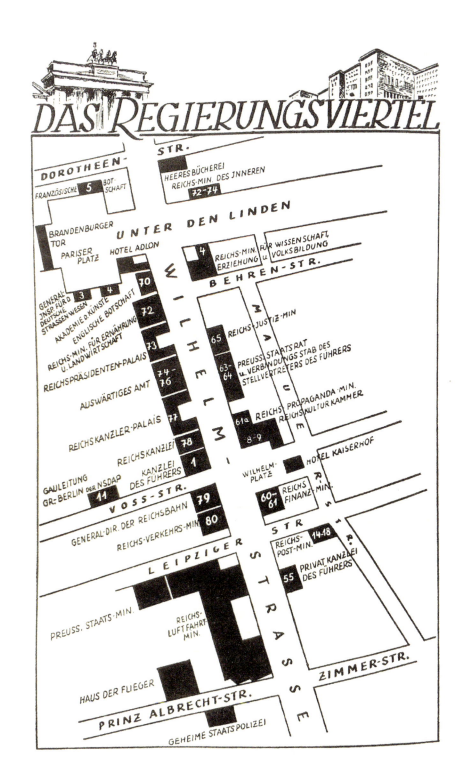

DAS REGIERUNGSVIERTEL

DOROTHEEN- STR.

FRANZÖSISCHE **5** BOT·SCHAFT

HEERES BÜCHEREI
REICHS-MIN. DES JNNEREN
72-74

UNTER DEN LINDEN

BRANDENBURGER TOR
PARISER PLATZ   HOTEL ADLON

4 REICHS-MIN. FÜR WISSENSCHAFT, ERZIEHUNG u. VOLKSBILDUNG

BEHREN-STR.

GENERAL-JNSP. FÜR D. DEUTSCHE STRASSENWESEN **3**
AKADEMIE D. KÜNSTE **4**
ENGLISCHE BOTSCHAFT **70**
REICHS-MIN. FÜR ERNÄHRUNG U. LANDWIRTSCHAFT **72**
REICHSPRÄSIDENTEN-PALAIS **73**

REICHS JUSTIZ-MIN **65**

PREUSS. STAATS RAT u. VERBINDUNGS STAB DES STELLVERTRETERS DES FÜHRERS **63-64**

AUSWÄRTIGES AMT **74-76**

REICHST. PROPAGANDA·MIN. REICHSKULTUR KAMMER **61a**
8·9

REICHSKANZLER·PALAIS **77**

REICHSKANZLEI **78**

KANZLEI DES FÜHRERS **1**

WILHELM·PLATZ   HOTEL KAISERHOF

GAULEITUNG GR. BERLIN DER NSDAP **11**

VOSS-STR.

REICHS FINANZ·MIN. **60-61**

GENERAL-DIR. DER REICHSBAHN **79**
REICHS-VERKEHRS-MIN **80**

REICHS-POST-MIN. **14-18**

PRIVAT. KANZLEI DES FÜHRERS **55**

LEIPZIGER

PREUSS. STAATS·MIN.

REICHS-LUFTFAHRT MIN.

ZIMMER-STR.

HAUS DER FLIEGER

PRINZ ALBRECHT-STR.

GEHEIME STAATS POLIZEI

62. Berlin's government quarter depicted in a map probably prepared for visitors to the Berlin Olympic Games in August 1936.

guests, the crowds outside were thrilled at the chance of seeing Hitler on the Chancellery balcony further down the street.[7]

Not all were impressed by the embassy party. 'Originally just a small meal, then it became a massive reception. A thousand people and a thousand nonsenses'[8] was how Goebbels ungenerously remembered the event (despite his inability to understand much of what was said), while 'Chips' Channon described it as 'boring, crowded and inelegant.'[9] Goebbels did, however, find Lady Vansittart 'charming' and the seventy-seven-year-old Sir James Rennell Rodd, now Baron Rennell and back in the building he had first known fifty years earlier, 'very nice'. Goebbels' host, the Ambassador, concerned about events in Spain, he thought 'stupid.'[10] There was to be no rest for the embassy staff afterwards, for Phipps gave another reception the following evening, this time for members of the British Olympic Team who had completed their events.[11] Meanwhile, Sir Robert Vansittart was taking advantage of his presence in Berlin to meet the Nazi regime's underdogs, a number of Jews making furtive visits to the Embassy. Amongst them was the wealthy Anglophile Wilfred Israel, who pleaded with Vansittart for the British to take a firmer line with Germany over their persecution of Jews, a plea to which Vansittart was able only to make a half-hearted response.[12] During the Vansittarts' visit to Berlin, which lasted nearly a fortnight, Sir Robert met 'almost every important member of the German regime, some of them several times', and *The Times* optimistically hoped that 'Although the talks appear to have remained on the whole general in character, there is no doubt that they must have been of considerable value in dispelling misconceptions and in opening up possibilities for easier Anglo-German cooperation in future.'[13]

In typically basic terms, Ribbentrop recalled that 'The sporting events offered a very favourable opportunity to make contacts with politicians and prominent men in the most diverse camps.'[14] Taking advantage of the presence of such an influential group of international VIPs, prominent members of the Nazi Government tried to outdo each other in holding extravagant and lavish entertainments to impress them. Goering held a kind of *fête champêtre* in the grounds of the Haus der Flieger,* an evening event tastefully lit by searchlights, and, on a separate evening, a lavish dinner at the State Opera House. At their house in Dahlem, the Ribbentrops held their own party for five hundred guests; Ribbentrop also gave a private lunch for Vansittart at the Kaiserhof Hotel, but 'felt from the start as if [he] were addressing a wall'.[15] Not to be outdone by his colleagues, Goebbels' party was held on the Pfauinsel in the Wannsee.†
The French Ambassador, for one, was under no illusions as to the ulterior

---

* Part of a complex of air ministry buildings built and improved in 1935–6 under Goering's direction located between Leipzigerstrasse and Prinz Albrecht Strasse. Goering also had an official residence there; remodelled by Albert Speer, the hall featured the enormous painting *Diana at the Stag Hunt* by Rubens which Goering had 'persuaded' the Director of the Kaiser Friedrich Museum to lend him. The painting could be dramatically raised when required to expose openings behind for a film projector (*Inside the Third Reich: Memoirs of Albert Speer*, p. 37).
† 'Peacock Island', a favourite resort of the imperial family. By this time the Wannsee had been developed as an extremely popular lakeside resort, its beach having been artificially extended in 1929–30; it was where Sir Horace Rumbold had rented a bolthole away from the city. In January 1942 a villa in the area served as the site of the infamous conference on the Nazi Government's 'final solution' to the issue of the Jewish population of German-occupied Europe.

motives behind these generous treats: 'How, one wondered, could these men, so obviously pleased with this fashionable and exquisite entertainment be the persecutors of Jews and the torturers of the concentration camps?'[16] Indeed, some members of the British establishment refused to accept the Nazi regime's excessive hospitality: at a lunch party given by Ribbentrop, the Channons came across Lady Austen Chamberlain, learning from her that her husband, who had such fond memories of Berlin and the Embassy as a young man fifty years earlier, now refused even to set foot in Germany.[17]

Hitler himself gave a grand reception and dinner in the Reich Chancellery. Lady Vansittart was seated next to the Chancellor and got along well with him, spending half an hour alone with Hitler in his study after the meal. Unity and Diana Mitford were the Goebbels' guests at their country house during the Games and were daily chauffeured to the sporting events – but, even with the attraction of the frequent presence of the Führer, they found the Games boring. Both of them went to some of the official parties; Unity, invited for coffee after Hitler's banquet, was breathlessly envious of the Vansittarts: 'Oh, how lucky to have dined with the Führer,' she told them.[18] But while the Vansittarts were not taken in by their surroundings, predictably, some British visitors were: the Channons, for example, were impressed by the improvements to Germany under Nazi rule. Given a 'magnificent suite of rooms' at the Eden Hotel and ferried to and from the Olympic Stadium 'in a grand car with a Storm Trooper at the wheel',[19] it is perhaps unlikely that they would have come to any other conclusion.

The Channons were also – at least initially – impressed by Joachim von Ribbentrop, whom they had met in London along with others sympathetic to the Nazi regime and who had invited them to the Games.[20] Under Hitler's patronage, Ribbentrop had managed to establish his own rival organisation to the German Foreign Office. Although he had been used by Hitler on various short-lived diplomatic missions to London, by the first half of 1936, lacking progress on Germany's behalf with people with real power and influence in Great Britain (i.e. members of the Government and the Prime Minister), Ribbentrop had begun to be disillusioned with the British. The professional diplomats of the German Foreign Office, for their part, loathed him, and, following the death of the German Ambassador to London in April 1936, in a bid to remove Ribbentrop from the Berlin scene and consequent daily influence over Hitler, the former wine merchant was nominated for the post.[21] It was not an honour that Ribbentrop welcomed, precisely because it did remove him from Hitler and Berlin; the posting was announced the same day as his Olympic reception in Dahlem. His wife Annalies was apparently delighted, however. On 21 October Phipps entertained Ribbentrop to a farewell dinner at the Embassy before his departure for London. Ribbentrop arrived late, 'dazed and rather deaf … having flown to and from the Führer at Berchtesgaden since breakfast!' Personally, Phipps had little time for him. Reflecting the opinions of many at the time he regarded him as 'a lightweight (I place him near the bottom of the handicap), irritating, ignorant and boundlessly conceited,'[22] and 'few things depress me more than a conversation with him on subjects other than the weather. He emits a woolly feeling of resistance without consistence, and imposes an unfair strain on the temper.'[23]

Leaving Berlin on the overnight Nord Express* on 25 October, one of the first things the new German Ambassador to the Court of St James did was to pay a call on Anthony Eden, now Foreign Secretary, pompously and patronisingly endeavouring to impress upon him how fortunate the British Government was that the new German Ambassador was so close to the centre of power in Germany – the Führer himself. Eden politely informed him that Ribbentrop had misunderstood the position of an ambassador: it was Phipps' duty in Berlin to report the German Government's opinions to the British; it was Ribbentrop's to report those of the British Government to Hitler.[24] It was also unfortunate for Ribbentrop that many of the members of the British Establishment whom he had sought to woo and who had been initially impressed by his outward charm, were by this stage, as a result of increased exposure to his character, revising their opinions. His crude efforts to win people round and his diplomatic *faux pas* – famously he was to give the Nazi salute to King George VI at a reception – were to alienate many. Unity and Diana Mitford, at least on one occasion, even disparaged him in front of Hitler himself.[25] More dangerously for the future, Ribbentrop was constantly to misunderstand and misreport to Hitler the British political situation.

***

In the summer of 1934 Phipps had written to the Foreign Office in London that lack of space at 70 Wilhelmstrasse due to an increasing staff complement was fast becoming intolerable, and had over the course of time required the division of some of the Chancery accommodation into ever-smaller rooms. Even some of the bedrooms had had to be colonised by embassy staff, including the Financial Advisor,† the office of the Press Attaché and the typists, who had to work alongside a small goods lift. Additionally, Phipps (inaccurately) reported, 'I am the first Ambassador at this post, it seems, with a family,' thereby putting further pressure on the private and bedroom accommodation upstairs. The Phippses had six children, including a son born in Berlin in April 1936, attracting Hitler's personal congratulations. The small children needed to occupy one of the few rooms that received any sunlight, a room unfortunately located next to the typists. 'Needless to say both parties complain about the noise made by their neighbours and both are probably justified.' The whole situation verged on farce when the Ambassador and his wife needed to take a bath, Strousberg's famed numerous and *en suite* facilities long since done away with:

> I have first to see that the screen which marks the room at the end of the section of trench now occupied by the enemy, namely, the Financial Advisor's room, is well and truly placed across the passage so that Dr. Schacht or some other financial magnate is not embarrassed by a sudden encounter with myself or my wife carrying sponge and towel.[26]

There were also more serious matters to contemplate: the very problems the embassy staff had foreseen in the late 1920s. 'Since the Nazis took office espionage is rampant, telephones are tapped,' and the geographical separation

* The overnight train service between Paris and Warsaw, via Berlin.
† The post of Embassy Financial Advisor was staffed by a Treasury official, not a diplomat.

of the three service attachés at 17 Tiergartenstrasse meant that Phipps had to 'arrange an interview every time I wish to discuss something with them'[27]: he would much prefer them to be under one roof. Phipps had considered trying to move the entire Embassy to another building, but, as ever in Berlin, prices for suitable buildings were extortionate. 'The risk of serious prejudice to the official conduct of the business of the Embassy is not one which Sir John Simon is prepared to take in the existing international situation,' the Foreign Office impressed upon the Ministry of Works in August 1934,[28] but, in the end, Phipps compromised and gave up yet more private space. 'I have decided to cede another of my private rooms to the offices thereby providing proper accommodation for the Financial Adviser', and the former 'musicians gallery' above the ballroom was converted into additional accommodation for the typists: 'I can't pretend that the solution is an ideal one, but it saves money and we shall be able to carry on for the present …. Next year all I ask is for the house to be painted outside.'[29]

There were also accommodation problems at the Consulate-General. In February 1935 the Air Ministry in London wrote to the Office of Works requesting more space at 17 Tiergartenstrasse, due to the increased amount of work that the Air Attaché in Berlin found he needed to manage. One solution was for Timothy Breen to move out of the flat he occupied in the building, allowing it to be converted into offices, but Phipps disagreed, thinking it advisable for security purposes that a member of the embassy staff be resident in the building.[30] Presumably with some basis for the accusation, Edward Muir of the Office of Works in London pointed out in an internal minute that 'the porter in the basement is a Nazi, so that if he were alone on the premises the secret police wd [sic] have the run of them at night. The answer to this is that a British subject shd [sic] be employed as a porter, and the F.O. are going to write to the Ambassador accordingly.'[31]

Basil Newton, the Counsellor, pointed out that this would not be an easy task. But the British Consul in Berlin had a straightforward approach to the issue, which Newton duly reported back to London. In the first place, the German porter had undertaken the job since the British had acquired the building in 1920: they would have to pay him some form of compensation for dismissal as well as having to pay a British-based porter a larger salary. He was moreover good value for money, undertaking cleaning duties in addition, and engaging female servants for 'charring'. The accommodation on offer was unsuitable 'for an Englishman', and if the German porter were to be dismissed they would risk alienating him 'and giving a willing agent to the German authorities if they did want to gain access'. Finally, it was difficult to find 'a suitable Englishman who speaks German. This is essential'. The Consul also made the logical point that when Phipps was away from Berlin 'no British subject sleeps in the Embassy which is much less fully equipped than the Consulate with such security devices as steel shutters.'[32] Breen duly moved out, his flat being converted to additional office accommodation, but as a compromise some of the area was converted into a smaller flat suitable for a British-based bachelor, not necessarily always a man – Miss C. Molesworth of the Passport Control staff occupied the flat from 1 April 1937.[33]

'I realise that in our free country the Government cannot always prevent Mayfair from rushing Hitlerwards, but if some of the visitors could be choked off I think it would be a good thing'[34]: Phipps had a dim view of the gullible members of the British Establishment who visited Berlin and Germany during his ambassadorship. One of them was Lord Londonderry, who had rejoined the British Government as Secretary of State for Air in 1931. Sharing with many of his aristocratic millionaire contemporaries a personal interest in the developing technology of flight, he was an energetic advocate of rearmament and of increasing the size of Britain's air force. But after an unfortunately judged speech in the House of Commons that appeared to condone the concept of air bombing to maintain political power, he lost much support, and when Stanley Baldwin became Prime Minister in June 1935 Londonderry was moved aside to the post of Lord Privy Seal and Leader of the House of Commons. He stood down from Parliament after the General Election of November 1935.

Bitter that he was no longer in public office, concerned about the mounting evidence of Germany's increasing air power, and as distrustful of professional diplomats as he had been in 1920, Londonderry became convinced that he could broker an understanding between Germany and Great Britain in an unofficial capacity. He, his wife and youngest child, Mairi,* made a personal visit to Berlin early in 1936, where, staying at the Adlon Hotel, they were invited to attend the third anniversary torchlight procession of Hitler's chancellorship. The procession once again took place along Wilhelmstrasse, the Londonderrys viewing it from the Reich Chancellery, followed by dinner with Hitler in the Presidential Palace. Further fraternisation and talks with senior Nazis (including Hitler) featured the standard outing to Goering's estate at Carinhall to participate in blood sports, and to the Winter Olympics at Garmisch in Bavaria.[35] Ribbentrop, who hosted the Londonderrys at Dahlem, was their guest at their London and country houses, visiting Mount Stewart (near Belfast) that Whitsun.

The Nazis' international public relations success at the Olympic Games encouraged more British visitors to visit Germany, with several British VIPs attending the September 1936 Nazi Party Congress at Nuremberg. These included Unity Mitford, her brother Tom and sister Diana Mosley, who had also been guests of the Goebbels at the Wagner Festspiel at Bayreuth. Former Prime Minister Lloyd George, one of the signatories of the 1919 Treaty of Versailles, even paid a call on Hitler at Berchtesgaden, where the Führer made a favourable impression, while Lord Londonderry continued his personal trips to Germany to meet Nazi top brass whom he regarded as influential.

The Embassy's relationship with these semi-official British visitors was a difficult one; Phipps felt that in many respects they were undermining his own position *vis à vis* the Nazi regime, giving the German Government cause to hope that the visitors' impressed and less than robust attitudes towards Hitler represented the official British position, rather than that of the Embassy in

---

* Lady Mairi Bury. She died in November 2009 aged eighty-eight, the last British person known to have met these Nazi leaders.

Berlin and the Foreign Office in London. Ribbentrop had been cultivated by the Londonderrys in the interests – from their point of view – of nurturing good British–German relations and so was Goering: Phipps was concerned by the possibility of Goering's presence at the 1937 Coronation of King George VI[†] in London as Londonderry's guest. Such an invitation would have been a propaganda coup for the Nazi regime and its prospect caused a flurry of indignation in the British press at the time. However, Goering, a frequent correspondent with the Londonderrys, informed Lady Londonderry that as a matter of personal pride, in view of the anti-German reports and opinions in the British press he could hardly come to London to attend the Coronation.[36] In the end, it was Field Marshal von Blomberg who did so. Londonderry's feelings on the matter were unequivocal: 'The Foreign Office seems quite incapable of doing anything right and goes out of its way to estrange our would-be friends. I feel that we are heading for disaster.'[37] Meanwhile, Phipps felt that even 'friendly and private' conversations that he held in the Embassy with German Government officials as part of his official duties were by now being deliberately misconstrued by them, for example believing that Hjalmar Schacht had misreported the subject of a discussion they had had on 29 October 1936, for propaganda purposes.[38]

In January 1937 Phipps was relieved to be able to report in his diary that he had been offered the post of Ambassador to Paris (he had been lobbying for the appointment since at least the early months of 1934[39]). On hearing this news plenty of German acquaintances expressed pity at his having to leave Berlin. Having spent a large amount of his career in the French capital and a self-confessed Francophile, Phipps was, in contrast, delighted: 'We do not share that opinion, for we regard the *Ville Lumière* as the hub of civilization.'[40] They left Berlin on 24 April, Phipps much relieved to be able to get away from a regime and people he increasingly despised. His anti-German feelings were certainly beginning to be seen by some parties in London as a hindrance to progress,[41] yet at the same time he was criticised for having 'too much wit and not enough warning'[42] in his failure to regard the threats posed by the Nazi regime as soberly as his predecessor Sir Horace Rumbold had done. Phipps' posting to Paris lasted until his retirement in October 1939; he died in August 1945.

Martha Dodd was fond of both Phipps and his wife. A frequent embassy guest, she left a vivid account of their behaviour on the diplomatic social circuit: '[Y]ou could not tell, from the expressions of his face, what [Phipps] was thinking, feeling, or even saying … He rarely smiled, he rarely quipped, he rarely did anything socially or conversationally except listen intently with owl-like seriousness to everything you said.' At receptions he seemed 'as nervous as a cat, bounced around with his crooked walk – one shoulder hunched up, making one leg seem shorter than the other – his head carried to the side, jerking from one group of his guests to another, emitting almost inaudible "Yes, yes, how interesting" sounds.' Meanwhile, Phipps' wife, Frances, 'stood quietly in one spot, leaving all the introducing and ceremonial formalities to her husband. She was serene, untalkative, a little cold, shy and sweet in manner … A short, slender woman, completely without make-

† To be held on 12 May 1937, the same day set for the Coronation of King Edward VIII, who had abdicated in December 1936.

up, with a face more beautiful and wholesome than a Madonna's.' She 'made no pretensions about liking diplomatic parties. She hated and felt uncomfortable at them,' confessing to Mrs Dodd that she 'gave as few parties as she could, and tried to meet all her obligations by giving large affairs where she would not have to mingle intimately with too many people. The small parties she reserved for people she really liked and could be natural with.'[43] (Interestingly, whatever impression she made during diplomatic parties, Hitler's nickname for Lady Phipps was apparently 'sob sister'.[44])

What the Dodds greatly admired in Phipps was his robust attitude towards the Nazi regime. 'To watch him with the Nazis, to overhear his conversation with men it was openly known he despised, was a lesson in the veneer of conventional diplomacy …. Underneath this magnificent stage-play was an intense hatred and contempt for the Nazis and their stooges, whoever they might be and no matter how highly placed.'[45] This was echoed by François-Poncet, the French Ambassador: 'I appreciated the delicacy of his feelings, his deep kindness, his playful humour, his unfailing amiability …. Possessed of a very steady and lucid judgement, he had seen through Hitler's real nature and had never been the dupe of the Third Reich.'[46] This reputation was, however, not to last once Phipps was Ambassador to François-Poncet's home country: his analysis of the political situation in Paris during the Munich Crisis, for example, was seen in London as hysterical and defeatist.[47]

But, if nothing else, Phipps had the measure of Goering. On one occasion shortly after the 'Night of the Long Knives' Goering arrived late for a dinner at the British Embassy, boasting that he had only just got back from a shooting trip. Phipps politely asked him, 'Animals, this time, I hope?'[48]

CHAPTER 16
1937: 'The Post-War Cinderella of Our Missions Abroad'

'The post of Ambassador in Germany was thoroughly uncongenial to me, and one for which I felt myself very unworthy and unsuited,'[1] confessed Sir Nevile Henderson. As British Ambassador to Argentina, he was informed by the Foreign Office in January 1937 that he was to succeed Sir Eric Phipps as Ambassador to Berlin. Given the political circumstances and the challenging personalities involved, it would have been understandable had his reaction to the appointment been similar to that of Sir Edward Goschen in 1908. As it was, writing in December 1939, Henderson admitted that he first of all felt inadequate 'for what was obviously the most difficult and most important post in the whole of the diplomatic service.'[2] However, he also felt – at least with hindsight and certainly not without immodesty – that he had been 'specially selected by Providence for the definite mission of, as I trusted, helping to preserve the peace of the world.'[3]* As we know, his hope was to be in vain.

Henderson was an example of how the personnel of the upper echelons of the diplomatic service had changed since Odo Russell's day sixty years before. He did not come from an aristocratic and diplomatic background but from a moneyed middle-class one: his father, whose family had established a successful business in Glasgow and who died in Henderson's childhood, was a director at the Bank of England. Henderson was not particularly academic, and would have preferred a military career. Instead, under family pressure, after leaving Eton he crammed for the diplomatic service examinations, and, succeeding, joined the service in May 1905. Six months later he was sent off on his first posting, to St Petersburg. Henderson never worked at the Foreign Office in London again and would confess in his memoirs that 'To all intents and purposes and except for varying pieces of leave … I left England for good that December until I returned from Berlin in September 1939.'[4] He slowly climbed up the diplomatic service ladder through a series of postings that included Tokyo (serving with Horace Rumbold), Rome (under Sir James Rennell Rodd), Niš,† Paris (where he was present at the Versailles peace negotiations) and Constantinople in 1920, where he again served with Rumbold, whose conduct in the post Henderson held in such high regard that he came to regard him almost as a mentor.[5] He then worked in Cairo and then as Minister in Paris in 1928, serving as Head of Mission in Belgrade from 1929 to 1935 before being sent – somewhat unexpectedly – to Buenos Aires.

---

* This remark was echoed in Henderson's autobiography, *Water under the Bridges*: '… I was presumptuous enough to think, or rather to pray, that I had been selected, under Providence, for the post for the sole purpose, for I could see no other, of helping avert world war. I based my whole attitude, while I was in Berlin, on that presumption. I believed that to be my mission, and I failed' (p. 209).
† In Serbia.

Almost from the moment it was made, debate has raged as to the reasons behind Henderson's appointment to Berlin. Apparently, it was on the recommendation of the Head of the Foreign Office, Sir Robert Vansittart,[6] but Sir Anthony Eden later expressed his regrets over the decision, describing it as 'an international misfortune.'[7] Eden's Private Secretary, Oliver Harvey, however, confessed in his diary that 'there really is not anybody else obvious to send.'[8] Henderson was thought to have shown some competence in dealing with difficult autocrats during his long service in Belgrade, and certainly appeared able to get along with them on a social level, becoming a close personal friend of King Alexander of Yugoslavia. Some were to question whether he was sufficiently able to step back from such close relationships and sympathies with the interests of the country in which he was posted and prevent himself from falling into that potential diplomatic pitfall of 'going native', but rather, to think objectively and remember that his duties were to represent Britain's interests in that country, and not the other way round.

An elegant and suave man, in appearance and outward behaviour the epitome of a British gentleman, Henderson wore a buttonhole almost every day during his ambassadorship, Hitler disparagingly referring to him as 'the man with the carnation.'[9] Martha Dodd described him as 'Tall, slender, dark, with a gaunt face, slick hair and a little jet-black moustache ….. the Beau Brummel of the [diplomatic] corps, convivial, overflowing with good spirits, enthusiasms, and seemingly hearty frankness. It would have been difficult to find a more complete antithesis to the dignified, quiet, and restrained Phipps.'[10] 'A great many people are surprised to find that Sir Nevile Henderson, our dark, good-looking, Scottish Ambassador to Berlin … is a bachelor,' gossiped *The Sunday Times* in September 1938.[11] Unusually for an ambassador – even fifty years on from Sir Edward Malet's time – Henderson was not, and never had been, married. This would have placed him in a position of some everyday practical difficulty as a head of mission, where, as we have seen, entertaining plays a key role in representational work; in Buenos Aires Henderson's divorced sister, Lady Leitrim, acted as hostess for the first six months of his posting.[12] Bachelorhood was a state Henderson appears, however, not in principle to have chosen. In the early 1930s he became very close to Irene Ravensdale, the eldest daughter of Lord Curzon, the former Viceroy of India and Foreign Secretary, who herself had never married. In August 1934, after they had become close, she had spent a short holiday with Henderson in Cornwall, where she refused his proposal of marriage. While she had had a number of close relationships, including a brief fling with her own brother-in-law Oswald Mosley, in truth she appears to have found Henderson something of a wimp. All the same, she could understand his theoretical attraction, as she confessed in her diary:

> Oh, oh dear! Why do I feel so violently that if he touched me or kissed me I would shudder and yet he is so sweet with all his conceits and tics and would make some less strong-minded woman blissful. I walked to and fro with him beating around the marriage question. When we sat on the lawn before tea he was touching, calling me My Sweet and kissing my fingers and saying how he loved me being with him and it does not move a tremor in me. Oh dear![13]

It must have been the case that the lack of a close and intimate supportive daily companion in the form of a wife only added to the stress Henderson was to experience in dealing with the appalling challenges and atmosphere he faced during his Berlin posting, and his failure to persuade Irene to marry him is poignant. On his appointment to Berlin, she wrote him a letter of congratulations. Her private remarks in her diary at that time echoed Elizabeth Bennett's thoughts in *Pride and Prejudice* on first seeing Pemberley: 'And I might have been Ambassadress there, if I had married Nevile.'[14] Ironically, she was no stranger to Germany, having been 'finished' in Dresden before 'coming out' in the summer of 1914, and could speak fluent German; with her extensive establishment connections and reputation as a generous hostess she would have made an ideal diplomatic wife.

Henderson left Buenos Aires in the middle of March 1937, deciding to travel on a German liner across the Atlantic in order to improve his rusty German. A spectacular event during the voyage – and one which must have enlivened his reading of *Mein Kampf* as psychological preparation for his new posting – was a brief encounter with the German airship *Hindenburg* on its way back to Germany from South America. The airship momentarily hovered over the liner before speeding on its way.[15] A swift round of preparatory meetings in London followed Henderson's arrival back in London, at least one of which seems to have been with Neville Chamberlain (who was to become Prime Minister on 28 May), over which there has been considerable debate. Chamberlain may have given Henderson some personal instructions as to how he should conduct his 'mission' in Germany and, in particular, how he should manage Adolf Hitler. It was subsequently claimed by Professor Conwell-Evans (based in Germany) that Henderson was indeed taking his orders directly from Chamberlain.[16] But no documentary evidence for this has survived, speculation ensuing as to the possible loss of personal correspondence between Henderson and Chamberlain when Henderson left Berlin as Ambassador at the outbreak of war in early September 1939. Time would in any case demonstrate that the new Prime Minister's ideas on how to deal with the fast growing threat of German expansion diverged from those of several senior members of the British Government, of Parliament, the Foreign Office and, indeed, with at least some of the embassy staff in Berlin.

It was during this period that Foreign Secretary Anthony Eden and Henderson were King George VI's overnight guests at Windsor. Oliver Harvey recorded that Eden was 'rather aghast at the nonsense [Henderson] was talking about what he was going to do in Germany. It seems quite to have gone to his head …. I hope we are not sending another Ribbentrop to Berlin.'[17] Henderson arrived at Friedrichstrasse Station in Berlin a week later on 30 April 1937 on the overnight sleeper train and like his predecessors was met at the station by a senior member of the embassy staff. On this occasion it was Sir George Ogilvie-Forbes, who had arrived in Berlin himself as the new Counsellor only shortly before Henderson, together with Ivone Kirkpatrick, the First Secretary, who had already served in Berlin for three and a half years.

Henderson naturally had to present his 'letters of credence' to the Head of State – Adolf Hitler – before he could serve as Ambassador in an official capacity. But events in Britain made the timing inconvenient: the Coronation of King George VI was set for 12 May, and that placed essential duties of diplomatic protocol on the

63. Sir Nevile Henderson in diplomatic uniform at the Embassy with his beloved dog Hippy, in a photograph probably taken on his diplomatic presentation day in May 1937.

Ambassador and his staff. Henderson therefore had to break with procedure and invite certain diplomatic guests to the celebration in the English Church before presenting his letters of credence, inviting Field Marshal von Blomberg and the two other delegates to the Coronation for lunch at the Embassy before their departure[18]; they were Henderson's first German guests after his arrival in Berlin. When Henderson finally did manage to meet and present his official diplomatic credentials to Hitler, the Chancellor was in a distracted mood, shocked and suspecting foul play after the news that the much-lauded *Hindenburg* airship had crashed in the United States.[19] It was an inauspicious start to what was to be a difficult relationship.

As the normal diplomatic cycle of the year progressed in what was to be the last summer of relative calm in Germany before the outbreak of the Second World War, on 9 June Henderson held the traditional annual party for the King's birthday. As there was no embassy garden, the inconvenience of entertaining a large number of guests indoors on what was a very hot day doubtless confirmed Henderson's dim views on the quality of 70 Wilhelmstrasse as an embassy. The gathering was as large as the Olympic reception on 8 August 1936, but was this time mainly composed of guests from the British community in Berlin of some 1,500 persons. Henderson remarked that this 'colony' was 'an extremely poor one,'[20] believing this to be the reason why the guests tucked into so much of the food that was on offer. Whatever the building's limitations, Henderson averred that he could recall no other party which had given him so much pleasure to hold as this one, able as he was to make full use of the large ballroom/banqueting room to show the forty-minute colour film of the Coronation that he had been able to borrow. The film was shown at three sittings that afternoon, so that all the many guests could see it.[21]

The film also came in useful the following day when Henderson held his diplomatic *entrée* party at the Embassy. This time two performances were given to 'about seven hundred Nazi functionaries and diplomats.'[22] 'The captions, being American, were excellent propaganda, and better than they would have been if the film had been British. I was hopeful that what they saw and heard about the British Monarchy and Empire might be instructive and salutary for the Nazi officials, few of whom had ever visited London.'[23] A large luncheon party was held later in June, when Henderson entertained the Prime Minister of Canada, Mackenzie King, who was in Berlin following the Imperial Conference in London. Several top Nazi officials attended, including Goering and his wife, Emmy, the first time Henderson met her; during the meal they discussed the relative vanities of men and women.[24]

***

Henderson found fault with most of the buildings in which he served during his diplomatic career. His main gripe was usually – and not, it has to be said, unfairly – with the Treasury in London, whose penny-pinching attitudes he felt actually damaged Britain's international prestige. Unconsciously echoing Lord Odo Russell's views on the subject sixty years before, Henderson thought that '... in peace time it is the hardest thing in the world to get the Treasury to spend money abroad. Our parsimony in this respect is in glaring contrast to what poorer countries such as the French, Italians or Germans used to spend on any purpose calculated to increase their prestige or serve as propaganda.'[25] This was exemplified in Belgrade, 'one of the latest Office of Works constructions'[26] with 'very inadequate reception-rooms.' It was 'of a suburban-villa type … it gave one the impression of having had as little spent on it as possible' and contrasted sharply with the new Italian Legation, which was the largest in Belgrade.[27] Worse was to come for Henderson in Buenos Aires, a building that was a 'shoddy affair.'[28]

In his memoirs and other documents Henderson gave a lengthy description of his problems with 70 Wilhelmstrasse, peddling a story of how when it was first acquired by the British Government in the 1870s, it had a rear garden that had been sold off in Sir Frank Lascelles' time in order to build the Adlon Hotel, Lascelles possibly being pressurised to do so by the Emperor Wilhelm II himself.[29] In fact, as we have seen, Strousberg's mansion had never had a back garden, while its rear terrace and much of the central courtyard garden it had overlooked were swallowed up when the Embassy's large ballroom was constructed thirty years before the Adlon was built. The story has over time been embellished with reference to a mythical 'carp pond' in the 'garden' to the rear, possibly some kind of atavistic memory of the water feature behind the demolished Palais Redern. Exactly why or when these particular myths grew up is unknown, but they are still current,[30] an example of how, in the closed psychological confines of diplomatic buildings, inaccurate stories about those buildings and their contents can over the years become accepted as verity and are overturned only with the greatest difficulty, if at all. Henderson regarded these 'facts' as catastrophic. 'Shut off on the south from the sunlight by the great edifice of the Adlon and sullied by the smoke from the hotel's vast kitchen chimney, the house was always dark and always dirty.'[31] It was a view echoed over sixty years later by Henderson's Private Secretary Geoffrey Harrison's wife, Katherine. She remembered that 'There were hardly any trees and food smells were always drifting over from the kitchens of the Hotel Adlon next door …. You didn't get a feeling of wellbeing there.'[32]

Since, unlike his predecessor, he had neither wife nor family to fill them, it was surprising that Henderson also found fault with the fact that the building had 'only about half a dozen' bedrooms.* Indeed, he marvelled at how Sir Eric Phipps can have managed: he 'can barely have had more than one guest-room available for visitors.' As previously discussed, there had originally been more guest rooms but as the number of embassy staff had greatly increased over the years they were gradually converted into office accommodation, so that, in Henderson's words, the Chancery rooms were 'inadequate and unhygienic. Those who imagine that the diplomatic secretaries and personnel of His Majesty's Embassies abroad work in the utmost luxury and comfort are under a grave misconception,'[33] Henderson assured his readers.

By now there were not far off one hundred embassy staff members in Berlin.[34] Repeating the complaints the staff had made in the late 1920s and those of his predecessors, Henderson lamented the fact that the consular, attaché, commercial and passport staff were based at 17 Tiergartenstrasse, 'about a kilometre away.'[35] This was extremely inconvenient, if not insecure, as economic and political cooperation at the closest level was required if the Embassy was to operate efficiently, and in Berlin, and as Phipps had described, 'the telephone can only be used as contact in respect of matters of an entirely non-confidential character.'[36] Henderson felt that Berlin was 'in many respects the post-War Cinderella of our Missions abroad.'[37] But he did achieve something, however prosaic, recording for posterity that he had installed a refrigerator in the kitchens, and a downstairs toilet for guests. With regard to improvements to facilities, like many ambassadors on arrival at post Henderson marvelled that his predecessors had not done something so obvious before. Strousberg's former palatial townhouse had once contained so many lavatories as to cause plumbing problems, but in recent decades visitors needing toilet facilities had been directed upstairs by a servant;[38] one wonders how the thousand guests at the Olympic reception the previous year coped.

Henderson began making representations to London about the Embassy's perceived shortcomings within a few months of his arrival in Berlin. One of these shortcomings was the Embassy's proximity to the Chancellery a little further down the street and the crowd-pulling appeal of the charismatic leader of the promised 'Thousand Year Reich':

> There are many occasions under the present regime when the Wilhelmstrasse is blocked, for it is the principal route for every procession and the chief avenue of assembly for any crowd which may gather to see

* Sir Horace Rumbold described eight bedrooms (see below).

or listen to the Chancellor should he appear on his balcony. On such occasions it is invariably impossible to approach the Embassy on foot and often with extreme difficulty.[39]

Henderson's complaints continued over the following months. In his later account of his Berlin ambassadorship, he explained that London had accepted and recognised the problems and that he had been authorised to try to find a new embassy building.[40] Indeed, detailed plans of the Embassy's four floors were drawn up in November 1937,[41] implying that Henderson's complaints about the building's shortcomings were receiving at least some attention in London.

For Henderson, the positive factors that had convinced Odo Russell to persuade the British Government to acquire 70 Wilhelmstrasse were no longer relevant. The world of the 1930s was of course very different from that of the 1870s, and Henderson admitted that 'From a sentimental point of view, it would have been sad to leave the historic building in the Wilhelmstrasse, but from the point of view of work it was essential.'[42] In contrast, the 'Court and Society' gossip column in *The Sunday Times* for 4 September 1938 described how the embassy building was known to many Germans as the '*Englische Torte* ("English Cake") because its front is so decorative and it has a most imposing façade, with heavy pillars on either side of the entrance. Sir Nevile has given most successful entertainments here.'[43] But for Henderson even the building's external appearance posed diplomatic problems, particularly the design of the metal grille on the Embassy's front door on to Wilhelmstrasse: according to him the Germans cited the use of the French motto in the royal coat of arms as evidence that the British Government had always been in cahoots with Germany's traditional enemy.[44]

Earlier in the 1930s Henderson had drawn attention to the money lavished on foreign missions by the fascist Italian Government: 'Mussolini is no fool and there is a sense and foresight behind the new Italian Embassies and Legations which he stole from Austria or has since created. In Belgrade this was noticeable and I find the same thing here [Buenos Aires] where the Italian Embassy is far the best …'[45] 'I fear it must be admitted that dictators seem to appreciate far better than democratic Governments the importance and ultimate profit of outward display, and its face value abroad,' he later stated.[46] Sometimes, however, such state-sponsored splendour could have the opposite psychological effect to that intended. It certainly did for the sober attitudes of the American Ambassador in Berlin Professor William Dodd, who was shocked at the extravagance shown by the Italian Government on building a brand new embassy in the 1930s:

> The palace is a wonderfully elaborate and roomy house, representing a great cost for a country that owes the United States two billions or something like that and never even apologizes for not paying any part of the interest due. The furniture and paintings are very valuable, everything beautiful and in good taste, but I would be ashamed, if I were the Ambassador, to invite an American official to the place.[47]

***

'The great eye-sore of the house is the truly ghastly stair-case, lit by tall brass lamps with white glass globes all the way up', the library was 'dark and hideous' and the

64. The staircase hall in 1939.

overall impression of the house 'rather Victorian', Lady Rumbold opined to her daughter and mother about 70 Wilhelmstrasse.[48] Indeed, the historical and decorative interior decoration of the British Embassy would have appeared very old-fashioned and fussy, if not completely tasteless and ugly in the 1920s and 1930s to those enamoured of the fashionable and sleek modernist interiors of the period, or even, for that matter, the stark neoclassical lines favoured by Hitler and Albert Speer ('ocean-liner style', as Speer himself described it[49]). Goebbels, for example, had controversially had the historic interior decorations of the building used for the Propaganda Ministry on Wilhelmplatz streamlined to his tastes.[50] Harold Nicolson may have been effusive in his praise of D'Abernon as British Ambassador, but not of his surroundings, the description of which was, of course, based on Nicolson's intimate personal experience. The Ambassador's study had 'three gaunt windows gaping upon the Wilhelmstrasse, with ... ugly panelling and ... grim leather chairs.'[51]

'The house is tolerably well furnished, the O. of W. having provided us with a good deal last year but, as you know, it is a big place with room for a good deal of your own stuff if you care to bring it along,'[52] Sir Ronald Lindsay advised his successor, Sir Horace Rumbold, in March 1928. Rumbold, who was later to describe the building as 'gloomy,'[53] replied that he remembered 'the Embassy house very well and the rooms certainly take a bit of filling. We have a fair amount of things of our own which can go in the drawing-rooms ...'[54] 'The whole of the downstairs part of the Embassy is practically arranged as is also some of the upstairs part', Rumbold reported to his daughter in mid-September 1928, soon after their arrival in Berlin.[55] Before leaving post, Rumbold, in turn, advised his successor, Sir Eric Phipps, that he also might prefer to make use of his own furniture and store at least some of the government-provided items. This was especially the case in his office, which contained 'practically nothing but my own furniture at the moment, as well as my own bookcases, as there is only one very small bookcase belonging to the Government. The original furniture will, of course, be put back, but it is very old and rather uncomfortable.'[56]

While his predecessors had made do with the perceived shortcomings of the building and its fittings, by taking advantage of Hitler's plans to aggrandise Berlin Henderson hoped to build a completely new embassy and give up 70 Wilhelmstrasse, which he was sure would immediately be snapped up by the Nazi regime for use as government offices. He could then move the Embassy and Consulate-General to 'some large site on a corner of one of Hitler's new thoroughfares' on which to build an embassy 'suitable for all modern requirements.'[57] This would indeed have matched Hitler's plans for the city. Proposals to redevelop Berlin actually dated back to Weimar days, but fitted in well with Hitler's ambitions to make the city truly a world capital on the scale of ancient Rome. In plans first submitted to the public in January 1938, Albert Speer was to propose no less than a vast rebuilding of Berlin's city centre dominated by north–south and east–west axes, featuring new railway stations, vast triumphal arches and the 'Great Hall of the People', the largest domed building in the world. The city would feature sectors for government, hotels and entertainment, as well as a defined 'diplomatic quarter' located to the west of the north–south axis, in the Tiergarten area. This part of Hitler's and Speer's plans were already underway by Henderson's time, with new embassies/residences being built for Spain, Denmark, Norway, Yugoslavia, Spain, Japan and Italy,* all in a monumental neoclassical style designed by Speer's architectural office.[58] Had Hitler and Speer had the time and opportunity to complete their plans, and the British given the building up, it is likely that 70 Wilhelmstrasse would have been demolished; plenty of historical buildings in the government quarter were already being swept away by the Nazi regime in order to build the grandiose and modern expressions of that regime's power.

Henderson took the matter very seriously, discussing it with Goering, a lunch guest at the Embassy early in November 1937. Goering assured him that the Führer would look favourably upon finding a suitable new site on the grand new north–south avenue; indeed, Henderson 'would be amazed at the generous manner in which Hitler would help.'[59] Interestingly, Goering's remarks imply that the Nazi Government would have contemplated placing the British Embassy not in the defined diplomatic quarter, but right in the thick of things in one of the main new state avenues. He later described how he also told Ribbentrop of the proposal, asking him to tell Hitler he was contemplating it, hoping that 'it would form part of a general understanding with Germany', but Henderson never got the chance to discuss it with Hitler in person.[60]

The matter of the British Embassy's future rumbled on at the Office of Works throughout 1938 and into 1939, by which time the Government had finally realised that a proper strategy was required. Foreign Secretary Lord Halifax wrote to Sir Philip Sassoon, First Commissioner of the Office of Works, on 6 January 1939, based on personal knowledge of the building: 'As you know we are carefully considering just how best we can push British propaganda abroad …. The Berlin Embassy … is really very unsatisfactory and I cannot but help feeling that it would create a very good impression if we could acquire, or build, a new house there.'[61] Ironically for Henderson, the Office of Works was spending money on a new embassy at the time – in Buenos Aires.

***

* Only the Japanese and Italian Missions survived the Second World War.

65. Sir Horace Rumbold in his study at the Embassy with two paintings from his family collection displayed on the wall behind him.

The D'Abernons, as we have seen, supplied some of their own works of art for the Embassy building, and so did the patrician Sir Horace Rumbold whose tastes, in so far as they are documented, consisted of Venetian baroque masters. A photograph of Rumbold sitting in his office in Berlin shows two paintings with labels bearing the name [Giovanni Battista] Piazzetta hanging behind his desk, and in July 1931 Rumbold referred to a 'Canaletto picture' on display in the building.[62] The Rumbolds had also been portrayed by the fashionable society artist Philip de László while serving in Madrid, and these portraits may very well have been displayed in Berlin. But by the 1930s the long-held policy of relying upon ambassadors to provide pictures for official residences (and/or negotiate loans of suitable works) was finally regarded as no longer practical. While the British would never imitate Hermann Goering's unattractive practice of siphoning off large quantities of art treasures from public collections for display in his personal and official residences, some of the British national collections had always lent a few works of art for display in major government buildings in London, including Downing Street. In 1935 Sir Lionel Earle's hopes in this direction were finally realised when the National Galleries Overseas Loans Act officially enabled British national collections to lend pictures from their collections to diplomatic buildings overseas. In the same year the Treasury also granted the Office of Works £250 specifically to purchase works for display in British missions abroad.

Armed with its new budget, the Office of Works immediately began to acquire suitable pictures. Henderson himself had been one of the early beneficiaries of this policy when he was Ambassador in Buenos Aires. Amongst his many complaints about that building had been its lack of pictures, and he was particularly exasperated that it did not qualify for suitably large state portraits.[63] In 1936 a large painting of the *Arch of Constantine, Rome* by Viviano Codazzi was sent from London for display in the building and remains in Buenos Aires to this day. The new 'Picture Fund' also provided suitable works for Copenhagen, Athens and Paris, while Berlin was another natural candidate for attention. Additionally, in February 1939 Sir Stephen Gaselee of the Foreign Office and Edward Muir of the Ministry of Works earmarked for Berlin three suitable paintings from the Royal Collection at Hampton Court Palace that the King was prepared to lend for such a purpose. These were *The Death of Saint Mark* by Bassano,[*] *A Carpenter in Lamplight* by Honthorst[†] and *The Holy Family* by Romano.[‡][64]

Had they been despatched to Berlin (and fortunately it appears they were not), these 'Old Masters' would have fitted in well with the ornamental interior of the Embassy and with D'Abernon's Ruysdael and Vrancx, but one work that was selected for Berlin from the new purchases the Office of Works made in this period may have seemed a little out of place. *Capri – Sunrise*, an early landscape painting by Sir Frederic (later Lord) Leighton, was bought by the Office of Works at auction in London in April 1937, a few days before Henderson's arrival in Berlin. It was an unusual purchase for the time, the art of the Victorian period (like the architecture) having fallen out of favour by the 1920s and 1930s. One of the first works of art by a major British artist that the Office of Works purchased for display abroad, by early that summer the decision had been made to send it to Berlin,[65] the exact reason unknown. Did Henderson personally choose it or was he persuaded to take it? Was it an attempt to make a cultural link with Germany?[§] Under Rodd's ambassadorship, Henderson had spent a happy time in 1914 at the summer residence of the British Embassy in Rome at Posillipo,[¶] overlooking the Bay of Naples.[66] Two and a half decades later, did he choose this painting as a souvenir? Its relatively small size and composition would not immediately suggest its suitability for the lofty proportions of the Embassy's reception rooms, and exactly where the painting was displayed is unknown, but its size suggests that it may have been placed in the more intimate surroundings of a smaller room, perhaps the Ambassador's office/study itself, where Henderson would naturally have received many high ranking visitors.

The Embassy's ballroom had evidently altered little in appearance from the late nineteenth century and would have remained an imposing (if by that stage very old-fashioned) sight. 'A reception at the British Embassy always draws a

---

[*] *The Martyrdom of St Mark* (RCIN402877).
[†] Probably *Christ in the Carpenter's Shop*, subsequently reattributed to Tromphime Bigot (RCIN404753).
[‡] Possibly *The Holy Family*, subsequently reattributed to Garofalo (RCIN406923).
[§] Leighton had spent some of his early years in Germany and, coincidentally, had visited the Embassy.
[¶] The Villa Delahunte had been donated to the British Government in 1909 by Lord Rosebery, who had purchased it in 1897, but after the Great War the British had given it back to the family, who, in turn, had given it to Mussolini. 'I sometimes think with despair of the chances which H.M. Treasury has squandered on the ground that the upkeep would be too heavy,' Henderson bewailed (*Water under the Bridges*, p. 69).

66. The ballroom in 1939, showing the state portraits of British Monarchs.

great crowd, and the stateliness of the great ballroom, with its royal portraits, including a picture of Queen Victoria as a girl* makes a beautiful setting,' the *Daily Mail* had reported in 1934.[67] By the mid-1930s the room housed state portraits of Queen Victoria, her son, her grandson, and their consorts. On 1936 plans were naturally afoot to send the official state portrait of the new King Edward VIII to diplomatic missions, but his abdication that December made them redundant. Attention the following year necessarily turned to the despatch of a portrait of the new Monarch, King George VI (the former Duke of York), who, unlike his brother, had married. Concerns were expressed over transport costs for state portraits of both King and Queen,[68] but Berlin was naturally slated to receive a pair.

Like most ambassadors, Henderson carried with him a number of possessions acquired at his various diplomatic postings; unlike most ambassadors, he had nowhere else to put them. With neither wife nor family, he had no 'base' back in England and his beloved parental home, Sedgwick Park (near Horsham in Sussex), with its spectacular gardens and views, was sold by his sister-in-law after his mother's death in 1931. Henderson took much of his own furniture to Berlin, enough to fill two rooms. One of the pieces was a reading table given to him shortly before his posting to Belgrade by Queen Mary from the furniture shop she sponsored.[69] He also displayed a portrait of his late mother in the Embassy.[70]

* The portrait after Winterhalter.

228

67. One of the last official photographs taken of the Embassy by the Ministry of Works in 1939: a reception room with a footman.

Henderson lacked assistance with interior decoration in the shape of a wife. However, he could call upon an old friend, Mademoiselle Germaine Lens,[†] who 'had a genius for such things'[71] and had helped him with the layout of his apartment during his posting to Paris. She 'arranged' the Embassy in Berlin for Henderson, who later recalled how the Embassy's own honorary *décorateur*, a Jew 'Aryanized by the Nazis because of his indispensable skill in such matters' was much impressed by her efforts, stating that 'even in Lady D'Abernon's day the Embassy had never looked so well'.[72] This man's fate in Germany after 1939 is unknown.

† The name is given as 'Germaine Lens' in Henderson's will; but as 'Germaine Leus' in *Water under the Bridges*, quite possibly a misreading of Henderson's very cursive handwriting by Henderson's literary agent/executor after his death. The author has so far been unable to discover anything else about her.

CHAPTER 17
1937–1938: 'A Soul Scarifying Job'

Henderson believed he had to make efforts to understand the Nazi Government and negotiate with it from a position of knowledge and strength. So, unlike his predecessors Rumbold and Phipps, he sought – and gained – permission from London to attend the annual Nuremberg Nazi Party Congress of 6–13 September 1937. To avoid the appearance of a Franco-British diplomatic split, the French Ambassador André François-Poncet went too, but for one day only.[1] This was the first time the British and French Ambassadors had been to the event (although other foreign delegations, with the exception of the American one, had attended previous congresses), and Henderson, who stayed for two days, was impressed by its well-planned theatrical qualities, particularly Speer's 'Cathedral of Light' created by hundreds of powerful searchlights directed upwards into the sky.[2] He was not the only British person there. Diana Mosley and Unity Mitford, together with their parents, Lord and Lady Redesdale, were present, having revised their previous opinions about the 'murderous gang of pests'.

Back in Berlin, that October a new and unique diplomatic challenge presented itself to the Embassy: how to deal, from the point of view of official protocol, with the forthcoming visit to the capital by the former King Edward VIII (now the 'Duke of Windsor') and his new Duchess. Since his abdication in December 1936 the Duke had consistently expressed a naive kind of patriotic-inspired sympathy for Hitler's regime in Germany, principally as a bulwark against the threat of communism. Ribbentrop had exploited this sympathy, boasting to Hitler of his own self-professed close social connections with both Edward[*] and his former mistress Wallis Simpson. In the end, Ribbentrop completely misread the constitutional conundrum posed by Edward's wish to marry the American divorcée and the former King's own influence over British diplomatic affairs, concocting a conspiracy theory that he had been forced to abdicate by the anti-German faction in the Foreign Office and British Establishment.

In May 1937 Edward VIII's successor, his brother, King George VI, had asked the Foreign Office to prepare guidance for British Ambassadors as to how they should behave as regards the former King and his wife-shortly-to-be (they were to marry on 3 June). It was a delicate situation and in the end it was decided that the couple could be entertained privately, but not officially, and that embassy staff should not arrange for them to take part in official events in their host countries. This all became disturbingly close to home for Henderson and his staff when

---

[*] His full name was Edward Albert Christian George Andrew Patrick David, but his preferred name – and as he was known to family and friends – was his last name, David. He had first visited the Embassy in Berlin in August 1913.

the Duke announced that he wished to visit Germany to make a study of the country's social housing (one of his special interests) and endeavour to promote harmony between the two countries, exploiting his unique family background and connections. It was Henderson who first told the British Government about the proposed visit, having received a letter from the Duke informing him that the visit would essentially be private but 'organised under the auspices of the Reich.'[3] He would arrive in Berlin on the Nord Express on Monday, 11 October and requested the services of an English-speaking attaché.

In view of the Duke's unique constitutional position and obvious remaining 'clout' in Germany, both the Foreign Office and the King were against the visit. It was an understandably difficult issue for the Embassy: given the circumstances, on their arrival in Berlin the couple could hardly be met 'officially' by the Ambassador or stay and be entertained as honoured guests in the Embassy itself (the case had a British monarch or other member of the royal family made a state or private visit to the country). Nor, considering who the Duke was, could the couple be completely ignored. Henderson himself had a cast-iron excuse: he would be on leave. The Foreign Office in London was definitely of the opinion that the couple should not be met at the railway station, but Henderson's number two Sir George Ogilvie-Forbes was in a quandary, writing to London on 1 October: 'It will be extremely embarrassing and painful for me if I am instructed to ignore his Royal Highness's presence, for this will not be understood here.'[4] In the end, a compromise was reached: a junior member of the embassy staff met the couple at the station, and Ogilvie-Forbes called on them later in their hotel (the Kaiserhof). While in Germany, the Windsors took meals with Hess and Goering and met Hitler at Berchtesgaden, Ribbentrop continuing to convince himself that the former King's sympathies towards what appeared to be the more positive aspects of the Nazi regime would have a constructive effect on official British foreign policy.

On leave in England, Henderson was spending time with the closely connected Establishment circles of the period and on 12 October was a luncheon guest of the Duke and Duchess of Kent at Bryanston Square in London. Irene Ravensdale was there, and Henderson told her and his hosts all about his experiences, so far, in Berlin. On the 23rd he was amongst Nancy Astor's guests at one of her house parties at the luxurious Astor family home at Cliveden. Other guests included Foreign Secretary Anthony Eden and his wife, the editor of *The Times*, Geoffrey Dawson, Lord Lothian, Sir Alexander Cadogan, Tom Jones, Irene Ravensdale and her younger sister, Lady Alexandra Metcalfe. In the clipped upper-class accents of the period, Henderson and the assembled guests talked much about his German experiences and views; Dawson's *The Times* editorial of a few days later was apparently heavily influenced by these conversations.

Lady Alexandra Metcalfe met Henderson for the first time at the house party. Irene found discussions with Henderson 'very interesting to the degree Baba wondered whether I had been wrong in refusing him.'[5] Indeed, she had to endure bouts of teasing to this effect from several of the female guests. Lady Alexandra (known as 'Baba' to friends) was closely associated with the Duke of Windsor, having married Captain Edward Dudley Metcalfe ('Fruity') in 1925; Fruity became the then Prince of Wales' equerry and long-term close companion. The marriage was not entirely successful, however, and Baba had gone on to enjoy a long affair with Oswald Mosley, an affair which began with almost indecent haste after the death of his wife, Irene and Baba's sister 'Cimmie' in 1933. It also coincided with Mosley's relationship with Diana Guinness (née Mitford). Lady Alexandra's intimacy with Mosley earned her the 'malicious' soubriquet 'Ba-ba Black-shirt' as 'Chips' Channon noted.[6] Another example of 'Mayfair rushing Hitlerwards', as Phipps had described it, Baba attended the opening of the Olympics in Berlin in August 1936. The following June she and Fruity were amongst the select number of guests who attended the former King Edward VIII's wedding to Wallis Simpson in France, Fruity acting as Edward's best man. Such was her rapport with Nevile Henderson at the Cliveden weekend that he invited Baba to stay at the Embassy after her visit a few weeks later to see her niece Vivien, Cimmie's daughter, who was being 'finished' in Munich.

In an attempt to promote British–German understanding through 'soft' diplomacy, Henderson had suggested that Britain participate in the international hunting exhibition to be held in Berlin in November 1937. The event was dear to Henderson's heart as he numbered hunting amongst his keen outdoor pursuits (as François-Poncet remarked, Henderson was 'an enthusiast of the chase, of dogdom and of golf'[7]). Indeed, far from sharing Phipps' caustic opinions of his hunting fixations, Henderson enjoyed a genuine friendship with Goering over this shared 'sport', spending time stag shooting at Goering's estate at Rominten[*] in East Prussia early that October. Henderson secured the participation in the hunting exhibition of Lord Halifax,[†] then Lord President of the Council, who visited Berlin from 17 to 21 November. Ostensibly, Halifax was there in his capacity as a Yorkshire Master of Foxhounds (English hunting traditions were greatly admired in Germany), and, certainly, from the exhibition point of view, the event appeared to be a success. Halifax was not the only British participant: Lord Londonderry had made a fresh visit to Berlin on 5 November, attending the opening banquet of the exhibition and lodging at the Embassy where he had a discussion with Henderson.[8]

Henderson gave a large dinner party attended by most of the 'leading Nazi Ministers and personalities,'[9] in Halifax's honour, enabling Halifax to make informal diplomatic contact with members of the German Government along the lines that Neville Chamberlain desired might be a useful outcome of the visit. Halifax also visited Hitler at Berchtesgaden, attended Holy Communion[‡] in the English Church, attended several formal and informal embassy lunches, and, on the last day of his visit, took tea at the Embassy with Joseph and Magda Goebbels together with 'leading personalities of the National-Socialist Party.'[10] Goebbels made quite an impression, Halifax confessing in his memoirs that he liked him.[11] (Henderson did, too: he described Goebbels as 'probably the most intelligent, from a purely brain point of view, of all the Nazi leaders'[12]). Baba Metcalfe was staying as Henderson's guest, and she and Lady Leitrim (once again temporarily acting as Henderson's chatelaine) entertained Frau Goebbels while her husband and Halifax held their discussions.[13] Baba had no idea that just a short distance away from the Embassy

[*] Now Krasnolesye in Russia.
[†] A story got out in the press that Halifax had been at Cliveden before going out to Germany on this visit – which was not the case – and that therefore his meetings with various Nazi leaders had been plotted by the members of the 'Cliveden Set'.
[‡] Halifax was a High Anglican; his nickname within government circles was 'The Holy Fox'.

the previous autumn the Goebbels had hosted the secret marriage between her lover Mosley and Diana Mitford, whom she and Irene both loathed, blaming her for luring Mosley away from their sister Cimmie. Baba returned to England full of the wonderful time she had had at the Embassy, but when, in November the following year she and her sister finally found out about the secret marriage, they were devastated.[*]

Another conjugal event took place on 11 January 1938 when Field Marshal von Blomberg, the Minister for War, married his mistress at the War Ministry in Bendlerstrasse (very close to the British Consulate at 17 Tiergartenstrasse). Much to Hitler's apparent consternation it turned out that von Blomberg's new wife was an ex-prostitute.[†] Henderson first learned about the marriage during a dinner at the Ministry of Propaganda on 12 January 1938, and von Blomberg's resignation in disgrace began a chain of political events. Adding to his responsibilities as both President and Chancellor of Germany, Hitler himself now took personal command of the German military, moving von Neurath from the post of Foreign Minister. The latter was replaced by Ribbentrop, whom Hitler recalled from his post as Ambassador to London after only just over a year in post; Herbert von Dirksen took his place. After this government reshuffle Henderson feared for the worst: Blomberg and Neurath had still commanded some respect (at least in his opinion), two of the 'moderates' whom he believed at that stage could still influence Hitler.

Henderson's fears for the future of the peace of Europe under Hitler were soon realised, for on 11 March news reached Berlin of German troop movements towards the Austrian border. Colonel Mason-MacFarlane, the British Military Attaché who had joined the embassy staff in January 1938, did some reconnoitring and ascertained that, contrary to official denials, the troop movements were indeed taking place: Hitler's forces were invading Austria.[14] First Secretary Ivone Kirkpatrick left the Embassy and gate-crashed Goering's thousand-guest diplomatic party at the Haus der Flieger dramatically to hand Henderson a telegram instructing him to see von Neurath – who was still Foreign Minister – immediately. As a small gesture of disapproval over Germany's Anschluss with Austria, Henderson subsequently refused to attend the anniversary commemoration for the dead of the Great War and ostentatiously paid a visit to the Austrian Ambassador, the Union Jack flying from his official car bonnet[‡] – only to find the Ambassador about to leave for the ceremony, where he was to make his own position on the 'invasion' clear by giving the Nazi salute.[15]

The next German-speaking area of Europe slated to be reunited with the Fatherland under Hitler, thereby putting to rights the Treaty of Versailles, was the Sudetenland area of Czechoslovakia, in which, according to the Treaty's

[*] Baba subsequently became extremely close to Lord Halifax for a number of years including the period after he became British Ambassador to Washington in January 1941.

[†] The not-so-happy couple honeymooned on the isle of Capri a few weeks later, continuing a long tradition in German Establishment circles of 'escape' there. Fritz Krupp, heir to the steel empire and a good friend of the Emperor Wilhelm II, maintained an erotic homosexual grotto on the island and committed suicide in 1902 rather than face trial in Berlin. The island remained a fashionable resort for the German well-to-do – Goering visited it in January 1937. It is tempting to think that Lord Leighton's painting *Capri – Sunrise* (see Chapter 16), on display in the Embassy, might have sparked off conversations about such topics.

[‡] William Shirer, the CBS correspondent in Berlin, reported that the British Ambassador's car was a familiar sight in Berlin and had the licence plate number 6 (*This is Berlin: A Narrative History, 1938–1940*, p. 64).

geographical terms, many ethnic Germans lived. In May 1938 rumours began to spread that an invasion of Czechoslovakia was imminent, apparently emanating from a German secret service agent working for the Czechs.[16] Henderson again despatched Mason-MacFarlane to find evidence of German troop movements in Saxony and Silesia, but this time he could find nothing: Henderson was instructed to deliver an official protest, but there was no invasion. This 'May Scare' indeed turned out to be merely a scare, but in response Chamberlain had stated in the House of Commons that, if Germany invaded Czechoslovakia, Britain would be bound to intervene.

Unfortunately, there was at the same time an episode of bathos at the Embassy that revitalised the pervading atmosphere of febrile rumour. According to Henderson, Thomas Troubridge, the Naval Attaché, had routinely made arrangements to return to England by train on leave with his family; another member of the embassy staff asked whether his own children might travel back with them. More seats had now been booked than were available on the train, so the railway made the eminently practical suggestion that a further coach might be added if those making the additional bookings could fill it. Two further staff members and their families duly agreed to return to England at the same time, and so the additional coach was booked. This innocent situation was interpreted by Hitler's Government and Henderson's diplomatic colleagues as British Embassy staff taking flight from Germany with their families. Henderson claimed he knew nothing about this until the French Ambassador intercepted him on the Embassy's steps and asked him whether it was true that he was 'evacuating the whole of the British Colony'. To add to the embarrassment, the Foreign Office in London got wind of what was going on and asked Henderson to cancel the arrangements, which he immediately did. Gallingly, the German Foreign Ministry suggested that Henderson should not be so 'alarmist.'[17]

But whether the 'May Scare' had a real basis in reality or not, in other ways the threat to the British, in particular, was real. On 17 August the Gestapo arrested the British Passport Control Officer in Vienna – Captain Thomas Kendrick – near Salzburg on charges of espionage and interrogated him for three days before deporting him. Kendrick had become Passport Control Officer in 1925; it was a post which, like that in Berlin, was a cover for the British Secret Service (the British gave up their Embassy in Vienna after the Anschluss of March 1938,[§] Henderson in Berlin becoming British Ambassador to the newly united Germany and Austria, but the PCO continued its duties in the city). As was the case in Berlin, the Office was flooded by applications from Jews desperate to escape from their increasingly hostile persecutors; in early August Kendrick had reported that his secret intelligence work was being badly affected partly because his staff were so overworked that 'they will burst into tears at the slightest provocation.'[18] Kendrick's arrest sparked a flurry of panicked destruction of files at the Vienna PCO in response to fears that the Gestapo might turn up at any moment and forcibly search the

§ Following the Anschluss the British Embassy/Residence at 6 Metternichgasse in Vienna was sold to the National Socialist Flying Club in a disadvantageous financial deal that raised eyebrows in London and inspired a parliamentary debate. After the war it was sold back to the British Government at the price it was sold for in 1938: it remains the Residence of the British Ambassador to Austria.

68. Sir Nevile Henderson amongst a group of foreign diplomats chatting informally to Hitler at the 1938 National Socialist Party Congress at Nuremberg, from *The Illustrated London News* of 17 September 1938.

premises: while embassies have always enjoyed protection from uninvited entry by local police and security services, the PCO did not.[19] Henderson's protests to the authorities were of little avail.

Henderson went to the Nuremberg Nazi Party Congress the following month, September 1938. There usually being insufficient hotel space in Nuremberg, diplomats visiting the Congress were forced to lodge in their train carriages.[20] Henderson was feeling unwell, and the experience of having to 'rough it' in this manner hardly improved matters, particularly as his stay lasted five days rather than the thirty-six hours he had originally intended.[21] After the experience, he was 'glad to get to Berlin and a bath. The discomforts of the diplomatic train are inconceivable.'[22] He was evidently not himself, even forgetting to bring writing materials for notes and reports, instead having to use blank pages torn from some detective novels he had with him.[23] His general feeling of psychological dislocation must have been worsened by a sudden encounter with the irrepressible and 'notorious' Unity Mitford at a party given by Heinrich Himmler. She 'squeaked out "Heil Hitler"' to Henderson, who was 'so dumbfounded that I forgot my usual retort which is "Rule Britannia". Except to shake her by the hand I didn't speak to her.'[24] Both Unity's parents were again at the event, staying at the Grand Hotel in Nuremberg and sitting with Unity in front-row seats at what one might term the Congress's 'plenary sessions'.

Hitler was now making increasingly volatile threats to come to the military aid of the ethnic German inhabitants of the Sudetenland, a situation which threatened to spiral out of control and ignite a European war. In the second half of September

1938 Henderson became deeply involved in Neville Chamberlain's historic personal summit diplomacy to try to avert that outcome, the Prime Minister determined to engage in one-to-one discussions with Hitler without the traditional accompaniment of ambassadors. Ulrich von Hassell, an old-school Prussian diplomat of the same generation as Henderson (and whom he had first met when posted to Belgrade), recently sacked by Ribbentrop as German Ambassador to Rome*, visited Henderson at the Embassy just before this period. Henderson was 'very frank and friendly, but at the same time visibly agitated'. Henderson explained to von Hassell that Britain would strive to its utmost to preserve peace in Europe, but that, if Germany were to use force, and France attempted to intervene, then Britain would support France. Negotiations for Chamberlain's visit to Hitler were at that point at a critical stage, and in von Hassell's presence Henderson telephoned Goering to intercede with Hitler.[25]

Visible in the background of many of the photographs and newsreels taken of the events, Henderson accompanied Chamberlain to meet Hitler at Berchtesgaden and was with him the following week at the Petersburg Hotel at Bad Godesberg on the Rhine during the negotiations over the Sudetenland. Hitler and his entourage stayed in the Hotel Dreesen on the opposite bank of the river, where, not reassuringly, they had plotted the 'Night of the Long Knives' in June 1934. Colonel Mason-MacFarlane returned to Berlin and drove to Czechoslovakia, risking life and limb in crossing the frontier to deliver the proposals for the revised frontier to the Czech Government. Not unreasonably, the Czechs refused to submit to the proposals, and so the French and British began to prepare for likely war. Chamberlain sent his special advisor, Sir Horace Wilson (who had been with him at Bad Godesberg), to Berlin with a personal letter from the Prime Minister to Hitler, urging him to rely on discussions to achieve his aims, rather than military might. Ivone Kirkpatrick attended Wilson's meeting with Hitler, where the situation was not resolved.

In what must have been an extraordinarily tense atmosphere, that evening Wilson stayed at the Embassy as Henderson's guest, Kirkpatrick remembering that 'Henderson and Wilson dined in the dining room, while I ate off a tray in front of the radio set.'[26] During the night instructions came through from Chamberlain in London to deliver yet another personal message to Hitler, which Wilson duly did the following day. Hitler was intransigent in his demands and so Wilson delivered an ultimatum to Hitler to the same effect that Henderson had told von Hassell: that, if Czechoslovakia were invaded and France supported Czechoslovakia, Britain would support France. That same afternoon, 28 September 1938, as Wilson flew back to London, all seemed lost.

In twenty-first-century terms the embassy staff had now reached psychological 'closure', Kirkpatrick later recalling that 'There was general satisfaction that the die had been cast.'[27] In preparation for evacuation the staff had already sought and been granted permission from London to start burning important embassy

---

* The German Embassy in Rome before the Second World War was the Villa Wolkonsky. After the war the building became – and remains – the British Ambassador's Residence; the Italian Old Master paintings donated by Lady D'Abernon (see Chapter 10) are located there.

69. Prime Minister Neville Chamberlain arrives at Munich on 28 September 1938 with Sir Nevile Henderson and Joachim von Ribbentrop.

documents.[28]* Suddenly, they became aware of a continuous vibration and rumbling outside in the street. Kirkpatrick went out on to the Embassy's front steps to see what it was: a mechanised division was moving past the government buildings and the Embassy, Hitler watching from the Reich Chancellery further down the street. The convoy was so long it took more than three hours to pass by. In a gesture of power to the watching world, Hitler was pointedly mobilising his army to move towards Czechoslovakia. What he did not bargain for, however, was the German reaction on the street which was not, as he might have expected, supportive and jingoistic, but silent and depressed. 'The picture which it represented was almost that of a hostile army passing through a conquered city. Hitler was deeply impressed.'[29]

After further deliberations amongst the Nazi top brass, and with Europe poised on the brink of a second world war, Hitler suddenly agreed to postpone his invasion of Czechoslovakia and to take up Chamberlain's suggestion – now supported by Mussolini – of a further face-to-face meeting. Henderson telephoned the Permanent Under-Secretary of the Foreign Office, Sir Alexander Cadogan,[†] from

* Almost all of the Embassy's archives concerning the period 1933–36 were destroyed in haste. This proved to be problematic after the likelihood of war receded following the Munich Agreement, so copies of certain documents had to be sent from London.

† Earlier that year the staunch anti-Nazi Sir Robert Vansittart had been 'booted upstairs' at the Foreign Office to the toothless position of 'Chief Diplomatic Advisor' and replaced as Permanent Under-Secretary by Sir Alexander Cadogan.

the Embassy with a message that Hitler was inviting Chamberlain to a conference the following morning at Munich, a message that was rapturously received in the House of Commons as the Prime Minister was summing up the depressing international situation.

Henderson was present at the negotiations in Munich[‡] and witnessed the signing of the agreement transferring the Sudetenland to Germany; the issue of the ethnic German population in that part of the world apparently resolved as a result, Hitler agreed that he had no further European territorial ambitions. Henderson had left Munich by the following morning and so was not present at the private meeting between Chamberlain and Hitler at which the British Prime Minister persuaded Hitler to sign a pre-prepared further, more informal, agreement that Britain and Germany would never go to war. This was the piece of paper that Chamberlain waved to a jubilant crowd at Heston Aerodrome on his return from Munich and which he later waved from one of the first floor front windows of 10 Downing Street, unwisely, as it turned out, describing events as 'peace in our time'. It was the same window from which Lord Beaconsfield had leaned in July 1878 on his return from the Congress of Berlin, promising the jubilant crowds below 'peace with honour'.

Kirkpatrick remembered that during these weeks of crisis in September 1938 he had found it easier to live in the Embassy where he could be immediately on hand for all emergencies and deal with the 'ceaseless flow of messages.'[30] Sir Horace Rumbold's and his colleagues' stressful experiences in exactly the same rooms a quarter of a century earlier were repeated as embassy staff worked frantic twelve-hour days. Kirkpatrick remembered how he barely left the building for three weeks, 'and almost every night was broken by the arrival of urgent telegrams.'[31] He found the building did not encourage an optimistic atmosphere: 'The Embassy itself was the gloomiest house I have ever inhabited and it was something of a relief to have a change of treadmill' (he accompanied Henderson and Chamberlain to Bad Godesberg).[32]

Through secret visits to the Embassy, certain high-ranking members of the German army concerned about the direction in which Hitler was leading their country had let it be known that they would be prepared to overthrow Hitler if guaranteed support by the British Government. The latter's response[33] was, however, that, if the German Generals were to take the initiative and rise against Hitler themselves, then the British Government would support them. But the Munich Agreement effectively put paid to the idea. That October the former Emperor Wilhelm II wrote to the widowed Queen Mary congratulating her country on the negotiations, which he hoped would prevent a second world war.

On his return to Berlin from Munich Henderson took part in the first meeting of the international commission set up to oversee the implementation of the agreement, a task that he found 'distasteful,'[34] and he left for England as soon as possible afterwards. Since the mid-1930s he had felt there was something wrong with his health,[35] and now his medical condition had been judged serious enough for him spend four months in a nursing home, during which time he underwent throat surgery. Given the turn of world events, with hindsight he described those

‡ At the newly completed Führerbau, now the Hochschule für Musik und Theater.

four months' absence as a 'minor disaster.'[36] At first received with so much relief, the popularity of the Munich Agreement quickly palled as it became evident that Hitler's ambitions to dominate Europe had been halted only temporarily, at great cost to the Czechs and to British honour. After less than a year's posting to Berlin, Embassy Third Secretary Con O'Neill resigned from the Foreign Office in disgust. O'Neill's father, Hugh (a Privy Counsellor and senior Conservative MP), appealed to Sir Horace Wilson, who had met Con in Berlin, to dissuade his son from this decision: Con was a Fellow of All Souls in Oxford and had a highly promising diplomatic career in front of him. On the contrary: Wilson disliked and distrusted professional diplomats and believed that Con should indeed leave the service. Speaking decades afterwards, Wilson's attitude towards 'the hot-tempered young man' remained breathtakingly arrogant: 'What had it to do with him. He was addressing envelopes or something. He didn't matter a row of beans.'[37]*

The unpalatable nature of the Nazi regime revealed itself once again with the widespread officially inspired pogrom against the Jews of 9 November 1938 (popularly known as Kristallnacht) in retaliation for the murder of a German diplomat by a Jewish student in Paris the previous day. The events of that date traumatised Katherine Harrison. Moments after she had walked out of a shoe shop on Tauentzienstrasse a lorry drew up and uniformed men rushed into the premises, dragging the old shopkeeper out by her hair. Later that day Nazi soldiers entered the Harrisons' own apartment block and carried off their landlord to a concentration camp.[38]

***

During Henderson's absence from Germany Counsellor George Ogilvie-Forbes acted as Chargé d'Affaires. Kirkpatrick, who had served at the Embassy since September 1933, left post in December 1938 to become Head of the Central Department of the Foreign Office in London, probably gratefully, in view of the circumstances. A study of embassy correspondence in this four-month period – during which time Ogilvie-Forbes produced the Embassy's annual report for 1938 – has given rise to debate that he managed to at least partially reverse Henderson's apparent pro-'appeasement' stance.[39] In January 1939 Ogilvie-Forbes and Military Attaché Mason-MacFarlane sent London reports, based on pro-British Nazi intelligence received the previous month, that Hitler was about to go on the offensive, including planning a surprise air attack on London. These warnings, however, Chamberlain appeared not to take particularly seriously,[40] although the Foreign Office was to recommend an increasingly tougher line against Germany.

Henderson returned to Berlin in the middle of February 1939. He later described himself at that point as 'physically ... still unfit', but not as pessimistic about events as he had been in the previous autumn.[41] He did, however, take exception to the apparent change of policy under his deputy, gathering his chancery staff together in order to inform them of his displeasure. According to Mason-MacFarlane,

---

* According to his obituary in *The Times* (12 January 1988) O'Neill attempted to rejoin the Foreign Office after the outbreak of war, only for Wilson to block his appointment. Instead he joined the Intelligence Corps, succeeding in rejoining the Foreign Office in 1947.

[Henderson] considered that we were appreciating the situation wrongly and misinforming HMG. He wished us to understand that in future all reports emanating from the Embassy would have to be strictly in accordance with his personal opinions. There was little to be said on our side except to point out to him that we remained in disagreement with his views on Hitler and on the course which Nazi Germany was likely to pursue.[42]

Ian Colvin, Central European correspondent for the *News Chronicle* from 1937 to 1939 and a close friend of Ogilvie-Forbes, strongly disagreed with Henderson's views. He recorded that when he wanted to discuss German affairs with a British diplomat, he preferred to do so with Ogilvie-Forbes, in his office in the embassy building. This had to be in lowered voices, however, for Henderson's deputy was sure that there were listening devices in the party wall with the Adlon Hotel, certain areas of which were increasingly being used for Nazi Government purposes.[43]

According to several accounts Henderson did not get on well with all of his British-based staff in Berlin. Given the pressures under which everyone was working; the increasingly appalling circumstances and sense of powerless responsibility for a drift to another European conflict; and the need to deal with the unpredictable and often callous behaviour of the Nazis and their followers, the stresses on everyone must however have been immense. By this stage merely commuting between the Embassy and home must have been a daily trial for staff. Official and many private buildings (indeed entire streets) were draped in swastikas and portraits of Hitler; military music and parades of uniformed troops and youth brigades could scarcely be avoided; there were rumours of terrible things happening at Gestapo headquarters a short distance to the south; permanent hoardings advertising the contents of the rabidly anti-Semitic publication *Die Stürmer* were everywhere, as was direct evidence for and rumour of violence and atrocities, on a daily basis. According to Hugh Greene, Berlin correspondent for *The Daily Telegraph*, it was 'rather like living in a lunatic asylum where everybody's got megalomania and persecution complex combined. One can never escape a feeling of being in an enemy country.'[44] Indeed, there was no escape from any of this other than to leave Germany. And in contrast to the pressured atmosphere the embassy staff's predecessors had experienced for a few weeks in the same building a quarter of a century earlier, all of this went on for years and continued to worsen.

Technology had also moved on since 1914: Hitler's hysterical, rabble-rousing speeches were broadcast everywhere on the radio, via loudspeakers in the streets and in the cinema. 'The loud, excitable, ranting voice of Hitler each time one turned on the radio did not help allay feelings of alarm and apprehension,' Katherine Harrison remembered.[45] There must also have been nagging doubts that members of the Embassy's locally engaged staff might be under pressure to serve more than one master. There was no sense how long it might last or where it might lead or end, so it would hardly have been surprising had there been only occasional outbursts of temper amongst the embassy staff. With the odds that were at stake, it was understandable that Henderson described his post as a 'soul scarifying job.'[46] Even worse, the illness from which he was suffering had been diagnosed as cancer.

There were other pressures, too. Martha Dodd was convinced that the embassies of the non-Axis powers and their staff were being constantly spied upon, even to the extent of opening documents sent in the diplomatic bag. Diplomats and officials could talk freely in the Tiergarten, but she believed that the American Embassy (on Pariser Platz) was being bugged by the German Government, so that the Ambassador and his family could not even talk freely amongst themselves or on the telephone.[47] The atmosphere and pressures, the 'strain and terror' under the Nazi regime, even for a foreign ambassador, were so much to bear that she believed they effectively killed her mother: within four months of the family's return to the United States in late 1937 Mrs Dodd died of a heart attack.[48] She was not alone in such a reaction: Norman Ebbutt, chief Berlin correspondent for *The Times* and a virulent critic of the Nazi regime, suffered a major stroke a month after being expelled from Berlin in August 1937.

But whatever the mitigating circumstances, Henderson did have a reputation for arrogance and could be overbearing and self-important. Con O'Neill resigned and Ogilvie-Forbes requested a transfer to another post.[49] Working as Assistant Military Attaché under Mason-MacFarlane, Kenneth Strong, writing a generation later, described the position in suitably diplomatic language: 'The policy of the British Embassy under Sir Nevile Henderson did not always seem to the attachés to be consistent with the available military information.'[50] The fact that the attachés were physically separated at 17 Tiergartenstrasse from the Ambassador and chancery staff at 70 Wilhelmstrasse cannot have helped matters either, as Henderson himself acknowledged. On the other hand, despite disagreeing with his views, Ivone Kirkpatrick later recorded that he had liked Henderson 'very much. He was a human chief for whom it was a pleasure to work, and except for a few angry outbursts when I tried to prove that war was inevitable he never was anything but kind and appreciative.'[51] It is noticeable that Henderson himself later admitted that he relied very much on Kirkpatrick and not on Ogilvie-Forbes: when Henderson returned to the Embassy in February 1939 he must have missed Kirkpatrick's presence.

Some Americans based in Berlin at the time were damning about Henderson. William Shirer, the CBS reporter in the city, commented, 'From the moment of [Henderson]'s arrival in Berlin he struck me as being not only sympathetic to Nazism, but to Nazism's aims.'[52] Martha Dodd had at first been open-minded about the Nazi regime, even enjoying romantic attachments with several of its prominent members, but as time went on during the four years she spent in Germany her opinions hardened, particularly in relation to Phipps' successor. Writing in 1939 she described Henderson's apparent 'fondness for Nazi leaders' as 'brash, brazen and disgusting …. It indicated that the English … had lost hold on themselves.' 'Everyone in the diplomatic corps marvelled and gossiped about the ease and facility with which Henderson was held tight and without protest to the Nazi breast.' He was the 'Beau Brummel representative of Mr. Chamberlain.'[53] On the British side, Robert Bruce Lockhart recalled a brief encounter with Henderson in Berlin shortly after the 1938 German Anschluss with Austria. After lunch with Ogilvie-Forbes, Lockhart walked through the Tiergarten to the Embassy to see the Ambassador, who was 'just recovering from "flu" and had a huge fire, central heating and himself two waistcoats.' According to Lockhart, Henderson was pleased that the Nazi sceptic Anthony Eden had recently resigned as Foreign Secretary* and was in favour of 'making the Czechs give way. Says cannot possibly go to war over Sudeten Germans.'[54] Many years later Iverach McDonald, another *Times* correspondent in Berlin, recalled how the

> British embassy in Berlin … was led by that most headstrong and purblind of all the appeasers, Sir Nevile Henderson; he more than once warned me, with his eye on the latest issue of *The Times* on his desk, about the dangers of picking out German events which did not fit in with the picture of the amenable Reich which he saw and which he commended to London. Although there were good men on the ambassador's staff, I have never been so out of touch with a British embassy as I was then.[55]

Henderson would surely not have been flattered to learn that, of the three British Ambassadors of Hitler's Chancellorship, he 'left the most favourable impression' on Hitler himself.[56][†]

Attempts have been made to rehabilitate Henderson's long-held notorious reputation as an arch-appeaser who did not sufficiently stand up to the threat to world peace that was literally on his doorstep.[57] Given the circumstances and personalities involved, it is fair to say that he was probably out of his depth, but those who actually had to deal with those momentous and terrifying circumstances in person were not of course blessed with our hindsight: for example, with Hitler's unpredictability in mind, Henderson persuaded the British Government not to issue a formal warning to the German Chancellor at Nuremburg in 1938.[58] It is, however, true that several members of Henderson's staff did have a more robust attitude at the time to the situation in which they all found themselves and to the daily atrocities taking place around them than Henderson appeared to possess. Mason-MacFarlane, whose residence was located at Sophienstrasse[‡] in the Tiergarten, very close to the one of the regular sites of Hitler's endless military parades on the Charlottenburger Chausee,[§] reportedly once told Ewan Butler, another *Times* correspondent, how he might use the location of his residence to practical advantage during one of Hitler's forthcoming birthday parades. '"Easy rifle-shot," [Mason-MacFarlane] said laconically, "I could pick the bastard off from here as easy as winking, and what's more I'm thinking of doing it."'[59] Self-restraint must have got the better of him, although his hatred for Hitler and the Nazi regime was more than just professional. Shortly after Hitler's triumphant return from the newly won Sudetenland in September 1938, his wife was harangued by a group of Hitler Youth demanding to know why her house did not exhibit a swastika. She saw them off, the group 'mouthing insults against her and everything British.'[60]

---

* On 20 February that year; he was replaced by Lord Halifax.
† In this particular monologue (16 May 1942, at the 'Wolf's Lair' in East Prussia) Hitler also described Rumbold as 'wrapped permanently in the haze of intoxication' and Phipps as 'a complete thug' (*Hitler's Table Talk*, p.488).
‡ The campus of the Technical University of Berlin now covers the site of this street.
§ Now Strasse des 17. Juni.

CHAPTER 18
1938–1939: 'FAILURE
OF A MISSION'

> Jews trying to find a way out of Germany queued in their hundreds outside
> the British Consulate, clinging to the hope that they would get a British
> passport or a visa. Day after day we saw them standing along the corridors,
> down the steps and across the large courtyard waiting their turn to fill in
> the forms that might lead to freedom. In the end, that queue grew to be a
> mile long. Some were hysterical. Many wept. All were desperate.[1]

The British Consulate-General at 17 Tiergartenstrasse had been dealing with
Jewish asylum applications since Hitler's rise to power in 1933, but after
Kristallnacht in November 1938 it was besieged by Jews desperate to leave
Germany; it was increasingly difficult for consular staff even to enter the building
owing to the press of people outside. Frank Foley now had to balance his 'day job'
with his secret intelligence duties to an even greater degree. As long queues built
up, Foley arranged for three night porters to come over from the Embassy to help
with crowd control.[2] He worked processing asylum applications from seven in the
morning until ten at night, and in the end helped probably tens of thousands of
Jews to leave Germany, almost certainly saving their lives. In 2004, on what would
have been his 120th birthday, a monument to Foley was unveiled at the new British
Embassy in Berlin, while on the seventieth anniversary of Kristallnacht in
November 2008 a further memorial was unveiled at the Foreign Office in London
commemorating the embassy staff's efforts during this period. Henderson's name
appears on neither tribute.

The secret intelligence service station in Berlin continued to operate under
cover of the British Passport Control Office, but after the events in Austria the
previous August there was growing apprehension of imminent hostile intervention
by the Gestapo. Passport Control Office staff were not classified as diplomatic
staff and hence not protected by the same diplomatic immunity or privileges,
and Henderson refused to allow them to be granted this status in Berlin.[3] Agents
continued to operate in increasingly difficult circumstances: Baron William de
Ropp worked for the British and passed information from members of the Nazi
regime until he relocated to Switzerland in August 1938, fearing his cover was about
to be blown. Dr Karl Krüger was another agent who gave the British information
about German U-boat development but was assumed to have been betrayed and
killed. An anonymous source, 'Jones' left packets of documents with various British
Consuls in Germany and Switzerland; again suddenly this source dried up when
he felt he was coming under suspicion from the authorities.[4]

While the Gestapo increased its surveillance over foreign missions in Berlin
and their staff, the Embassy's internal security was itself a worry for the British
Foreign Office. In February 1937 Deputy Head of the Secret Intelligence Services

70. The Embassy photographed in the last few months before the Second World War.

Major Valentine Vivian was sent on a security inspection of the Embassy in Rome. What he found was not reassuring. It was the perennial issue of overdue reliance upon locally engaged staff, which for an Embassy operating in a country with a hostile government posed a major risk. In July 1937 he made a similar inspection of the facilities in Berlin. Echoing the concerns that had previously been voiced about the security at 17 Tiergartenstrasse given the employment of a German caretaker, Vivian reported that the Embassy was vulnerable to infiltration by the German porter, especially during Henderson's summer leave period. He concluded that the Gestapo could easily gain access to secret papers, going so far as to state that in view of 'the situation in Berlin and the German mentality, it would be sheer lunacy not to act on the assumption that … the porter is in the pay of the Gestapo.'[5] He strongly recommended the employment of British-based staff in this regard. Reiterating former guidance on this subject, he advised that 'It follows that, if an Embassy staff contains natives of the country or persons belonging to the British community domiciled in the country, the task of the "enemy" intelligence will be obviously much simpler and the danger to state secrets much greater.'[6] But, despite this recommendation, no British-based porter appears to have been appointed, just as none was appointed at 17 Tiergartenstrasse in 1935. Nor was Vivien content to reserve his criticisms to the porters: he was also reproachful about Henderson's own tendency to indiscretion.

Considering the mental stresses and demands of this posting above all others at the time, quite why Henderson was sent back to Berlin following surgery for cancer has always been something of a mystery, not least to Henderson himself. But sent back there he was. The anxieties he had been experiencing the previous year were evident to Irene Ravensdale. Calling on her when he was back in London following the Munich Agreement, she recorded that 'he was so strung up that he could not rest, and nearly wore the carpet out with his pacings to and fro.'[7]

Before Henderson had left Berlin in October 1938 some more 'soft' diplomacy had been organised: a visit had been arranged for the President of the Board of Trade and the Secretary of the British Overseas Trade Department. Henderson hoped that, as with the Hunting Exhibition the previous year, a banquet at the Embassy for these two British VIPs and the opportunity to meet German trade representatives in more relaxed circumstances would help lead to greater mutual cooperation and understanding. But it was not to be. On 14 March 1939 President Hácha of Czechoslovakia and his daughter were summoned to Berlin and lodged at the Adlon. The frail old man was kept waiting by Hitler (who had been watching a trashy film) in his new Reich Chancellery further down Wilhelmstrasse for an all-night meeting at which he was bullied into signing his country over to Germany, and collapsed as a result. Waiting anxiously up the street in the Embassy, Henderson came to the bitter realisation that Hitler had now 'crossed the Rubicon' and that there was no hope of world peace.[8] All promises that he had no further territorial ambitions after securing the Sudetenland had evidently been false. All the efforts and reputational risk that the Ambassador and Neville Chamberlain had put into preserving European peace were left in tatters.

As a gesture of protest against the German invasion of the rest of Czechoslovakia – Hitler's ambitions of German expansion into non-germanophone countries now laid bare – the official visit from London was cancelled and the Foreign Office recalled Henderson to London on an indefinite basis. He was to write later that he left Berlin 'feeling that I might very well never return there.'[9] In fact, given that all he had been striving for had been dashed when Hitler had invaded Czechoslovakia, he felt that it might have been best to replace him as Ambassador. This opinion was shared by Oliver Harvey, now Foreign Secretary Lord Halifax's Private Secretary. For him, Henderson's reports were 'bad, and had a bad effect here, whilst his attitude in Berlin had the effect of convincing the Germans we were flabby …. But it is complicated. No Ambassador can do any good in Berlin at present'. Nonetheless, other possible candidates were discussed.[10]* In the end, however, Henderson was sent back to Berlin, to send the Foreign Office 'streams of hysterical telegrams and letters' according to Harvey[11] within only a few weeks of his return.

Henderson was not of course privy to the Foreign Secretary's deliberations as to whether or not he should be replaced and he reasoned later that the British Government preferred not to make so drastic a change in the middle of the serious international situation. On 25 April he returned to Berlin after five weeks in London spent, like the rest of the British population, in 'suspense and anxiety.'[12] Harvey thought he looked 'very shattered' on his return to the Foreign Office in London,[13] and he was 'sad, disillusioned and could see no daylight', according to Irene Ravensdale. But the scales had apparently not fallen from his eyes quite yet. 'He definitely felt the out-and-out lefters, Goebbels, Streicher and Himmler, had rushed Hitler into this.'[14] In the early summer she came to realise that Henderson did 'not see the Germans' fault enough. His spectacles are too rosy and it pains me.'[15] But the invasion of Czechoslovakia (if not Kristallnacht the previous November) was indeed the Rubicon for many in Britain. Having made a much-criticised personal visit to Munich at the time of the negotiations, Lord Londonderry had written a strongly critical letter to Goering, who never replied. Many of the so-called 'Cliveden Set', who had faced condemnation for 'defeatist' attitudes which many felt had helped encourage a British climbdown at Munich, now reversed their former optimism and pro-isolationist stance and openly deplored Hitler's behaviour. The national mood had changed. Many, as Harold Nicolson observed, 'were startled to observe that their conception of "the future" had suddenly been altered. Until that dreadful hour† the thought of spring and summer had been illumined by gay enterprises and delights; suddenly they found themselves wincing away from the implications of May or June.'[16]

---

* According to Harvey, two possible candidates for the job were Archibald Clerk Kerr (1882–1951), recently appointed as Ambassador to China (as Lord Inverchapel, he was later to serve as Ambassador to Washington) and Horace Seymour (1885–1978), then serving as Minister to Tehran (he later served Ambassador to China).
† The invasion of Czechoslovakia.

Henderson's return to Berlin took place a few days after its population – and that of the entire country – had spent 20 April celebrating Hitler's fiftieth birthday. The capital ground to a halt for a four-and-a-half-hour military parade (the largest peacetime display of military power yet seen) along the east–west axis* in the Tiergarten, overseen by the Führer. Government, public and private buildings and entire streets were draped in swastikas and portraits of Hitler.[17] The previous evening crowds had wandered through a Tiergarten, Pariser Platz and Unter den Linden spectacularly lit up by illuminated pillars surmounted by spread eagles and burning torches. On the birthday morning there was a small parade on Wilhelmstrasse and later Hitler's route to and from the main parade took him past the Embassy. Turning right along Unter den Linden and then doubling back in front of the Lustgarten, Hitler's convoy again crossed the junction with Wilhelmstrasse, where the Embassy can briefly be seen in the official film of the event.[18]

Following Germany's occupation of Czechoslovakia, together with France the British Government had pledged to support Poland in the event of Hitler's invasion of that country, assumed to be his next goal of conquest given that Danzig, located in the 'Polish Corridor' separating Germany from East Prussia, was in his sights. During the course of that summer the British attempted to negotiate agreements with other European powers to act as a block against and deter Germany. Slowly, over the summer, Turkey, Greece and Romania signed up to support France and Britain against further German continental aggression. German preparations for a war footing were increasingly evident as more and more reservists were called up, including, just as had been the case in the run up to the Great War, two of the locally engaged embassy footmen. Gradually Henderson found himself frozen out of the diplomatic networks he had striven to build since his arrival in Berlin in May 1937. In early June, ostensibly because of the busy number of engagements organised by the Nazi regime, Henderson was unable to invite the Prince Regent of Yugoslavia to a banquet at the Embassy during his state visit to Berlin, an event otherwise to be expected in other, normal, circumstances considering his dynastic connections with the British royal family and Henderson's personal friendship with the Yugoslavian monarchy. On 9 June Henderson hosted the traditional King's birthday celebration, attended by three to four hundred British nationals. The following day was Henderson's birthday; that evening he held a dinner party, inviting a selection of foreign diplomats he could trust and some of the embassy staff.[19] These were to be the last representational events of any size ever held in the building.

At one o'clock in the morning on 7 July 1939 Ogilvie-Forbes was woken by the South African Minister to be told that the British Consulate at 17 Tiergartenstrasse was on fire (the Minister lived in the adjacent building). The fire was extinguished that afternoon, discovered to have been caused by smouldering papers in the boiler room chimney; already busy burning official documents in preparation for the worst, consular staff had failed to use a newly installed incinerator.[20] Fortunately, Miss Molesworth of the Passport Control Office (who had resided in the building since April) escaped unhurt, and there were no casualties. The Office of Works in

---

* An early element in Hitler and Speer's planned remodelling of Berlin.

London began repairs, most of which, with unfortunate timing, were completed in early September.

Henderson returned to London privately in early July to see his doctor. On the 15th Oliver Harvey took the opportunity to send the following note to Lord Halifax:

> The almost hysterical note of Henderson's letters, quite apart from the defeatist nature of their substance, does seem to me evidence that he is no longer physically equal to the strain of the coming months. I'm afraid I do regard him rather as a public danger! Although you at this end can discount what he says, we know he is the most indiscreet of men and certainly talks to others as he writes to you. Moreover, he is the symbol of 'appeasement', and so long as he is at his post Berlin will believe that 'appeasement' is not dead. His withdrawal would be a piece of that ocular evidence which we are always being advised to give in order to convince Hitler that we mean business. Nor is it quite fair to Henderson himself, who has always believed sincerely and passionately in appeasement, to expect him to carry out with conviction the complete reversal of policy which has come about.[21]

Nonetheless, Henderson did return to Berlin.

***

'[T]o cross the border into Germany was enough to be caught up immediately in a horrifying atmosphere fraught with impending catastrophe,' wrote Christabel Bielenberg[†] of the summer of 1939.[22] On the pretext of coming to the aid of beleaguered ethnic Germans, Hitler planned to invade Poland on 26 August, and on the 21st there came stunning news: the German Government announced that Foreign Secretary Ribbentrop was shortly to fly to Moscow to sign a German–Russian pact, the high point in his uneven career; the end-game in Britain's diplomatic dealings with the Third Reich had now begun. Meanwhile, Ribbentrop's consistent advice to Hitler was that, given their form up until now, the British would not go to war to prevent his invasion of Poland. The following day, Henderson flew to see Hitler at Berchtesgaden with another personal message from Neville Chamberlain, and on 25 August an Anglo-Polish agreement was signed in London.

All British nationals still in Berlin and all Germans in the UK were advised to leave the country. Via Henderson, Hitler asked Britain not to support the Poles. The Ambassador duly relayed the British response that Poland and Germany should negotiate. Hitler called off his planned invasion date of the following day, and moved it to 1 September. On 29 August Hitler demanded that Henderson and the British Government ensure that a suitable representative from the Polish Government be in Berlin the following day; as Henderson received Hitler's response to British proposals only at 7.15 that evening, this was a physical impossibility. When Henderson pointed out that the demand sounded like an ultimatum, Hitler commenced one of his famed hysterical tirades, but this time Henderson had finally had enough and shouted back.[23] He requested Halifax to endeavour to organise for a Polish negotiator

† British Christabel Bielenberg (1909–2003) had married a German law student in 1934 and was to spend the Second World War in Germany.

to fly to Berlin to discuss Hitler's terms, but Halifax refused. The deadline for the appearance of such a negotiator expired at midnight on 30 August, when Ribbentrop referred to – but never showed – a set of sixteen points for negotiation.

A full-scale slanging match between Henderson and Ribbentrop now ensued. Henderson retired to the Embassy up the street greatly upset, taking three hours to calm down before he contacted Halifax in London to report on events.[24] The following day – 31 August – von Hassell went to see Henderson at the Embassy, finding him at breakfast, not having gone to bed until four o'clock that morning. Henderson told von Hassell that he was 'above all, shocked at Ribbentrop's rudeness.'[25] During the course of the day von Hassell met Henderson again on the street in front of the Embassy, as von Hassell, without success, tried to act as a go-between between the German administration and Henderson to summon a Polish negotiator, sabotaged by Ribbentrop who refused to hand over the 'sixteen points.'[26]

The strain and weight of personal responsibility that Henderson was feeling at this stage – even without the burden of cancer – must have been enormous. The First Secretary at the Polish Embassy described him on 31 August as looking 'at least ten years older' and 'worn out.'[27] Indeed, the past few days had seen him working non-stop as a go-between, flying between Berlin and the Cabinet in London as necessary, Oliver Harvey unsympathetically remarking that 'N.H.'s very presence here is a danger as he infects the Cabinet with his gibber.'[28] Short-notice shuttle diplomacy between European capitals had now become the norm, politicians and diplomats no longer having to rely on prolonged train and ferry journeys for face-to-face meetings. But there were downsides to the benefits brought about by the advancing technology: shuttle diplomacy demanded commensurately faster responses, and to add to the worries the German Research Office in Berlin could by this time monitor telephone calls from the Embassy on a regular basis.[29]

Hitler's vast new Reich Chancellery, designed by Speer, had been completed in record time by January 1939 and occupied the entire block of Vossstrasse from the corner of Wilhelmstrasse.* Once darkness had fallen, moving between it and its close neighbour the British Embassy for meetings was by this stage more difficult than normal as the street was in complete darkness, Berlin undergoing a trial series of blackouts in advance of possible air attacks. 'A considerable but quite expressionless crowd had collected in the square opposite the entrance to the courtyard [of the Reich Chancellery], into which my car had to drive. Though the people were silent, they gave me no sensation of hostility,'[30] Henderson remembered. Emerging from the car, his route to Hitler's study in the vast new building had not been designed to calm nerves:

> From Wilhelmplatz an arriving diplomat drove through great gates into a court of honour. By way of an outside staircase he first entered a medium-sized reception room from which double doors almost seventeen feet high opened into a large hall clad in mosaic. He then ascended several

---

* Speer claimed in his memoirs (*Inside the Third Reich*, p.29) that a passage existed all the way along the attics of the buildings lining the west side of Wilhelmstrasse between the Reich Chancellery and the Adlon Hotel, created as an escape route during the unrest in Berlin in 1918–19 and which Hitler promptly had walled up on coming to power. There was indeed a heavy concentration of German Government buildings along the street, but as such a passage would have led straight through the attic of the British Embassy the claim is far-fetched.

steps, passed through a round room with domed ceiling, and saw before him a gallery four hundred eighty feet long … twice as long as the Hall of Mirrors at Versailles … Only then came Hitler's reception hall …. 'On the long walk from the entrance to the reception hall they'll get a taste of the power and grandeur of the German Reich! [Hitler told Speer].[31]

The slippery marble floors along the route met with Hitler's approval: "'That's exactly right; diplomats should have practice in moving on a slippery surface.'" The Führer's desk at the end of his vast study was inlaid with a design that might have made even Wilhelm II blush: a sword half-drawn from its sheath. "'Good, good … when the diplomats sitting in front of me at this desk see that, they'll learn to shiver and shake,'" said Hitler.[32]

On the day that Hitler finally invaded Poland – Friday, 1 September – Halifax sent instructions to Henderson to tell the German Government that if Germany did not immediately withdraw its forces from the country, Britain and France would have to honour the treaty they had made with Poland to go to war with Germany. Henderson visited the Foreign Ministry further down Wilhelmstrasse and gave this message to Ribbentrop. Taking a realistic view of the way events were likely to go, Halifax also instructed the Ambassador to make arrangements with the American Chargé d'Affaires Alexander Kirk to take responsibility for the British Embassy in the event of war. 'All ciphers and confidential documents were burnt and the whole of the Staff left their normal residence and were concentrated in the Adlon Hotel next door or in the Embassy itself,' Henderson recalled.[33]

Having sent his wife, Katherine, and his young son back to England that June, Geoffrey Harrison packed what he could and left his apartment to lodge at the Embassy. The Consulate-General had been closed on about 25 August, and most of the female staff had left for England, together with many of the remaining personnel. As was the case in 1914, there was no time to make arrangements for heavy baggage to be returned home, and so staff made individual arrangements for the care of the possessions they were forced to leave behind. Many stored what they could in the Embassy: William Shirer, passing by the building on 31 August, noticed that he could see luggage piled up inside.[34] Henderson ascribed the smooth running of these operations to the efficiency of Adrian Holman, who had succeeded Kirkpatrick as Head of Chancery in 1938.

The preparations continued the next day, Saturday, 2 September, when Henderson took the opportunity to leave the Embassy building and stroll up to Unter den Linden. The general mood was, he noticed, in stark contrast to that of early August 1914. This time there was no howling mob, no feeling of menace against the British, just miserable and morose resignation. A couple of days later he was to notice that the traffic policeman at the junction, who had so often saluted him, turned away rather than face him. In search of painkillers Henderson entered a pharmacy. The 'lugubrious' pharmacist agreed to let Henderson have the tablets without prescription when the Ambassador drily remarked that, if the drugs ended up doing him harm, the German Government would probably feel that the pharmacist had done Germany a favour.[35]

Late that night Henderson received a further instruction from the British Government in London – to arrange to meet Ribbentrop at nine o' clock the following morning and to deliver a further message. Eventually arrangements were made for Paul Schmidt, Hitler's long-suffering interpreter who had been present at so many meetings between Hitler, Chamberlain, Phipps, Henderson, and other British VIPs, to receive the message. That Sunday morning was bright and sunny, and shortly before nine Henderson left the Embassy for the short journey south along Wilhelmstrasse to the Foreign Ministry, Schmidt, who had overslept,[36] arriving slightly after Henderson. The Ambassador delivered to him Chamberlain's ultimatum: that if no positive reply to Britain's demands that the German army withdraw immediately from Poland was received by eleven o'clock that morning,* Britain would declare war on Germany.

Returning to the Embassy, Henderson and his remaining staff waited as time ticked by. There was no communication from the German Government. At 11.10 the Foreign Secretary got through to the Embassy and was told that no reply had been received.[37] Shortly afterwards Neville Chamberlain made his famous, sonorous, broadcast to the nation, beginning with the words:

> I am speaking to you from the Cabinet Room at 10 Downing Street. This morning the British Ambassador in Berlin handed the German Government a final note stating that, unless we hear from them by 11 o'clock that they were prepared at once to withdraw their troops from Poland, a state of war would exist between us. I have to tell you now that no such undertaking has been received, and that consequently this country is at war with Germany.

Chamberlain concluded his announcement with a prayer: 'Now may God bless you all. May He defend the right. For it is evil things that we shall be fighting against – brute force, bad faith, injustice, oppression and persecution – and against them I am certain that right will prevail.'[38] Paul Schmidt later related how, when he informed Hitler and Ribbentrop of Britain's declaration of war, Hitler, up to that time mollified into believing Ribbentrop's assurances that Britain would not go to war, turned to Ribbentrop and asked, 'Now what?'[39]

* * *

Finally, in Kirkpatrick's words, 'the die had been cast'[40]: it was time for the British to leave. Henderson saw Ribbentrop for the last time at 11.30 that morning, never again encountering any representatives of German officialdom apart from railway staff. Hitler gave a rousing speech to the German people broadcast on the radio and on the streets via loudspeakers, but the popular reaction remained extremely muted. That lunchtime, Henderson dined at the Adlon with the French Ambassador Robert Coulondre (who had taken over from François-Poncet in 1938), the American Chargé, and other remaining British Embassy staff,[41] and at four o'clock that afternoon the Embassy's telephone lines were cut. The German diplomatic protocol department made arrangements for a train the following morning for the embassy staff to leave Berlin for England via the Hook of Holland. That day, in Munich, Unity Mitford made an unsuccessful attempt at suicide.

From a purely personal point of view, Henderson now had a 'hateful' decision to make. He had brought two pet dogs with him to Berlin: 'Hippy', a cross

* British Summer Time.

71. Sir Nevile Henderson at Charlottenburg Station with Sir George Ogilvie-Forbes and Hippy on 4 September 1939 on his way back to England, photographed by Heinrich Hoffmann.

between a dachshund and a small Bavarian bloodhound (acquired during Henderson's posting to Belgrade), and 'Rah', a red setter. Despite the sylvan delights of the nearby Tiergarten, Henderson could never safely allow them off their leads in the urban forest, for fear of their being shot, like Crown Princess Vicky's cat, by some 'zealous forester or game warden.'[42] The dogs did, however, enjoy two walks there every day, in the morning with an embassy footman, and with Henderson himself in the afternoon. Hippy had a special place in Henderson's heart: the Ambassador was photographed with him on a corner banquette in the Embassy soon after his arrival in Berlin (probably on the day of his official diplomatic presentation ceremony), and after his return to England even wrote a short 'biography' of him.[†] As Henderson had no permanent base in England, and as there might well be objections to the presence of two dogs in any property he might rent, Henderson came to the painful conclusion that he would have to leave one pet behind in Berlin, in the knowledge, given the circumstances, that he would almost certainly never see it again. In the end, he chose Hippy to accompany him to England, leaving Rah with Rüger, the embassy butler, who had taken quite a fancy to him, allowing the dog to sleep in his family quarters in the embassy basement.

The German lawyer Helmuth von Moltke opposed Hitler's regime and found the outbreak of war unbearably depressing, corroborating Henderson's observations about the popular atmosphere, which Moltke told his wife was '... terrible. A mixture of resignation and mourning.'[43] 'I happened to pass when Henderson left the Wilhelmstrasse yesterday. There were about 300 to 400 people, but no sound of disapproval, no whistling, not a word to be heard; you felt that they might applaud any moment. Quite incomprehensible.'[44] What he witnessed on Monday, 4 September 1939 was the remaining British Embassy staff – thirty men, seven women and two dogs[45] (one of them Hippy) – together with what luggage they could carry with them, leaving the Embassy for Charlottenburg Station for the special train to the Dutch coast.

During the past seven decades the walls of the Embassy's rooms had echoed to the voices of Bethel Henry Strousberg, Benjamin Disraeli, Otto von Bismarck, Crown Princess Victoria, the Emperor Wilhelm II, Sir Arthur Conan Doyle, Lord and Lady Randolph Churchill, Cecil Rhodes, King Edward VII, Augustus John, Albert Einstein, Charlie Chaplin and, more recently, Hermann Goering, Joseph Goebbels and Adolf Hitler, to name but a few. But now the front doors were closed behind the departing embassy staff, and the lofty rooms were finally silent.

---

† *Hippy: In Memoriam: The Story of a Dog* (1943). Advertised by Hodder and Stoughton as 'Sir Nevile Henderson's touching and sympathetic story of his dog', it was on sale for 3s.6d.

CHAPTER 19
1939–1945: 'A HURRICANE OF FIRE'

72. Sir Nevile Henderson on 14 February 1940 with the typescript of his shortly-to-be-published book *Failure of a Mission*.

The journey to the Dutch coast was uneventful apart from a delay of several hours at the German border waiting for the embassy staff's counterparts from the German Embassy in London to cross over. Reaching Rotterdam, Henderson and Ogilvie-Forbes lodged at the British Legation at The Hague, the rest of the staff accommodated in the nearby seaside town of Scheveningen. Finding a Dutch ship, *Batavier V*, to take them to Gravesend, they were escorted over the Channel by three British destroyers. During the voyage, a sudden commotion brought the passengers running up on deck: the destroyers had dropped three depth charges. A member of the embassy staff later informed a reporter from *The Daily Telegraph*[1] that a German U-boat had been attempting to torpedo them. The accuracy of this observation is difficult to assess, but German U-boats had indeed sunk the SS *Athenia* on the very day that war had been declared, with over one hundred casualties. The embassy staff finally reached Victoria Station at eight o'clock on 7 September,[2] the journey from Berlin – normally one of about twenty-four hours without any breaks – having taken three days and eight hours.

Henderson initially went to live at his aunt's house, Rauceby Hall, near Sleaford in Lincolnshire. Almost immediately he put pen to paper, first of all to submit an official report on events in Berlin to the Foreign Office. *The Sunday Times* praised 'our tall, well-dressed envoy in Berlin' who had come out of 'the whole affair with both diplomatic and literary distinction. To paraphrase Anatole France: "He has become a moment in history."'[3] By December 1939 Henderson had completed his book *Failure of a Mission*, written, he claimed, in response to a question from the stationmaster at Grantham railway station as to why the war had started.[4] Serialised in the *Daily Herald* from 5 March 1940, the book was published by Hodder & Stoughton on 15 April.* It sold extremely well, Henderson directing that all current and future profits

---

* A précis of the book was published in three weekly parts in the American magazine *Life* from 25 March

go towards a trust fund for British refugees from Germany.[5] Perhaps courageously given the circumstances, in neither his official report nor his book did Henderson, with hindsight, attempt to repent of his pro-appeasement stance and efforts.

**

Left hundreds of miles away in Berlin were the contents of the British Embassy and the personal possessions of Henderson and his staff. Naturally, on their departure from Germany no one had any notion of how long hostilities might last or how serious they might be, and most of the staff had neither the time nor the opportunity to despatch their possessions to London or dispose of them locally. Those staff members who stayed to the end and left Berlin with Henderson in early September were able to take only a few items of luggage with them. Geoffrey Harrison took two suitcases crammed with possessions, some silver and his wife's evening dresses.[6] Henderson described in *Failure of a Mission* that possessions were loaded on to vans outside the Embassy,[7] watched by a morose crowd, but the individual ownership of this property is unclear. Some of the staff left their possessions – including cars – in the apartments and garages they had rented in Berlin, relying in some cases on the goodwill of their German landlords to care for it. One staff member even left an aircraft behind. Some had managed to make personal arrangements with American diplomatic colleagues and friends to leave their property in their care, while others had been able to leave possessions inside the large rooms and cellars of the Embassy or at the British Consulate-General.[8] At least some of the Embassy's contents – furniture, silver and large paintings – remained in the building, and this evidently included some of Henderson's own furniture. But he had been quick enough off the mark to organise the shipment of a portrait of his mother to London: it arrived soon after his own return there.[9]

A year later, in September 1940, the Foreign Representation Section of the American Embassy in Berlin confirmed to the authorities in London[10] the arrangements for the care and maintenance of the Embassy and Consulate-General buildings. In the days leading up to the outbreak of war the British Embassy requested the German Foreign Office to permit three locally based members of the embassy and consular staff – Artur Rüger, the embassy butler (who was then in his early fifties); Fritz Stenzel, the Chancery servant (then forty-five years of age; he had served the British Embassy since just after the end of the Great War); and Otto Neumann, the embassy porter – to continue to look after the Embassy once the British staff had departed. Rüger was officially appointed 'caretaker' of the building by the American Embassy on 6 April 1940, with Fritz Stenzel acting as his assistant. There had been some concern in the UK as to whether Stenzel might be called up. However the Americans assured the British that this was unlikely to be the case for either man, as general liability for military

---

to 8 April 1940 as 'War's First Memoirs'. The articles included photographs of Henderson talking to the stationmaster at Grantham; with his aunt at Rauceby Hall; at the British Legation at The Hague in September 1939; and several shots of Hippy. A photograph of Henderson appeared on the front cover of the 25 March edition of the magazine.

service in Germany ceased at the age of forty-five. Hermann Neumann,* an embassy porter, was detailed to look after the British Consulate-General building. One George Böhlke was appointed to assume Otto Neumann's duties when he left for another job.

Rüger and his family continued to live in the building together with Böhlke and an American Vice-Consul. Stenzel apparently preferred to live elsewhere in Berlin, but given his long and intimate knowledge of the Embassy buildings he was given the responsibility (under American supervision) of inspecting 17 Tiergartenstrasse at regular intervals. The Americans reported however that 'he has found the actual duties of caretaking uncongenial – in the experience of the [American] Embassy he is satisfactory in his own calling but quite unsuited for the responsibilities of management or supervision.'[11] Stenzel had therefore requested work similar to the type he had previously undertaken – as messenger in the British Interests Section of the American Embassy, but with the additional duty of frequent inspections of the two buildings.

British instructions had been to retain Rüger as butler, and he had evidently impressed the Americans:

> the Embassy may state that [his] presence in the British Embassy has assured its proper care and that of the furniture and effects stored therein (the Embassy contains almost all of the personal property of the former Embassy and Consulate personnel). He has shown himself to be thoroughly honest, very resourceful and motivated by the highest sense of loyalty. In addition, his life-time training as a butler in looking after large establishments has fitted him well for his present task.[12]

The winter of 1939–40 was the coldest in northern Germany for over a century,[13] but 'Rüger's actions saved the Embassy and its contents from the severe damage suffered by practically all the other buildings in the Wilhelmstrasse. His precautions against the possibility of damage from air raids and his coolness and concern for the Embassy's welfare during these raids deserve special note.' Apparently, he never left the building unless one of the others was there, never went away at night and refused to take any holidays.[14]

Henderson shared the Americans' high opinion of Rüger; indeed, in the absence of a wife to undertake, as Lady D'Abernon had put it, the *Hausfrau* side of things at 70 Wilhelmstrasse, for much of his ambassadorship he would have had to rely particularly heavily on him to manage the domestic and entertaining side of his representational duties. On his departure from Berlin on 4 September 1939 the Ambassador had personally left the butler with money to look after the building[15] and Rah. He also left him with a supply of coal, an extremely valuable commodity that hard winter. 'I trusted Rüger implicitly,' he told the Chief Clerk of the Foreign Office in December 1940. 'My whole idea was that the house should be properly looked after, with all its contents, for the duration of the war, & my sole concern was that Rueger should be in a position to go on living there for this purpose.'[16] The possibility that, as a German, the butler's political loyalties might lie elsewhere (as the British security advisor had previously suspected of the Embassy's porter) or be under some pressure to do so seems to have been disregarded. On the contrary: Henderson

---

* Possibly a relation of Otto Neumann, but the surname is not uncommon.

was worried that the Gestapo might 'interfere' with Rüger, 'the one German I really trusted', 'an absolutely honest man.'[17] Geoffrey Harrison had written to the Foreign Office at the end of September 1939 that Henderson was anxious about Rüger: 'He is rather afraid that the German authorities may wish to remove Herr Rüger and may in fact have done so.'[18]

***

Through a reciprocal arrangement with the German Embassy in London, it was at first intended that embassy and staff property left behind in Berlin would be gathered together and shipped back to England at the same time as the property of the German Embassy and its staff in London was moving in the opposite direction. As the 'phoney war' of late 1939 and early 1940 progressed, negotiations for this went forward. The property concerned included several cars (eight of which had been parked in the Embassy garage, the former coach yard). A complication was that since September 1939 several British staff members who had left possessions behind in Berlin had been posted elsewhere: by November Ogilvie-Forbes, for example, was in Oslo, and Miss Molesworth was in Geneva.

These arrangements naturally included Henderson's own possessions, although exactly what these consisted of is unclear. According to Henderson, Rüger, the butler, was personally involved in the packing of certain items, either in early September 1939 or afterwards. A special arrangement was negotiated for his property to be 'exchanged' with that of Dirksen, the German Ambassador in London.[19] By the end of April 1940 all the arrangements for this were in place, and four railway vans[20] containing property left Berlin for Rotterdam and shipment to England. The timing was unfortunate: the vans were still on their way to the Dutch border when Hitler invaded Holland that May. Reaching Wiesbaden, they were turned back to Berlin, which at least spared the contents from damage or destruction during the German bombardment of Rotterdam.

Within a few weeks Germany had invaded France for the third time in seventy years: the French were humiliatingly compelled to surrender to Germany in the same railway carriage in which Germany had signed the 1918 Armistice. Delirious crowds massed along Wilhelmstrasse and outside the Reich Chancellery to celebrate an extraordinary military achievement, and one that allowed Hitler to prepare to invade England. It was now out of the question for the vans to travel across the Channel and so it was agreed that they be sent to neutral Switzerland for storage in a furniture warehouse. They reached Berne in January 1941; the German Ambassador's property was sent to Dublin.[21] There was apparently no attempt to return or move the possessions of the rest of the embassy staff to England, which remained in Berlin.

Whether or not the vans containing Henderson's and/or embassy property were opened in Berne during the war – and if so whether the contents were interfered with – has become a matter for conjecture. On his escape from Colditz in January 1942 Airey Neave took one of the standard escape routes to England via Switzerland and, like several of his fellow escapees (according to some reports) the British Embassy in Berne supplied him with articles of

Henderson's clothing.* After the war was over and it was possible once again to travel to Switzerland, the vans were opened by Henderson's beneficiaries. Henderson claimed that the diaries and other papers he wished he had had with him when he was writing his autobiography, *Water under the Bridges*,[22] were amongst the contents of these vans, but when the vans were opened after the war they were not inside.

Given the stresses of the late summer of 1939 when Henderson – not a well man by any means – was intimately involved in the countdown to the Second World War, it would hardly have been surprising for him to have been mistaken in his memory about what was in the consignment, although he did claim that Rüger provided him with a detailed list.[23] Henderson did bring some confidential documents back to England, for he quoted them in *Failure of a Mission* and they were subsequently handed over to the Foreign Office by his literary executor. There has been considerable speculation[24] that the butler may have stolen and/or destroyed certain documents (including Henderson's diaries and confidential written instructions from Neville Chamberlain), perhaps working for an unknown third party, giving rise to speculation that he was indeed a Nazi spy. A less exciting explanation may of course simply be that the documents were accidentally left behind in the Embassy or deliberately destroyed by embassy staff along with everything else a few days before war broke out.

In a letter of April 1940 Rüger sent Henderson some news about Rah: the dog was 'fit and well, thanks partly to food supplied by the US Embassy,'[25] and that December he reported that Rah was 'well and happy and that however short rations might be he would get his share of them.'[26] Henderson tried to picture Rüger's routine in Berlin, imagining that he 'was doing his best in difficult circs to look after the Embassy & all that is in it. I do not expect that he leaves it much – except to exercise my dog.'[27] But by July 1942, in his book about his beloved Hippy, Henderson confessed that he had heard no news about Rah since 1940, and that by then he was 'afraid of getting it'. Following six months' quarantine Hippy had come to live with him at Rauceby Hall, but had died only four months later. Henderson was distraught: 'For nine years and more he had been part of my life and a very big part of it, and when he died something went out of it which I know I can never find again. None can ever take his place and I can hardly conceive of another life unless Hippy be waiting there to share it with me.'[28]

These words are poignant. Henderson knew that the throat operation he had endured in the winter of 1938–39 had not cured him and that his condition was terminal. He wrote his autobiography, *Water under the Bridges*, partly as an attempt to distract his mind from the situation, confessing to his literary agent (whom he appointed his literary executor) that 'the doctors here say that my case is such

---

* This story featured in the 1990 obituary of Sir Clifford Norton, British Minister in Berne from 1942: 'Fortunately the Germans had dropped the effects of Sir Nevile Henderson, British Ambassador to Berlin at the outbreak of war, into Switzerland, so there was a good supply of Savile Row suits for the former prisoners-of-war. Most thoughtfully, the Germans had also conveyed Sir Nevile's wine cellar to Switzerland' (*Daily Telegraph*, 13 December 1990). Airey Neave himself was not so specific about the matter: after debriefing at the British Legation in Berne he 'was led into a cellar beneath the Legation where a pile of second-hand men's suits was laid out as if for a village jumble sale. I selected a green tweed creation with baggy trousers', (*Saturday at M.I.9: A History of Underground Escape Lines in North-West Europe in 1940–5 by a Leading Organiser in M.I.9*, p. 39).

that there is nothing which can be done. They give me about six months to live, possibly less; at most a month or so more'[29]: the book was eventually published in July 1945. Oliver Harvey had seen him in April 1940, when Henderson had told him he was travelling to the south of France for his health. 'I am afraid he is not very well and also that he realises it himself. Rather sad.'[30]

By August 1942 Henderson had moved into the Dorchester Hotel on Park Lane, his friend Germaine Lens (or Leus) domiciled in an apartment in the new block of flats next door.[31] Opened in 1931, the Dorchester, or 'Dorch' as it was known to many of its exclusive clientele, was built in a fashionable modernist style, almost as if the owners had known that the Blitz was coming. Its structure was made entirely of reinforced concrete, including a twelve foot deep basement. During the war the 'Dorch' became the chosen place of residence and evening entertainment for the rich, who held lavish parties as German bombs fell on London. The Halifaxes stayed in a suite on the sixth floor, and the socialite Emerald Cunard on the seventh. Other regular guests included the Duff Coopers, ex-Ambassador to Paris Sir George Clerk, and Chief of the Air Staff Lord Portal, Irene Ravensdale and Baba Metcalfe. 'Chips' Channon recorded the affluent hedonism in the hotel on a night during the Blitz:

> London lives well: I've never seen more lavishness, more money spent or more food consumed than tonight, and the dance floor was packed. There must have been a thousand people…. The contrast between the light and gaiety within, and the blackout and the roaring guns outside was terrific: but I was more than a little drunk.[32]

Henderson died in his suite upstairs on 30 December 1942, never knowing what would ultimately happen to his property, Rah or the Embassy building in Berlin; never knowing, as the bombs fell outside, what would be the outcome of the war, in the start of which he had been so intimately involved; like Neville Chamberlain (who himself died of cancer in 1940) never having the opportunity to defend his record with the benefit of real hindsight. In Germany, Ulrich von Hassell sadly recorded in his diary on hearing of Henderson's death, 'The official German press lied shamelessly. This man, who worked to preserve peace up to the very last minute in August 1939, if also understandably without belief in success, they now call a 'saboteur' of peace …. One witness less, one gentleman less!'[33] Von Hassell himself would survive his friend by less than two years: implicated in the July 1944 von Stauffenberg plot to assassinate Hitler, he was executed that September. He went the same way as Helmuth von Moltke, who had witnessed Henderson's departure from the Embassy on 4 September 1939 and who in January 1944 was arrested for his opposition to the Government. In January 1945 he was put to death.

***

The former British Embassy staff's personal familiarity with the Nazi hierarchy acquired during their postings to Berlin came in useful for the British Government in unexpected ways during the war. On 10 May 1941 Hitler's deputy Rudolf Hess sensationally flew to Scotland, claiming that since German victory was inevitable he had come to negotiate an honourable peace. Ivone Kirkpatrick, by now working as Controller of the BBC's European services, was brought in to identify and help interrogate him: he had met Hess on many social and official occasions during his posting in Nazi Germany. Former Foreign Secretary Sir John Simon (who had met Hess at the Embassy in March 1935) took the role of an 'official' high-ranking government negotiator (as Hess demanded) with former Passport Control Officer Frank Foley present at the interviews. It became apparent that Hess remained under the erroneous impression that previously pro-German British sympathisers like Lord Londonderry still had influence in the British Government and might organise a coup in order to sue for peace with Hitler.[34] The unstable Hess was kept in custody for the remainder of the war before being sentenced to life imprisonment at the Nuremberg Trials of 1945–46. Amongst other former Nazi visitors to the Embassy in the 1930s, Kirkpatrick was to meet General Goering again in the run-up to the Trials, at which Goering and Ribbentrop were sentenced to death. Unlike Ribbentrop, Goering managed to escape the hangman's noose by committing suicide shortly before his execution.

Back in Berlin, by 1941, if he had not already done so as a precaution, it would have been sensible for Rüger to have moved whatever property he could down to the embassy cellars. But he may very well have been unable to move the largest pieces of furniture and paintings, including the full-length state portraits in the ballroom. The first RAF bombing raid on Berlin took place on 27 August 1940. The raids continued into 1941, with some damage inflicted on the Wilhelmstrasse area that September. For protection, some of the city centre was draped in camouflage netting, and flak batteries and anti-aircraft guns were mounted at strategic points. The damage to the German capital to that point was minor compared to what the Luftwaffe were inflicting on London and other British cities over the same period, but in December 1941, as the United States entered the conflict, the war escalated; care of the British Embassy and Consulate-General buildings was handed over to the neutral Swiss Government. Under the direction of Sir Arthur Harris, and with the increased range possibilities of British aircraft including the Lancaster bomber, the RAF began a renewed strategy of bombing Berlin on 18 November 1943. The RAF's most effective raid on Berlin took place a few days later, the night of 22–23 November.

The Palais Strousberg was now to pay the ultimate price for its builder's decision to locate it in the heart of Berlin's government district. Using the technique of 'carpet bombing', the RAF did not aim at specific targets, but blanketed a demarcated area with hundreds of tons of bombs. They knew exactly which parts of Berlin on which to use these tactics, and unfortunately for the Embassy, it was right in the centre of it: there was no escape from the incendiary bombs that rained down that night. Together with a 'high explosive bomb', fire raged through the building. Rüger and his family survived, but lost most of their possessions.[35] They may well have fled to the nearby Adlon Hotel air-raid shelter, an enormous underground structure with several entrances that had been built beneath Pariser Platz. Rah's fate is unknown.

Sheltering in the bunker in Wilhelmplatz, Joseph Goebbels described the effect of the attacks on the government district: 'The picture that greeted my eye in the Wilhelmplatz was one of utter desolation. Blazing fires everywhere …. Although damage in the Reich Chancellery is quite heavy, it is nothing compared with other ministries.' He then described a further attack:

Large bombs and land mines were dropped over the whole government quarter. They destroyed everything around the Potsdamer Platz. The pressure was so strong that even our bunker, though constructed deep underground, began to shake .... Devastation is again appalling in the government section as well as in the western and northern suburbs .... Mines and explosive bombs keep hurtling down upon the government quarter. One after another of the most important buildings begins to burn .... The Kaiserhof was hit by countless incendiary bombs and soon went up in flames. Although the largest fire-fighting units were put to work there, the edifice could not be saved; it burned to the ground. Nothing but the outer walls remain standing. ... The government quarter is nothing short of an inferno .... The Wilhelmplatz and the Wilhelmstrasse present a gruesome picture .... How beautiful Berlin was at one time and how run-down and woebegone it now looks![36]

The British were not the only foreign power whose embassy buildings were destroyed or damaged: the French, Italian and Japanese Embassies were also hit. Goebbels recorded that 'The diplomatic quarter along the Tiergarten looks like one gigantic heap of rubble. One can hardly pass through the streets, so deeply are they covered with debris.'[37] The British Consulate at 17 Tiergartenstrasse, already affected by the raid of 22–23 November 1943, was bombed again in another heavy attack during the night of 18–19 January 1944, when the next door South African Legation was destroyed. Crown Princess Vicky's English Church and the Royal Schloss were also badly damaged. Then, in the spring of 1944, the US Air Force began daylight raids on the city in addition to the British night raids; in all over 67,000 tons of Allied bombs were dropped on to the German capital.

In response to enquiries from London, the Swiss Embassy in Berlin tried to ascertain what had survived the destruction, and in September 1944 was able to produce a report. The possibility of opportunistic looting in the meantime of whatever remained in the buildings cannot of course be discounted. At the Consulate-General building, 'the government-owned furniture and files ... as well as the effects which British officials had stored ... in the building were completely destroyed by fire and water in November, 1943, and January, 1944 ... nothing of the contents of this building could be saved, except for [a] few motor cars ...'[38] Four cars belonging to consular staff, including one belonging to Miss Molesworth, had been left parked in the courtyard behind the building and were now covered by and surrounded by debris and were all badly damaged. The property of thirteen members of staff had been destroyed.[39]

So far as the British Embassy building at 70 Wilhelmstrasse was concerned, six cases of embassy silver, packed into wooden crates, had been salvaged and moved to the strong room of the basement of the American Embassy at 2 Pariser Platz, around the corner from the British Embassy,[40] and for which the Swiss were also now responsible as the 'protecting power'. The cases mostly contained the poignant remnants of the Embassy's once large collection of 19th century tableware:

Case 1: 84 meat plates, 48 soup plates
Case 2: 14 oval platters, 4 round platters, 8 vegetable dishes, 4 round vegetable dishes with covers, 3 oval vegetable dishes with covers, 6 bottle trays

Case 3: 4 soup tureens with covers, 8 sauce tureens with covers, 12 salt cellars, 1 cream jug, 1 sugar basin, 1 milk jug, 1 coffee pot, 1 tea pot, 4 candlesticks, 1 cruet stand (vinegar and oil)

Case 4: 2 Gloschen [sic], 1 cruet stand (4 bottles), 4 vegetable dishes with covers, 6 plate-warmers, 2 2-light candlesticks, 2 small trays, 2 gold fruit trays, 1 large silver dish, 1 samovar in 2 parts

Case 5: 6 gold soup ladles ['spoons'], 9 salt spoons, 37 fruit knives, 27 small table knives, 96 large table forks, 87 large table knives, 36 dessert forks, 36 dessert spoons, 60 soup spoons, 40 gold dessert spoons, 50 gold forks, 24 gold coffee spoons, 36 silver coffee spoons, 6 'helping' spoons, 8 sauce ladles, 4 gold 'helping' spoons, 4 gold sugar spoons, 2 pairs of grape scissors, 3 sugar tongs, 3 soup ladles, 6 large knives, 6 large forks, 11 wine labels, 1 cruet stand (3 bottles)

Case 6: 1 gold platter [there were also various pieces of silverware belonging to the former Embassy Counsellor Adrian Holman]

There was also some furniture: 'Dining Room chairs, partly broken, 1 table, round, … 5 chandeliers (brackets), 1 cupboard, 1 desk, 1 leather sofa, 1 large green carpet, 1 office carpet, 1 oriental carpet.' Two paintings were also listed: those by Ruysdael and Vrancx 'bought from Lord D'Abernon' (twenty years after their acquisition, it is interesting that this is how these two paintings were still identified). As a sad souvenir of the Embassy's long history of large parties, there were also ninety-five gilt chairs. Some of these items had been stored in a room on the ground floor of the American Embassy, and some in the basement of the British Embassy which was 'still intact and can be locked safely; another part has been evacuated into the country under the supervision of the Swiss Legation'. There were some additional articles stored in the basement of the British Embassy, noted as being without damage, and from the kitchen: 3 warming stoves, 4 kitchen tables, 1 large kitchen stove, 1 cupboard, 1 refrigerator plant, a heating plant (2 boilers), a water elevator plant, 1 oval table, 1 round table seating 12, 3 chests of drawers, 3 long tables, 5 bedside tables, 10 chairs, and 'quantities of letter heads, envelopes and courrier [sic] bags'.[41] All in all, it did not add up to much. If the large state portraits had remained on the walls, they were almost certainly destroyed in the bombing, fire and/or water from fire hoses.

A list was also provided of articles, apparently the property of some individual embassy staff members (implying that everything had been efficiently labelled): Adrian Holman, Colonel Daly (the former Military Attaché) and Miss Reid; these had also been stored partly in the basements of the American Embassy and partly 'in the country under the supervision of the Swiss Legation.'[42] Rüger had submitted a list of former embassy staff whose property had been completely destroyed, including Geoffrey Harrison, Frank Foley and Sir George Ogilvie-Forbes.[43]

**

Following Hitler's declaration of war against Russia and the Battle of Stalingrad of 1942–43, the course of the war in Europe turned against Germany. The Red Army pushed the Germans westwards, while in June 1944 the British and Americans invaded the Continent from Normandy and began to move east. For weeks, the

73. The Embassy in ruins in a photograph taken in 1946.

inhabitants of Berlin lay in dread of the Red Army pressing ever westwards across East Prussia and towards their goal of their mortal enemy's capital. The Wilhelmstrasse area was within the range of Russian artillery fire from 21 April as Soviet troops closed in on the ruined city, and, street by street, building by building, moved their tanks and troops closer to the government district where Hitler and his remaining associates were sheltering in the bunker underneath the Reich Chancellery. The area around the Reichstag took heavy pounding from artillery, as did the buildings in the government district, which was being heavily garrisoned by some 10,000 retreating German troops. A 1946 photograph shows the Embassy roofless, its façade pockmarked with shrapnel. The portico's right-hand column had vanished, and a huge hole, two storeys in height, had been blasted into the façade to the left, suggesting that a sniper or snipers might have been hiding amongst the ruins, shooting at the Russian tanks passing by on Wilhelmstrasse, which then fired defensive salvos directly into the Embassy's façade.

Some of the remaining Nazi top brass and their military support staff took their own lives in the nearby Reich Chancellery bunker and Chancellery gardens. Refusing to surrender, Hitler and his new wife, Eva Braun, killed themselves on 30 April, Joseph Goebbels and his wife the day after, but not before murdering their six children. The adults' bodies were set alight in the Chancellery gardens so as not to become objects of curiosity and triumph for the Russians. That day Soviet troops let forth a 'hurricane' of fire[44] on the district and on 2 May entered the Reich Chancellery. The Adlon Hotel, up until this time remarkably unscathed and whose basement served as an emergency hospital, was entered by Russian troops and suddenly went up in flames. Nurses from the Reich Chancellery (also in use as a hospital) rushed up Wilhelmstrasse past the Embassy to save whomever they could.[45] The Hotel's owner was taken away by Russian troops; his wife, Hedda, later found him dead.[46]

Germany signed an unconditional surrender at Potsdam on 8 May 1945, but it was not until the first week of July that the occupying Soviet forces allowed western troops into the capital. In September, the war in Europe and the Far East over, the British Government in London again asked the British Control Commission authorities based in Berlin to investigate the fate of the remaining British Embassy property in Berlin. Unfortunately, the list of items they sent for checking, based on that provided by the Swiss authorities the previous year, was inaccurate (one of D'Abernon's paintings, the 'Sebastian Franks [Vrancx]' was – mistakenly or not – left off the list).[47] Eventually, on 18 October, Ivor Pink of the Control Commission for Germany reported to Ernest Bevin, the Foreign Secretary of the new Labour Government, what had happened, enclosing witness statements from Fritz Stenzel and Wladislau Peplinksy, the caretaker of the American Embassy.[48]

Stenzel and Wadislau Peplinsky (a locally engaged American Embassy steward) and their colleagues from the American Embassy* had taken refuge from the advancing Soviet army in the shelters under that Embassy on Pariser Platz, where the boxes of British Embassy silver had been taken for safekeeping. But then the American Embassy caught fire; the staff only just managed to escape and flee to the nearby Adlon shelter. On 2 May they emerged, to be placed under the custody of the Russians, only then realising that the Embassy was 'totally burned out' (it had been destroyed by Russian artillery on 29 April). Placed under Russian custody in a building near Tempelhof Aerodrome,† they were released on 11 May, returning to the Embassy to see what could be salvaged from the ruins. Almost everything appeared to have been burned or looted, but the safe containing the valuables was intact: Peplinsky and some of his colleagues worked for two days with their bare hands to try to free it from the surrounding rubble of the building, only to find that the safe's key no longer worked, probably because the interior mechanism had been damaged by the heat of the raging fires.

Suddenly, five Russian soldiers appeared demanding to know what they were doing, ignoring Peplinsky's pleas that the building belonged to an Allied power, over which the Red Army had no jurisdiction. Threatening to shoot Peplinsky and his colleagues, using brute force the Russian soldiers succeeded in opening the safe themselves. Peplinsky begged some Russian superior officers to intervene, which they did, ordering the men away. But this proved only a brief respite. The following day the same men returned, this time with reinforcements, superior officers once more ordering them away. Peplinsky tried to make arrangements to take whatever was left in the safe to the Swiss Embassy for protection.

The Soviet authorities now raided Peplinsky's home, taking him and his family for interrogation at the remains of the Reich Chancellery, where, understandably, they feared for their lives. They were, however, released, and Peplinsky's suspicion that they had been conveniently removed from the vicinity of the American

---

* Stenzel had been working for the Americans as well as the British – see earlier.
† According to Peplinsky, to Köpernick, a Berlin suburb to the east of the city.

Embassy proved correct, for, when they returned to the site it was to find that the safe had been broken into and the contents looted: 'All cases, trunks, and cupboards were broken open'. 'Due to my daily observations,' Stenzel affirmed, 'I noticed that russian [*sic*] soldiers took away and transported all the Table-Silver, unpacked, on Thursday 22 May, about 5 o'clock in the afternoon. As I were [*sic*] alone and without any protection, I regret to say that it was impossible to do anything against this transport.' Peplinsky discovered that the contents of the Swiss Embassy had also been pillaged. Stenzel confirmed that the British Consulate-General at 17 Tiergartenstrasse had also been destroyed by bombing, but, poignantly, he reported that had managed to salvage five British passports from the building, which he handed over to the authorities.[49]

On the basis of the evidence of these witnesses Pink affirmed to the Foreign Secretary that

> both those [i.e. the British and the American] Embassy buildings and that of the British Consulate-General, together with the contents of all three buildings, were destroyed. The destruction of the buildings and their contents has been confirmed by members of my staff who are also satisfied, from personal investigation, that any property that may eventually be discovered after the removal of the vast amount of rubble, will be unfit for further use.[50]

Subsequent investigations concerning Embassy property evacuated by the Swiss in 1944 described as having been sent to the countryside determined that this had consisted 'mostly of office furniture and was limited in extent'. It was now doubtful that it could ever be recovered as the area outside Berlin to which it had been evacuated 'was of course subsequently overrun by Soviet troops.'[51]

Nothing that individual members of the embassy staff in the days leading up to the beginning of the war had hurriedly stored in the British Embassy and Consulate-General in Berlin appeared to have survived – at least in a fit state to be of any use. Some had left possessions in the rented apartments they had had to vacate so quickly in 1939. One of these was Mr C. H. F. Hardy, the Assistant Archivist, who wrote to the British Government in September 1945 asking whether the fate of his belongings could be checked. Hardy's lodgings had been in an apartment at 10 Schaperstrasse, where he lodged with the Henschel family, with whom he had evidently been on friendly terms. Miss Henschel reported back to the British Control Commission what had happened: Hardy's things had largely survived the war, despite the fact that they had been bombed out of their home on the same night that the British Embassy had been hit, 22–23 November 1943. Miss Henschel's father remained living in the same area (15 Schaperstrasse); unfortunately, she chose to go and check on his welfare just as the Soviets finally took Berlin and looting started, 30 April and 1 May. She assured the British that she had repaired Mr Hardy's things and had kept them for his hoped-for eventual return. Miss Henschel explained that 'she was held back for another day or two after the fighting' was over, with her father.[52]

According to a newspaper story published a decade and a half later, when Frank Foley returned to Berlin in 1945 to work for the Allied Control Commission, he went to visit the ruins of his former workplace at 17 Tiergartenstrasse. According to the report, quite by chance he stumbled across 'his old safe still intact and containing some of the valuables he and Kay [his wife] had been forced to leave behind in August 1939'. They were all neatly catalogued and labelled: Foley ascribed this to the legendary efficiency of the German authorities,[53] but it is far more likely to have been the work of Stenzel or Rüger, who, judging from the surviving evidence, dutifully labelled the property that individual members of staff both in the Embassy and Consulate had left behind.

But despite the Soviets' depredations, a small amount of the embassy silver had survived, a few pieces engraved with the name of the mission and the date 1816 and in use throughout the time 70 Wilhelmstrasse was the British Embassy. Together with some other pieces from the English Church, it was stored in a district bank in Charlottenburg, now in the British Sector of Berlin. In November 1945 a Mr Langmaid of the Ministry of Works visited Berlin and inspected the silver and he confirmed that 'Unfortunately there is very little indeed …. of the former British Embassy Plate and nothing in condition fit for immediate use, except the Communion Plate' [54] (from the English Church). There was also some silver that had been the property of the Egyptian Embassy in Berlin.* The remaining silver was collected and returned to London in March 1946.[55]

The accounts of what had survived and what had been destroyed in the British and American Embassies paint a very confusing picture. This is hardly surprising given the nightmarish circumstances of intense bombing and shelling, loss of life and everyday pillage and destruction. And whatever the Soviet soldiers had looted from these embassies, it represented but a tiny fraction of the vast quantity of cultural goods removed from Germany to Russia at this period. The possibility that some items (other than the silver) may have been looted rather than destroyed – or even moved to safety somewhere within ultimate British control and not immediately reported – was neither raised nor discussed by the British authorities at the time, nor does there seem to have been any further discussion – at least in the surviving documents – about what happened to any remaining property at 70 Wilhelmstrasse. What had obviously survived and was salvageable from that building, however, was the ornate grille from the front door, eventually placed in the headquarters of the British Military Government in West Berlin, which, somewhat ironically in view of the Nazis' investment in overt political power and splendour on the site for the 1936 Games, came to be based at the Olympic Stadium complex.

---

* It seems possible that the early nineteenth century Ancient Egyptian-inspired designs of several of the components of the British Embassy silver collection made those not familiar with it mistakenly believe that these pieces were in fact the property of the Egyptian Embassy in Berlin.

Epilogue
1945–2010: 'The Colourful House'

The Berlin that Stenzel lived in in late 1945 was a massive, devastated ruin that shocked visitors. Geoffrey Harrison, who had returned to Berlin as part of Winston Churchill's British delegation to the Potsdam Conference, flew over the city with a member of the RAF who had served on bombing raids. 'The destruction was quite indescribable. I don't think there is an undamaged house in the whole area. The trees in the Tiergarten are just skeletons. The whole place was like those pictures of battlefields of the last war.' For him the sight was 'absolutely staggering, it will surely take decades to rebuild, even to clear.'[1] Visiting what was left of the Embassy building, he found the wreckage of his car in the garage.

Under the terms of the Yalta Agreement of February 1945 Germany was divided into three (later four) zones, with Berlin itself split into four separate sectors: the Soviets in the East, and the British, French and Americans in the West. Originally intended to be a temporary measure, the Federal Government of Germany was established in May 1949 with its capital in the cultured but anonymous city of Bonn, on the Rhine. In 1953 the Ministry of Works' in-house architects erected a set of offices in Bonn at 77 Friedrich Ebert Allee, in a very austere, functionalist style; a 'temporary' set of offices that served as the British Embassy to West Germany for nearly fifty years. David Cornwell served as Embassy Second Secretary in this building in the late 1950s and early 1960s, evocatively describing its plain styling and Cold War atmosphere in his 1965 novel (written under his *nom de plume* John Le Carré) *A Small Town in Germany*.

In West Berlin the British Consulate-General re-established itself at 7–8 Uhlandstrasse. East Germany, the 'German Democratic Republic' was formed in October 1949, with its capital as (East) Berlin. The buildings of Wilhelmstrasse, once the proud centre of the Prussian, German, Weimar and, finally, Nazi, Governments, stood in ruins for several years. Amongst them, sadly, were the remains of Strousberg's grand Berlin mansion, open to all weathers. The building's geographical location was once more profoundly to affect its fate. The boundary between East and West Berlin was fixed to run north–south through the line of the Brandenburg Gate, placing the old Embassy just in the Eastern Sector of the city, while the ruins of the Consulate-General lay not far inside the Western Sector.

In ruins, the buildings associated with the British over the previous eight decades finally ceased to exist as the authorities in both East and West Berlin undertook programmes of demolishing and rationalising what remained of the former government district in the Wilhelmstrasse area and elsewhere. In February 1951[2] reports came through that the East Berlin authorities were unilaterally demolishing 70 Wilhelmstrasse, despite its designation as an historic monument. British officials quickly ascertained what legal claim they had over the site – which was, after all, British Government property. Most of the shell of the Adlon Hotel on Pariser Platz was also demolished at this time; the south, 'service' wing continued to be used as a hotel for some years, but in 1984 what remained was pulled down. In its turn, the remains of the English Church were demolished and a new St George's Church built in West Berlin, near the Olympic Stadium as a garrison church for British military personnel,* while in 1955 the dangerous remains of the British Consulate-General at 17 Tiergartenstrasse were, in their turn, torn down. Gradually the ministry buildings that characterised the Wilhelmstrasse area were moved further east; humiliatingly, by 1955 the former site of the Embassy was in use as an official car park for one government ministry that was still located in the area.[3] British title to the property remained unchallenged, although the British authorities felt that the site was too small to be reused for an embassy in the future. What they felt might be possible, however, would be to sell that particular site and use the money to purchase additional plots next to the old 17 Tiergartenstrasse.

In the late 1940s and 1950s a growing number East Germans voted with their feet against the East German regime and crossed permanently into the West; in 1960 alone some 360,000 people left the GDR, while tensions between East and West escalated. Early in the morning of 13 August 1961 barbed wire was strung across the boundary between East and West Berlin, completely sealing off the latter, while the Brandenburg Gate was to become the symbolic centre of violent protest for Berliners against the East Berlin authorities' unilateral action in dividing the city: the Gate was closed as a crossing point for what turned out to be almost thirty years. Two parallel walls with associated trenches, barbed wire and watchtowers were erected in September, with entire streets on the border evacuated and sealed, and in certain areas an open 'no man's land' was created by demolishing buildings next to the wall to improve security and prevent illegal crossings. The Brandenburg Gate became part of the wall's north–south axis, next to what was the most photogenic piece of no man's land, the former now-empty and windswept Pariser Platz, where what remained of the former structures of imperial Berlin in the Pariser Platz had been razed to the ground. The former busy and glamorous shopping and hotel district around Potsdamer Platz and Leipzigerstrasse had also been swept away, leaving a vast empty space to serve as part of what became know as the 'death strip'.

Diplomatic relations were not established between the UK and East Germany until 1973, the Quadripartite Agreement on Berlin of 1971 finally recognising the GDR as a separate political entity. Retaining their historic diplomatic association with the old government district, the British acquired offices in a modern block at 32–34 Unter den Linden to serve as an embassy, with a residence in the suburb of Pankow. By this stage much of the historic government district of Berlin and its surroundings had completely disappeared. The Russians, the superpower of Eastern Europe, reoccupied and rebuilt their former Embassy site, 7 Unter den Linden, extending into the plot next door formerly occupied by the Hotel Bristol. To its south, the site of Bleichröder's luxurious palace at 63 Behrenstrasse was covered by a grey and dreary 1960s apartment block. On Wilhelmstrasse, slightly to the south of

*Following Reunification, in 1994 the Church became a civilian one.

the former British Embassy site, unattractive apartment buildings, shops, schools and car parks were erected in the 1980s using prefabricated concrete blocks, for occupation by East German 'persons of merit'. Built partly on the site of the Reich Chancellery, Hitler's bunker and part of the gardens of the ministerial buildings on the west side of Wilhelmstrasse, they remain to this day. The area that was once the bustling Whitehall of Berlin within a few decades had completely changed in character, and even now, a quarter of a century after Reunification, this area has still to shrug off an atmosphere of bombed desolation and Cold War shabbiness.

The empty site of 70 Wilhelmstrasse was a flat, grassy, nondescript piece of land, but was so close to the Berlin Wall and to the hated 'death strip', that there was neither desire to redevelop it, nor practical hope of doing so. Berlin's 'temporary' division between East and West lasted for more than forty years, but in 1989, on 9 November, that portentous date in the calendar in twentieth-century German history[†] the crossing points into the west were reopened, with mass celebrations at the Brandenburg Gate. The historic structure finally reopened on 22 December. The East German Government quickly collapsed; East and West Germany were formally reunited on 3 October 1990; in its 'Resolution on Completion of German Unity' of 20 June 1991 the Bundestag voted to move the seat of government back to the former capital of Germany.

After more than four decades the return of a powerful, united Germany could be interpreted as a worrying prospect for the balance of power that had come about during that period through the development of NATO and the European Community. It was a concern that Prime Minister Mrs Thatcher asked a group of historians to address at a special meeting at Chequers on 24 March 1990. However it was envisaged that about 150 of the embassies located in Bonn would indeed move back to Berlin.[4] Britain was amongst them, with plans for a new, purpose-built embassy in the old capital. 70 Wilhelmstrasse was to rise again.

The decision was taken to build a new embassy on the empty plot of land on which the former Embassy building had stood. In this way, the British could symbolically return to the situation that had existed before the outbreak of the Second World War and at the same time demonstrate confidence in the new Germany by returning to business in the same place in Berlin's former government district. The British were not the only ones to enact this symbolic return to the old Berlin: with varying degrees of architectural merit the Adlon Hotel, the American and the French Embassies were all to be rebuilt on their former plots on the nearby Pariser Platz as much of the old street pattern that had existed before the war was recreated. Having been renamed Otto Grotewohl Strasse (after an East German Prime Minister) during the Cold War, in 1993 Wilhelmstrasse returned to its historic name.

The Berlin planning authority wanted to avoid a repeat of the brutalistic and totalitarian architectural horrors that had been inflicted on the capital since the devastation of the Second World War, especially in the heart of the government

---

[†] The date of 9 November has also witnessed the end of the German monarchy with Karl Liebknecht's declaration of the formation of a free socialist republic in 1918 (from the Berlin Schloss) and Philipp Scheidemann's declaration of a new German democratic republic from the Reichstag on the same day; Hitler's Beer Hall Putsch of 1923 in Munich; and Kristallnacht in 1938.

74. Michael Wilford and Partners' spectacular new British Embassy. The section of Wilhelmstrasse in front of the Embassy was blocked off to traffic in November 2003 to provide additional security.

quarter of old Prussian Berlin, where strict guidelines were created to govern the proportions, height and appearance of the street frontages of the new buildings, all of which were to have a strict architectural relationship with the Brandenburg Gate. In a move that would have delighted many former ambassadors, the British had planned that should East and West ever be reunited, the new British Embassy should house not only the Chancery but all the functions that had once been located in the Consulate-General building on Tiergartenstrasse: the attachés, passport and visa offices, the commercial offices, and so on. However, in keeping with the times, the new building would not also double up as the Residence. On 21 October 1992, in preparation for this symbolic move back to its historic past, Her Majesty Queen Elizabeth II unveiled a plaque on the site recording her visit to 'the site of the future British Embassy to Germany.'[5] Once again, this time in its rebuilt form, the Adlon Hotel was to exert an influence over the building. After reunification the former hotel site was bought by an investment firm which planned to recreate it, and construction was begun on the north and west boundaries of the 70 Wilhelmstrasse site. When the first hotel had been built in the early 1900s, the British Embassy had had no choice but to accept the constraints of its own site, but now there was a second chance. Accordingly, the British purchased the next-door plot to the south of the embassy site.[6]

The enlarged dimensions of the site having been worked out, there remained the important question of an architect and a design for this symbolic and prestigious new building, and in 1994–95 the Foreign and Commonwealth Office held an international architectural competition to find both. The construction of new embassy buildings affords a valuable opportunity for cultural diplomacy through the work of that country's prestigious architects, and the British Embassy in Berlin was to be one of a series of such *grands projets* undertaken by the Foreign Office in the 1990s and early 2000s. The competition for the new British Embassy in Berlin was to be a closed – but symbolic – one, restricted to British architects who had experience in working in Germany, and German architects who had experience in working in the United Kingdom. Reduced to a shortlist of nine contenders, all major players in the international architectural scene, the competition was won by Michael Wilford and Partners. But in a way that would have seemed wearily familiar to Odo Russell and Nevile Henderson, the Treasury's traditional reluctance to spend public money on property overseas once again resurfaced: the project was funded by the 'Private Finance Initiative' (PFI), the first, and (at the time of writing) so far the only, new British diplomatic building to be funded in this complicated manner. As Ambassador, Sir Paul Lever reported back to the Foreign Office in London that he had moved from Bonn back into full diplomatic residence in Berlin (symbolically on the sixtieth anniversary of the outbreak of the Second World War on 3 September 1999). I remember standing in the middle of the building site of the new Embassy, the UK Government Art Collection planning for a series of site-specific commissioned works of art for the new structure.

It was the architect's intention for the new Embassy to symbolise not only cooperation between Germany and the United Kingdom, but also 'openness', with a striking and innovative façade made of the same local Berlin sandstone with which the Brandenburg Gate was constructed. With the same cornice line as the next door rebuilt Adlon Hotel to the north (i.e. higher than the original Embassy) and repeated rows of windows, the building gives more than a nod to the same classical style of the original Embassy. However, where the classical portico of the former building projected into Wilhelmstrasse, 'an abstract collage of coloured

75. Part of the Wintergarden of the new British Embassy. Tony Cragg's sculpture *Dancing Columns*, in the middle foreground, was commissioned for the building by the UK Government Art Collection. Embassy staff soon gave the sculpture the unofficial title 'Two Diplomats: Bitter and Twisted'.

forms, hinting at the special places within'[7] now juts out through a gaping, symbolic 'hole' in the façade.

In contrast to the two entrances to the historic embassy building, Wilford's design provided one door for all staff and visitors. Passing through this open courtyard, visitors enter the building proper through a revolving door into an entrance hall which immediately gives a sense of lofty space. The core of the building is a huge and dramatic first-floor, glass-covered atrium known as, in an echo of Strousberg's building, the 'Wintergarden', reached by an elegant wide staircase. The staircase and atrium feature an enormous and dramatic wall painting by David Tremlett and a

76. HM Queen Elizabeth II opens the new British Embassy in Berlin on 18 July 2000, greeted by the architect Michael Wilford.

sculpture by Tony Cragg, both commissioned by the UK Government Art Collection. The Wintergarden is intended to be the public centre of the building, the location for functions and parties filled with light, an area provided with seating to enable visitors to stop and ponder their surroundings.

To the left of a large purple 'drum' containing conference facilities is located a room that can be used as a dining room for entertaining. Although the Embassy is intended principally to function as an office, the inclusion of a large interior reception space (vital for Berlin's harsh winters) and a dining room gives recognition to the fact that, just as Strousberg intended and Lord Odo Russell recognised, from an entertaining point of view the site has an unbeatably convenient location in central Berlin. This is in contrast to the current Residence, acquired in the 1950s and located several kilometres from central Berlin in the leafy suburb of Grünewald in the former Western Sector.

The new Embassy was officially opened on 18 July 2000 by Her Majesty Queen Elizabeth II and H.R.H. The Duke of Edinburgh. She was the first reigning British Monarch to enter the embassy site since her grandfather King George V, and the first British Monarch ever officially to open such a building. In an echo of visits to the same spot of land by her predecessors, the Queen drew up outside the new building in a Rolls-Royce flying the Royal Standard, with large cheering crowds of onlookers lining Wilhelmstrasse. In her speech the Queen stated that 'Berlin will no longer be an outpost, but a geographic centre of the Continent. Where formerly East and West confronted each other, they can come together here.' Like so many events in that same space in the decades before the Second World War, that same day she attended a dinner party hosted by the Ambassador, amongst the guests the German Chancellor Gerhard Schroeder.

In June 2010 the Embassy celebrated its tenth anniversary. Berliners had by that stage come to describe the building as 'the colourful house'. Much acclaimed, the Embassy remains one of the most dramatic and inspiring of the many contemporary buildings in Berlin, where, in the past two and a half decades so much has risen, phoenix-like, from the ashes of history.

***

Acting on the advice of the officials on the spot in the ruined Berlin of 1945 that nothing had – or indeed could have – survived from the old Embassy, after the end of the Second World War the Ministry of Works had recorded *Capri – Sunrise*, the painting by Frederic, Lord Leighton that had been sent to Berlin in 1937 as destroyed. But in June 2000 the painting suddenly re-materialised in the London salerooms. Because it had always been recorded as no longer in existence, neither the Ministry of Works nor its successor organisation the UK Government Art Collection ever searched for it – not even a photograph of it was extant – and the sale by auction went through without objection. Exactly how the painting survived the Second World War and what happened to it afterwards have not yet been definitely established, and it may well have remained somewhere in Continental Europe for decades. In the course of researching what might have happened to it I discovered that, contrary to the reports in 1945, it was not alone in surviving the conflict.

Lord D'Abernon's eighteenth-century topographical prints of Berlin are still hanging in the Ambassador's current Residence, their survival never having been reported to the Ministry of Works in 1945. In that building are located three other historic paintings almost certainly either acquired by him or by another British Ambassador to Berlin before the Second World War. The existence, somewhere in the world, of the two works Lord D'Abernon purchased for the Embassy – the Salomon Ruysdael and the Sebastian Vrancx – therefore cannot also be ruled out, despite the accounts of what had happened to property from the British Embassy in early May 1945, and research continues.

These survivals are examples of the fact that no work of art can ever be assumed to have been definitively destroyed merely on the basis of documentary evidence, however apparently authoritative that evidence may appear. They are also, in a small way, an illustration of how, even though so much was destroyed in Berlin in the Second World War, nothing in that remarkable city should ever be completely written off. A windswept, almost empty space for decades, Berlin's government quarter now follows its historic street plan, Pariser Platz, 'Berlin's drawing room', is back, and the new British, American and French Embassies occupy their former sites. Just as it was in the 1930s, although mercifully without the menacing presence of the Third Reich, it is once more possible to sit outside the Adlon Hotel* sipping cocktails on summer evenings, contemplating the Brandenburg Gate, and meet diplomats and journalists in the Hotel's bar before walking round the corner to meet the British Ambassador.

The only substantial pre-war government building to survive in Berlin's government district – apart from the Brandenburg Gate – is, ironically, Goering's Air Ministry, since 1999 the German Ministry of Finance. The beautiful gardens backing on to the Tiergarten, with their trees and pools, together with Goebbels' residence where Diana Mitford and Oswald Mosley married, are sadly long gone, nowadays in part covered by Peter Eisenman's spectacular Memorial to the Murdered Jews of Europe. Covered by car parks and dreary 1980s apartment blocks, there is no trace above ground of Hitler's new Reich Chancellery. The Tiergarten is

---

* Few commentators seemed to have had a kind word for the rebuilt Adlon Hotel, the edition of *Die neuen Architekturführer* on the British Embassy (No.23) describing it as 'a replica of pompous Wilhelminian architecture with its low, artificially lit interiors and fountain-splashing atmosphere', in contrast to the light-filled, open and dramatic spaces of the Embassy.

77. The former Embassy's front gates are now installed in the Wintergarden of the new British Embassy.

much the same, however, as is the leafy atmosphere of Tiergartenstrasse on which brand-new (and some restored) embassy buildings are located in what remains a major diplomatic quarter of the city, close to the old Bendlerblock, once the close neighbour of the British Consulate-General at 17 Tiergartenstrasse and where von Stauffenberg was executed after the failed 20 July plot against Hitler in 1944.

The new, purpose-built British Embassy in Berlin is very different in spirit from its historic predecessor on the same site, and operates in a Germany and a Europe* that is for the most part far more peaceful than was the case in the period this book covers. Within its walls one can only imagine the variety of events and emotions experienced long ago, in exactly the same spot. But something more tangible does remain from the past. Mounted on one of the walls of the Wintergarden at the top of the grand staircase are the metal grilles of the old Embassy's front doors, complete with their re-gilded royal mottos and coats of arms. Saved from the former Embassy's ruins in 1945, Anthony Eden, Sir John Simon and Adolf Hitler once stood in fron t of them. They were only the most latter examples of the great, the good, the famous – and the infamous – who passed through those doors on their way to see the British Ambassador.

---

* The long-term effect of 'Brexit' on UK/German diplomatic relations is, of course, a story that has yet to be told.

References

ATUBUB = Architekturmuseum des Technischen Universität Berlin in der Universitätsbibliothek, Berlin
BAL = British Architectural Library, Royal Institute of British Architects, London
BL = British Library, London
Bod Lib = Bodleian Library, University of Oxford
CACC = Churchill Archives Centre, Churchill College, University of Cambridge
GAC = UK Government Art Collection, London
TNA = The National Archives, London

CHAPTER 1

1. Much of the account of Strousberg's career and the Palais Strousberg in this chapter and the description of the house that follows is taken from Joachim Borchart, *Der europäische Eisenbankönig Bethel Henry Strousberg* (C.H. Beck 1991)
2. *Valuation of His Majesty's Embassy* House at Berlin dated 31 March 1913, TNA, WORK 10/488
3. Deutscher Architekten und Ingenieuverband, *Berlin und seine Bauten* (Berlin 1877), 409
4. Shephard Thomas Taylor, *Reminiscences of Berlin during the Franco-German War of 1870–71* (Griffin, Farran & Co. 1885), 175
5. Quoted in Borchart, op. cit., 141
6. 'Der grösste Mann in Deutschland ist unbedingt der Strousberg. Der Kerl wird nächstens deutscher Kaiser .... Sein Hauptprinzip ist: nur Aktionäre zu prellen, mit Lieferanten und anderen Industriellen aber kulant sein', Friedrich Engels to Karl Marx, 5 September 1869, quoted in Borchart, op. cit., 83
7. See Fritz Stern, *Gold and Iron: Bismarck, Bleichröder and the Building of the German Empire* (Allen & Unwin1977)
8. See G. M. Mork, 'The Prussian Railway Scandal of 1873: Economics and Politics in the German Empire', *European Studies Review* Vol. 1, No. 1 (1971)
9. Report on the debate in the Lower House of the Prussian Parliament made by Mr Dering of the British Embassy, Berlin for the Foreign Secretary in London, 7 February 1873, TNA, FO 64/767
10. Otto Glagau, *Der Börsen und Gründungschwindel in Berlin* (1874), quoted in Jonathan Steinberg, *Bismarck: A Life* (Oxford University Press 2011), 394
11. Strousberg to Lasker, 7 February 1876, quoted in Mork, op. cit., 41
12. Quoted in *The Times*, 27 October 1876
13. 'A Railway King', *The Times*, 27 October 1876
14. Quoted in Borchart, op. cit., 239
15. *The Times*, 4 March 1876
16. Borchart, op cit, 237. *The Times* (4 March 1876) in London reported that, at least initially, the purchaser was the German banker Baron Moritz von Cohn.
17. Bismarck to the Comte de Saint-Vallier, the French Ambassador to Berlin, 26 February 1879 (Archives du Ministère des affairs étrangères, Correspondence Politique, Allemagne, XXVII), quoted in Fritz Stern, 'Money, Morals and the Pillars of Bismarck's Society', *Central European History* Vol. III, No. 1/2 (1970), 55-6 (Note 7)
18. Ibid.
19. Quoted in *The Times*, 27 October 1876
20. Strousberg's Obituary, *The Times*, 2 June 1884
21. 'die Aktien aller Eisenbahnen des Strousbergschen Reichs und noch eine Welt von Wertpapieren aufzunehmen', quoted in Joachim Borchart, op. cit., 95 and see 94-7

CHAPTER 2

1. Odo Russell to Earl Granville, 3 October 1871, *Letters from the Berlin Embassy: Selections from the Private Correspondence of British Representatives at Berlin and Foreign Secretary Lord Granville, 1871–1874, 1880–1885*, ed. Paul Knaplund, Annual Report of the American Historical Association for the Year 1942, Vol. II (Washington, DC 1944), 47 (note)
2. Lady William Russell to Lord Lynedoch, 22 March 1830, quoted in Georgiana Blakiston, *Lord William Russell and his Wife, 1815–1846* (John Murray 1972), 210, Woburn Abbey Collection.
3. Lord William Russell to Lord John Russell, 19 December 1838, quoted in ibid., 414, Woburn Abbey Collection
4. Ibid., 394
5. Sir James Rennell Rodd, *Social and Diplomatic Memories, 1884–1893* (3 vols, Edward Arnold, 1922–25), Vol. I, 45
6. Odo Russell to Lady Salisbury (with whom he had previously been in love), 13 January 1868, quoted in Karina Urbach, *Bismarck's Favourite Englishman: Lord Odo Russell's Mission to Berlin* (Tauris 1999), 21
7. Quoted in Hannah Pakula, *An Uncommon Woman: The Empress Frederick* (Weidenfeld & Nicolson 1996), 141
8. Crown Princess Victoria of Prussia to Queen Victoria, 4 July 1868, in *Your Dear Letter: Private Correspondence of Queen Victoria and the Crown Princess of Russia, 1865–1871*, ed. Roger Fulford (Evans Brothers 1971), 198
9. *The Diplomatic Reminiscences of Lord Augustus Loftus 1862-1879* (2 vols, Cassell 1894), Vol. I, 360-1
10. Letter to Queen Victoria from Earl Granville, 31 August 1884, quoted in Raymond Jones, *The British Diplomatic Service, 1815–1914* (Smythe, Gerrards Cross 1983), 177
11. Russell to his brother Hastings, 7 July 1871, Urbach, op. cit., 76

12. Lady Emily Russell to Lady William Russell, November 1870, TNA, FO 918/85, quoted in Urbach, op. cit., 54

13. Odo Russell to his brother Arthur, 24 March 1870, TNA, FO 918/84

14. Georgiana Blakiston, *Woburn and the Russells* (Constable 1980), 129

15. Lord William Russell to Lady William Russell, 1839, quoted in Georgiana Blakiston, *Lord William Russell and his Wife, 1815–1846*, 420, Woburn Abbey Collection.

16. Lord Derby, referring to the Berlin 'season' of 1873, *Lord Derby's Diary*, quoted in Urbach, op. cit., 79

17. Russell's claim is filed under TNA, FO 64/743, 24 April 1872

18. Russell to the Marquess of Salisbury, 22 April 1878, printed in *Correspondence respecting the Repairs and the Supply and Maintenance of Furniture at certain of Her Majesty's Embassies and Legations* (TNA, WORK 10/255)

19. Russell to Earl Granville, 2 July 1872, TNA, FO 64/745. Odo and his brothers were very familiar with this spa town, having spent several summers there in childhood.

20. Russell to Earl Granville, 5 July 1872, TNA, FO 64/745; how this issue was resolved is not clear.

21. Russell to Earl Granville, 9 July 1872, TNA, FO 64/745

22. Harold Nicolson, Sir Arthur Nicolson Bart, *1st Lord Carnock: A Study in the Old Diplomacy* Constable 1930), 14–15

23. Russell to Earl of Derby, 18 May 1874, TNA, FO 64/804

24. *The Times*, 26 August 1884

25. Edmund Hammond to Russell, 5 August 1871, TNA, FO 918/38

26. Russell to Earl Granville, 27 February 1873, TNA, 64/768

27. Russell to Earl of Derby, 10 April 1874, TNA, FO 64/803

28. Mark Bertram, *Room for Diplomacy: Britain's Diplomatic Buildings Overseas, 1800–2000* (Spire Books 2011), 112-13

29. Russell to Earl Granville, 27 February 1873, TNA, 64/768

30. Russell to Earl Granville, 31 January 1873, TNA, 64/767

31. Russell to Earl Granville, 2 April 1873, TNA, 64/770

32. Russell to Earl Granville, 14 June 1873, TNA, 64/769

33. Russell to Earl Granville, 22 November 1873, TNA, 64/777

34. Russell to Earl Granville, 4 January 1874, TNA, FO 64/801

35. Russell to Earl of Derby, 9 February 1875, TNA, 64/1612

36. HM Treasury to the Foreign Office, 16 March 1875, TNA, FO 64/1612. At the same time Stephenson was also working on the acquisition of a British Embassy building in Rome.

37. Correspondence between HM Treasury, Russell and Earl of Derby, 16 March, 30 April and 18 October 1875, TNA, FO 64/1612

38. Russell to Earl of Derby, 18 October 1875, TNA, FO 64/1612

39. According to Boyce's report of October or December 1883 TNA, WORK 10/488; Stephenson's report of 1875 does not appear to have survived.

40. Russell to Earl Granville, 5 April 1872, TNA, FO 64/743

41. Russell to Earl Granville, 11 May 1872, TNA, FO 64/744

42. Russell to Earl of Derby, 1 June 1876, TNA, FO 64/852

43. Russell to Sir Francis Beilby, 3 June 1876, TNA, FO 64/853

44. Discussions in late 1884, TNA, WORK 10/488

45. Russell to Earl of Derby, 29 November 1875, TNA, FO 64/831

46. According to a young witness of one conversation (Baron von Eckardstein, *Ten Years at the Court of St. James's* (Thornton Butterworth 1921)), 19

47. W. F. Monypenny & G. E. Buckle, *The Life of Benjamin Disraeli, Earl of Beaconsfield*, Vol. VI: 1876–1881 (John Murray1920), 311-12; 'Monty Corry, Lord Rowton', in Sir Charles Petrie, *The Powers behind the Prime Ministers* (MacGibbon & Kee 1958), 22.

48. *The Times*, 9 July 1878

49. Beaconsfield to Queen Victoria, 12 June 1878, quoted in Monypenny & Buckle, op. cit., 317

50. *The Illustrated London News*, 25 November 1893

51. *The Graphic*, Saturday, 29 June 1878, 631

52. Beaconsfield's diary for 24 June 1878, quoted in Monypenny & Buckle, op. cit., 327

53. Ibid.

54. 'The banqueting hall, very vast and very lofty, and indeed the whole of the mansion, is built of every species of rare marble, and, where it is not marble, it is gold', Beaconsfield to Queen Victoria, quoted in Fritz Stern, *Gold and Iron: Bismarck, Bleichröder and the Building of the German Empire* (Allen & Unwin 1977), 478

55. Monypenny & Buckle, op. cit., Vol. IV, 341

56. Monypenny & Buckle, op. cit., Vol. VI, 346

57. Russell to his brother 9th Duke of Bedford, 27 June 1878, Woburn Archive, quoted in Urbach, op. cit., 198.

58. Russell to the Duke of Bedford, 19 June 1878, Woburn Archive, quoted in Urbach, op. cit., 13

59. Beaconsfield to Lady Bradford, 26 June 1878, quoted in Monypenny & Buckle, op. cit., 329

60. Quoted in Lady Gwendolen Cecil, *The Life of Robert, Marquis of Salisbury, Vol. II* (Hodder & Stoughton 1921), 288

CHAPTER 3

1. *The Times*, 12 June 1879.

2. Odo Russell to Earl of Derby, 18 May 1874, TNA, FO 64/804

3. Russell to Edmund Hammond, 22 March 1875, TNA, FO 391/22, quoted in Karina Urbach, *Bismarck's Favourite Englishman: Lord Odo Russell's Mission to Berlin* (Tauris 1999), 85

4. *The Times*, 9 February 1880

5. Crown Princess Victoria to Queen Victoria, 17 September 1880, *Beloved Mama: Private Correspondence of Queen Victoria and the German Crown Princess, 1878–1885*, ed. Roger Fulford (Evans Brothers 1981), 89

6. Russell to Earl Granville, 1 February 1873, TNA, FO 64/767

7. Copy of a note from the Emperor Wilhelm I to Emily, Lady Russell, 1 February 1873, enclosed with letter from Russell to Earl Granville, 1 February 1873, TNA, FO 64/767

8. Russell to his brother Arthur, undated, TNA, FO 918/84

9. Charles Lowe, *The German Emperor William II* (Bliss, Sands & Foster 1895), 103

10. Urbach, op. cit., 103

11. Russell to Earl Granville, 18 December 1880, *Letters from the Berlin Embassy: Selections from the Private Correspondence of British Representatives at Berlin and Foreign Secretary Lord Granville, 1871–1874, 1880–1885*, ed. Paul Knaplund, Annual Report of the American Historical Association for the Year 1942, Vol. II (Washington, DC 1944), 172.

12. Crown Princess Victoria to Queen Victoria, 24 May 1880, *Beloved Mama: Private Correspondence of Queen Victoria and the German Crown Princess 1878–1885*, ed. Roger Fulford, 79

13. Russell to Earl Granville, 5 March 1873, TNA, 64/768

14. Lady Emily Russell to Queen Victoria, 15 March 1873, *The Letters of Queen Victoria, Second Series, 1862–1878* (2 vols, John Murray 1926), ed. G.E. Buckle, Vol. II, 247

15. Russell to Earl Granville, 12 November 1881, Knaplund, op. cit. 233

16. As told to Earl Granville by Odo Russell, 4 March 1882, Knaplund, op. cit., 254-5

17. See D. C. M. Platt, *The Cinderella Service* (Longman 1971), 37-8. A popular view was that the British Consular service was 'riddled with foreigners who occupied numerous honorary and unpaid posts', *Stranger Within: Autobiographical Pages by Sir Francis Oppenheimer CMG* (Faber 1960), 162

18. Oppenheimer, op. cit., 146–7

19. Odo Russell to Viscount Enfield, 28 September 1872. TNA, FO 64/749

20. Winifred Taffs, *Ambassador to Bismarck: Lord Odo Russell, First Baron Ampthill* (Frederick Muller 1938), 374

21. *The Times* of 26 May 1884 gives an account of the occasion.

22. Sir James Rennell Rodd, *Frederick: Crown Prince and Emperor: A Biographical Sketch Dedicated to his Memory* (D. Stott 1888), 156

23. According to Joachim Borchart (*Der Europäische Eisenbahnkönig Bethel Henry Strousberg* (C.H. Beck 1991), 322, Note 57), Ujest had become the sole owner of the property from at least 1881.

24. Odo Russell to Earl Granville, 16 October 1883, TNA, WORK 10/488

25. Mark Bertram, *Room for Diplomacy: Britain's Diplomatic Buildings Overseas, 1800–2000* (Spire Books 2011), 85–6

26. HM Treasury to Board of Works, 13 November 1883, TNA, WORK 10/488

27. R. H. Boyce, *Further Report on Berlin Embassy*, 4 December 1883, TNA, WORK 10/488

28. Ibid.

29. Ibid.

30. Ibid.

31. Ibid.

32. Ibid.

33. Odo Russell to Earl Granville, 20 October 1883, Knaplund, op. cit., 300

34. Odo Russell, 27 January 1884, TNA, WORK 10/488

35. Odo Russell to Earl Granville, 23 February 1884, TNA, FO 64/1612

36. Boyce's report of 7 March 1884, TNA, WORK 10/488

37. Ibid.

38. Odo Russell to Earl Granville, 26 March 1884, TNA, WORK 10/488

39. Ibid.

40. Ibid.

41. Russell to Earl Granville, 9 June 1884, TNA, FO 64/1612

42. George Shaw-Lefevre, First Commissioner of Works to HM Treasury, 3 July 1884, TNA, WORK 10/488. His

view proved prescient.

43. Ibid.

44. *Foreign Office, Diplomatic and Consular Sketches reprinted from 'Vanity Fair'* (Allen & Co. 1883), 104-5.

45. Urbach, op. cit., 102 (Bleichröder Archive, Harvard University)

46. *The Times*, 26 August 1884

47. Ibid.

48. Charles Scott to Earl Granville, 25 August 1884, TNA, FO 64/1051

49. Charles Scott to Sir Thomas Sanderson (Earl Granville's Private Secretary), 23 August 1884, Knaplund, op. cit., 341

50. Charles Scott to Earl Granville, 25 August 1884, TNA, FO 64/1051

CHAPTER 4

1. Charles Scott to Earl Granville, 25 August 1884, TNA, FO 64/1051

2. Ibid.

3. Note (dated 29 September 1884) on Charles Scott's minute to Earl Granville, 23 September 1884, TNA, FO 64/1051

4. Crown Princess Victoria to Queen Victoria, 26 April 1873, *Darling Child: Private Correspondence between Queen Victoria and the Crown Princess of Prussia, 1871–1878*, ed. Roger Fulford (Evans 1976), 89

5. Crown Princess Victoria to Queen Victoria, 12 July 1876, ibid., 218

6. Charles Scott to Earl Granville, 1 September 1884, TNA, FO 64/1051

7. Russell's obituary, *The Times*, 26 August 1884

8. Sir Charles Scott to Earl Granville, 1 September 1884, TNA, FO 64/1051

9. Quoted in Winifred Taffs, *Ambassador to Bismarck: Lord Odo Russell, First Baron Ampthill* (Frederick Muller 1938), 391

10. Ibid., 53

11. Sir James Rennell Rodd, *Frederick: Crown Prince and Emperor: A Biographical Sketch Dedicated to his Memory* (D. Stott 1888), 163

12. Sir James Rennell Rodd, *Social*

and Diplomatic Memories,
1884–1893 (3 vols, Edward
Arnold 1922–25), Vol. I, 54

13. Crown Princess Victoria to
Queen Victoria, 24 May 1880,
*Beloved Mama: Private
Correspondence of Queen
Victoria and the German
Crown Princess, 1878–1885*,
ed. Roger Fulford (Evans
1981), 79

14. Crown Princess Victoria to
Queen Victoria, 7 August 1880,
ibid., 86

15. Charles Scott to Earl
Granville, 30 August 1884,
TNA, FO 64/1051

16. Ibid.

17. *The Times*, 4 September 1884

18. *The Spectator*, 30 August 1884

19. Lord Beaconsfield to the Earl
of Derby, 13 September 1877,
quoted in G. E. Buckle & W.
F. Monypenny, *The Life of
Benjamin Disraeli, Earl of
Beaconsfield* (Vol. VI, John
Murray 1920), 178

20. Jonathan Steinberg, *Bismarck:
A Life* (Oxford University
Press 2011), 351–2

21. Odo Russell to Earl of Derby,
16 October 1874, TNA,
FO 64/806

22. *The Graphic*, 30 August 1884,
'Topics of the Week'

23. *The Spectator*, 30 August 1884

24. E. C. C. Corti, *The English
Empress: A Study in the
Relations between Queen
Victoria and her Eldest
Daughter, Empress Frederick of
Germany* (Cassell 1957), 224

25. Georgiana Blakiston, *Woburn
and the Russells* (Constable
1980), 219

26. Quoted in Raymond Jones,
*The British Diplomatic Service,
1815–1914* (Smythe, Gerrards
Cross 1983), 182

27. Austen Chamberlain, *Down
the Years* (Cassell 1935), 30–31

28. Letter from Sir Hughe
Knatchbull-Hugessen to
Sir Alexander Cadogan,
Permanent Under–Secretary
of the Foreign Office, 20
January 1939, quoted in full in
D. C. M. Platt, *The Cinderella
Service: British Consuls since
1825* (Longman 1971), 240–42

29. Earl Granville to Queen
Victoria, quoted in Jones,
op.cit., 183

30. Malet to Earl Granville, 11
October 1884, *Letters from the
Berlin Embassy: Selections from
the Private Correspondence of
British Representatives at Berlin
and Foreign Secretary Lord
Granville, 1871–1874,
1880–1885*, ed. Paul Knaplund,
Annual Report of the
American Historical
Association for the Year 1942,
Vol. II (Washington, DC
1944), 347

31. Charles Scott, 31 March 1885,
TNA, WORK 10/488

32. Hon. F. H. Villiers to Sir F. B.
Alston, 7 September 1884,
TNA, FO 64/1612

33. This is demonstrated by
comparing (1) plans of the
house published in *Berlin und
seine Bauten* (1877 edn.) and
(2) Boyce's sketch plan of the
house's 'footprint' made during
his visit in the autumn of 1883
(TNA, WORK 10/488); an
undated plan of the reception
floor made by August Orth
which shows the placing of
Ampthill's furniture
(ATUBUB, reproduction of a
drawing, inv. no. F5551); and
plans published in *Berlin und
seine Bauten* (1896 edn.).

34. August Orth, *Der grosse
Saal im englischen
Gesandschaftsgebäude in
Berlin* [the large room in
the English Legation in
Berlin] (Architektonisches
Skizzenbuch H. 183/6, 1883,
ATUBUB, drawing, inv.
no. B3533)

35. August Orth, *Wohnhaus
Wilhelmstrasse 70, Berlin,
Entwurf zu einem Tanzaal,
Kellergschoss* [design for a
ballroom: basement], dated
21 March 1876 (ATUBUB,
drawing, inv. no. 14431)

36. August Orth, *Wohnhaus
Wilhelmstrasse 70, Berlin,
Umbau, Bauerlaubnisgesuch
zum Bau eines Tanzaales:
Vorderansicht, Längsschnitt und
Querschnitt* [building licence
application to erect a ballroom:
front elevation, side elevation,
cross section], dated 1 July
1876 (ATUBUB, drawing,
inv. no. 14434)

37. Joachim Borchart, *Der
Europäische Eisenbahnkönig

Bethel Henry Strousberg*
(C.H. Beck 1991), 322 note 57
(Bleichröder Archive, Harvard
University)

38. R. H. Boyce, 8 October 1884,
TNA, WORK 10/488

39. Minute, R. H. Boyce, 2
January 1885, TNA,
WORK 10/488

40. Borchart, op. cit., 96

41. Minute, R. H. Boyce, 2
January 1885, TNA, WORK
10/488

42. Hannah Pakula, *An
Uncommon Woman: The
Empress Frederick* (Weidenfeld
& Nicolson 1996), 110. She
was not alone in this opinion:
'England has led all the
continental countries in
developing the bathroom. The
presence of a bathroom was
taken for granted in England
at a time when it was still an
exception in the German
house', Hermann Muthesius,
The English House, (Berlin
1904, 1905, unabridged English
version, Vol. III, 235, published
by Frances Lincoln Ltd.,
copyright © 2007 Reproduced
by permission of Frances
Lincoln Ltd)

43. Muthesius, op. cit., 239

44. Minute, R. H. Boyce, 2
January 1885, TNA,
WORK 10/488

45. Ibid

46. Ibid

47. Boyce to Treasury, 30 January
1885, TNA, WORK 10/488

48. Malet to Earl Granville,
26 February 1885, TNA,
FO 64/1612

49. August Orth, *Wohnhaus
Wilhelmstrasse 70 (Villa
Strousberg), Grundriss
Erdgeschoss* [ground floor
plan], 1867 (ATUBUB,
drawings, inv. nos. 14414,
14417); and see illustration
number 2.

50. In a plan of the ground floor
of the building by Orth dated
21 March 1876, incorporating
his earlier ballroom design,
the left drawing room remains
undivided, *Wohnhaus
Wilhelmstrasse 70, Entwurf zu
einem Tanzaal* [design for a
ballroom] (ATUBUB, drawing,
inv. no. 14432)

51. Malet to Earl Granville,

26 February 1885, TNA, FO 64/1612

52. Malet to Earl Granville, 26 May 1885, TNA, FO 64/1612

53. See the 1937 plans of the Residence reproduced in A. J. Gordon's unpublished thesis *A New British Embassy in Berlin*, Welsh School of Architecture, 1948 (BAL, ref. X.M.S. 725-125 (43B): 72.064)

54. Malet to the Office of Works, 18 October 1890, TNA, FO 64/1613

55. Sir Edward Malet, *Shifting Scenes or Memories of Many Men in Many Lands* (John Murray 1901), 166

56. Sir James Rennell Rodd, *Social and Diplomatic Memories, 1884–1893*, Vol. I, 57

57. Bismarck to Sir Alexander Russell, 2 October 1884, Knaplund, op.cit., 347–8

58. *The Illustrated London News*, 25 November 1893. As we have seen, the Russell connection with the Embassy in Berlin actually dated back to when Odo's father had the post of Minister to the Court of Prussia in Berlin from 1835 to 1841.

CHAPTER 5

1. Austen Chamberlain, *Down the Years* (Cassell 1935), 33–6

2. Ibid, 31

3. Sir James Rennell Rodd, *Social and Diplomatic Memories, 1884–1893* (3 vols, John Murray 1922–25), Vol. I, 57

4. Ibid, 93

5. Odo Russell to Earl of Derby, 1 June 1875, TNA, FO 64/828

6. Charles Lowe, *The Tale of a 'Times' Correspondent: Berlin, 1878–1891* (Hutchinson 1927), 196

7. Rodd, op.cit., 71

8. Katie Hickman, *Daughters of Britannia: The Lives & Times of Diplomatic Wives* (Flamingo 2000), 142

9. Malet to Earl Granville, 18 April 1885, *Letters from the Berlin Embassy: Selections from the Private Correspondence of British Representatives at Berlin and Foreign Secretary Lord Granville, 1871–1874, 1880–1885*, ed. Paul Knaplund,

Annual Report of the American Historical Association for the Year 1942, Vol. II (Washington, DC 1944), 397

10. *Old Diplomacy: The Reminiscences of Lord Hardinge of Penshurst* (John Murray 1947), 25

11. Ibid., 28

12. Rodd, op.cit., 98–9

13. Hardinge, op. cit., 28

14. Princess Victoria of Prussia, *My Memoirs* (Eveleigh Nash and Grayson 1929), 61–2

15. Malet to Lord Salisbury, 24 October 1885, TNA, FO 64/1612

16. Ibid

17. Report by David Grove (Friedrichstrasse 94, Berlin SW), 23 October 1885, TNA, FO 64/1612

18. Malet to Lord Salisbury, 24 October 1885, TNA, FO 64/1612

19. Malet to Lord Salisbury, 24 December 1885, TNA, FO 64/1612

20. HM Treasury to the Foreign Office, 29 January 1886, TNA, FO 64/1613

21. Malet to Lord Iddesleigh, 15 December 1886, TNA, FO 64/1612

22. Malet to Lord Salisbury, 13 July 1887, TNA, FO 64/1613

23. Office of Works to HM Treasury, 14 July 1887, TNA, FO 64/1613

24. Leonée and Richard Ormond, *Lord Leighton* (Yale University Press 1975), No.85

25. Simon Reynolds, *William Blake Richmond: An Artist's Life, 1842–1921* (Michael Russell 1995), 208

26. *The Athenaeum*, 2 June 1888. The New Gallery on Regent Street in London had only just opened; admission to the summer exhibition of 1888 was one shilling. While welcoming the gallery to the London art scene, the publication sniffily opined that 'No good is done to anybody by the exhibition of works which are below mediocrity. How small is the number of fine paintings which even the good taste and rare opportunities of the directors have gathered will

appear from the following notes' (*The Athenaeum* 19 May 1888).

27. *The Illustrated London News*, 12 May 1888

28. Rodd, op.cit., 118

29. Reynolds, op. cit., 209–211

30. Queen Victoria to the Prince of Wales, 3 January 1888, quoted in Robert Rhodes James, *Lord Randolph Churchill* (Weidenfeld & Nicolson 1959), 327

31. Lord Randolph Churchill to the Prince of Wales, 29 December 1887, *The Letters of Queen Victoria, Third Series, 1886–1901*, ed. G. E. Buckle (John Murray 1931), Vol. I, 367–9

32. Mrs George Cornwallis-West, *The Reminiscences of Lady Randolph Churchill* (Edward Arnold 1908), 194

33. René Kraus, *Young Lady Randolph: The Life and Times of Jennie Jerome, American Mother of Winston Churchill* (Jarrolds 1944), 145

34. Quoted in Winston Churchill, *Lord Randolph Churchill* (Macmillan 1906), Vol, I, 368–9. Reproduced with permission of Curtis Brown, London on behalf of the Estate of Winston S. Churchill, © The Estate of Winston S. Churchill). Randolph thought that Prince von Bismarck had shunned him on purpose.

35. *The Letters of the Empress Frederick*, ed. Sir Frederick Ponsonby (Macmillan 1928), 227–9 and see Frank L. Müller, *Our Fritz: Emperor Frederick III and the Political Culture of Imperial Germany* (Harvard University Press 2011)

36. *The Illustrated London News*, 17 March 1888

37. Hannah Pakula, *An Uncommon Woman: The Empress Frederick* (Weidenfeld & Nicolson 1996), 466

38. Rodd, op. cit., 131

39. Queen Victoria's journal, RA VIC/MAIN/QVJ (W) Wednesday 25 April 1888 (Princess Beatrice's copies) [retrieved 19 October 2015]

40. '… it was terrible to see her standing there in tears, while the train moved slowly off, &

to think of all she was suffering, & might have to go through', Queen Victoria's journal, RA VIC/MAIN/QVJ (W) Thursday 26 April 1888 (Princess Beatrice's copies) [retrieved 19 October 2015]

41. Pakula, op. cit., 476.

42. Malet to Salisbury, 19 November 1887, Royal Archives I 55/78, quoted in J. C. G. Röhl, *Young Wilhelm: The Kaiser's Early Life, 1859–1888* (Cambridge University Press 1998), 688

43. Queen Victoria to her private secretary Lord Ponsonby, 13 December 1887, Royal Archives Add. A12/1509, quoted in Röhl, op. cit., 689.

44. *The Letters of the Empress Frederick*, ed. Sir Frederick Ponsonby, 339–41

45. German Empress Victoria to Queen Victoria, 2 May 1888, Royal Archives Z41/42 & 12 & 13 June 1888, Royal Archives Z41/61–2: Röhl, op. cit., 679, 824

46. Rodd, op.cit., 158–9

47. Telegram from Malet to Queen Victoria, 14 June 1888, Royal Archives Z41/61–2; Röhl, op. cit., 824

48. Rodd, op. cit., 143

49. *The Illustrated London News*, 30 June 1888

50. Malet to Salisbury, 24 June 1888, Royal Archives VIC/Z/MAIN/68/131, quoted in Miranda Carter, *The Three Emperors: Three Cousins, Three Empires and the Road to World War I* (Fig Tree 2009), 90

51. For example: 'Few great leaders can show such an unvarying record of successes, and none have possessed in a higher degree the most indispensable quality of the successful soldier, the power of attaching to himself the love and confidence of his followers … His thought was always for others, never for himself.' Sir James Rennell Rodd, *Frederick: Crown Prince and Emperor: A Biographical Sketch Dedicated to his Memory* (D. Stott 1888), 138

52. Malet to Lord Salisbury, 30 March 1889, *The Letters of Queen Victoria, Third Series, 1886–1901*, ed. G. E. Buckle, Vol. I, 485

53. Malet to Queen Victoria, 30 March 1889, quoted in Carter, op. cit., 103–4

54. *The Graphic*, 29 March and 5 April 1890

55. E. C. C. Corti, *The English Empress: A Study in the Relations between Queen Victoria and her Eldest Daughter, Empress Frederick of Germany* (Cassell 1957), 335

56. 'Our Ambassadors: No.1', *The Illustrated London News* 25 November 1893. Despite the article's title, the series on British ambassadors was not continued in successive issues.

57. Hardinge, op. cit., 24

58. Charles Lowe, *The Tale of a 'Times' Correspondent: Berlin, 1878–1891* (Hutchinson 1927), 196

59. Hardinge, op. cit., 24

60. Carter, op. cit., 189

61. Corti, op. cit., 351

62. Spring-Rice to his brother Stephen, *The Letters and Friendships of Sir Cecil Spring-Rice: A Record*, ed. Stephen Gwynn (2 vols, Constable 1929), Vol. I, 180–81

63. Spring-Rice to his brother, 2 November 1895, Ibid., 182

64. Rodd, op cit., 162

65. Hardinge, op. cit., 24

66. Rodd, op. cit., 160

CHAPTER 6

1. *The Times*, 3 January 1920

2. Queen Victoria's journal, RA VIC/MAIN/QVJ (W) Tuesday 6 August 1895 (Princess Beatrice's copies) [retrieved 19 October 2015]

3. Lord Salisbury to Bigge, 16 August 1895, quoted in Raymond Jones, *The British Diplomatic Service, 1815–1914* (Smythe, Gerrards Cross 1983), 190. This remark seems somewhat at odds with reports that Salisbury was also apparently seriously considering appointing Lord Beaconsfield's former trusted private secretary Montagu Corry, Lord Rowton, to the position (Sir Charles Petrie, *The Powers behind the Prime Ministers* (MacGibbon & Kee 1958), 13)

4. Based on Lord Lansdowne to Queen Victoria, 7 August 1895; correspondence between Queen Victoria, Lord Lansdowne, Lord Salisbury and Sir Arthur Bigge, 8-12 August 1895; Queen Victoria to Wilhelm II, 28 August 1895, *The Letters of Queen Victoria, Third Series, 1886-1901* (John Murray 1931), ed. G.E. Buckle, Vol. II, 545–6; 547–9; 560–61.

5. *The Diplomatic Reminiscences of Lord Augustus Loftus 1862-1879* (2 vols, Cassell 1894), Vol. I, 375

6. All quotes taken from Spring-Rice's letter, 14 March 1896, to The Hon. Francis Hyde Villiers at the Foreign Office, *The Letters and Friendships of Sir Cecil Spring-Rice: A Record*, ed. Stephen Gwynn (2 vols, Constable 1929), Vol. I, 200

7. Madame Morel [Comtesse Clare Morel des Boullets], *From an Eastern Embassy: Memories of London, Berlin and the East* (Herbert Jenkins 1920), 135

8. Lady Susan Townley, *'Indiscretions' of Lady Susan* (T. Butterworth 1922), 43

9. Lamar Cecil, 'History as Family Chronicle: Kaiser Wilhelm II and the Dynastic Roots of the Anglo-German Antagonism', *Kaiser Wilhelm II: New Interpretations: The Corfu Papers* (Cambridge University Press 1982), 94–6. The issue is dealt with extensively by J. C. G. Röhl in *Young Wilhelm: The Kaiser's Early Life, 1859–1888* (Cambridge University Press 1998).

10. Townley, op. cit., 43

11. Ibid., 44

12. This was related to Lady Susan by her husband (Townley, op. cit., 47–8). The Berlin–Baghdad Railway was built from 1903.

13. Townley, op. cit., 54

14. J. C. G. Röhl, *The Kaiser and his Court: Wilhelm II and the Government of Germany* (Cambridge University Press 1994), 79–96

15. *Berlin and its Environs: Handbook for Travellers by Karl*

Baedeker (5th edn, Karl Baedeker 1912), 68–9

16. James W. Gerard, *My Four Years in Germany* (Hodder & Stoughton 1917), 7–8. See Chapter 7 for Beresford Hope's remarks on what crafty guests did in order to secure a seat at supper.
17. Major-General Lord Edward Gleichen, *A Guardsman's Memories: A Book of Recollections* (W. Blackwood & Sons 1932), 255–6
18. Gerard, op. cit., 9–10
19. Röhl, op.cit., 94
20. Townley, op. cit., 61–2
21. Spring-Rice to his brother, 2 January 1897, *The Letters and Friendships of Sir Cecil Spring-Rice: A Record*, ed. Stephen Gwynn (2 vols, Constable 1929), Vol. I, 216–17
22. Sir James Rennell Rodd, *Social and Diplomatic Memories 1884–1893* (3 vols, Edward Arnold 1922–25), Vol. I, 124
23. D. S. MacDiarmid, *The Life of Lieut. General Sir James Moncrieff Grierson KCB CVO CMG ADC* (Constable 1923), 113
24. Jones, op. cit., 191
25. Quoted in Matthew S. Seligmann, 'Military Diplomacy in a Military Monarchy? Wilhelm II's Relations with the British Service Attachés in Berlin, 1903–1914', *The Kaiser: New Research on Wilhelm II's Role in Imperial Germany* ed. Annika Mombauer and Wilhelm Diest (Cambridge University Press 2003), 177
26. J. C. G. Röhl, *Young Wilhelm: The Kaiser's Early Life, 1859–1888* (Cambridge University Press 1998), 440–41
27. Several entries are quoted in MacDiarmid, op. cit.,
28. Spring-Rice to Theodore Roosevelt, 18 July 1896, *The Letters and Friendships of Sir Cecil Spring-Rice*, Vol. I, 207
29. Spring-Rice to his brother Stephen, 7 July 1897, ibid., 222
30. Spring-Rice to Theodore Roosevelt, 18 July 1896, ibid., 208
31. Christopher Clark, *Kaiser Wilhelm II: A Life in Power*

(paperback edn, Penguin 2009), 64

32. Spring-Rice to Lady Helen Ferguson, 26 December 1896, *The Letters and Friendships of Sir Cecil Spring-Rice*, Vol. I, 214
33. Townley, op. cit., 65
34. Lascelles told what appears to be the same story to the British Consul-General in Frankfurt, Sir Francis Oppenheimer (*Stranger Within: Autobiographical Pages by Sir Francis Oppenheimer KCMG* (Faber 1960), 168. The account also appears in the unpublished memoirs of Richard Seymour, a young attaché at the Embassy at this time (Miranda Seymour, *Noble Endeavours: The Life of Two Countries, England and Germany, in Many Stories* (Simon & Schuster 2013), 134. Although it would appear to have all the hallmarks of an after-dinner story, quite possibly with some later embellishments, Lascelles' daughter Florence was a witness to the event (see later note).
35. Townley, op. cit., 65–7
36. As she recalled to Lady Rumbold on a visit to the Embassy in May 1933 (Lady Rumbold to her mother Lady Fane, 16 May 1933, Rumbold Family Papers)
37. Quoted in MacDiarmid, op. cit., 148
38. Townley, op. cit., 67–9
39. *The Times*, 22 January 1901
40. *The Times*, 23 January 1901
41. *The Times*, 4 February 1901
42. *The Times*, 9–11 April 1901
43. *The Times*, 27 January 1902
44. Spring-Rice to Eleanor Roosevelt, 20 January 1904, *The Letters and Friendships of Sir Cecil Spring-Rice*, Vol. I, 376
45. *Old Diplomacy: The Reminiscences of Lord Hardinge of Penshurst* (John Murray 1947), 120
46. Madame Morel, op. cit., 136
47. HRH Princess Marie Louise, *My Memories of Six Reigns* (Evans Brothers 1956), 90
48. Gleichen, op. cit., 257
49. Lady Edward Cavendish to Florence Spring-Rice, 7 & 12

March 1905, CACC, Spring-Rice Papers (CASR II 1/5)

50. Jones, op. cit., 193. King Edward VII & Charles Hardinge, by then the Foreign Office Permanent Under-Secretary, blocked the appointment. Sir Francis Bertie was appointed instead.
51. Sir Frank Lascelles to Florence Spring-Rice, 28 February 1908, CACC, Spring-Rice Papers (CASR II 1/2)
52. Sir Francis Bertie to Louis Mallett, 11 June 1904, quoted in Zara Steiner, *The Foreign Office and Foreign Policy, 1898–1914* (Cambridge University Press 1969), 66
53. 1 January 1908, *British Documents on the Origins of the War 1898-1914* (HMSO 1928), Vol. III, Appendix A, 408
54. Steiner, op.cit., 115, 178
55. *The Times*, 3 January 1920

CHAPTER 7

1. *The Diary of Edward Goschen, 1900–1914*, ed. C. H. D. Howard (Royal Historical Society, Camden Fourth Series, 1980), 175–6 (entry for 12 August 1908)
2. Ibid.
3. Wickham Steed, 'Some Incidents in Vienna', letter to *The Times*, 22 May 1914
4. Frank Lascelles to Florence Spring-Rice, 15 & 23 August 1908, CACC, Spring-Rice Papers (CASR II 1/2)
5. *The Diary of Edward Goschen*, 177 (entry for 7 November 1908)
6. Ibid., 178 (entry for 8 November 1908)
7. Ibid.
8. See catalogue number 118 of Michael Snodin (ed.), *Karl Friedrich Schinkel: A Universal Man*, exh. cat., Victoria & Albert Museum (Yale University Press 1991) for elevations, cross-sections and views of the interior of this lost building.
9. Hedda Adlon, *Hotel Adlon: The Life and Death of a Great Hotel* (Barrie Books 1958), 18–19
10. Lady Edward Cavendish to Florence Spring-Rice,

12 January 1907, CACC, Spring-Rice Papers (CASR II 1/5)

11. Philip Magnus, *King Edward the Seventh* (John Murray 1964), 398–9

12. Harold Nicolson, *Sir Arthur Nicolson Bart, 1st Lord Carnock: A Study in Old Diplomacy* (Constable 1930), 290

13. Cartwright was also favoured by Sir Charles Hardinge (Zara Steiner, *The Foreign Office and Foreign Policy, 1898–1914* (Cambridge University Press 1969), 178

14. Quoted in Gordon Brook-Shepherd, *Uncle of Europe* (Collins 1975), 299

15. 'This was certainly my own view, and I had no ambition to return', James Rennell Rodd, *Social and Diplomatic Memories*, (3 vols, Edward Arnold 1922-5) Vol. III, 91

16. Jonathan Steinberg, 'The Kaiser and the British: the State visit to Windsor', November 1907, ed. J.C.G. Röhl and N. Sombart, *Kaiser Wilhelm II: New Interpretations: The Corfu Papers* (Cambridge University Press 1982), 136

17. *Old Diplomacy: The Reminiscences of Lord Hardinge of Penshurst* (John Murray 1947), 159

18. Raymond Jones, *The British Diplomatic Service, 1815–1914* (Smythe, Gerrards Cross 1983), 192

19. Goschen's obituary, *The Times*, 21 May 1924

20. Emperor Wilhelm II to von Bülow, 12 and 13 August 1908, quoted in J. C. G. Röhl, *Kaiser Wilhelm II, 1859–1941: A Concise Life* (Cambridge University Press 2014), 96

21. Baron von Eckardstein, *Ten Years at the Court of St. James's, 1895–1905* (Thornton Butterworth 1921), 245

22. *The Diary of Edward Goschen 1900-1914*, 187 (entry for 10 February 1909)

23. Princess Marie Radziwill to General di Robilant, 9 February 1909, *This Was Germany: An Observer at the Court of Berlin: Letters of Princess Marie Radziwill to General di Robilant KCB GCMG, One-time Italian Military Attaché at Berlin (1908–1915)*, trans. and ed. Cyril Spencer Fox (John Murray 1937), 70–71

24. Quoted in Lamar Cecil, 'History as Family Chronicle: Kaiser Wilhelm II and the Dynastic Roots of the Anglo-German Antagonism', ed. J.C.G. Röhl and N. Sombart, *Kaiser Wilhelm II: New Interpretations: The Corfu Papers* (Cambridge University Press 1982), 107

25. *Memoirs of Field-Marshall Lord Grenfell* (Hodder & Stoughton 1925), 183–4

26. Princess Marie Radziwill to General di Robilant, 9 February 1909, *This Was Germany*, 70

27. Princess Marie Radziwill to General di Robilant, 19 February 1909, ibid., 71

28. Ibid.

29. *Daisy, Princess of Pless: By Herself* (Murray 1929), 176

30. Lord Grenfell, op. cit., 186

31. Hardinge, op. cit., 174. Unsurprisingly, witness accounts of this dramatic event, most of them written a number of years after the event, differ slightly. For example, Pless (op. cit., 176) records that it was she – together with Queen Alexandra – who undid the King's collar (apparently with some difficulty) and then made him sit on a higher seat than the low sofa.

32. Princess Marie Radziwill to General di Robilant, 13 February 1909, *This Was Germany*, 71

33. Lord Grenfell, op. cit., 186

34. Hardinge, op. cit., 174

35. Brook-Shepherd, op. cit., 342

36. Princess Marie Radziwill to General di Robilant, 13 February 1909, *This Was Germany*, 71–2

37. Hardinge, op. cit., 174. Pless however records that the King did see the German doctor she recommended, and that 'it had done him good too and that he is seeing him again tomorrow' (Pless, op. cit., 177)

38. Sir Frederick Ponsonby, *Recollections of Three Reigns* (Eyre & Spottiswoode 1951), 258

39. *The Graphic*, 20 February 1909, 228

40. Princess Marie Radziwill to General di Robilant, 19 February 1909, *This Was Germany*, 72-3

41. *The Diary of Edward Goschen, 1900–1914*, 199 (entry for 7 February 1910)

42. Ibid., 203 (entry for 6 May 1910)

43. Ibid. (entry for 7 May 1910)

44. Quoted in H. W. Law & I. Law, *The Book of the Beresford Hopes* (Heath Cranton 1925), 250

45. Quoted in ibid., 251–2

46. Quoted in ibid., 253

47. *The Diary of Edward Goschen*, 256 (entry for 1 January 1912)

48. H. J. Bruce, *Silken Dalliance* (Constable 1946), 118

49. Ibid., 130–31

50. Quoted in Law, op. cit., 254

51. David Duff, *Alexandra: Princess and Queen* (London 1980), 76

52. H.J. Bruce, op.cit., 121, 131–3

53. *Richard Burdon Haldane: An Autobiography* (Doubleday, Doran & Co. 1929), 240

54. From Haldane's diary of his visit to Berlin, in Sir Frederick Maurice, *Haldane 1856–1928: The Life of Viscount Haldane of Cloan KT, OM* (2 vols, Faber & Faber 1937, 1939), Vol. I , 302

55. From Haldane's letter to his mother on his way back from Berlin (quoted in Maurice, op. cit., 294–7)

56. *The Diary of Edward Goschen*, 264 (entry for 9 March 1913)

57. Law, op. cit., 261

58. Ponsonby, op. cit., 294, 298

59. Sir Francis Oppenheimer, *Stranger Within: Autobiographical Pages by Sir Francis Oppenheimer KCMG* (Faber 1960), 225

60. Ibid.

61. *The Diary of Edward Goschen*, 277 (entry for 30 August 1913)

62. Frank Rattigan, *Diversions of a Diplomat* (Chapman & Hall 1924), 115

63. See *Prussian Aggrandisement and English* Policy, a pamphlet by Sir Horace Rumbold Senior published in 1870; Martin

Gilbert, *Sir Horace Rumbold: Portrait of a Diplomat, 1869–1941* (Heinemann 1973), 103. In 1895 Rumbold Senior had been a potential candidate as Ambassador to Berlin instead of Lascelles.

64. *The Times*, 4 February 1914
65. *The Illustrated London News*, 21 January 1888 ('Sketches in Berlin')
66. *Inside Asquith's Cabinet: From the Diaries of Charles Hobhouse*, ed. Edward David (John Murray 1977), 163
67. Ibid.
68. *The Diary of Edward Goschen*, 284 (entry for 3 March 1914)
69. Steiner, op.cit., 197
70. Oppenheimer, op. cit., 161
71. Gilbert, op.cit., 105

CHAPTER 8

1. Sir Horace Rumbold to his wife, 30 July 1914, Bod Lib, Rumbold Papers, Box 16, ff 203–06
2. Martin Gilbert, *Sir Horace Rumbold: Portrait of a Diplomat, 1869–1941* (Heinemann 1973), 105–06
3. Ibid., 109
4. Rumbold to his wife, 25 July 1914, Bod Lib, Rumbold Papers, Box 16, ff 190–93
5. Quoted in Gilbert, op. cit., 112
6. Quoted in ibid., 113
7. Quoted in ibid., 114
8. Rumbold to his wife, 30 July 1914, Bod Lib, Rumbold Papers, Box 16, ff 203–06
9. Quoted in Gilbert, op. cit., 116
10. Rumbold to his wife, 1 August 1914, Bod Lib, Rumbold Papers, Box 16, ff 207–09
11. Quoted in Gilbert, op. cit., 118
12. Frank Rattigan, *Diversions of a Diplomat* (Chapman & Hall 1924), 134
13. *The Illustrated London News*, 1 August 1914, 171
14. Rumbold to his wife, 2 August 1914, Bod Lib, Rumbold Papers, Box 16, ff 210–11
15. James W. Gerard, *My Four Years in Germany* (Hodder & Stoughton 1917), 89
16. Sir Francis Oppenheimer, *Stranger Within: Autobiographical Pages by Sir Francis Oppenheimer KCMG* (Faber 1960), 229
17. Rumbold to Godfrey Thomas,

17 December 1926, quoted in Gilbert, op. cit.,121 (note)
18. Gerard, op. cit., 91
19. *Dispatch from the British Ambassador in Berlin*, Parliamentary Paper Cd 7445, 8 August 1914 (reprinted in *The Times*, 28 August 1914)
20. Ibid.
21. Sir Horace Rumbold, *The War Crisis in Berlin, July–August 1914* (new edn, Constable 1944), 313
22. Gerard, op. cit., 91
23. Rumbold, op. cit., 323
24. Rumbold (op. cit., 324) claimed that he telephoned; Goschen claimed that he did (*Dispatch from the British Ambassador …*)
25. Rumbold, op. cit., 323
26. *The Illustrated London News*, 15 August 1914, 269
27. Rumbold, op. cit., 324
28. Rumbold, op. cit., 325 and *Dispatch from the British Ambassador…*
29. Gerard, op. cit., 92
30. Rumbold, quoted in Gilbert, op. cit., 122
31. Rumbold, op. cit., 323
32. *The Illustrated London News*, 15 August 1914
33. *Dispatch from the British Ambassador …*
34. Gerard, op. cit., 93
35. Ibid.
36. It was past midnight according to Rumbold's retrospective account (op. cit., 324).
37. *Dispatch from the British Ambassador …*
38. It was Rumbold's butler, rather than a maid, according to his later account (op. cit., 326)
39. Rumbold, op. cit., 327. In 1916 they were to be returned to him via the American Embassy in Berlin, sent to Rumbold in Berne where he was by that time Head of Mission. 'Not a thing was missing.'
40. *The Graphic*, Saturday 8 August 1914, Supplement, 7. Accounts of the timing of the German Ambassador's return home that evening are confused. Harold Nicolson (*Sir Arthur Nicolson Bart, 1st Lord Carnock: A Study in the Old Diplomacy* (Constable 1930), 425) relates that the Ambassador was already in his

bedroom at the Embassy shortly after 11.00 p.m.
41. Harold Nicolson, op. cit., 424–6.
42. Gilbert, op cit, 122
43. *Dispatch from the British Ambassador …*
44. Ibid.
45. Rumbold, op. cit., 328
46. Ibid., 329
47. Gilbert, op. cit., 123
48. As told by Valentine Chirol to Sir Charles Hardinge, *The Diary of Edward Goschen 1900–1914*, ed. H. D. Howard (Royal Historical Society, Camden Fourth Series, London 1980), 50; Oppenheimer, op. cit., 234
49. Joseph C. Grew, *Turbulent Era: A Diplomatic Record of Forty Years*, Vol. I: 1904–1945, ed. Walter Johnson (Hammond & Hammond 1953), 138 (entry for 5 August 1914)
50. Gilbert, op. cit., 123
51. Gerard, op. cit., 94
52. Quoted in Gilbert, op. cit., 124
53. As recounted to Sir Charles Hobhouse by Rumbold (*Inside Asquith's Cabinet: From the Diaries of Charles Hobhouse*, ed. Edward David (John Murray 1977), 185. Writing a few weeks later, Rumbold also recalled the event (Gilbert, op. cit., 124).
54. *Dispatch from the British Ambassador …*
55. Oppenheimer, op. cit., 234
56. *Dispatch from the British Ambassador …*

CHAPTER 9

1. Diary of King George V, entry for 9 November 1918, Royal Archives, quoted in Kenneth Rose, *King George V* (Weidenfeld & Nicolson 1983), 229
2. Sir Horace Rumbold to King George V, 24 October 1928, Bod Lib, Rumbold Papers, Box 36, ff 79–84
3. Copy of a letter from Abrahamson, British Red Cross representative in Berlin, to Lord Kilmarnock, 9 January 1919, forwarded to Lord Curzon, TNA, FO 371/3776. One of the main concerns for the Allies was to 'help solve the food problem in Germany' in

order to discourage the spread of Bolshevism.

4. Ibid.
5. *The Diaries of a Cosmopolitan: Count Henry Kessler, 1918–1937*, trans. and ed. Charles Kessler (Weidenfeld & Nicolson 1971), 54
6. Kessler's diary, quoted in Laird McLeod Easton, *The Red Count: The Life and Times of Harry Kessler* (University of California Press 2002), 289
7. Kessler, op. cit., 93
8. Gaynor Johnson, *The Berlin Embassy of Lord D'Abernon, 1920–1926* (Palgrave Macmillan 2002), 19–20
9. Sydney Waterlow, Central European Department, Foreign Office, quoted in Johnson, op. cit., 20–21
10. Correspondence between Lord Kilmarnock and Lord Curzon, the Foreign Secretary, June 1920, TNA, T162/997
11. Ibid.
12. Lady Susan Townley, *'Indiscretions' of Lady Susan* (T. Butterworth 1922), 311
13. *Hansard*, 19 February 1919, Vol. 112, cc918–20
14. Townley, op. cit., 308
15. Ibid., 311
16. Martin Gilbert, *Sir Horace Rumbold: Portrait of a Diplomat, 1869–1941* (Heinemann 1973), 180
17. *Old Diplomacy: The Reminiscences of Lord Hardinge of Penshurst* (John Murray 1947), 249
18. *An Ambassador of Peace: Pages from the Diary of Viscount D'Abernon* (3 vols, Hodder & Stoughton 1929–30), Vol. I, 53 (entry for 25 June 1920)
19. Hardinge, op. cit., 249. However, Johnson (op. cit., 18, 22) opines that Curzon was quite content for the appointment to go ahead as it was in line with the recommendations of the MacDonnell Commission, with Lloyd George taking the blame for it.
20. Johnson, op. cit., 26
21. Johnson, op. cit., 23
22. *The Times*, 29 June 1920
23. Lord Londonderry to Lord D'Abernon, 4 July 1920, BL, D'Abernon Papers, © The British Library Board, Add. MSS 48939
24. As reported in *The Times*, 2 July 1920
25. Rumbold to Sir Charles Hardinge, 28 August 1920, quoted in Gilbert, op. cit., 214
26. Townley, op. cit., 306
27. *Berliner Tageblatt*, 8 October 1926
28. *René Gimpel: Diary of an Art Dealer*, trans. from the French by John Rosenberg (Hodder & Stoughton 1966), 148–9 (entry for 8 October 1920)
29. Sargent's first rendition of Lady D'Abernon apparently portrayed her in a white satin dress, but he soon changed it to a black and white one. In early 1926 the portrait featured in a monographic exhibition on the recently deceased artist at the Royal Academy in London. In 1941 it was on display in the drawing room of the D'Abernons' home at Stoke D'Abernon in Surrey (*Country Life*, 28 November 1941); Richard Ormond & Elaine Kilmurray, *John Singer Sargent: Complete Paintings Vol. III: The Later Portraits* (Yale University Press 2003), 122, 124, cat. no. 466). After Lady D'Abernon's death in 1954 the portrait passed to her nephew and was eventually sold at Christie's on 1 June 1984, purchased by the Birmingham Museum of Art, Alabama. Sargent also made a later charcoal sketch of Lady D'Abernon (now in York City Art Gallery).
30. Ormond & Kilmurray, op. cit., cat. no. 524, p. 178. In 1941 this portrait was also on display in the drawing room at Stoke D'Abernon (*Country Life*, 28 November 1941). It is now in a private collection.
31. *The Diaries of Cynthia Gladwyn*, ed. Miles Jebb (Constable 1995), 67 (entry for 5 October 1947)
32. Ibid., 68
33. Ibid.
34. Ibid.
35. Edgar Stern-Rubarth, *Three Men Tried … Austen Chamberlain, Stresemann, Briand and their Fight for a New Europe: A Personal Memoir* (Duckworth 1939), 36
36. Ibid.
37. Gimpel, op. cit., 148–9 (entry for 8 October 1920)
38. *The Times*, 5 July 1920
39. *The Illustrated London News*, 17 July 1920
40. *The Times*, 8 December 1919
41. Account in *The Times*, 8 December 1919
42. *Red Cross and Berlin Embassy, 1915–1926: Extracts from the Diaries of Viscountess D'Abernon* (John Murray 1946), 59
43. Ibid., 60 (entry for 4 August 1920)
44. Ibid.
45. Ibid., 71 (entry for 31 October 1920)
46. Ibid., 60-61 (entry for 4 August 1920)
47. Ibid., 61
48. Ibid., 64 (entry for 7 August 1920)
49. Hardinge, op. cit., 237
50. Rumbold to his wife, 5 August 1920, quoted in Gilbert, op. cit., 206
51. Hardinge, op. cit., 237
52. Gilbert, op. cit., 218
53. According to Lady D'Abernon in *Red Cross and Berlin Embassy …*, 68 (entry for October 1920). However, *The Times* of 22 October 1920 gives the date of their arrival on the previous day, Thursday 21 October. The dates in both Lord and Lady D'Abernon's memoirs sometimes conflict with those given in contemporary sources.
54. Minute from Johnson, Foreign Office, April 1922, TNA, T/162/997
55. *Red Cross and Berlin Embassy…*, 70 (entry for 30 October 1920)
56. A printed invitation to the D'Abernons' diplomatic reception in the D'Abernon Papers at the British Library (Add. MSS 48939) gives the date for this as 21 October, which, if the couple had indeed arrived in Berlin on that day, seems unlikely, and may have been some kind of example copy or one discarded as the date had been wrongly printed. *The Times* of 1 November confirms the date for this event as Saturday, 30 October,

reporting that both the diplomatic corps and the Heads of the Inter-Allied Missions in Berlin were invited.

57. *Red Cross and Berlin Embassy ...*, 70 (entry for 31 October 1920)

58. BL, D'Abernon Papers, © The British Library Board, Add. MSS 48939

59. *Red Cross and Berlin Embassy ...*, 71 (entry for 31 October 1920)

60. Lady D'Abernon remarked that 'It is rather surprising that [the silver] should have lain safe and uninjured in the basement of the Embassy all through the War' (ibid.)

61. Ibid.

62. Ibid.

CHAPTER 10

1. Harold Nicolson, *The Spectator*, 27 January 1939 ('People and Things')

2. Foreign Office Circular to Heads of Missions from Lord Curzon, 14 February 1922, TNA, FO 366/798

3. D'Abernon to Lord Curzon, 30 August and 2 November 1921, TNA, FO 366/792.

4. D'Abernon to Lord Curzon, 8 April 1922, TNA, FO 366/798

5. Ibid.

6. Sir Lionel Earle, *Turn over the Page* (Hutchinson 1935), 183

7. Sir Frank Lascelles to the Marquess of Lansdowne, 27 February 1904, TNA, FO 64/1613

8. Keith Jeffery, *MI6: The History of the Secret Intelligence Service* (Bloomsbury paperback edn, 2011), 193–4

9. Michael Smith, *Foley: The Spy who Saved 10,000 Jews* (Hodder & Stoughton 1999), 63.

10. Harold Nicolson, *Diplomacy* (Harcourt, Brace 1939), 167

11. Ibid.

12. '10.30 every day General Sir Richard Ewart, I and Lieutenant Breen go to a meeting at the Interallied Conference in the French Legation at Pariserplatz', Abrahamson to Lord Kilmarnock, 9 January 1919, TNA, FO 371/3776.

13. *Red Cross and Berlin Embassy, 1915–1926: Extracts from the Diaries of Viscountess D'Abernon* (John Murray 1946), 118 (note)

14. The information in this paragraph is taken from documents in TNA, T162/997.

15. Note typed by May Wilson, 30 July 1925, TNA, T162/997

16. *Red Cross and Berlin Embassy ...*, 69–70 (entry for 30 October 1920)

17. Ibid., 72 (entry for 6 November 1920)

18. Ibid., 85 (entry for 3 February 1921)

19. Ibid., 86

20. Ibid.

21. Ibid., 87 (entry for 24 February 1921)

22. Ibid., 94 (entry for 4 June 1921)

23. William (Lord) Strang, *The Foreign Office* (George Allen & Unwin 1955), 101

24. Lady Curzon to Lady D'Abernon, written from the Ritz Hotel, Paris, 17 October 1921, BL, D'Abernon Papers, © The British Library Board, Add. MSS 48939

25. Marchioness Curzon of Kedleston to her husband Lord Curzon, *Reminiscences* (Hutchinson 1955), 129

26. Ibid.

27. Ibid.

28. Michael Bloch, *Ribbentrop* (Bantam Press 1992), 20

29. *Red Cross and Berlin Embassy ....* 103 (entry for 1 February 1923)

30. 1-2 March 1923, *Champion Redoubtable: The Diaries and Letters of Violet Bonham-Carter, 1914–1945*, ed. Mark Pottle (Weidenfeld & Nicolson 1998), 141

31. Ibid.

32. *Red Cross and Berlin Embassy ...* 105 (entry for 7 March 1923)

33. Viscountess D'Abernon quoted Violet Bonham-Carter's letter to her of 19 March 1923 in full (*Red Cross and Berlin Embassy ...*, 106–7)

34. Ibid., 113 (entry for 17 October 1923)

35. Ibid., 112

36. Ibid., 114 (entry for 2 November 1923)

37. Ibid., 117 (entry for 10 November 1923)

38. Ibid.

39. Ibid., 124 (entry for 27 November 1923)

40. Ibid., 130 (entry for 12 January 1924)

41. *The Sunday Times*, 20 January 1924 ('The Social Season: Jubilant Berlin')

42. *An Ambassador of Peace: Pages from the Diary of Viscount D'Abernon* (3 vols, Hodder & Stoughton 1929–30), Vol. II, 290 (entry for 31 December 1923)

43. In September 1924 D'Abernon announced that he would resign from the ambassadorship (*The Times*, 20 September 1924) but was persuaded to remain in Berlin.

44. Augustus John, *Chiaroscuro: Fragments of Autobiography: First Series* (Jonathan Cape 1952), 144

45. Ibid., 144–6

46. Viscount D'Abernon, *Portraits and Appreciations* (Hodder & Stoughton 1931), 140–41

47. *An Ambassador of Peace ...*, Vol. III, 152–3 (entry for 19 March 1925) and 222

48. John, op. cit., 143. The portrait is now in the collection of the Albright-Knox Art Gallery, Buffalo, NY, USA

49. *An Ambassador of Peace ...*, Vol. III, 153, 222

50. *The Times*, 26 October 1925

51. 'Politics Forgot', Pathé newsreel 428.29, 2 November 1925

52. *An Ambassador of Peace ...*, Vol. III, 153 (entry for 19 March 1925). D'Abernon was, however, shocked to learn the following April that Germany and the Soviet Union had signed a treaty reaffirming commercial links. D'Abernon's long-acclaimed success in the diplomatic negotiations in which he was involved over the years of his ambassadorship has undergone some recent revision (for example, Gaynor Johnson, *The Berlin Embassy of Lord D'Abernon, 1920–1926* (Palgrave Macmillan 2002))

53. Count Henry Kessler to his sister, quoted in Laird McLeod Easton, *The Red Count: The Life and Times of Harry Kessler* (University of California Press 2002), 368

54. D'Abernon to Lloyd George, 16

January 1926, BL, D'Abernon Papers, © The British Library Board, Add. MSS 48939

55. Ralph Stevenson to D'Abernon, written from the British Legation, Sofia, 4 November 1925, BL, D'Abernon Papers, © The British Library Board, Add. MSS 48939

56. *The Times*, 16 July 1926

57. A more recent interpretation of this event, in contrast to the hagiographies that traditionally surround D'Abernon's role in international diplomacy at this time has been that Germany was keen to enter the League for cynical motives, so that she could be treated as having equal status as the other members and begin to renegotiate the terms of the Treaty of Versailles (Johnson, op. cit., 142).

58. *The Times*, 9 October 1926

59. As reported in *The Times*, 9 October 1926. In *Red Cross and Berlin Embassy* .... Lady D'Abernon wrongly claims that this even took place in late September (140–41).

60. It dated from 1768 according to *The Times* of 9 October 1926

61. Red Cross and Berlin Embassy ..., 139

62. *The Times*, 7 October 1926

63. *The Times*, 11 October 1926. Lady D'Abernon gives the date for their departure from Berlin as 6 October (*Red Cross and Berlin Embassy* ..., 141)

64. *Red Cross and Berlin Embassy* ..., 141

65. *The Times*, 11 October 1926

66. Ibid.

67. *The Illustrated London News*, 23 October 1926

68. *The Sunday Times*, 10 October 1926

69. *The Diaries of Cynthia Gladwyn*, ed. Miles Jebb (Constable 1995), 67 (entry for 5 October 1947)

70. GAC File 4002/24. Amongst Lady D'Abernon's bequests after her death, she gave her husband's personal papers to the British Museum, portraits by Reynolds and Gainsborough to the National Gallery in London, and a black and white crayon drawing of herself by John Singer Sargent to York City Art Gallery ('Latest Wills', *The Times*, 22 July 1954).

CHAPTER 11

1. Sir Edward Malet, *Shifting Scenes or Memories of Many Men in Many Lands* (John Murray 1901), 165–66

2. Lord Odo Russell to the Marquess of Salisbury, 22 April 1878, printed in *Correspondence respecting the Repairs and the Supply and Maintenance of Furniture at certain of Her Majesty's Embassies and Legations* (TNA, WORK 10/255)

3. Ibid

4. Minute from R.H. Boyce, 2 October 1884, TNA, WORK 10/488

5. Ibid

6. 'Schedule of Furniture and Fittings the property of the late Lord Ampthill proposed to be purchased by Her M's Government, Sept.r 84', TNA, WORK 10/488

7. *The Illustrated London News*, 25 November 1893

8. Hannah Pakula, *An Uncommon Woman: The Empress Frederick* (Weidenfeld & Nicolson 1996), 144

9. *The Illustrated London News*, 25 November 1893

10. In an amateur watercolour of 1882 (at Woburn Abbey) by Ermytrude Russell's sister Ela, the portrait, in the same elaborate frame in which it appears in *The Illustrated London News* picture, is shown hanging above a fireplace in the Saloon at Woburn Abbey.

11. *The Illustrated London News*, 25 November 1893

12. Sir Lionel Earle, *Turn Over the Page* (Hutchinson 1935), 150, 251

13. Correspondence in TNA, FO 64/1613

14. Lady Edward Cavendish to Florence Spring-Rice, 1 October 1905, CACC, Spring-Rice Papers (CASR II 1/5)

15. Lady Edward Cavendish to Florence Spring-Rice, 1 November 1905, CACC, Spring-Rice Papers (CASR II 1/5)

16. Lady Edward Cavendish to Florence Spring-Rice, 12 January 1907, CACC, Spring-Rice Papers (CASR II 1/5)

17. *An Ambassador of Peace: Pages from the Diary of Viscount D'Abernon* (3 vols, Hodder & Stoughton 1929, 1930), Vol. III, 36–7 (entry for 15 January 1924)

18. *Red Cross and Berlin Embassy, 1915–1926: Extracts from the Diaries of Viscountess D'Abernon* (John Murray 1946), 61 (entry for 4 August 1920). The photographs were included in A. J. Gordon's unpublished thesis 'A New British Embassy in Berlin', Welsh School of Architecture, 1948 (BAL, ref. X.M.S. 725-125 (43B): 72.064)

19. Dated 1816 according to sources in the National Archives

20. TNA, WORK 68/3. Photographs of representative items were placed in an album in the 1930s (TNA, WORK 68/11)

21. *Red Cross and Berlin Embassy* ..., 61 (entry for 4 August 1920)

22. Ibid., 94 (entry for 4 June 1921)

23. *An Ambassador of Peace* ..., Vol. III, 37 (entry for 15 January 1924)

24. *Ambassador Dodd's Diary, 1933–1938*, ed. by W. E. Dodd & M. Dodd (Victor Gollancz 1941), 66–7 (entry for 31 October 1933)

25. Lord Esher, First Commissioner, Office of Works to Francis Mowatt, Permanent Secretary, HM Treasury, 5 December 1899, TNA, WORK 54/50

26. 'Queen Victoria's portrait when young is well lit, and hangs at the end of the room, and the other 4 Sovereigns, on the walls around', Lady Rumbold to Lady Fane, 18 June [or possibly January] 1930, Rumbold Family Papers

27. *The Diaries of a Cosmopolitan: Count Henry Kessler, 1918–1937*, ed. Charles Kessler (Weidenfeld & Nicolson 1971), 278

28. The D'Abernon Papers at the

British Library contain much correspondence and invoices on D'Abernon's art collecting activities during this period.

29. D'Abernon to Crichton Brothers, London, 25 October 1925, BL, D'Abernon Papers, © The British Library Board, Add. MSS 48933

30. BL, D'Abernon Papers, © The British Library Board, Add. MS 48933

31. This is from a typed list, 'PICTURES etc. / the Property of Lord D'Abernon' with a note from the Ambassador dated 4 December 1923 (TNA, T161/76). Presumably, D'Abernon meant the art dealer Wertheimer who operated in Berlin (and London). D'Abernon was later influential in acquiring Sargent's portraits of members of the Wertheimer family for the Tate Gallery in London. Samuel Wertheimer had settled in England from Germany in 1830 and had created a successful business in dealing in fine art, his clients including the Rothschilds. However it is not impossible that D'Abernon did indeed mean Wertheim's, the large luxury department store in Berlin which coincidentally was built on the same site as the previous Embassy building, on the corner of Leipzigerstrasse and Leipziger Platz. Unfortunately, despite D'Abernon's promise in this document that the receipt for this purchase was enclosed, which would have settled the matter, a note on the document states that the receipts had not been received in London.

32. René Gimpel, *Diary of an Art Dealer*, trans. from the French by John Rosenberg (Hodder & Stoughton 1966), 148 (entry for 8 October 1920)

33. 'PICTURES etc. / the Property of Lord D'Abernon' with a note from the Ambassador dated 4 December 1923, TNA, T161/76; the painting's title is not listed.

34. Ibid.

35. 'It will be a pretty monstrous thing if the picture is bought by the Chantrey Bequest Committee. D'Abernon wants to reimburse himself at the expense of the Bequest ... I thought he was going to present it to the Tate. Surely Chantrey meant his Bequest to benefit the artist rather than the sitter.' Augustus John to Sir Gerald Kelly, 21 December 1931, Tate Archive, TGA803. The Tate's portrait is inventory number N05936.

36. Erroneously recorded as 1924 in Earle's autobiography *Turn Over the Page*, 181

37. Earle did make other visits to Berlin, during which time he visited art collections with D'Abernon (Chapter 9)

38. Earle, op. cit., 181–2

39. McAdam to Sir G. L. Barstow, HM Treasury, 21 December 1923, TNA, T161/76

40. D'Abernon to Sir Lionel Earle, 4 December 1923, TNA, T161/76

41. Sir Lionel Earle to Sir G. L. Barstow, Controller of Supply Services at HM Treasury, 17 December 1923, TNA, T161/76

42. Sir Charles Holmes, National Gallery, to Sir G. L. Barstow, HM Treasury, 28 December 1923, TNA, T161/76

43. BL, D'Abernon Papers, © The British Library Board, Add. MSS 48933

44. Sir Charles Holmes, National Gallery, to Sir G. L. Barstow, HM Treasury, 28 December 1923, TNA, T161/76

45. Leitch, Office of Works, to HM Treasury, 21 February 1924, TNA, T161/76

46. D'Abernon to Cassirer Gallery, Berlin, 9 October 1926, BL, D'Abernon Papers, © The British Library Board, Add. MS 48933

47. Earle to Lady D'Abernon, 19 November 1926, D'Abernon, Papers, BL, © The British Library Board, Add. MS 48939

48. As they had never been given a catalogue number and there is no mention of them in any of the Government Art Collection's own files, the GAC was completely oblivious to the existence of these paintings until 2009 when the author discovered the papers concerning them in the National Archives, filed amongst Treasury papers rather than Ministry of Works ones.

CHAPTER 12

1. Vita Sackville-West to Harold Nicolson, 12 July 1928, *Vita and Harold: The Letters of Vita Sackville-West and Harold Nicolson*, ed. Nigel Nicolson (paperback edn, Phoenix 1993), 198

2. Sackville-West to Virginia Woolf, 29 February, 1928, written from Nicolson's apartment at 24 Brücken Allée, Berlin NW23, *The Letters of Vita Sackville-West to Virginia Woolf*, ed. Louise DeSalvo & Mitchell A. Leaska (Hutchinson 1984), 271–3

3. Sackville-West to Woolf, 14 March 1928, Ibid., 276–8

4. He served as 'a valuable and efficient assistant' as Embassy Secretary under Lord Loftus (*The Diplomatic Reminiscences of Lord Augustus Loftus 1862-1879* (2 vols, Cassell 1894), Vol. I., 374

5. Lionel Earle, Office of Works to C. H. Montgomery, Foreign Office, 12 January 1927, TNA, File WORK 10/279

6. Letter signed by the Commercial Secretary, Naval and Military Attachés, TNA, File WORK 10/279

7. Quoted in Michael Smith, *Foley: The Spy who Saved 10,000 Jews* (London 1999), 156

8. Sir Lawrence Evelyn ('L.E.') Jones, *Georgian Afternoon* (Rupert Hart-Davis 1958), 109

9. Harold Nicolson to Sackville-West, 7 November 1927, *Vita and Harold …* , 186

10. Nicolson to Sackville-West, 11 February 1928, ibid., 192

11. Nicolson to Sackville-West, 14 April 1928, ibid., 192–3

12. Nicolson to Sackville-West, 16 May 1928, ibid.,195

13. Nigel Nicolson, *Portrait of a Marriage* (Weidenfeld & Nicolson 1973), 213

14. Ibid.

15. Sackville-West to Woolf, 25 January 1929, *The Letters of Vita Sackville-West to Virginia Woolf*, 325–6

16. Harold Nicolson to his parents, 30 June 1928, *Harold Nicolson Diaries and Letters 1907–1964*, ed. Nigel Nicolson (paperback edn, Phoenix 2005), 64

17. Harold Nicolson, *Sir Arthur Nicolson Bart, First Lord Carnock: A Study in the Old Diplomacy* (Constable 1930).

18. Bella Fromm, *Blood and Banquets: A Berlin Social Diary* (Geoffrey Bles 1942), 28 (entry for 1 February 1930)

19. Sir Robert Vansittart to Sir Horace Rumbold (undated, early March 1928), Bod Lib, Rumbold Papers, Box 35, f 235

20. Rumbold to Sir Ronald Lindsay, 24 March 1928, Bod Lib, Rumbold Papers, Box 35, ff 270–76

21. Ibid.

22. Martin Gilbert, *Sir Horace Rumbold: Portrait of a Diplomat, 1869–1941* (Heinemann 1973), 323. 'Today we are lunching with some Germans called Ribbentrops who have a pretty house not far from here and very good tennis', Lady Rumbold reported to her daughter in a letter of 25 April 1930 (Rumbold Family Papers).

23. Nicolson to Sackville-West, 3 August 1928, *Harold Nicolson Diaries and Letters*, 65

24. Ibid.

25. As reported in *The Times*, 11 August 1928

26. Sackville-West to Woolf, 21 August 1928, *The Letters of Vita Sackville-West to Virginia Woolf*, 293–5

27. Lady Rumbold to her daughter, 19 September 1928, Rumbold Family Papers

28. Rumbold to his daughter, 17 September 1928, Bod Lib, Rumbold Papers, Box 36, ff 56–7

29. Rumbold to his stepmother, 23 September 1929, Bod Lib, Rumbold Papers, Box 37, ff 42–5. The Rumbolds also brought with them a butler named Hansen who had accompanied them on several postings (Rumbold family information).

30. Sackville-West to Nicolson, 12 July 1928, *Vita and Harold*, 198 (from the same letter quoted at the beginning of this chapter)

31. Sackville-West to Woolf, 3 1 August 1928, *The Letters of Vita Sackville-West to Virginia Woolf*, 296–7

32. The quotations in this paragraph are taken from *Confidential Report from Daniel A. Binchy to Joseph P. Walshe*, Documents on Irish Foreign Policy, Vol. III, 1926-1932 (Dublin, 2002), Document 373, Binchy to Walshe, 27 May 1930.

33. Nicolson to Sackville-West, 18 September 1928, Nicolson Papers, quoted in Gilbert, op. cit., 318

34. Nicolson to Sackville-West, 11 May 1929, quoted in James Lees-Milne, *Harold Nicolson: A Biography*, Vol. I 1886-1929, 342–3

35. André François-Poncet, *The Fateful Years: Memoirs of a French Ambassador in Berlin, 1931–1938* (Victor Gollancz 1949), 112

36. *Old Diplomacy: The Reminiscences of Lord Hardinge of Penshurst* (John Murray 1947), 236–7

37. Gilbert, op. cit., 320

38. Oswald Mosley, *My Life* (Nelson 1968), 243

39. Quoted in Humphrey Carpenter, *W. H. Auden: A Biography* (George Allen & Unwin 1981), 90

40. Mosley, op. cit., 243

41. Ibid.

42. Nicholas Mosley, *Rules of the Game: Sir Oswald and Lady Cynthia Mosley, 1896–1933* (Secker & Warburg 1982), 110

43. Diana Mosley, *A Life of Contrasts: The Autobiography* (Hamish Hamilton 1977), 72

44. Rumbold to his stepmother, 8 March 1929, Rumbold Papers, Bod Lib, Box 36, ff 212–14

45. Lady Rumbold to her mother Lady Fane, 7 November 1928, Rumbold Family Papers

46. Rumbold to his stepmother, 22 December 1928,Rumbold Papers, Bod Lib, Box 36, ff 135–6

47. Sackville-West to Woolf, 12 January 1929, *The Letters of Vita Sackville-West to Virginia Woolf*, 323–4

48. *The Diary of Virginia Woolf*, Vol. III, 1925–1930, ed. A. O. Bell (Hogarth Press 1980), 218

49. Frances Spalding, *Vanessa Bell* (Weidenfeld & Nicolson 1983), 227–8

50. *The Diaries of a Cosmopolitan: Count Henry Kessler, 1918–1937*, ed. Charles Kessler (Weidenfeld & Nicolson 1971), 362

51. Ibid., 361

52. Sackville-West to Woolf, 29 January 1929, *The Letters of Vita Sackville-West to Virginia Woolf*, 326-7

53. Sackville-West to Woolf, 31 January 1929, ibid., 328–30

54. Sackville-West to Woolf, 4 February 1929, ibid., 333–34

55. David Herbert, *Second Son: An Autobiography* (Peter Owen Ltd 1972), 35–6

56. Ibid., 37

57. Ibid., 39

58. *Cyril Connolly: Journal and Memoir*, ed. David Pryce-Jones (Collins 1983), 142–5

59. *The Romantic Friendship: The Letters of Cyril Connolly to Noel Blakiston*, ed. Noël Blakiston (Constable 1975), 320 (letter of 3 June 1928, written c/o British Embassy, Berlin)

60. Lady Rumbold to her daughter, 18 March 1929, Bod Lib, Rumbold Papers, Box 36, ff 220–22

61. Sir Horace Rumbold to his daughter, 20 March 1929, Bod Lib, Rumbold Papers, Box 36, ff 225–6

62. Rumbold to his daughter, 24 March 1929, Bod Lib, Rumbold Papers, Box 36, ff 227–8

63. Nicolson to Sackville-West, 10 April 1929; James Lees-Milne, *Harold Nicolson: A Biography*, Vol. I 1886–1929, 366

64. Nicolson to Sackville-West, 12 and 16 April 1929, *Harold Nicolson Diaries and Letters*, 69

65. Lees-Milne, op.cit., 371

66. As reported by Nicolson to Sackville-West, 22 July 1929, *Vita and Harold*, 219

67. Sackville-West to Woolf, 29 February 1928, *The Letters of Vita Sackville-West to*

Virginia Woolf, 271–3
68. Sackville-West to Woolf, 12 January 1929, ibid., 323–4
69. Sackville-West to Woolf, 23 February 1929, ibid., 346–7
70. Sackville-West to Nicolson, 15 November 1928, quoted in Nigel Nicolson, *Portrait of a Marriage* (Weidenfeld & Nicolson 1973), 212
71. Nicolson to Sackville-West, 8 August 1929, *Harold Nicolson Diaries and Letters*, 73
72. Nicolson to R.B. Lockhart, 22 July 1929, *The Diaries of Sir Robert Bruce Lockhart*, ed. Kenneth Young (2 vols, Macmillan 1973), Vol. I, 99
73. Sackville-West to Woolf, 13 September 1929, *The Letters of Vita Sackville-West to Virginia Woolf*, 368–9; *The Diaries of Sir Robert Bruce Lockhart*, Vol. I, 107 (entry for 16 September 1929)
74. Nicolson to Sackville-West, 2 September 1929, Nicolson Papers, quoted in Gilbert, op. cit., 325
75. Gilbert, op. cit., 325 (note)
76. Rumbold to his stepmother, 12 October 1929, Bod Lib, Rumbold Papers, Box 37, ff 73–6
77. Nicolson to Sackville-West, 16 December 1929, *Vita and Harold …*, 225
78. Nicolson to Sackville-West, quoted in Nigel Nicolson, *Portrait of a Marriage* (London 1973), 214
79. Nicolson (diary entry for 19 December 1929), *Harold Nicolson Diaries and Letters*, 75. '[H]uge and most fierce looking', the cactus was a gift from the German Foreign Office. For Nicolson, 'The greatest enigma of the German character is their strange love of cacti' (Lady Rumbold to Lady Fane, 22 December 1929, Rumbold Family Papers)

CHAPTER 13

1. Lady Rumbold to her daughter, 7 January 1931, Rumbold Family Papers; Midge Gillies, *Amy Johnson* (Weidenfeld & Nicolson 2003), 189
2. *The Times* 11 October 1930
3. Sir Horace Rumbold to Harold Nicolson, 18 January 1930, Bod Lib, Rumbold Papers, Box 37, ff 120–23
4. Margaret Lane, *Edgar Wallace: The Biography of a Phenomenon* (William Heinemann 1938), 357
5. E. V. Wallace, *Edgar Wallace by his Wife* (Hutchinson 1932), 180–81
6. Rumbold to Nicolson, 18 January 1930, Bod Lib, Rumbold Papers, Box 37, ff 120–23
7. Rumbold to his son, 23 June 1930, quoted in Gilbert, op. cit., 318, Note 3
8. Rumbold to his son, 10 March 1931, Bod Lib, Rumbold Papers, Box 38, ff 167–8
9. Hedda Adlon, *Hotel Adlon: The Life and Death of a Great Hotel* (Barrie Books 1958), 193
10. Rumbold to his son, 10 March 1931, Bod Lib, Rumbold Papers, Box 38, ff 167–8
11. Rumbold Family Papers and information
12. Rumbold to Sir Francis Lindley, British Ambassador to Tokyo, 24 February 1932, quoted in Martin Gilbert, *Sir Horace Rumbold: Portrait of a Diplomat, 1869–1941* (Heinemann 1973), 346–7 (Note).
13. Rumbold to his wife, 30 July 1931, Bod Lib, Rumbold Papers, Box 38, ff 212–19
14. Ibid.
15. Ibid.
16. Ibid.
17. Rumbold to Viscount D'Abernon, 9 September 1930, BL, D'Abernon Papers, Add. MS 48939
18. Quoted in Gilbert, op.cit., 351 Note 1
19. Ibid., 333
20. Rumbold to his stepmother, 20 December 1931, Bod Lib, Rumbold Papers, Box 39, ff 72–4
21. Nicolson to Vita Sackville-West, 25 January 1932, written from the Prinz Albrecht Hotel, Berlin, *Vita and Harold: The Letters of Vita Sackville-West and Harold Nicolson*, ed. Nigel Nicolson (paperback edn, Phoenix 1993), 232–3
22. Ibid.
23. André François-Poncet, *The Fateful Years: Memoirs of a French Ambassador in Berlin, 1931–1938* (Victor Gollancz 1949), 48
24. Lady Rumbold to her mother Lady Fane, 2 February 1933, Rumbold Family Papers
25. Gilbert, op. cit., 367
26. As recounted by Rumbold to his stepmother, 14 February 1933, Bod Lib, Rumbold Papers, Box 40, ff 112–15
27. As Lady D'Abernon had described him in 1923
28. Rumbold to Geoffrey Knox, President of the Saar Governing Commission, 28 February 1933, Bod Lib, Rumbold Papers, Box 40, ff 131–6
29. Rumbold to Geoffrey Knox, President of Saar Governing Commission, 11 April 1933, quoted in Gilbert, op. cit., 376
30. Rumbold to Sir Godfrey Thomas, 15 March 1933, Bod Lib, Rumbold Papers, Box 40, ff 158–9
31. Gilbert, op. cit., 375
32. Nicholas Mosley, *Rules of the Game: Sir Oswald and Lady Cynthia Mosley, 1896–1933* (Secker & Warburg 1982), 110
33. Oswald Mosley, *My Life* (Nelson 1968), 243
34. Rumbold to Sir Clive Wigram, 28 June 1933, quoted in Gilbert, op. cit., 383
35. Gilbert, op.cit., 377–8
36. *The Times*, 28 June 1933
37. *The Times*, 1 July 1933
38. Lady Rumbold to Lady Fane, 7 March 1933, Rumbold Family Papers
39. Rumbold to Sir Eric Phipps, 2 June 1933, Bod Lib, Rumbold Papers, Box 40, ff 230–34
40. Harold Nicolson, *Diplomacy* (Harcourt, Brace 1939)
41. Harold Nicolson, Introduction to Sir Horace Rumbold, *The War Crisis in Berlin July August 1914* new edn, (Constable 1944), xxvi
42. Ibid., xxi
43. Gilbert, op. cit., 453
44. Anthony Eden to Lady Rumbold, quoted in Gilbert, op. cit., 454

CHAPTER 14

1. *Our Man in Berlin: The Diary of Sir Eric Phipps, 1933–1937*, ed. Gaynor Johnson (Palgrave

Macmillan 2008), 23 (18 October 1933), all extracts reproduced with permission of Palgrave Macmillan

2. Sir Ivone Kirkpatrick, *The Inner Circle* (Macmillan 1959), 49

3. As reported by Phipps to Sir John Simon, 24 October 1933, *Our Man in Berlin*, 25

4. Harold Nicolson, *Diplomacy* (Harcourt, Brace 1939)

5. Martha Dodd, *My Years in Germany* (Victor Gollancz 1939), 297

6. *Ambassador Dodd's Diary, 1933–1938*, ed. W. E. Dodd & M. Dodd (Victor Gollancz 1941), 202–3 (entry for 17 November 1934)

7. Kirkpatrick, op. cit., 53

8. *The Sunday Times* 29 October 1933

9. *Our Man in Berlin*, 40 (24 February 1934)

10. *The Eden Memoirs: Facing the Dictators* (Cassell 1962), 64

11. Kirkpatrick, op. cit., 70

12. Eden, op.cit., 64

13. Ibid., 67

14. Ribbentrop to Hitler, 21 February 1934, quoted in Martin Bloch, *Ribbentrop* (Bantam Press 1992), 51

15. Ibid.

16. Eden, op.cit., 69

17. Martha Dodd, op. cit., 189.

18. From Phipps' 'Bison Dispatch' of 13 June 1934, *Our Man in Berlin*, 58

19. Bella Fromm, *Blood and Banquets: A Berlin Social Diary* (Geoffrey Bles 1942), 148 (entry for 16 June 1934)

20. 'Register of Cards', CACC, Phipps Papers (PHPP III 6/5)

21. *Our Man in Berlin*, 68 (17 July 1934)

22. Phipps to Sir John Simon, Foreign Secretary, 4 July 1934, *Our Man in Berlin*, 63–4

23. *The Times*, 1 February 1935. See also J. R. M. Butler, *Lord Lothian (Philip Kerr)* (Macmillan 1960), 202. Apparently the visit was also suggested by T. P. Conwell-Evans, visiting lecturer in diplomatic relations at Königsberg University and pro-German sympathiser.

24. *Our Man in Berlin*, 85 (31 January 1935)

25. Ibid.

26. Ibid., 87 (28 February 1935)

27. *The Times*, 26 March 1935

28. Eden, op. cit., 139

29. There is some confusion over the timing of this event. Contemporary newspaper accounts described a lunch at the British Embassy, while the seating plan preserved in the Churchill Archives described the event as an *Abendtafel*. Adding to the confusion, Eden did not mention this event in his memoirs, although he is shown on the seating plan placed on the large central table, between the Princess of Hesse and Lady Phipps, with Hitler seated to the Ambassadress's left. He did, however, mention the small dinner that night with Hitler (Eden, op.cit., 141).

30. Seating plan in CACC, Phipps Papers (PHPP III 5/11). Ribbentrop was the only member of this select group to be seated (at least according to the plan) away from the main table.

31. *The Times*, 27 March 1935

32. Ibid.

33. *Our Man in Berlin*, 93

34. Ibid., 94 (28 March 1935)

35. *Retrospect: The Memoirs of the Rt. Hon. Viscount Simon GCSI, GCVO* (Hutchinson 1952), 202

36. *Our Man in Berlin*, 90 (16 March 1935)

37. Ibid., 100 (17 April 1935)

38. Christopher Isherwood, *Mr. Norris Changes Trains* (London 1935)

39. *Ambassador Dodd's Diary*, 245 (entry for 20 April 1935)

40. *The Times*, 12 May 1935

41. *The Thirties in Colour*, BBC TV 2009, Episode 4

42. As recollected by Lady Phipps and quoted in David Pryce-Jones, *Unity Mitford: A Quest* (Weidenfeld & Nicolson 1976), 99. Pryce-Jones discusses the background to his research and this book in his memoir *Fault Lines* (Criterion Books 2015)

43. Lord Redesdale to his daughter Diana Guinness, née Mitford, quoted in Jan Dalley, *Diana Mosley: A Life* (Faber & Faber 2000), 152

44. Pryce-Jones, op. cit., 149

45. Ibid., 99

46. Ibid.

47. Seating Plan, CACC, Phipps Papers (PHPP II 7/1)

48. Pryce-Jones, op. cit., 144

49. Ibid., 149

50. Diana Mosley, *A Life of Contrasts: The Autobiography* (Hamish Hamilton 1977) 141–2

51. Ibid., 142

52. *The Times*, 26 November 1935

53. *Our Man in Berlin*, 160 (23 January 1936)

CHAPTER 15

1. *Daily Telegraph*, 3 August 1936

2. André François-Poncet, *The Fateful Years: Memoirs of a French Ambassador in Berlin, 1931–1938* (Victor Gollancz 1949), 203–4

3. Ian Colvin, *Vansittart in Office* (Victor Gollancz 1965), 104

4. As remembered by Lady Vansittart (Duff Hart-Davis, *Hitler's Games: The 1936 Olympics* (Century 1986), 204)

5. Guy Walters, *Berlin Games: How Hitler Stole the Olympic Dream* (John Murray 2006), 252

6. *Daily Telegraph*, 11 August 1936

7. Ibid.

8. 'Zuerst ein kleines Essen, und dann ein Reisenempfang. Tausend Leute, tausend Quatsch'. *Die Tagebücher von Joseph Goebbels*, Teil I, Band 3/ II (K.G. Saur 2001), 153–4, (entry dated Sunday 9 August 1936)

9. *Chips: The Diaries of Sir Henry Channon*, ed. Robert Rhodes James (Weidenfeld & Nicolson 1967), 108 (entry for Saturday 8 August 1936)

10. 'Lady Vansittard [sic] ist bezaubernd …. Sehr sympatisch ist Lord Renell [sic]. Phipps ist dumm. Jetzt hat er Angst um Spanien.' *Die Tagebücher von Joseph Goebbels*, op. cit., 153–4 (entry dated Sunday 9 August 1936)

11. *Morning Post*, 10 August 1936

12. Norman Rose, *Vansittart: Study of a Diplomat* (Heinemann 1978), 199

13. *The Times*, 14 August 1936

14. Quoted in Colvin, op. cit., 107

15. *The Ribbentrop Memoirs* (Weidenfeld & Nicolson 1954), 64–5

16. François-Poncet, op. cit., 206
17. Channon, op.cit., 108 (entry for 8 August 1936)
18. Quoted in Colvin, op. cit., 109
19. Channon, op. cit.,106, 107 (entries for 5 and 6 August 1936)
20. Michael Bloch, *Ribbentrop* (Bantam Books 1992), 94–5
21. Ibid., 96–7
22. *Our Man in Berlin: The Diary of Sir Eric Phipps 1933–1937*, ed. Gaynor Johnson (Palgrave Macmillan 2008), 182 (21 October 1936)
23. Ibid., 106 (15 May 1935)
24. Bloch, op. cit., 112
25. Mary S. Lovell, *The Mitford Girls: The Biography of an Extraordinary Family* (paperback edn, Abacus 2002), 207. The incident took place at a lunch party at Goebbels' home.
26. The quotes in this paragraph are taken from Phipps' letter to Foreign Secretary Sir John Simon, 19 July 1934, TNA, FO 366/926
27. Ibid.
28. C. Howard Smith, Foreign Office, to Office of Works, 3 August 1934, TNA, FO 366/926
29. Phipps to C. Howard-Smith, 10 November 1934, TNA, FO 366/926
30. Phipps to Simon, 10 May 1935, TNA, WORK 10/280
31. Minute from Edward Muir, Office of Works, 21 June 1935, TNA, WORK 10/280
32. Basil Newton to Foreign Office, 4 July 1935, TNA, WORK 10/280
33. Note in File, TNA, WORK 10/280
34. *Our Man in Berlin*, 188 (10 November 1936)
35. Ian Kershaw, *Making Friends with Hitler: Lord Londonderry and Britain's Road to War* (Allen Lane 2004), 134–9
36. Anne de Courcy, *Circe: The Life of Edith, Marchioness of Londonderry* (Sinclair-Stevenson 1992), 279
37. Quoted in Kershaw, op. cit., 200
38. *Our Man in Berlin*, 190 (9 December 1936). Schacht had claimed in his speech that a *Menschenfreund* [friend of

mankind], a 'foreign diplomatist' had advocated German birth control in response to Germany's claim that she had too little space for its population. The claim to greater *Lebensraum* [living space] was to help justify the later German invasions of Poland and Russia.
39. John Herman, *The Paris Embassy of Sir Eric Phipps: Anglo–French Relations and the Foreign Office, 1937–1939* (Sussex Academic Press 1998), 8
40. *Our Man in Berlin*, 194–5 (3 February 1937)
41. Argued, for example, in Vaughan B. Baker, 'Nevile Henderson in Berlin: A Re-Evaluation', *Red River Historical Journal of World History* Vol. II, No. 4 (Winter 1977), 341 & Note 1
42. Sir Robert Vansittart, *The Mist Procession: The Autobiography of Lord Vansittart* (Hutchinson 1958), 445; he ascribed the comment to Stanley Baldwin.
43. These quotations are taken from Martha Dodd, *My Years in Germany*, 283–5
44. David Pryce-Jones, *Unity Mitford: A Quest* (London 1976), 99
45. Ibid., 283–4
46. François-Poncet, op. cit., 112
47. Herman, op.cit., 100–126
48. Various sources cite this episode, for example Ivone Kirkpatrick, *The Inner Circle* (Macmillan 1959), 90

CHAPTER 16

1. Sir Nevile Henderson, *Water under the Bridges* (Hodder & Stoughton 1945), 206
2. Sir Nevile Henderson, *Failure of a Mission* (Hodder & Stoughton 1940), 13
3. Ibid.
4. *Water under the Bridges*, 23
5. Henderson himself claimed responsibility for the idea of moving Rumbold from Warsaw to be as Ambassador to Constantinople, after a key conversation with D'Abernon on a journey from Paris to London in 1920 (*Water under the Bridges*, 99)
6. Vaughan B. Baker, 'Nevile Henderson in Berlin: A

Re-Evaluation', *Red River Historical Journal of World History* Vol. II, No. 4 (Winter 1977), 342–3; Peter Neville, 'The Appointment of Sir Nevile Henderson, 1937: Design or Blunder?', *Journal of Contemporary History* Vol. 33, No. 4 (1998): Berlin was 'surely the most sensitive posting in 1937', 617.
7. *The Eden Memoirs: Facing the Dictators* (Cassell 1962) 503–4
8. *The Diplomatic Diaries of Oliver Harvey, 1937–1940*, ed. John Harvey (Collins 1970), 41 (entry for 23 April 1937)
9. Peter Neville, 'Sir Neville Meyrick Henderson', *Oxford Dictionary of National Biography* (Oxford 2004)
10. Martha Dodd, *My Years in Germany* (Victor Gollancz 1939), 288
11. *The Sunday Times*, 4 September 1938 ('Court and Society')
12. *Water under the Bridges*, 199
13. Quoted in Anne de Courcy, *The Viceroy's Daughters: The Lives of the Curzon Sisters* (Weidenfeld & Nicolson 2000), 208
14. Quoted in ibid., 253
15. *Failure of a Mission*, 15–16.
16. Peter Neville, 'The Appointment of Sir Nevile Henderson …', 617 (Note 61)
17. *The Diplomatic Diaries of Oliver Harvey*, 41 (entry for 23 April 1937). Indeed, the early summer of 1937 was to see the new Ambassador voicing a number of apparently pro-German opinions, to the surprise of his diplomatic colleagues in London (Peter Neville, *Appeasing Hitler: The Diplomacy of Sir Nevile Henderson 1937-1939* (Macmillan 2000), 26–31)
18. *Failure of a Mission*, 47
19. Ibid., 48–49
20. Ibid., 55
21. Ibid.
22. Ibid.
23. Ibid.
24. Ibid., 83
25. *Water under the Bridges*, 142
26. Ibid., 172
27. Ibid., 174
28. Sir Nevile Henderson to Sir Robert Vansittart, Permanent

Under-Secretary, Foreign
Office, 11 August 1936, GAC,
File AA3006/1 Part 1

29. *Failure of a Mission*, 52–3
30. See, for example, the booklet
on the new British Embassy
(2000) and several British and
German newspaper articles
published the same year.
31. *Failure of a Mission*, 53
32. 'Nur die Treppenhaus war
elegant', *Berliner Zeitung*
19 July 2000. The article
wrongly describes Katherine
Harrison as Henderson's
daughter.
33. These quotes are taken from
Failure of a Mission, 53
34. *Water under the Bridges*, 29
35. *Failure of a Mission*, 54
36. Ibid. See also Martha Dodd's
comments on embassy security
in Chapter 17.
37. Ibid., 53–4
38. *Water under the Bridges*, 166–7
39. Henderson, 20 July 1937, TNA,
FO 366/995
40. *Failure of a Mission*, 54
41. Photographs of these plans are
included in A. J. Gordon's
unpublished thesis 'A New
British Embassy in Berlin',
Welsh School of Architecture,
1948 (BAL, ref. X.M.S. 725-125
(43B): 72.064)
42. *Failure of a Mission*, 54
43. *The Sunday Times*, 4
September 1938 ('Court and
Society')
44. *Water under the Bridges*, 112
45. Henderson (when Ambassador
to Buenos Aires) to Sir Robert
Vansittart, Permanent Under–
Secretary, Foreign Office,
11 August 1936, GAC, File
AA3006/1 Part 1
46. *Water under the Bridges*, 174
47. *Ambassador Dodd's Diary,
1933–1938*, ed. W. E. Dodd
& M. Dodd (Victor Gollancz
1941), 284 (entry for 16
November 1935)
48. Lady Rumbold to her daughter,
16 September and 10 October
1928; Lady Rumbold to Lady
Fane, 18 June [possibly
January] 1930; she also found
the historic English Church
'hideous', 'full of brass, and
terra-cotta tiles and plush and
bad wood-work', Rumbold
Family Papers
49. *Inside the Third Reich:*

Memoirs by Albert Speer
(English trans., Weidenfeld
& Nicolson 1970), 26
50. Ibid.
51. Harold Nicolson, *The
Spectator,* 27 January 1939
('People and Things')
52. Sir Ronald Lindsay to Sir
Horace Rumbold, 18 March
1928, Bod Lib, Rumbold
Papers, Box 35, ff 260–61
53. Sir Horace Rumbold, *The
War Crisis in Berlin, July –
August 1914* (new edn,
Constable 1944), 7
54. Rumbold to Sir Ronald
Lindsay, 24 March 1928,
Bod Lib, Rumbold Papers,
Box 35, ff 270–76
55. Rumbold to his daughter,
17 September 1928, Bod Lib,
Rumbold Papers, Box 36,
ff 56–7
56. Rumbold to Sir Eric Phipps,
20 May 1933, Bod Lib,
Rumbold Papers, Box 40,
ff 220–21
57. *Failure of a Mission*, 54
58. Sebastian Redecke & Ralph
Stern (eds), *Foreign Affairs:
New Embassy Buildings and
the German Foreign Office in
Berlin* (Birkhäuser Verlag
1997), 15–19
59. Henderson, 9 November 1937,
TNA, FO 366/995
60. *Failure of a Mission*, 54
61. Lord Halifax to Sir Philip
Sassoon, 6 January 1939, TNA,
FO 366/1049
62. Rumbold to Lady Rumbold, 30
July 1931, Bod Lib, Rumbold
Papers, Box 38, ff 212–19
63. Correspondence with
Henderson in GAC File 3006/1
Part 1
64. Correspondence in TNA,
FO 366/1055
65. *List of Pictures sent to
Embassies and Legations*
(annotated), sent with letter
from Edward Muir of 5 June
1937, GAC File AA 634/1
66. *Water under the Bridges*, 69
67. *Daily Mail*, 26 May 1934
68. 'Presentation of Royal Portraits
to HM Missions Abroad, 1937',
TNA, FO 366/987
69. *Water under the Bridges*, 178
70. Correspondence, TNA,
FO 372/3329
71. *Water under the Bridges*, 166
72. Ibid.

CHAPTER 17

1. André François-Poncet,
*The Fateful Years: Memoirs
of a French Ambassador in
Berlin, 1931–1938* (Victor
Gollancz 1949), 211
2. 'The effect, which was both
solemn and beautiful, was like
being inside a cathedral of
ice.', Sir Nevile Henderson,
Failure of a Mission (Hodder
& Stoughton 1940), 71
3. Quoted in Philip Ziegler,
*Edward VIII: The Official
Biography* (Collins 1990), 388
4. Quoted in ibid., 390
5. Irene Curzon's diary, quoted in
Anne de Courcy, *The Viceroy's
Daughters: The Lives of the
Curzon Sisters* (Weidenfeld &
Nicolson 2000), 274
6. *Chips: The Diaries of Sir
Henry Channon*, ed. Robert
Rhodes James (Weidenfeld
& Nicolson 1967), 22 (entry
for 18 January 1935)
7. François-Poncet, op. cit., 113
8. Ian Kershaw, *Making Friends
with Hitler: Lord Londonderry
and Britain's Road to War*
(Allen Lane 2004), 207–8
9. *Failure of a Mission*, 98
10. *The Times*, 22 November 1937
11. The Earl of Halifax, *Fulness
of Days* (Collins 1957), 191
12. *Failure of a Mission*, 76
13. Ibid., 98
14. Ibid., 123
15. Ibid., 127
16. Wesley K. Wark, *The Ultimate
Enemy: British Intelligence
and Nazi Germany, 1933–1939*
(I.B. Tauris 1985), 103
17. *Failure of a Mission*, 137–8; it
was known as the story of the
'special train'. Others naturally
had different accounts of the
sequence of events. According
to 'Atticus' in *The Sunday
Times* of 29 May 1938, alarm
had spread as a result of
Henderson's interview with
Ribbentrop concerning the
rumoured troop movements
and 'a number of the wives
of British journalists and of
members of the staff at the
British Embassy prepared to
leave the country at once. …
The Germans … have
denounced it as a diplomatic
manoeuvre to create prejudice
against their Government.

Whatever the facts may be I offer this as another example of that drama from which the theatre offers almost our only escape.'

18. Quoted in Keith Jeffery, *MI6: The History of the Secret Intelligence Service, 1909–1949* (paperback edn, Bloomsbury 2011), 301
19. Ibid.
20. François-Poncet, op. cit., 211
21. *Failure of a Mission*, 145
22. Henderson to Lord Halifax, 13 September 1938, *Documents on British Foreign Policy 1919–1939*, 3rd Series, Vol. II (HMSO 1949), 654
23. *Failure of a Mission*, 145
24. Henderson to Lord Halifax, 13 September 1938, *Documents on British Foreign Policy, 1919–1939*, 3rd Series, Vol. II, 654; *Failure of a Mission*, 48
25. *The Ulrich von Hassell Diaries, 1938–1944: The Story of the Forces against Hitler inside Germany*, trans. Geoffrey Brooks (Frontline Books 2011), 2 (retrospective entry written on 17 September 1938)
26. Sir Ivone Kirkpatrick, *The Inner Circle* (Macmillan 1959), 124
27. Ibid., 126
28. Peter Neville, *Appeasing Hitler: The Diplomacy of Sir Nevile Henderson, 1937–1939* (Macmillan 2000), 125 and note 22; correspondence between Sir George Ogilvie-Forbes and Foreign Office, London, 8–19 September 1938 (TNA, FO 370/564); British Embassy, Berlin to Foreign Office, 20 October 1938, TNA, FO 370/565
29. *Failure of a Mission*, 161
30. Kirkpatrick, op. cit., 112–13
31. Ibid.
32. Ibid.
33. As related by Sir Frank Roberts in 'The Wrong War', Episode 3 of *The Nazis: A Warning from History*, BBC TV 1997
34. *Failure of a Mission*, 168
35. A remark made by Henderson to Eden, 21 June 1937. Peter Neville, *Appeasing Hitler*, 37
36. *Failure of a Mission*, 171
37. Quoted in Martin Gilbert, 'Horace Wilson: Man of Munich?', *History Today* October 1982, 8. The remark is undated but, judging from information in the article, was probably made to Gilbert in 1962.
38. Katherine Harrison, *On the Fringe: Living in the Realms of Hitler and Stalin* (Book Guild Publishing 2007), 13–14
39. Discussed in Bruce Strang, 'Two Unequal Tempers: Sir George Ogilvie-Forbes, Sir Nevile Henderson and British Foreign Policy, 1938–1939', *Diplomacy and Statecraft*, Vol. 5, No. 1 (March 1994)
40. Ibid.
41. *Failure of a Mission*, 183
42. Quoted in Neville, *Appeasing Hitler*, 137–8
43. Ian Colvin, *Vansittart in Office* (Victor Gollancz 1965), 210; Hedda Adlon, *Hotel Adlon: The Life and Death of a Great Hotel* (Barrie Books 1958), 206
44. Quoted in Jeremy Lewis, *Shades of Greene: One Generation of an English Family* (Jonathan Cape 2010), 160
45. Harrison, op. cit., xiii
46. Henderson to Lord Halifax, Foreign Secretary, 15 March 1939 *Documents on British Foreign Policy, 1919–1939*, 3rd Series, Vol. IV (HMSO 1951), 595–6
47. Martha Dodd, *My Years in Germany* (Victor Gollancz 1939), 236–8
48. Ibid., 316–17
49. Vaughan B. Baker, 'Nevile Henderson in Berlin: A Re-evaluation', *Red River Historical Journal of World History*, Vol. II, No. 4 (Winter 1977), 347–8
50. Major-General Sir Kenneth Strong, *Intelligence at the Top: The Recollections of an Intelligence Officer* (Cassell 1968), 25
51. Kirkpatrick, op. cit., 91
52. William J. Shirer, *Twentieth Century Journey: A Memoir of a Life and the Times Vol. II: The Nightmare Years, 1930–1940* (Little, Brown & Company 1984), 447–8 (note)
53. Martha Dodd, op. cit., 287–8, 305
54. *The Diaries of Sir Robert Bruce Lockhart*, ed. Kenneth Young (2 vols, Macmillan 1973), Vol.I, 387–8 (entry for 21 March 1938)
55. Iverach McDonald, *A Man of The Times: Talks and Travels in a Disrupted World* (Hamish Hamilton 1976), 20
56. Comments made by Hitler at dinner, 16 May 1942, *Hitler's Table Talk*, trans. N. Cameron and R.H. Stevens (Weidenfeld & Nicolson 1953), 488
57. For example, Vaughan B. Baker, op. cit., and Peter Neville, *Appeasing Hitler*
58. *Failure of a Mission*, 147
59. Ewan Butler, *Mason-Mac: The Life of Lieutenant-General Sir Noël Mason-MacFarlane* (Macmillan 1972), 75. The German magazine *Der Spiegel* reported in 1969 that MacFarlane had written about this in an article in 1952. His daughter recalled that Whitehall had apparently vetoed his proposal as 'unsportsmanlike'. Recounted in *The Times* on 5 August 1969, the story gave rise to a leader the following day ('Should he have shot Hitler?') and a flurry of letters to the newspaper.
60. Ibid., 87

CHAPTER 18

1. As recalled by Mrs Foley; quoted in Michael Smith, *Foley: The Spy who Saved 10,000 Jews* (Hodder & Stoughton 1999), 134
2. Ibid., 132
3. Keith Jeffery, *MI6: The History of the Secret Intelligence Service* (paperback edn, Bloomsbury 2011), 302
4. Ibid., 295–8
5. Vivian, 'Security Measures at B.E. Berlin', 22 July 1937, TNA, FO 850/2, quoted in Christopher Andrew, *Secret Service: The Making of the British Intelligence Community* (Heinemann 1985), 405
6. Ibid., 406
7. *In Many Rhythms: An Autobiography by Baroness Ravensdale* (Weidenfeld & Nicolson 1953), 210
8. Sir Nevile Henderson, *Failure of a Mission* (Hodder & Stoughton 1940), 205

9. Ibid., 215
10. *The Diplomatic Diaries of Oliver Harvey, 1937–1940*, ed. John Harvey (Collins 1970), 274 (entry for 6 April 1939)
11. Ibid., 286 (entry for 3 May 1939)
12. *Failure of a Mission*, 215
13. *The Diplomatic Diaries of Oliver Harvey*, 264 (entry for 19 March 1939, referring to the previous day)
14. Irene Curzon's diary, quoted in in Anne de Courcy, *The Viceroy's Daughters: The Lives of the Curzon Sisters* (Weidenfeld & Nicolson 2000), 293
15. Ibid., 295
16. Harold Nicolson, *The Spectator*, 24 March 1939 ('People and Things')
17. Roger Moorhouse, *Berlin at War: Life and Death in Hitler's Capital, 1939–45* (paperback edn, Vintage 2011), 1–11
18. *Berlin feiert den Führergeburtstag, 1939* (www.History-Films.com)
19. *Failure of a Mission*, 234
20. Sir George Ogilvie-Forbes to Lord Halifax, 10 July 1939, TNA, WORK 10/280
21. 15 July 1939; quoted in Appendix Q of *The Diplomatic Diaries of Oliver Harvey*, 435
22. Christabel Bielenberg, *The Past Is Myself* (Chatto & Windus 1968), 46.
23. Peter Neville, *Appeasing Hitler: The Diplomacy of Sir Nevile Henderson 1937-1939* (Macmillan 2000), 164
24. Michael Bloch, *Ribbentrop* (Bantam Books 1992), 256–7
25. *The Ulrich von Hassell Diaries, 1938–1944: The Story of the Forces against Hitler inside Germany*, trans. Geoffrey Brooks (Frontline Books 2011), 45 (entry for 31 August 1939)
26. Ibid., 45–6
27. *Diplomat in Berlin: Papers and Memoirs of Józef Lipski, Ambassador of Poland*, ed. Wacław Jędrzejewicz (Columbia University Press 1968), 569
28. *The Diplomatic Diaries of Oliver Harvey*, 307–8 (entry for 27 August 1939)
29. Neville, *Appeasing Hitler*, 164
30. *Failure of a Mission*, 263

31. *Inside the Third Reich: Memoirs by Albert Speer* (English edn, Weidenfeld & Nicolson 1970), 103
32. Ibid., 113–14
33. *Failure of a Mission*, 279
34. William J. Shirer, *Twentieth Century Journey: A Memoir of a Life and the Times Vol. II: The Nightmare Years, 1930–1940* (Little, Brown & Company 1984), 439
35. *Failure of a Mission*, 288
36. Paul Schmidt, *Hitler's Interpreter* (William Heinemann 1951), 157
37. *The Diplomatic Diaries of Oliver Harvey*, 316 (entry for 3 September 1939)
38. The typescript of the speech is reproduced at bbc.co.uk/archives/ww2outbreak/7957.shtml. The words vary very slightly from Chamberlain's actual delivery.
39. Schmidt, op. cit., 158
40. Sir Ivone Kirkpatrick, *The Inner Circle* (Macmillan 1959), 124
41. Helmuth James von Moltke, *Letters to Freya, 1939–1945*, ed. and trans. B. R. von Oppen (Collins Harvill 1991), 33 (letter of 4 September 1939)
42. Sir Nevile Henderson, *Hippy: In Memoriam, The Story of a Dog* (Hodder & Stoughton 1943), 42.
43. Von Moltke, op. cit., 32 (letter of 3 September 1939)
44. Ibid., 33 (letter of 5 September 1939)
45. *Failure of a Mission*, 289

CHAPTER 19

1. *The Daily Telegraph*, 8 September 1939. The story was repeated in part three of the *précis of Failure of a Mission* that was published in *Life* magazine, 8 April 1940 (see later note)
2. Ibid.
3. *The Sunday Times*, 22 October 1939 ('Men, Women and Memories' by 'Atticus')
4. Sir Nevile Henderson, *Failure of a Mission* (Hodder & Stoughton 1940), Introduction
5. *The Diplomatic Diaries of Oliver Harvey, 1937–1940*, ed. John Harvey (Collins 1970), 350 (entry for 22 April 1940).

Henderson apparently expected the book to raise some £40,000. The book's retail price was 7s.6d.
6. Katherine Harrison, *On the Fringe: Living in the Realms of Hitler and Stalin* (Book Guild Publishing 2007), 21
7. *Failure of a Mission*, 289
8. Miscellaneous correspondence, TNA, FO 372/3331, 3332
9. Correspondence between Foreign Office, London, and Sir Nevile Henderson, 20–22 September 1939, TNA, FO 372/3329
10. The information in this paragraph is taken from 'American Embassy, Berlin, Foreign Representation Section, Memorandum to the Foreign Office in London', 17 September 1940, TNA, FO 366/1091
11. Ibid.
12. Ibid.
13. Roger Moorhouse, *Berlin at War: Life and Death in Hitler's Capital, 1939–45* (paperback edn, Vintage 2011), 74
14. American Embassy, Berlin, Foreign Representation Section, Memorandum, 17 September 1940, TNA, FO 366/1091
15. These funds were apparently exhausted by April/May 1940 (ibid.)
16. Henderson to Ashton-Gwatkin, writing from Rauceby Hall, Sleaford, 3 December 1940, TNA, FO 366/1091
17. Sir Nevile Henderson, *Hippy: In Memoriam: The Story of a Dog* (Hodder & Stoughton 1943), 44–5
18. G. W. Harrison to Mr. Cleobury, 30 September 1939, TNA, FO 372/3330
19. Information kindly supplied by the Foreign Office Historical Department, from destroyed Foreign Office archives
20. Described by Henderson as 'lift vans' in *Hippy: In Memoriam*, 45, and 'military lorries' in *Failure of a Mission*, 289
21. *Hippy: In Memoriam*, 45
22. Letter from Henderson to his literary editor, 24 April 1942, reproduced in Sir Nevile

Henderson, *Water under the Bridges*, (Hodder & Stoughton 1945), 5–6

23. *Hippy: In Memoriam*, 45
24. For example, in Vaughan B. Baker, 'Nevile Henderson in Berlin: A Re-evaluation', *Red River Historical Journal of World History*, Vol. II, No. 4 (Winter 1977), 352 Note 54
25. *Hippy: In Memoriam*, 45
26. Ibid.
27. Henderson, 15 July 1941, TNA, FO 366/1173
28. *Hippy: In Memoriam*, 47
29. *Water under the Bridges*, 5. At this stage (April 1942) Henderson's address was Ruthin Castle, North Wales. His Aunt Sylvia, the owner of Rauceby Hall, died in 1940; it was subsequently taken over as an RAF hospital and in the autumn of 1941 he moved away (*Hippy: In Memoriam*, 46).
30. *The Diplomatic Diaries of Oliver Harvey, 1937–1940*, ed. John Harvey (Collins 1970), 350 (entry for 22 April 1940)
31. Henderson's Last Will and Testament, dated 25 August 1942
32. *Chips: The Diaries of Sir Henry Channon*, ed. Robert Rhodes James (Weidenfeld & Nicolson 1967), 272 (entry for 5 November 1940)
33. *The Ulrich von Hassell Diaries, 1938–1944: The Story of the Forces against Hitler inside Germany*, trans. Geoffrey Brooks (Frontline Books 2011), 182 (entry for 31 December 1942)
34. Keith Jeffery, *MI6: The History of the Secret Intelligence Service* (paperback edn, Bloomsbury 2011), 758
35. Telegram, 10 December 1943, TNA, WORK 10/487
36. Joseph Goebbels, *Diaries*, trans. and ed. Louis P. Lochner) (Hamish Hamilton 1948), 425–33 (entries for 24 and 25 November 1943)
37. Ibid., 435 (entry for 27 November 1943)
38. Memorandum from Swiss authorities in Berlin, 19 September 1944, TNA, FO 366/1351
39. Ibid.
40. This was confirmed in

Wadislau Peplinsky's statement of 13 July 1945; he affirmed that silver from other sources, including the Egyptian Embassy and the English Church, was put into his custody (TNA, FO 1049/210).
41. Memorandum from Swiss authorities in Berlin, 19 September 1944, TNA, FO 366/1351
42. Ibid.
43. Ibid.
44. Quoted in Antony Beevor, *Berlin: The Downfall 1945* (paperback edn, Penguin 2007), 369
45. Ibid., 391
46. Hedda Adlon, *Hotel Adlon: The Life and Death of a Great Hotel* (Barrie Books 1958), 255
47. List enclosed with letter from J. Wilson, Foreign Office, to Chief of Staff, Control Commission, Berlin, 7 September 1945, TNA, FO 1049/210
48. Ivor Pink, Control Commission for Germany, Berlin, to Ernest Bevin, Foreign Secretary, 18 October 1945, TNA, 1049/210
49. This account of events is taken from witness statements given by Fritz Stenzel and Wadislau Peplinksy, Berlin, 12 and 13 July 1945, TNA, FO 1049/210
50. Ivor Pink to Ernest Bevin, 18 October 1945, TNA, 1049/210
51. Ivor Pink, 17 November 1945, TNA, FO 1049/210
52. Information in this paragraph taken from correspondence in TNA, FO 1049/210
53. *Sunday Mercury*, 7 May 1961, as reported in Michael Smith, *Foley: The Spy who Saved 10,000 Jews* (Hodder & Stoughton 1999), 263
54. Report by Langmaid, Ministry of Works, November 1945, TNA, FO 1049/210
55. TNA, FO 1049/489; the subsequent fate of this silver is unknown.

EPILOGUE

1. 1074 Quoted in Katherine Harrison, *On the Fringe: Living in the Realms of Hitler and Stalin* (Book Guild Publishing 2007), 23–4

2. TNA, FO 1008/72
3. Minute from E. A. Webb, 30 September 1955, with reports on the sites of 17 Tiergartenstrasse and 70 Wilhelmstrasse, TNA, WORK 10/489
4. Sebastian Redecke and Ralph Stern (eds), *Foreign Affairs: New Embassy Buildings and the German Foreign Office in Berlin* (Birkhäuser Verlag 1997), 11. A number of less affluent countries have as yet been unable to move their embassies to Berlin.
5. Mark Bertram, *Room for Diplomacy: Britain's Diplomatic Buildings Overseas, 1800–2000* (Spire Books 2011), 440
6. Ibid.
7. *Michael Wilford: Selected Buildings and Projects, 1992–2012* (Artifice 2014), 17

SOURCES

ARCHIVES

D'Abernon Papers, British Library, London

Foreign Office Papers, National Archives, London

UK Government Art Collection, London (Department for Culture, Media & Sport), Archives

Augustus John Papers, Tate Archive, London

Sir Gerald Kelly Papers, Tate Archive, London

Lascelles Papers, Churchill Archive Centre, University of Cambridge

August Orth Materials, Architekturmuseum der Technischen Universität Berlin in der Universitätsbibliothek, Berlin

Phipps Papers, Churchill Archives Centre, Churchill College, University of Cambridge

Rumbold Papers, Bodleian Library, University of Oxford

Rumbold Family Papers

Spring-Rice Papers, Churchill Archives Centre, Churchill College, University of Cambridge

HM Treasury Papers, National Archives, London

Queen Victoria's Journals, Royal Archives online RA VIC/ MAIN/QVJ (W) (Princess Beatrice's copies) (www. queenvictoriasjournals.org)

Ministry of Works Papers, National Archives, London

Miscellaneous Papers, British Architectural Library, Royal Institute of British Architects, London

PRINTED SOURCES

Adlon, Hedda, *Hotel Adlon: The Life and Death of a Great Hotel* (Barrie Books 1958)

Andrew, Christopher, *Secret Service: The Making of the British Intelligence Community* (Heinemann 1985)

Baedeker, Karl, *Berlin and its Environs: Handbook for Travellers* (Karl Baedeker 1912)

Baker, Vaughan B., 'Nevile Henderson in Berlin: A Re-Evaluation', *Red River Historical*

Journal of World History Vol. II, No. 4 (Winter 1977)

Beevor, Antony, *Berlin: The Downfall, 1945* (Viking 2002, paperback edn, Penguin 2007)

Berberova, Nina, *Moura: The Dangerous Life of the Baroness Budberg* (English edn, Review Books 2005)

Bertram, Mark, *Room for Diplomacy: Britain's Diplomatic Buildings Overseas, 1800–2000* (Spire Books 2011)

Bielenberg, Christabel, *The Past is Myself* (Chatto & Windus 1968)

Confidential Report from Daniel A. Binchy to Joseph P. Walshe (Dublin), 27 May 1930 (Documents on Irish Foreign Policy No.373 NAI DFA EA 231/4/B, www.difp.ie)

Blakiston, Georgiana, *Lord William Russell and his Wife, 1815–1846* (John Murray 1972)

Blakiston, Georgiana, *Woburn and the Russells* (Constable 1980)

Bloch, Michael, *Ribbentrop* (Bantam Press 1992)

Champion Redoubtable: The Diaries and Letters of Violet Bonham-Carter, 1914–1945, ed. Mark Pottle (Weidenfeld & Nicolson 1998)

Borchart, Joachim, *Der europäische Eisenbahnkönig Bethel Henry Strousberg* (C.H. Beck 1991)

Bradford, Sarah, *Disraeli* (Weidenfeld & Nicolson 1982)

British Documents on the Origins of the War 1898-1914, Volume III (HMSO 1928)

Brook-Shepherd, Gordon, *Uncle of Europe* (Collins 1975)

Bruce, H. J., *Silken Dalliance* (Constable 1946)

Bülow, Prince von, *Memoirs* (volume for 1849–1897) (Putnam, New York 1931–32)

Butler, Ewan, *Mason-Mac: The Life of Lieutenant-General Sir Noel Mason-Macfarlane* (Macmillan 1972)

Butler, J. R. M., *Lord Lothian (Philip Kerr) 1882–1940* (Macmillan 1960)

Campbell, Sir Gerald, *Of True Experience* (Hutchinson 1949)

Carpenter Humphrey, *W. H. Auden: A Biography* (George Allen & Unwin 1981)

Carsten. F. L., *Britain and the*

Weimar Republic: The British Documents (Batsford Academic and Educational 1984)

Carter, Miranda, *The Three Emperors: Three Cousins, Three Empires and the Road to World War I* (Fig Tree 2009)

Cecil, Lady Gwendolen, *Life of Robert, Marquis of Salisbury* (4 vols, Hodder & Stoughton 1921)

Cecil, Lamar, 'History as Family Chronicle: Kaiser Wilhelm II and the Dynastic Roots of the Anglo-German Antagonism', J. C. G. Röhl and N. Sombart (eds), *Kaiser Wilhelm II: New Interpretations: The Corfu Papers* (Cambridge University Press 1982)

Chamberlain, Austen, *Down the Years* (Cassell 1935)

Chips: The Diaries of Sir Henry Channon, ed. Robert Rhodes James (Weidenfeld & Nicolson 1967)

Chaplin, Charles, *My Wonderful Visit* (Hurst & Blackett 1922)

Churchill, Winston, *Lord Randolph Churchill* (2 vols, Macmillan 1906)

Clark, Christopher, *Iron Kingdom: The Rise and Downfall of Prussia, 1600–1847* (Allen Lane 2006)

Clark, Christopher, *Kaiser Wilhelm II: A Life in Power* (Pearson 2000, paperback edn, Penguin 2009)

Cockett, Richard, *Twilight of Truth: Chamberlain, Appeasement and the Manipulation of the Press* (Weidenfeld & Nicolson 1989)

Cole, Terence F., 'The Daily Telegraph Affair and its Aftermath: The Kaiser, Bülow and the Reichstag, 1908–1909', J. C. G. Röhl and N. Sombart (eds), *Kaiser Wilhelm II: New Interpretations: The Corfu Papers* (Cambridge University Press 1982)

Colvin, Ian, *Vansittart in Office* (Victor Gollancz 1965)

The Romantic Friendship: The Letters of Cyril Connolly to Noel Blakiston, ed. Noel Blakiston (Constable 1975)

Cyril Connolly: Journal and Memoir, ed. David Pryce-Jones (Collins 1983)

Cornforth, John, 'The British Embassy, Vienna', *Country Life* 26 April 1990

Cornwallis-West, Mrs George, *The Reminiscences of Lady Randolph Churchill* (Edward Arnold 1908)

Corti, E. C. C., *The English Empress: A Study in the Relations between Queen Victoria and her Eldest Daughter, Empress Frederick of Germany* (Cassell 1957)

Craig, G. A., 'The British Foreign Office from Grey to Austen Chamberlain', in G. A. Craig & F. Gilbert (eds), *The Diplomats, 1919–1939* (Princeton University Press 1953, reprinted 1994)

Crewe. Marquess of, *Lord Rosebery* (2 vols, John Murray 1931)

Curzon of Kedleston, Marchioness, *Reminiscences* (Hutchinson 1955)

An Ambassador of Peace: Pages from the Diary of Viscount D'Abernon (3 vols, Hodder & Stoughton 1929, 1930)

D'Abernon, Viscount, *Portraits and Appreciations* (Hodder & Stoughton 1931)

Red Cross and Berlin Embassy, 1915–1926: Extracts from the Diaries of Viscountess D'Abernon (John Murray 1946)

Dalley, Jan, *Diana Mosley: A Life* (Faber & Faber 2000)

de Courcy, Anne, *Circe: The Life of Edith, Marchioness of Londonderry* (Sinclair-Stevenson 1992)

de Courcy, Anne, *Diana Mosley* (Chatto & Windus 2003)

de Courcy, Anne, *The Viceroy's Daughters: The Lives of the Curzon Sisters* (Weidenfeld & Nicolson 2000)

Deutscher Architekten und Ingenieuverband, *Berlin und seine Bauten* (Berlin 1877 & 1896)

Documents on British Foreign Policy, 1919–1939, ed. E. L. Woodward & R. Butler, Third Series, Volume II (HMSO 1949)

Documents on British Foreign Policy, 1919–1939, ed. E. L. Woodward & R. Bulter, Third Series, Volume IV (HMSO 1951)

Dodd, Martha, *My Years in Germany* (Victor Gollancz 1939)

Ambassador Dodd's Diary, 1933–1938, ed. W. E. Dodd & M. Dodd (Victor Gollancz 1941)

Duff, David, *Alexandra: Princess and Queen* (Collins 1980)

Earle, Sir Lionel, *Turn Over the Page* (Hutchinson 1935)

Easton, Laird McLeod, *The Red Count: The Life and Times of Harry Kessler* (University of California Press 2002)

Eckardstein, Baron von, *Ten Years at the Court of St. James, 1895–1905* (Thornton Butterworth 1921)

Eden, Anthony, *The Eden Memoirs: Facing the Dictators* (Cassell 1962)

Faber, David, *Munich: The 1938 Appeasement Crisis* (Simon & Schuster 2008)

Foreign Office, Diplomatic and Consular Sketches, reprinted from *Vanity Fair* (Allen & Co. 1883)

François-Poncet, André, *The Fateful Years: Memoirs of a French Ambassador in Berlin, 1931–1938* (Victor Gollancz 1949)

The War Diary of the Emperor Frederick, trans. & ed. A. R. Allinson (Stanley Paul 1927)

The Letters of the Empress Frederick, ed. Sir Frederick Ponsonby (Macmillan 1928)

Friedrich, Thomas, *A Photographic Portrait of Berlin in the Weimar Years, 1918–1933* (Tauris Parke 1991)

Friedrich, Thomas, *Hitler's Berlin: Abused City*, trans. Stewart Spencer (Yale University Press 2012)

Fritzinger, Linda B., *Diplomat without Portfolio: Valentine Chirol, his Life* and The Times (Tauris 2006)

Fromm, Bella, *Blood and Banquets: A Berlin Social Diary* (Geoffrey Bles 1942)

Gerard, James W., *My Four Years in Germany* (Hodder & Stoughton 1917)

Gilbert, Martin & Gott, Richard, *The Appeasers* (2nd edn, Weidenfeld & Nicolson 1967)

Gilbert, Martin, *Sir Horace Rumbold: Portrait of a Diplomat, 1869–1941* (Heinemann 1973)

Gilbert, Martin, 'Horace Wilson: Man of Munich?', *History Today* October 1982

Gillies, Midge, *Amy Johnson* (Weidenfeld & Nicolson 2003)

Gimpel, René, *Diary of an Art Dealer*, trans. John Rosenberg (Hodder & Stoughton 1966)

The Diaries of Cynthia Gladwyn, ed. Miles Jebb (Constable 1995)

Gleichen, General Lord Edward, *A Guardsman's Memories: A Book of Recollections* (W. Blackwood & Sons 1932)

Goebbels, Joseph, *Diaries*, trans. and ed. Louis P. Lochner (Hamish Hamilton 1948)

Die Tagebücher von Joseph Goebbels, Teil I, Band 3/II (K.G. Saur 2001)

The Diary of Edward Goschen, 1900–1914, ed. H. D. Howard (Royal Historical Society, Camden Fourth Series, 1980)

Letters from the Berlin Embassy: Selections from the Private Correspondence of British Representatives at Berlin and Foreign Secretary Lord Granville, 1871–1874, 1880–1885, ed. Paul Knaplund (*Annual Report of the American Historical Association for the Year 1942*, Vol. II, Washington, DC 1944)

Grenfell, Field-Marshall Lord, *Memoirs* (Hodder & Stoughton 1925)

Grew, Joseph C., *Turbulent Era: A Diplomatic Record of Forty Years; Volume I: 1904–1945*, ed. Walter Johnson (Hammond & Hammond 1953)

Richard Burdon Haldane: An Autobiography (Doubleday, Doran & Co. 1929)

Halifax, Earl of, *Fulness of Days* (Collins 1957)

Hamilton, Lord Frederick, *The Vanished Pomps of Yesterday: Being some Random Reminiscences of a British Diplomat* (Hodder & Stoughton 1919)

Old Diplomacy: The Reminiscences of Lord Hardinge of Penshurst (John Murray 1947)

Harrison, Katherine, *On the Fringe: Living in the Realms of Hitler and Stalin* (Book Guild Publishing 2007)

Hart-Davis, Duff, *Hitler's Games: The 1936 Olympics* (Century 1986)

The Diplomatic Diaries of Oliver Harvey, 1937–1940, ed. John Harvey (Collins 1970)

The Ulrich von Hassell Diaries, 1938–1944: The Story of the Forces against Hitler inside Germany, trans. Geoffrey Brooks (Frontline Books 2011)

Henderson, Sir Nevile, *Failure of a Mission* (Hodder & Stoughton 1940)

Henderson, Sir Nevile, *Hippy: In Memoriam: The Story of a Dog* (Hodder & Stoughton 1943)

Henderson, Sir Nevile, *Water under the Bridges* (Hodder & Stoughton 1945)

Herbert. David, *Second Son: An Autobiography* (Peter Owen Ltd 1972)

Herman, John, *The Paris Embassy of Sir Eric Phipps: Anglo-French Relations and the Foreign Office, 1937–1939* (Sussex Academic Press 1998)

Hickman, Katie, *Daughters of Britannia: The Lives & Times of Diplomatic Wives* (Harper Collins 1999, paperback edn. Flamingo 2000)

Hitler's Table Talk, 1941–1944, trans. N. Cameron and R.H. Stevens (Weidenfeld & Nicolson 1953)

Inside Asquith's Cabinet: From the Diaries of Charles Hobhouse, ed. Edward David (John Murray 1977)

Huggett, Frank E., *Life below Stairs: Domestic Servants in England from Victorian Times* (John Murray 1977)

James, Robert Rhodes, *Lord Randolph Churchill* (Weidenfeld & Nicolson 1959)

James, Robert Rhodes, *Rosebery: A Biography of Archibald Philip, 5th Earl of Rosebery* (Weidenfeld & Nicolson 1963)

Jebb, Gladwyn, *The Memoirs of Lord Gladwyn* (Weidenfeld & Nicolson 1972)

Jeffery, Keith, *MI6: The History of the Secret Intelligence Service* (Bloomsbury 2010, paperback edn, London 2011)

John, Augustus, *Chiaroscuro: Fragments of Autobiography: First Series* (Jonathan Cape 1952)

Johnson, Gaynor, *The Berlin Embassy of Lord D'Abernon, 1920–1926* (Palgrave Macmillan 2002)

Jones, Sir Lawrence Evelyn ('L.E.'), *Georgian Afternoon* (Rupert Hart-Davis 1958)

Jones, Raymond, *The British Diplomatic Service, 1815–1914* (Smythe, Gerrards Cross 1983)

Kershaw, Ian, *Making Friends with Hitler: Lord Londonderry and Britain's Road to War* (Allen Lane 2004)

The Diaries of a Cosmopolitan: Count Henry Kessler, 1918–1937, ed. Charles Kessler (Weidenfeld & Nicolson 1971)

Kirkpatrick, Sir Ivone, *The Inner Circle* (Macmillan 1959)

Kraus, René, *Young Lady Randolph: The Life and Times of Jennie Jerome, American Mother of Winston Churchill* (Jarrolds 1944)

Lane, Margaret, *Edgar Wallace: The Biography of a Phenomenon* (William Heinemann 1938)

Law, Henry W. & Irene, *The Book of the Beresford Hopes* (Heath Cranton 1925)

Lees-Milne, James, *Harold Nicolson: A Biography Volume I: 1886–1929* (Chatto & Windus 1980)

Lewis, Jeremy, *Shades of Greene: One Generation of an English Family* (Jonathan Cape 2010)

Diplomat in Berlin: Papers and Memoirs of Józef Lipski, Ambassador of Poland, ed. Wacław Jędrzejewicz (Columbia University Press 1968)

The Diaries of Sir Robert Bruce Lockhart, ed. Kenneth Young (2 vols, Macmillan 1973)

The Diplomatic Reminiscences of Lord Augustus Loftus 1862-1879 (2 vols, Cassell 1894)

Louvish, Simon, *Chaplin: The Tramp's Odyssey* (Faber 2009)

Lovell, Mary S., *The Mitford Girls: The Biography of an Extraordinary Family* (Little, Brown 2001, paperback edn, Abacus 2002)

Lowe, Charles, *The German Emperor William II* (Bliss, Sands & Foster 1895)

Lowe, Charles, *The Tale of a 'Times' Correspondent: Berlin, 1878–1891* (Hutchinson 1927)

MacDiarmid, D. S., *The Life of Lieut. General Sir James Moncrieff Grierson KCB CVO CMG ADC* (Constable 1923)

McDonald, Iverach, *A Man of The Times: Talks and Travels in a Disrupted World* (Hamish Hamilton 1976)

Magnus, Philip, *King Edward the Seventh* (John Murray 1964)

Malet, Sir Edward, *Shifting Scenes or Memories of Many Men in Many Lands* (John Murray 1901)

Manvell, Roger & Frankel, Heinrich, *Goering: The Rise and Fall of the Notorious Nazi Leader* (Simon & Schuster 1962, republished by Frontline Books/Skyhorse Publishing 2011)

Marie Louise, H.R.H. Princess, *My Memories of Six Reigns* (Evans Brothers 1956)

Masters, Anthony, *Nancy Astor: A Life* (Weidenfeld & Nicolson 1981)

Maurice, Sir Frederick, *Haldane 1856–1928: The Life of Viscount Haldane of Cloan KT, OM, Volume I* (2 vols, Faber & Faber 1937, 1939)

Metzger, Rainer, *Berlin in the 20s: Art and Culture, 1918–1933* (Thames & Hudson 2007)

Moltke, Helmuth James von, *Letters to Freya, 1939–1945,* ed. and trans. by B. R. von Oppen (Collins Harvill 1991)

Monypenny, W. F., &, Buckle, G. E. *The Life of Benjamin Disraeli, Earl of Beaconsfield* (6 vols., John Murray 1910–20)

Moorhouse, Roger, *Berlin at War: Life and Death in Hitler's Capital, 1939–45* (The Bodley Head 2010, paperback edn. Vintage 2011)

Morel, Madame [Comtesse Clare Morel des Boullets], *From an Eastern Embassy: Memories of London, Berlin and the East* (Herbert Jenkins 1920)

Mork, G. M., 'The Prussian Railway Scandal of 1873: Economics and Politics in the German Empire', *European Studies Review* Vol. 1, No. 1 (1971)

Mosley, Diana, *A Life of Contrasts: The Autobiography* (Hamish Hamilton 1977)

Mosley, Nicholas, *Rules of the Game: Sir Oswald and Lady Cynthia Mosley, 1896–1933* (Secker & Warburg 1982)

Mosley, Oswald, *My Life* (Nelson 1968)

Müller, Frank Lorenz, *Our Fritz: Emperor Frederick III and the Political Culture of Imperial Germany* (Harvard University Press 2011)

Muthesius, Hermann, *The English House* (Berlin 1904, 1905, unabridged English edn, 3 vols, Frances Lincoln 2007)

Neave, Airey, *Saturday at M.I.9: A History of Underground Escape Lines in North-West Europe in 1940–5 by a Leading Organiser in M.I.9.* (Hodder & Stoughton 1969)

Neville, Peter, 'The Appointment of Sir Nevile Henderson, 1937: Design or Blunder?', *Journal of Contemporary History* Vol. 33, No. 4 (1998)

Neville, Peter, *Appeasing Hitler: The Diplomacy of Sir Nevile Henderson 1937–1939* (Macmillan 2000)

Neville, Peter, 'The Foreign Office and Britain's Ambassadors to Berlin', *Contemporary British History* 18 (3), 2004

Nicolson, Harold, *Sir Arthur Nicolson Bart, 1st Lord Carnock: A Study in the Old Diplomacy* (Constable 1930)

Nicolson, Harold, *Diplomacy* (Harcourt, Brace 1939)

Nicolson, Harold, *King George the Fifth: His Life and Reign* (Constable 1952)

Harold Nicolson Diaries and Letters, 1907–1964, ed. Nigel Nicolson (Weidenfeld & Nicolson 2004, paperback edn, Phoenix 2005)

Nicolson, Nigel, *Portrait of a Marriage* (Weidenfeld & Nicolson 1973)

Nilsen, Micheline, *Railways and the Western European Capitals: Studies of Implantation in London, Paris, Berlin and Brussels* (Palgrave Macmillan 2008)

Stranger Within: Autobiographical Pages by Sir Francis Oppenheimer KCMG (Faber 1960)

Ormond, Leonée & Richard, *Lord Leighton* (Yale University Press 1975)

Ormond, Richard & Kilmurray, Elaine, *John Singer Sargent: Complete Paintings; Volume III: The Later Portraits* (Yale University Press 2003)

Oxford Dictionary of National Biography

Pakula, Hannah, *An Uncommon Woman: The Empress Frederick* (Weidenfeld & Nicolson 1996)

Parker, Peter, *Christopher Isherwood: A Life* (Picador 2004)

Peters, A. R., *Anthony Eden at the Foreign Office 1931-1938* (Gower 1986)

Petrie, Sir Charles, *The Powers behind the Prime Ministers* (MacGibbon & Kee 1958)

Pflanze, Otto, *Bismarck and the Development of Germany* (3 vols, Princeton University Press 1990)

Our Man in Berlin: The Diary of Sir Eric Phipps, 1933–1937, ed. Gaynor Johnson (Palgrave Macmillan 2008)

Platt, D. C. M., *The Cinderella Service: British Consuls since 1825* (Longman 1971)

Pless, Daisy, Princess of, *By Herself* (Murray 1929)

Ponsonby, Sir Frederick, *Recollections of Three Reigns*, ed. Colin Welch (Eyre & Spottiswoode 1951)

Price, George Ward, *Extra-Special Correspondent* (Harrap 1957)

Pryce-Jones, David, *Unity Mitford: A Quest* (Weidenfeld & Nicolson 1976)

Radziwill, Princess Catherine, *Memories of Forty Years* (Cassell 1914)

This was Germany: An Observer at the Court of Berlin: Letters of Princess Marie Radziwill to General di Robilant KCB GCMG, One-time Italian Military Attaché at Berlin (1908–1915), trans. and ed. Cyril Spencer Fox (John Murray 1937)

Ramm, Agatha, *Sir Robert Morier: Envoy and Ambassador in the Age of Imperialism, 1876–1893* (Clarendon Press 1973)

Rattigan, Frank, *Diversions of a Diplomat* (Chapman & Hall 1924)

In Many Rhythms: an Autobiography by Baroness Ravensdale (Weidenfeld & Nicolson 1953)

Reynolds, Simon, *William Blake Richmond: An Artist's Life, 1842–1921* (Michael Russell 1995)

The Ribbentrop Memoirs (Weidenfeld & Nicolson 1954)

Ritchie, Alexandra, *Faust's Metropolis: A History of Berlin* (Harper Collins 1998)

Rodd, Sir James Rennell, *Frederick, Crown Prince and Emperor: A Biographical Sketch Dedicated to his Memory* (D. Stott 1888)

Rodd, Sir James Rennell, *Social and Diplomatic Memories* (3 vols, Edward Arnold 1922–25)

Röhl, J. C. G, *The Kaiser and his Court: Wilhelm II and the Government of Germany* (Cambridge University Press 1994)

Röhl, J. C. G, *Young Wilhelm: The Kaiser's Early Life, 1859–1888* (Cambridge University Press 1998)

Röhl, J. C. G, *Wilhelm II: The Kaiser's Personal Monarchy, 1888-1900* (Cambridge University Press 2004)

Röhl, J. C. G, *Wilhelm II: Into the Abyss of War and Exile 1900-1941* (Cambridge University Press 2014)

Röhl, J. C. G, *Wilhelm II 1859–1941: A Concise Life* (Cambridge University Press 2014)

Rose, Kenneth, *King George V* (Weidenfeld & Nicolson 1983)

Rose, Norman, *Vansittart: Study of a Diplomat* (Heinemann 1978)

Rose, Norman, *The Cliveden Set: Portrait of an Exclusive Fraternity* (Cape 2000)

Rumbold, Sir Horace, *The War Crisis in Berlin, July–August 1914* (Constable 1940, new edn. 1944)

Russell, William, Berlin Embassy (M. Joseph 1942)

Sackville-West, Robert, *Inheritance: The Story of Knole and the Sackvilles* (Bloomsbury 2010)

The Letters of Vita Sackville-West to Virginia Woolf, ed. Louise DeSalvo & Mitchell A. Leaska (Hutchinson 1984)

Vita and Harold: The Letters of Vita Sackville-West and Harold Nicolson, ed. Nigel Nicolson (Weidenfeld & Nicolson 1992, paperback edn, Phoenix 1993)

Schmidt, Paul, *Hitler's Interpreter* (William Heinemann 1951)

Seligmann, Matthew S., 'Military Diplomacy in a Military Monarchy? Wilhelm II's relations with the British Service Attachés in Berlin, 1903–1914', Annika Mombauer and William Deist (eds.), *The Kaiser: New Research on Wilhelm II's Role in Imperial Germany* (Cambridge University Press 2003)

Seymour, Miranda, *Noble Endeavours: The Life of Two Countries, England and Germany in Many Stories* (Simon & Schuster 2013)

Shirer, William J., *Twentieth Century Journey: A Memoir of a Life and the Times*, Vol. II: *The Nightmare Years, 1930–1940* (Little, Brown & Company 1984)

Shirer, William J., *This is Berlin: A Narrative History, 1938–1940* (Hutchinson 1999)

Simon, Sir John, *Retrospect: The Memoirs of the Rt. Hon. Viscount Simon GCSI, GCVO* (Hutchinson 1952)

Smith, Michael, *Foley: The Spy who Saved 10,000 Jews* (Hodder & Stoughton 1999)

Spalding, Frances, *Vanessa Bell* (Weidenfeld & Nicolson 1983)

Inside the Third Reich: Memoirs of Albert Speer (English edn, Weidenfeld & Nicolson 1970)

The Letters and Friendships of Sir Cecil Spring-Rice: A Record, ed. Stephen Gwynn (2 vols, Constable 1929)

Steinberg, Jonathan, 'The Kaiser and the British: the State Visit to

Windsor, November 1907', J. C. G. Röhl and N. Sombart (eds), *Kaiser Wilhelm II: New Interpretations: The Corfu Papers* (Cambridge University Press 1982)

Steinberg, Jonathan, *Bismarck: A Life* (Oxford University Press 2011)

Steiner, Zara, *The Foreign Office and Foreign Policy, 1898–1914* (Cambridge University Press 1969)

Steiner, Zara & Dockrill, M. L., 'The Foreign Office Reforms, 1919–21', *The Historical Journal* Vol. 17, No. 1 (March 1974)

Stern, Fritz, 'Money, Morals and the Pillars of Bismarck's Society', *Central European History* Vol, 3, No. 1/2 (1970)

Stern, Fritz, *Gold and Iron: Bismarck, Bleichröder and the Building of the German Empire* (Allen & Unwin 1977)

Stern-Rubarth, Edgar, *Three Men Tried … Austen* Chamberlain, *Stresemann, Briand and their Fight for a New Europe: A Personal Memoir* (Duckworth 1939)

Strang, Bruce, 'Two Unequal Tempers: Sir George Ogilvie-Forbes, Sir Nevile Henderson and British Foreign Policy, 1938–1939', *Diplomacy and Statecraft* Vol. 5, No. 1 (March 1994)

Strang, William (Lord), *The Foreign Office* (George Allen & Unwin 1955)

Strauch, Rudi, *Sir Nevile Henderson: Britischer Botschafter in Berlin von 1937 bis 1939* (L. Böhrscheid 1959)

Strong, Major-General Sir Kenneth, *Intelligence at the Top: The Recollections of an Intelligence Officer* (Cassell 1968)

Taffs, Winifred, *Ambassador to Bismarck: Lord Odo Russell, First Baron Ampthill* (Frederick Muller 1938)

Taylor, Shephard Thomas, *Reminiscences of Berlin during the Franco-German War of 1870–71* (Griffin, Farran & Co. 1885)

Thacker, Toby, *Joseph Goebbels: Life and Death* (Palgrave Macmillan 2009)

Townley, Lady Susan, *'Indiscretions' of Lady Susan* (T. Butterworth 1922)

Trzebinski, Errol, *The Life and Death of Lord Erroll: The Truth behind the Happy Valley Murder* (Fourth Estate 2000)

Tusa, Ann, *The Last Division:*

Berlin and the Wall (Hodder & Stoughton 1996)

Urbach, Karina, *Bismarck's Favourite Englishman: Lord Odo Russell's Mission to Berlin* (Tauris 1999)

The Mist Procession: The Autobiography of Lord Vansittart (Hutchinson 1958)

Vickers, Hugo, *Queen Elizabeth the Queen Mother* (Hutchinson 2005)

The Letters of Queen Victoria, Second Series & Third Series, ed. George E. Buckle (John Murray 1926, 1931),

Your Dear Letter: Private Correspondence of Queen Victoria and the Crown Princess of Prussia 1865–1871, ed. Roger Fulford (Evans Brothers 1971)

Darling Child: Private Correspondence of Queen Victoria and the Crown Princess of Prussia, 1871–1878, ed. Roger Fulford (Evans 1976)

Beloved Mama: Private Correspondence of Queen Victoria and the German Crown Princess, 1878–1885, ed. Roger Fulford (Evans Brothers 1981)

Victoria, Princess, of Prussia, *My Memoirs* (Eveleigh Nash and Grayson 1929)

Wallace, E. V., *Edgar Wallace by his Wife* (Hutchinson 1932)

Walters, Guy, *Berlin Games: How Hitler Stole the Olympic Dream* (John Murray 2006)

Wark, Wesley K., *The Ultimate Enemy: British Intelligence and Nazi Germany, 1933–1939* (I.B. Tauris 1985)

Watt, Donald C., 'Chamberlain's Ambassadors', M. Dockrill & B. McKercher (eds), *Diplomacy and World Power: Studies in British Foreign Policy, 1890–1950* (Cambridge University Press 1996)

Williamson, D. G., *The British in Germany, 1918–1930: The Reluctant Occupiers* (Berg 1991)

Wise, Michael Z., *Capital Dilemma: Germany's Search for a New Architecture of Democracy* (New York 1998)

Wiskemann, Elizabeth, *The Europe I Saw* (Collins 1968)

The Diary of Virginia Woolf, Volume III, 1925–1930, ed. A. O. Bell (Hogarth Press 1980)

Wylie, Neville, *Britain, Switzerland and the Second World War* (Oxford

University Press 2003)

Ziegler, Philip, *Edward VIII: The Official Biography* (Collins 1990)

THE NEW BRITISH EMBASSY

Anon., 'Back in the high life'; 'Queen opens Berlin embassy' *BBC News Website,* 18 July 2000:

Anon., 'PFI saved money on Embassy' *Building,* 7 July 2000

Amery, Colin, 'Made in our own image', *Perspectives* (June/July 1997)

Barrie, Giles, 'Wilford's Design in Jeopardy', *Building,* 12 April 1996

Binney, Marcus, 'Grand style chosen for new embassy', *The Times,* 23 February 1995

Boyes, Roger, 'Britain has designs on Berlin', *The Times,* 23 February 1995

Finch, Paul, 'Berlin Game', *The Architects Journal,* 2 March 1995

Geipel, Kaye, 'Beyond the façade: Michael Wilford & Partners in Berlin', *Architecture Today* (November 2000)

Glancey, Jonathan, 'Shameful Foreign Policy', *The Guardian,* 24 July 2000

Gordon, A. J., 'The New British Embassy in Berlin: Report on Thesis Design' (unpublished thesis, Welsh School of Architecture, 2 Vols, 1948, British Architectural Library, Royal Institute of British Architects)

Hall, Allan, 'Queen lost for words over Berlin embassy', *The Times,* 19 July 2000

Helm, Toby, 'Embassy is a waste of space says Philip', *Daily Telegraph,* 19 July 2000

Jenner, Michael, 'Britische Botschaft, Berlin / British Embassy, Berlin', *Neue Britische Architektur in Deutschland / New British Architecture in Germany* (Prestel 2000)

Karacs, Imre, 'Embassy is a fittingly banal tribute to "Cool Britannia"', *The Independent,* 18 July 2000

Knutt, Elaine, 'Losing practices count cost of competing', *Building,* 3 March 1995

Melhuish, Clare, 'Berlin Embassy: pursuing a subtle diplomacy', *Building Design,* 3 March 1995

Redecke, Sebastian, & Stern Ralph (eds), *Foreign Affairs:*

New Embassy Buildings and the German Foreign Office in Berlin (Birkhäuser Verlag 1997)

Speller, Susan, 'Berlin's bright house', *Foreign Office News & Views* (July–September 2000)

Spring, Martin, 'Wilford brightens up Berlin', *Building*, 14 July 2000

Stungo, Naomi, 'Our man in Berlin', *RIBA Journal* (March 1995)

Sudjic, Deyan, 'It's what's on the inside that counts', *The Observer*, 16 July 2000

Weaver, Matt, 'Wilford's defends Embassy', *Building Design*, 7 July 2000

Watt, Nicholas, 'Tories launched cool Britannia', *The Times*, 6 March 1998

Wilford, Michael, *Michael Wilford: Selected Buildings and Projects, 1992–2012* (Artifice 2014)

Worsley, Giles, 'Blasting a hole in classicism', *Daily Telegraph*, 18 July 2000

NEWSPAPERS AND JOURNALS

The Athenaeum

The Daily Graphic

Daily Mail

The Daily Telegraph

The Graphic

The Illustrated London News

Morning Post

The Spectator

The Sunday Times

The Times

SELECT BRIEF BIOGRAPHIES

Other than members of the Royal and Imperial Families

Adlon, Lorenz (1949–21) German hotelier and restaurateur in Berlin from 1870s, father of **Louis Adlon** (1874–1945), who took over the business and married (2) **Hedda (Hedwig) Leythen** (1889–1967) in 1922

Ampthill, 1st Baron, see **Russell, Odo**

Angeli, Heinrich von (1840–1925) Austrian artist, highly successful society portrait painter who received many commissions from the British Royal Family

Arnim, Count Harry von (1824–81) German diplomat, German Ambassador to France 1872–74

Arnold, Matthew (1822–88) British poet and civil servant, son of headmaster of Rugby School Dr Thomas Arnold

Ashton-Gwatkin, Frank Trelawny Arthur (1889–1976) British diplomat from 1913, Assistant Under-Secretary and Chief Clerk, Foreign Office 1940–44

Astell, Richard John Vereker (1890–1969) British diplomat from 1913, at Berlin 1914, resigned 1919

Astor, Viscountess (Nancy Witcher) (1879–1964) American-born British politician and society hostess, the first woman to sit as a Member of Parliament

Auden, Wystan Hugh (1907–73) British poet and author

Baldwin, Stanley (1867–1947) British Politician, Conservative Prime Minister 1923–24, 1924–29, 7 June 1935 – 28 May 1937

Balfour, 1st Earl of (Arthur James Balfour) (1848–1930) British politician, Foreign Secretary 1916–19, Conservative Prime Minister 1902–5

Beaconsfield, Lord (Benjamin Disraeli) (1804–81) British Politician and author, Chancellor of the Exchequer 1858–59 and 1866–68, Conservative Prime Minister 1868, 1874–80

Bedford, 9th Duke of (Francis Charles Hastings Russell) (1819–91) Succeeded to dukedom in 1872, agricultural reformer, married Lady Elizabeth Sackville-West

(1818–97) in 1844, father of **Lady Ermyntrude Sackville Russell**

Beilby, Sir Francis (1820–1905) British diplomat, Chief Clerk at the Foreign Office 1866–90

Bell, Vanessa (1879–1961) British artist and designer, member of the 'Bloomsbury Group', sister of **Virginia Woolf**

Beresford, Charles William de la Poer, 1st Baron Beresford (1846–1919) British Admiral and MP, took part in General Gordon Relief Expedition in 1885, later Commander-in-Chief of the Mediterranean and Channel Fleets 1903–9

Beresford Hope, Harold Thomas (1882–1917) British diplomat, at Berlin early 1900s, later Second Secretary at Athens, where he died suddenly

Bertie, Sir Francis Leveson, 1st Viscount Bertie of Thame (1844–1919) British diplomat from 1863, attended 1878 Congress of Berlin, British Ambassador to Rome 1903–15, British Ambassador to Paris 1905–18

Bethmann-Hollweg, Theobald Theodor Friedrich Alfred von (1856–1921) German politician, Chancellor of Germany 1909–17

Bieberstein, Adolf Freiherr Marschall von (1842–1912) German politician, German Foreign Secretary 1890–97

Binchy, Daniel (1899–1989) Irish academic, Irish Ambassador to Berlin 1929–32

Bismarck Herbert, Prince von (1849–1904) German diplomat, son of **Otto von Bismarck**, German Foreign Secretary 1886–90

Bismarck, Otto, Prince von (1815–98) Prime Minister of Prussia 1873–90, Chancellor of Germany 1871–90, married **Johanna von Puttkamer** (1824–94) in 1847, father of **Herbert von Bismarck**

Bismarck, Otto Christian Archibald, Prince von (1897–1975) German diplomat, eldest son of **Herbert von Bismarck**, joined National Socialist Party 1933, served in Foreign Office in Berlin

1937–40, Rome 1940–43 and Head of Italian Department of German Foreign Ministry 1943–44

Bleichröder, Gerson von (1822–93) Influential Jewish German Banker and financier

Blomberg, Werner von (1878–1946) German army officer, War Minister and Commander-in-Chief of the German Army 1935–38

Bloomfield, John Arthur Douglas, 2nd Baron Bloomfield (1802–79) British diplomat, Envoy Extraordinary and Minister Plenipotentiary at Berlin 1851–60 and Vienna 1860–71

Bonar Law, Andrew (1858–1923) British politician, Chancellor of the Exchequer 1916–19, Conservative Prime Minister October 1922 – May 1923

Bonham Carter, Helen Violet (Baroness Asquith of Yarnbury) (1887–1969) British politician, daughter of Lord Asquith, President of Women's Liberal Federation 1923–25 and 1939–45, President of Liberal Party 1945–47

Borsig, August (1804–54) German railway entrepreneur and industrialist, founded locomotive factory in Berlin 1837

Boyce, Robert Henry (1834–1909) Principal Surveyor of HM Diplomatic and Consular Buildings, HM Office of Works

Breen, Timothy Florence (1885–1966) British civil servant, at British Military Mission in Berlin 1919, Press Attaché at Berlin 1921–37

Brockdorff, Countess Therese von (1840–1904), German aristocrat with title of 'Senior Mistress of the Court' to the Empress Augusta

Bruce, Henry James (1880–1951) British diplomat from 1904, at Berlin 1908–13, First Secretary and Head of Chancery at St Petersburg 1913–20

Brüning, Heinrich (1885–1970) German politician, Chancellor of Germany 1930–32

Budberg, Moura (Moura Platonovich Zahresky) (1892–1974) Russian socialite, became a British citizen in early 1930s

Bülow, Bernhard Ernst von (1815–79) German politician, Foreign Minister of Prussia 1873–79, Prussian Plenipotentiary at the 1878 Congress of Berlin, father of **Bernhard Heinrich Karl Martin von Bülow**

Bülow, Bernhard Heinrich Karl Martin von (1849–1929) German politician, Foreign Minister of Prussia and German Foreign Secretary 1897–1900, Minister–President of Prussia and Chancellor of Germany 1900–1909, married **Maria Beccadelli di Bologna** (1848–1929) in 1886

Burne-Jones, Sir Edward (1833–98) British artist and decorative arts designer, including stained glass and tapestries for William Morris & Company

Butler, Ewan (1911–74) British journalist and author, Assistant Correspondent for *The Times* at Berlin 1938–39

Cadogan, Sir Alexander George Montagu (1884–1968) British diplomat from 1908, British Ambassador to Peking 1933–36, Permanent Under-Secretary of State, Foreign Office 1938–46, UK Permanent Representative to the United Nations 1946–50

Caprivi de Montecuccoli, Georg Leo Graf von (1831–99) German General and politician, Chancellor of Germany 1890–94

Cartwright, Sir Fairfax Leighton (1857–1928) British diplomat from 1881, served in Berlin in 1880s, later British Ambassador to Vienna 1908–13

Cassel, Ernest Joseph (1852–1921) German-born merchant banker, capitalist and philanthropist, confidant of King Edward VII

Cassirer, Paul (1871–1926) German avant-garde art dealer in Berlin

Cavendish, Lady Emma Elizabeth (died 1920) elder sister of Sir Frank Lascelles, married Lord Edward Cavendish

Chamberlain, Joseph (1836–1914) British politician, Mayor of Birmingham, President of the Board of Trade, Secretary of State for the Colonies 1895–1906, father of **(Joseph) Austen Chamberlain** and **Neville Chamberlain**

Chamberlain, Sir (Joseph) Austen (1863–1937) British politician, Postmaster-General 1902–3, Chancellor of the Exchequer 1903–15, Secretary of State for India 1915–17, Lord Privy Seal 1921–22, Foreign Secretary 1924–29, signed Treaty of Locarno

in October 1925 for which he shared the Nobel Peace Prize, half-brother of **Neville Chamberlain**

Chamberlain, Neville (1869–1940) British politician, son of **Joseph Chamberlain** and half-brother of **Sir (Joseph) Austen Chamberlain**, Chancellor of the Exchequer 1923–24 and 1931–37, Prime Minister 1937–40

Channon, Sir Henry ('Chips') (1897–1958) American-born British politician and author, MP for Southend 1935–58, married **Lady Honor Guinness** in 1933

Chaplin, Charlie (1889–1977) British actor, entertainer and filmmaker

Chirol, Sir Ignatius Valentine (1852–1929) British journalist, historian and diplomat, at Foreign Office 1872–76, Berlin correspondent for *The Times* 1892–96, later director of foreign department at *The Times*

Churchill, Lord Randolph Henry Spencer (1859–95) British politician, Secretary of State for India 1885–86, Leader of the House of Commons 1886–87, Chancellor of the Exchequer August–December 1886. Married **Jeanette Jerome** (1854–1921) in 1874

Clarendon, 4th Earl of (George Frederick William Villiers) (1800–1870) British Whig politician and diplomat, Minister to Spain 1833–39, Viceroy of Ireland 1847–52, father of **Lady Emily Theresa Villiers** and **The Hon. Francis Hyde Villiers**

Colvin, Ian (1877–1938) British journalist, Central Europe correspondent for the *News Chronicle* 1937–39

Connolly, Cyril Vernon (1903–74) British literary critic and author

Conwell–Evans, T. Philip (1891–1968) British academic based in Germany, lecturer at University of Königsberg 1932–34 and Joint Secretary of Anglo–German Society 1934–39

Coulondre, Robert (1885–1959) French diplomat, French Ambassador to Berlin 1938–39

Coward, Sir Noël (1899–1973) British playwright, actor and entertainer

Cranborne, Viscount (Robert Arthur James Gascoyne-Cecil, 5th Marquess of Salisbury)

(1893–1972) British politician, Parliamentary Under-Secretary of State for Foreign Affairs 1935–38, later Leader of the House of Lords 1943–45, 1951–57, Lord President of the Council 1952–57

Cromer, 1st Earl of (Evelyn Baring) (1841–1917) Agent and Consul-General, Egypt, 1883–1907, married (1) **Ethel Stanley** (died 1898) in 1876

Crowe, Sir Eyre Alexander Barby Wichart (1864–1925) British diplomat, Permanent Under-Secretary at the Foreign Office 1920–25

Curtius, Julius (1877–1948) German politician, Minister for Economic Affairs 1926–9, Foreign Minister 1929–31, married **Adda Carp** in 1931

Curzon, George Nathaniel, 1st Marquess Curzon of Kedleston (1859–1925) British politician, Foreign Secretary 1919–24, Leader of the House of Lords 1916–24. Married (1) Mary Leiter (1870–1906) in 1895 and (2) Grace, née **Duggan** (1877–1958) in 1917, father (by first marriage) of **Irene Ravensdale, Cynthia Mosley** and **Alexandra Metcalfe**

D'Abernon, Viscount (Edgar Vincent) (1857–1941) British politician, diplomat and art collector, Governor of Imperial Ottoman Bank 1889–97, MP for Exeter 1899–1906, Chairman of Central Liquor Control Board 1915–1920, Inter-Allied Mission to Poland 1920, Ambassador to Berlin 1920–26, married **Helen Venetia Duncombe** (1866–1954) in 1890

Daly, Colonel Thomas Denis (1890–1956) British Army Officer, Military Attaché at Belgrade, Prague, Bucharest 1932–36, at Berlin, 1939, at Paris 1945–6, Chief of the Berlin Mission, Inter-Allied Reparation Agency 1946–8

Dawes, Charles (1865–1951) American banker and politician, joint winner of 1925 Nobel Peace Prize for work in resolving post-Great War German war reparations, US Vice-President 1925–9, American Ambassador to the UK 1929–32

Dawson, Geoffrey (1874–1944) British journalist, editor of *The Times* 1912–19, 1923–41

Derby, 15th Earl of (Edward Henry Stanley) (1826–93) British Secretary of State for Foreign Affairs 1866–68, 1874–78

Dirksen, Herbert von (1882–1955) German diplomat, Ambassador to London 1938–39

Dodd, Martha Eccles (1908–1990) daughter of **William Dodd**, migrated to Soviet Union in 1950s

Dodd, William Edward (1869–1940) American academic, American Ambassador to Berlin 1933–1937, married **Martha Johns** (died 1938) in 1901, father of **Martha Dodd**

Doyle, Sir Arthur Ignatius Conan (1859–1930) British author and physician

Earle, Sir Lionel (1866–1948) British civil servant, Permanent Secretary of HM Office of Works 1912–33

Ebbutt, Norman (1894–1968) British journalist, chief Berlin correspondent for *The Times* 1925–37, expelled from Germany

Ebert, Friedrich (1871–1925) German politician, President of Germany 1919–25

Eden, Anthony (1st Earl of Avon) (1897–1977) British politician, Parliamentary Under-Secretary of State at Foreign Office 1931–33, Lord Privy Seal 1934–35, Minister for the League of Nations 1935, Foreign Secretary 1935–38, 1940–45 and 1951–55, Prime Minister 1955–57

Einstein, Albert (1879–1955) German theoretical physicist, migrated to the United States in 1933

Ernst, Karl (1904–34) SA Grüppenführer and SA leader in Berlin, murdered during the 'Night of the Long Knives', 30 June 1934

Erroll, 22nd Earl of (Josslyn Victor Hay) (1900–1941) British diplomat, son of **4th Baron Kilmarnock**, Hon. Attaché at Berlin 1920–22, resigned to marry Lady Idina Sackville, moved to Kenya in 1924, died under mysterious circumstances on 24 January 1941

Eulenberg und Hertefeld, Philipp Frederick Alexander, Furst zu, Graf von Sandels (1847–1921) German politician and diplomat, close friend of **Emperor Wilhelm II**

Foley, Major Francis (Frank) Edward (1884–1958) British civil servant, Passport Control Officer and British intelligence officer at Berlin 1919–39, married Katharine Eva (died 1979) in 1921, father of **Ursula Foley**

François–Poncet, André (1887–1978) French diplomat, Ambassador at Berlin 1931–38

Frick, Wilhelm (1877–1946) German politician, Reich Minister of the Interior under Adolf Hitler 1933–43, tried at Nuremberg and sentenced to death

Friedländer-Fuld, Fritz von (1858–1917), German industrialist and coal-merchant, married **Milly Antonie Fuld** (1866–1943)

Galsworthy, Sir John (1867–1933) British novelist and playwright

Gainer, Sir Donald St Clair (1891–1966) British diplomat, served in Consular Service in Munich 1926–29, Bavaria 1932–38, and Austria 1938–39

Gaselee, Sir Stephen (1882–1943) British civil servant, Librarian and Keeper of Papers at the Foreign Office from 1920

Gerard, James Watson (1867–1951) American lawyer, member of the Supreme Court of New York, American Ambassador to Berlin 1913–17

Gimpel, René (1881–1945) French art dealer in Paris

Gladstone, William Ewart (1809–98) British politician, Chancellor of the Exchequer 1852–55, 1859–66, 1873–74, 1880–82, Liberal Prime Minister 1868–74, 1880–85, February–July 1886, 1892–94

Gleichen, Lord Edward (1863–1937) British army officer, son of Prince Victor of Hohenlohe-Langenberg, nephew of Queen Victoria, Military Attaché at Berlin 1903–1906 and at Washington, DC 1906–07

Goebbels, Joseph (1897–1945) German politician, Minister for Propaganda 1933–45 under Adolf Hitler, married **Magda Ritschel** (1901–45) in 1931, committed suicide May 1945

Goering, Hermann (1893–1946) German politician under Adolf Hitler, former Great War flying ace, Prime Minister of Prussia 1933, Commander-in-Chief of the German Air Force 1933–1945, Field

Marshal 1938, , married (2) **Emmy Sonnemann** (1893–1973) in 1935 tried at Nuremberg and committed suicide October 1946

Goschen, Sir (William) Edward (1847–1924) British diplomat from 1869, Minister to Belgrade 1898–1900, Minister to Copenhagen 1900–1905, Ambassador to Vienna 1905–8, Ambassador to Berlin 1908–14, married **Harriet ('Hosta') Clarke** (died 1912) in 1874

Gough, Hugh, 3rd Viscount Gough (1849–1919) British diplomat, Secretary at Berlin 1896–1901

Graef, Gustav (1821–95) German artist, based in Königsberg and Berlin, specialised in portraits and historical subjects

Grant, Duncan James Corrowr (1885–1978) British artist and designer, member of the 'Bloomsbury Group'

Granville, 2nd Earl (George Leveson Gower) (1815–91) British Secretary of State for Foreign Affairs 1851–52, 1870–74, 1880–85. His son Granville George Leveson Gower, the 3rd Earl (1872–1939) was a British diplomat from 1893, Second Secretary at Berlin in 1904, Counsellor at Berlin 1911–13, later (amongst other appointments) Ambassador to Brussels 1928–33

Greene, Hugh (1910–1987) British journalist, Berlin correspondent for the *Daily Telegraph* 1934, later Director-General of the BBC 1960–69

Grenfell, Francis Wallace, 1st Baron (1841–1925) British army officer, Field-Marshal, commanded forces in Egypt 1897–98, Governor and Commander-in-Chief at Malta 1899–1903, Commander of the 4th Army Corps 1903–4, Commander-in-Chief, Ireland, 1904–8

Grew, Joseph Clark (1880–1965) American diplomat, at Berlin 1912–17, later American Ambassador to Tokyo 1932–41

Grey, Edward, 1st Viscount Grey of Falloden (1862–1933) British politician, Foreign Secretary 1905–16, Ambassador to Washington, DC 1919–20

Grierson, Lt. General Sir James Moncrieff (1859–1914) British army officer, Military Attaché at Berlin 1896–1900, later served in South Africa, Director of Military

Operations at Headquarters 1904–06

Gurney, Sir Hugh (1878–1968) British diplomat from 1901, at Berlin 1914, later Ambassador to Rio de Janeiro 1935–39

Hácha, Emil (1872–1945) President of Czechoslovakia 1938–39

Haldane, Richard Burdon, 1st Viscount Haldane (1856–1928) British politician, Secretary of State for War 1905–12, Lord Chancellor 1912–15

Halifax, 1st Earl of (Edward Frederick Lindley Wood) (1881–1959) British politician, Lord Privy Seal 1935–37, Leader of the House of Lords 1935–38, Lord President of the Council 1937–38, Foreign Secretary 1938–40, later British Ambassador to Washington, DC 1940–46

Hammond, Edmund, 1st Baron Hammond (1802–90) Permanent Under-Secretary for Foreign Affairs 1854–73

Hanfstaengl, Ernst Franz Sedgwick ('Putzi') (1887–1975) German businessman, confidant of **Adolf Hitler**, Head of the Foreign Press Association at Berlin

Hansemann, Adolf von (1826–1903) Prussian banker, financier and railway entrepreneur

Hardy, C.H.F. British civil servant, Assistant Archivist at Berlin in late 1930s

Hardinge, Sir Charles, 1st Baron Hardinge of Penshurst (1858–1944) British diplomat from 1880, Permanent Under-Secretary at the Foreign Office 1906–1910, Ambassador to St Petersburg 1904–16, Viceroy of India 1910–16, Ambassador to Paris 1920–23

Harrison, Sir Geoffrey Wedgwood (1908–1990) British diplomat from 1932, at Berlin 1937–39, later British Ambassador to Moscow 1965–68, married **Amy Katherine Clive** (1913–2007) in 1936

Harvey, Sir Oliver Charles, 1st Baron Harvey of Tasburgh (1893–1968) British diplomat from 1919, Private Secretary to Foreign Secretary 1936–39 and 1941–43, British Ambassador to Paris 1948–54

Harvey, Roland British diplomat, Second Secretary at Berlin in 1914

Hassell, Ulrich von (1881–1944)

German diplomat, Ambassador at the Holy See 1932–38

Hatzfeldt zu Trachenberg, Melchior Hubert Paul Gustav, Graf von (1831–1901) German diplomat, Ambassador to Constantinople 1878–81, Foreign Secretary 1881–85, Ambassador to London 1885–1901

Henderson, Sir Arthur (1863–1935) Labour politician and Leader of the Labour Party, Home Secretary 1924, Foreign Secretary 1929–31

Henderson, Sir Nevile Meyrick (1882–1942) British diplomat from 1905, later British Minister to Belgrade 1929–34, Ambassador to Buenos Aires 1935–37, Ambassador to Berlin 1937–39, brother of **Violet Lina, Countess of Leitrim**

Herbert, The Hon. David Alexander Reginald (1908–95) British socialite and author, second son of the 15th Earl of Pembroke

Hess, Rudolf Walter Richard (1894–1987) German politician, joined National Socialist Party in 1920, close associate of Adolf Hitler, Deputy Führer 1933, tried at Nuremberg and imprisoned

Himmler, Heinrich (1900–1945) German civil servant, Head of the SS under Adolf Hitler 1929–45, Head of German Police 1936–45, committed suicide May 1945

Hindenburg, Paul Ludwig Hans Anton von (1847–1934) Prussian Field Marshal and German politician, recalled to military service in Great War as Chief of General Staff, President of Germany 1925–4 August 1934

Hitler, Adolf (1889–1945) Chancellor of Germany 1933–45, committed suicide 1945, married **Eva Braun** (1912–45) in 1945

Hobhouse, Sir Charles (Edward Henry) (1862–1941) British politician, Parliamentary Under-Secretary of State for India 1907–8, Financial Secretary, HM Treasury 1908–11, Chancellor of the Duchy of Lancaster 1911–14, Postmaster General 1914–15

Holman, Adrian (1895–1974) British diplomat, Head of Chancery in Berlin 1938–39, later British Ambassador to Havana 1950–54

Holmes, Sir Charles John (1868–1936) British artist and art historian, Director of National

Portrait Gallery 1909–16 and of National Gallery 1916–28

Hope-Vere, Edward James (1885–1924) British diplomat, Second Secretary at Berlin April – August 1914

Iddesleigh, 1st Earl of (Stafford Northcote) (1818–87) British politician, Chancellor of the Exchequer 1874–80, Foreign Secretary 1886–7

Isherwood, Christopher William Bradshaw (1904–86) British author, lived in Berlin 1925–33

Israel, Wilfred (1899–1943) German Jewish philanthropist involved in the rescue of Jews from Nazi Germany

Jagow, Gottlieb von (1863–1935) German diplomat, German Foreign Minister 1913–16

Jebb, Hubert Miles Gladwyn (1st Baron Gladwyn) (1900–1996) British diplomat from 1924, British Ambassador to the United Nations 1950–54, British Ambassador to Paris 1954–60, married **Cynthia Noble** (1898–1990) in 1929

John, Augustus (1878–1961) British (Welsh-born) artist of international repute and fashionable portraitist

Johnson, Amy (1903–41) British record-breaking aviator, died following a plane crash in the Thames Estuary in January 1941

Jones, Tom (1870–1955). Deputy Secretary to the Cabinet, accompanied Lloyd George on his visit to meet Hitler at Berchtesgaden in September 1936

Kapp, Wolfgang (1858–1922) German political activist, leader of failed coup against Weimar Republic in March 1920

Kendrick, Captain Thomas British Passport Control Office in Vienna in 1930s

Kessler, Harry Clemens Ulrich, Graf (1868–1937) Anglo–German Count, soldier, cosmopolitan and socialite, Director of the Museum für Kunst und Kunstgewerbe at Weimar, friend of many contemporary artists

Kilmarnock, 4th Baron (Victor Alexander Gerald Hay, 21st Earl of Erroll) (1876–1928) British diplomat from 1900, Chargé d'Affaires at Berlin 1920, Counsellor to 1921, British High Commissioner to Inter-Allied Rhineland High Commission to

1928, succeeded to Earldom 1927, father of **Josslyn Victor Hay, 22nd Earl of Erroll**

King, William Lyon Mackenzie (1874–1950) Canadian politician, Prime Minister of Canada 1935–48

Kirk, Alexander Comstock (1888–1979) American diplomat from 1915, American *Chargé d'Affaires* at Berlin 1939–1940, later American Ambassador to Rome 1944–46

Kirkpatrick, Sir Ivone (Augustus) (1897–1964) British diplomat from 1919, First Secretary and Head of Chancery at Berlin 1933–1938, Controller of BBC European Services 1941, later British High Commissioner in Germany 1950–1943, Permanent Under-Secretary, Foreign Office, 1953–1957, Chairman of Independent Television Authority 1957–1962

Knaus, Ludwig (1829–1910) German artist, settled in Berlin in 1874

Knollys, Francis, 1st Viscount Knollys (1st Baron Caversham) (1837–1924) Private Secretary to Edward, Prince of Wales, later King Edward VII and King George V

Krüger, Dr Karl German agent operating for the British in the 1930s

Landau, Henry (1892–1968) Passport Control Officer and intelligence officer in Berlin 1919–20

Langhorne, George American army officer, Military Attaché at Berlin in 1914

Lansdowne, 5th Marquess of (Henry Petty-Fitzmaurice) (1845–1927) British politician, Governor–General of Canada 1885–88, Viceroy of India 1888–94, Secretary of State for War 1895–99, Foreign Secretary 1900–1905

Lascelles, Florence Caroline (1876–1961) daughter **Sir Frank Lascelles**, married **Sir Cecil Spring–Rice** in 1904

Lascelles, Sir Frank Cavendish (1841–1920) British diplomat from 1861, at Berlin 1870–71, Ambassador to St Petersburg 1894, Ambassador to Berlin 1895–1908, married **Mary Emma Oliffe** (died 1897) in 1867, father of **Florence Lascelles** and brother of **Lady Emma Elizabeth Cavendish**

Lasker, Eduard (1829–84) German politician and jurist

László, Philip de (1869–1937) Hungarian-born fashionable society artist, became a British citizen in 1914

Lever, Sir Paul (born 1944) British diplomat, Ambassador to Germany 1997–2003 (resident in Berlin 1999–2003)

Leighton, Frederic, 1st Baron Leighton (1830–96) British artist, President of the Royal Academy of Arts 1878–96

Leitrim, Countess of (Violet Lina, née Henderson) (died 1943) elder sister of **Sir Nevile Henderson**, married Charles Clements, 5th Earl of Leitrim (1879–1952) in 1902, divorced 1932

Lens (or Leus), Germaine Friend and confidante of **Sir Nevile Henderson**

Lessing, Otto (1846–1912) German sculptor, worked in collaboration with architects in Berlin, produced work for the Reichstag, the Royal Schloss and many other buildings

Lewis, Harry Sinclair (1885–1951) American author and playwright, winner of the Nobel Prize for Literature in 1930

Liebermann, Max (1847–1935) German avant-garde artist

Liebknecht, Karl (1871–1919) German socialist, co-founder of Spartacist League 1914, declared formation of a Socialist Republic in Berlin 9 November 1918, killed during Spartacist uprising 15 January 1919

Lindsay, Sir Ronald Charles (1877–1945) British diplomat from 1898, at St Petersburg 1899–1903, later British Ambassador to Berlin 1926–28, Permanent Under-Secretary of State, Foreign Office 1928–30, British Ambassador to Washington, DC 1930–39

Lipski, Józef (1894–1958) Polish diplomat from 1925, Polish Ambassador to Berlin 1934–39

Lloyd George of Dwyfor (David Lloyd George) (1863–1945) British politician, Chancellor of the Exchequer 1908–15, Prime Minister 1916–22

Lockhart, Sir Robert Hamilton Bruce (1887–1970) British diplomat in Consular Service from 1911, at

Moscow and St Petersburg 1915–18, at Prague 1919–22, later journalist and Director-General of Political Warfare Executive

Loftus, Lord Augustus William Frederick Spencer (1817–94) British diplomat, Attaché at Berlin under Lord William Russell and John Fane, Lord Burghersh, later Ambassador to Berlin 1865–71, Ambassador to St Petersburg 1871–79, Governor of New South Wales 1879–85

Londonderry, 7th Marquess of (Charles Stewart Henry Vane-Tempest Stewart) (1878–1949) British politician, Parliamentary Under-Secretary of State for Air 1920–21, Governor of Northern Ireland 1921–26, First Commissioner of Works 1928–29 and 1931, Secretary of State for Air 1931–35, Lord Privy Seal and Leader of the House of Lords 1935, married **Edith Helen Chaplin** (1878–1959) in 1899, father of **Lady Mairi Elizabeth Vane-Tempest-Stewart** (1921–2009)

Lothian, 11th Marquess of (Philip Kerr) (1882–1940) British politician, Ambassador to Washington, DC 1939–40

Lowe, Charles (1848–1931) British author and journalist, *The Times* correspondent at Berlin late 1870s–1891

Lowry-Corry, Montagu William (Baron Rowton) (1838–1903) British civil servant, Private Secretary to Prime Minister Lord Beaconsfield 1866–68 and 1874–80

Luther, Hans (1879–1962) German politician, Chancellor of Germany January 1925 – May 1926

Lyall, George (1883–1959) British diplomat in Consular Service from 1917, British Consul in Berlin in 1926, Consul–General 1936–39

Lyons, Richard Bickerton Pernell (1st Viscount Lyons) (1817–87) British diplomat from 1839, later Ambassador to Paris 1867–87

MacDonald, Ramsay (1866–1937) British politician, Foreign Secretary 1929, Labour Prime Minister 1929–35

McDonald, Iverach (1908–2006) British journalist, *The Times* correspondent in Berlin 1937, later Associate Editor of *The Times* 1967–73

Mackenzie, Sir Morell (1837–92) British physician and pioneering larynx specialist

Magnus, Viktor Karl von (1828–72) Prussian banker, British Consul in Berlin

Malet, Sir Edward Baldwin, 4th Baronet (1837–1908), British diplomat from 1859, Agent and Consul-General at Cairo 1879–83, Ambassador to Brussels 1883–84, Ambassador to Berlin 1884–95, married Lady Ermyntrude Sackville Russell (1856–1927) in 1885

Marshall-Cornwall, Sir James Handyside (1887–1985) British army officer, Military Attaché at Berlin 1928–32, later Lieutenant General head of Western Command 1941–42

Mason-MacFarlane, Lt. General Sir Frank Noel (1889–1953) British Army officer, Military Attaché at Berlin 1937–39, later Head of British Military Mission to Moscow 1941–42, Governor at Commander-in-Chief, Gibraltar 1942–44

Maugham, W. Somerset (1874–1965) British author and playwright

Menzel, Adolph (1815–1905) German artist based in Berlin, specialising in highly detailed historical works and genre subjects

Metcalfe, Alexandra Naldera ('Baba') (1904–95) British socialite, third daughter of **Lord Curzon** and his first wife Mary Leiter, married **Captain Edward Dudley ('Fruity') Metcalfe** in 1925

Mitchell, Leslie British civil servant, at British Consulate-General 1920s/1930s

Mitford, Diana (1910–2003) British socialite and author, daughter of **2nd Baron Redesdale**, married (1) Bryan Guinness (1905–92) in 1929 (divorced), (2) **Oswald Mosley** in 1936

Mitford, Tom (1909–45) son of 2nd Baron Redesdale, killed in action in Burma in 1945

Mitford, Unity Valkyrie (1914–48) British socialite, daughter of **2nd Baron Redesdale**, attempted suicide 3 September 1939, died from later medical complications

Molesworth, Miss C. British civil servant, at British Passport Control Office at Berlin in late 1930s

Moltke, Helmuth Karl Bernhard, Graf von (1800–91) Chief of Staff of the Prussian Army and Field-Marshal

Moltke, Helmuth James, Graf von (1907–45) German lawyer and opponent of Nazi regime, executed January 1945

Monck, Sir John Berkeley (1883–1964) British diplomat, Honorary Attaché at Berlin 1908–14

Morier, Sir Robert Burnet David (1826–93) British diplomat, at Berlin 1858 and a number of minor German courts in 1860s, Chargé d'Affaires at Berlin 1867, later Ambassador to St Petersburg 1884–93

Mortimer, Raymond (1895–1980) British author, close associate of **Harold Nicolson** and **Vita Sackville-West**

Mosley, Oswald ('Tom') (1896–1980) British politician, formed British Union of Fascists 1933, married (1) Cynthia Curzon ('Cimmie') (1898–1933) daughter of **Lord Curzon** in 1920, (2) Diana Guinness (née Mitford) in 1936

Mounsey, Sir George Augustus (1879–1966) British diplomat from 1902, at Berlin in 1908, later Assistant Under-Secretary at the Foreign Office 1929

Muir, Sir Edward (1905–79) British civil servant in HM Office of Works from 1927, later its Permanent Secretary 1956–62

Münster, Georg Herbert zu German diplomat, Ambassador to London 1873–85

Neave, Airey Middleton Sheffield (1916–79) British Army officer and Colditz escapee, politician, assassinated by IRA car bomb March 1979

Neumann, Hermann German porter at British Embassy, Berlin 1930s/1940s

Neumann, Otto German porter at the British Embassy, Berlin 1930s/1940s

Neurath, Konstantin Hermann Freiherr von (1873–1956) German diplomat from 1903, Minister of Foreign Affairs 1932–38, Reichsprotektor of Bohemia and Moravia 1939–41

Newton, Sir Basil Cochrane (1889–1965) British diplomat from 1912, Counsellor at Berlin 1930–1935, Minister at Berlin 1935–1937, Minister to Prague 1937–39, Ambassador to Baghdad 1939–41

Nicolson, Sir Arthur (1st Baron Carnock) (1849–1928) British diplomat from 1870, at Berlin 1874–76, later Ambassador to Madrid 1904–5, Ambassador to St Petersburg 1906–10, Permanent Under-Secretary of State at the Foreign Office 1910–16, father of **Harold Nicolson**

Nicolson, Sir Harold George (1886–1968) British diplomat from 1909, author and politician, Counsellor at Berlin 1927–29, journalist for the *Evening Standard*, briefly stood for New Party, subsequently entered Parliament as Labour MP in 1935, Parliamentary Under-Secretary of State in the Coalition Government, 1940, son of **1st Baron Carnock**, married **Vita Sackville-West** in 1913

Norton, Sir Clifford John (1891–1990) British Army officer, diplomat from 1921, British Minister to Bern 1942–46, Ambassador to Athens 1946–51

Noske, Gustav (1868–1946) German politician, oversaw defeat of Spartacist uprising, German Minister of Defence 1919–20

Novello, Ivor (1893–1951) British composer and actor

O'Neill, Sir Con Douglas Walter (1912–88) British diplomat from 1936, Third Secretary at Berlin 1938, later Ambassador to Helsinki 1961–63, Ambassador to the European Communities in Brussels 1963–65

Ogilvie-Forbes, Sir George Arthur Drostan (1891–1954) British Army officer, British diplomat from 1919, Counsellor at Berlin 1937–39, later Ambassador to Caracas 1944–48

Oppenheimer, Sir Francis (Charles) (1870–1961) British diplomat, Consul-General at Frankfurt 1900–1911 and Commercial Attaché there 1912–14

Orth, August Friedrich Wilhelm (1828–1901) German architect based in Berlin, designed Palais Strousberg

Ovey, Marie-Armande, Lady (née **Vignat**) (died 1954) second wife of Sir Esmond Ovey (1879–1963), British diplomat from 1902, later British Ambassador to Moscow 1929–34, to Brussels 1934–37 and Buenos Aires 1937–42

Paget, Sir Augustus Berkeley (1823–96) British diplomat from 1843, at Berlin 1857–58, Minister

to Copenhagen 1859–66, later Ambassador to Vienna 1884–93, married **Walpurga Ehrengarde Helena, Gräfin von Hohenthal** (1839–1929) in 1860

Panter, Noël British journalist, *Daily Telegraph* correspondent in Munich to 1933

Peplinsky, Wadislau Steward at American Embassy, Berlin in 1940s

Peters, Wilhelm (c.1817–1903) German artist based in Berlin, specialised in history painting

Phipps, Sir Eric Clare Edmund (1875–1945) British diplomat from 1899, British Ambassador to Berlin 1933–37, to Paris 1937–39, married (2) **Frances Ward** (died 1988) in 1911

Piazzetta, Giovanni Battista (1682–1754) Venetian artist

Pink, Ivor (Thomas Montague) (1910–66) British diplomat from 1934, Control Commissioner for Germany at Berlin 1945–47

Pless, Daisy, Princess of (Mary Theresa Olivia Cornwallis-West) (1873–1943) British-born German society beauty, married Hans Heinrich XV, Prince of Pless of Fürstenstein (1861–1938) in 1891, divorced 1922; her brother George married **Jeanette Churchill** (née **Jerome**) in 1900

Plunkett, Rt. Hon. Sir Francis Richard (1835–1907) British diplomat from 1855, at Berlin early 1870s, later Ambassador to Vienna 1900–05

Ponsonby, Frederick Edward Grey (1st Baron Sysonby) (1867–1935) Assistant Private Secretary to Queen Victoria, King Edward VII and King George V (to 1912)

Rachsdorff, Julius Carl (1823–1914) Prolific German architect, designed Cathedral and St George's English Church in Berlin

Radolin, Hugo Julius Eduard Leszczyc Raoul, Prince von (1841–1917) German diplomat, Marshal of the Court 1884–88, later German Ambassador to Paris 1901–10

Radziwill, Princess Marie (Marie Dorothée Élisabeth, née Castellane) (1840–1915) French noblewoman, married Prince Antoine Radziwill (1833–1904) in 1857

Ratibor, Viktor Moritz Carl I, Herzog von, Fürst von Corvey, Prinz zu Hohenlohe-Schillingsfürst (1818–93) Prussian/Silesian aristocrat, associate of **Otto von Bismarck**

Rattigan, William Frank (1879–1952) British diplomat from 1903, Second Secretary at Berlin 1913–14

Ravensdale, 2nd Baroness (Mary Irene Curzon) (1896–1966) British socialite, eldest daughter of Lord Curzon and his first wife Mary Leiter, sister of **Cynthia** ('Cimmie') **Mosley** and **Alexandra** ('Baba') **Metcalfe**

Redesdale, 2nd Baron (David Freeman-Mitford) (1878–1958) British aristocrat, father of **Diana**, **Tom** and **Unity** Mitford, married **Sydney Bowles** ('Muv') (1880–1963) in 1904

Reid, Sir James (1849–1923) British physician, physician to Queen Victoria, King Edward VII and King George V

Rhodes, Cecil John (1853–1902) British imperialist, mining tycoon, railway developer and politician in Southern Africa

Ribbentrop, Joachim Ulrich Friedrich von (1893–1946) German businessman and politician, joined National Socialist Party 1933, German Ambassador to London 1936–38, German Foreign Minister 1938–45, tried and executed at Nuremberg, married **Annalies Henkell** (1896–1973) in 1920

Richmond, William Blake (1842–1921) British artist, son of artist George Richmond (1809–96)

Roberts, Sir Frank (1907–98) British diplomat from 1930, in Foreign Office Central Department in late 1930s, later Ambassador to Moscow 1960–62, Ambassador to Bonn 1963–68

Rodd, Sir James Rennell, 1st Baron Rennell (1858–1941) British diplomat, poet and classical scholar, at Berlin 1884–88, later Ambassador to Rome 1908–19

Röhm, Ernst (1887–1934) Joined Nazi Party 1919, SA Chief of Staff 1930–34, murdered during the 'Night of the Long Knives', 1 July 1934

Roon, Albrecht Theodor Graf von (1803–79) Prussian politician, Prussian Minister of War 1859–73, Minister-President of Prussia

January – November 1873

Ropp, Baron William Sylvester de (1886–1973) Lithuanian-born British agent operating in Germany in 1930s, became a British citizen in 1915

Rosebery, 5th Earl of (Archibald Philip Primrose) (1847–1929) British politician, Under-Secretary, Home Office 1881–83, Chief Commissioner of Works and Lord Privy Seal, 1885, Foreign Secretary 1886, Prime Minister 1892–95

Rüger, Artur (born c.1887) German butler at British Embassy, Berlin 1930s/1940s

Rumbold, Sir Horace, 8th Baronet (1829–1913) British diplomat, Ambassador to Vienna 1896–1900, father of **Sir Horace Rumbold, 9th Baronet**, married (2) **Louisa Anne Crampton** (died 1940) in 1881

Rumbold, Sir Horace George Montagu, 9th Baronet (1869–1941) British diplomat from 1888, Counsellor at Berlin 1913–14, Minister to Berne 1916, Minister to Warsaw 1920, Ambassador to Constantinople 1920–24, Ambassador to Madrid 1924–1928, Ambassador to Berlin 1928–33, married **Ethelred Constantia Fane** (1879–1964) in 1905, father of **Constantia Dorothy Rumbold** (1906–2001) and **(Horace) Anthony Claude** (1911–83)

Rumbold, Sir (Horace) Anthony ('Tony') Claude, 10th Baronet (1911–1983) British diplomat from 1935, later Ambassador at Vienna 1967–70, son of **Sir Horace Rumbold, 9th Baronet**

Russell, Alexander Victor Frederick Villiers (1874–1965) British Army officer, son of **Odo Russell, 1st Baron Ampthill**, Military Attaché in Stockholm and Berlin 1910–14

Russell, Odo William Leopold (1st Baron Ampthill) (1829–84) British diplomat from 1849, Envoy to the Holy See 1858–70, Special Mission to Versailles 1870–71, Ambassador to Berlin 1871–84, married **Lady Emily Theresa Villiers** (1843–1927) in 1868, father of **Alexander Russell**

Russell, Lord George William (1790–1846) Second son of John Russell, 6th Duke of Bedford and brother of Prime Minister Lord John Russell, British Army

officer, served under the Duke of Wellington in the Peninsular War, Minister to Berlin 1835–41, married **Elizabeth Ann Rawdon** (1793–1874) in 1817, father of **Hastings Russell, 9th Duke of Bedford** and **Odo Russell, 1st Baron Ampthill**

Ruysdael, Salomon van (c.1602–70) Dutch landscape artist based in Haarlem

Sackville-West, The Hon. Victoria (Vita) Mary (1892–1962) British author and garden designer, married Harold Nicolson in 1919, close confidante of **Virginia Woolf**

Salis, John Francis Charles, 7th Count de (1864–1939) British diplomat from 1887, Counsellor at Berlin 1906–11

Salisbury, 3rd Marquess of (Robert Gascoyne-Cecil) (1830–1903) British politician, Foreign Secretary 1878–80, 1885–86, 1887–92, 1895–1900, Conservative Prime Minister 1885–86, 1886–92, 1895–1902

Sampson, George Frederick (1883–1948) British civil servant, Archivist at Berlin in 1914

Sassoon, Sir Philip (1888–1939) British politician, Parliamentary Under-Secretary of State for Air 1924–29 and 1931–37, First Commissioner of Works 1937–39

Schacht, Hjalmar Horace Greeley (1877–1970) German economist and politician, President of Reichsbank 1923–31 and 1933–39, Reich Minister of Economics 1934–1937, tried at Nuremberg and acquitted

Schaller, Friedrich (1812–99) German genre and historical artist, based in Berlin

Scheidemann, Philipp (1865–1939) German politician, proclaimed German Republic 9 November 1918, Chancellor of Germany February – June 1919

Schleicher, Kurt von (1882–1934) German politician, Chancellor of Germany 1932–33, murdered with his wife Elisabeth during the 'Night of the Long Knives', 30 June 1934

Schmidt, Paul (1899–1970) German civil servant, professional translator in German Foreign Ministry 1923–45

Schinkel, Karl Friedrich (1781–1841) Prussian architect and city planner

Schleswig-Holstein, (Frederick Charles) Christian (Augustus), Prince of (1831–1917) German Prince, born in Denmark, married Queen Victoria's daughter Helena (1846–1923) in 1866

Schneider German servant at British Embassy, Berlin in 1920s

Schön, Wilhelm Eduard Freiherr von (1851–1933) German politician, German Foreign Secretary 1907–10

Schönemann German servant at British Embassy, Berlin from c.1880

Scott, Sir Charles Stewart (1838–1924) British diplomat from 1858, Embassy Secretary at Berlin early 1880s, later British Ambassador to St Petersburg 1898–1904

Shaw-Lefevre, George (1831–1928) British politician, First Commissioner of Works 1881–85 and 1892–94, Postmaster-General 1884–85, President of the Local Government Board 1894–95

Shirer, William Lawrence (1904–93) American journalist and radio reporter for CBS at Berlin 1934–40

Simon, Sir John (1873–1954) British politician, Home Secretary 1915–16 and 1935–37, Foreign Secretary 1931–35, Chancellor of the Exchequer 1937–40, Lord Chancellor 1940–45

Simons, Walter (1861–1937) German politician and lawyer, German Foreign Minister 1920–21, President of Imperial Court of Justice 1922–29

Speer, (Berthold Konrad Hermann) Albert (1905–81) German architect, joined Nazi Party in 1931, worked for Adolf Hitler and other members of Nazi government, later Minister of Armaments and War Production, tried at Nuremberg and imprisoned

Spring-Rice, Sir Arthur Cecil (1859–1918) British diplomat, at Berlin 1895–98, later Ambassador to Washington, DC 1912–18, married **Florence Lascelles** in 1904

Stanley, Sir Henry Morton (1841–1904) Journalist and African explorer, led the search to find David Livingstone in 1871–72

Stauffer, Viktor (1852–1934) Austrian artist, based in Vienna, known for genre subjects and portraiture

Steed, Henry Wickham (1871–1956) British journalist, foreign correspondent for *The Times* at Berlin 1896, Rome 1897–1902, Vienna 1902–13, editor of *The Times* 1919–22

Steffeck, Carl (1818–90) German artist working in Berlin, specialised in portraits, landscapes, historical and animal paintings

Stenzel, Fritz (born c.1895) German working at British Military Mission, Berlin from c.1918, later Chancery Servant at British Embassy, Berlin and messenger, British Interests Section, American Embassy, Berlin during Second World War

Stephenson, Charles surveyor at the Board of Works in the 1870s

Stevenson, Sir Ralph Clarmont Skrine (1895–1977) British diplomat from 1919, in Germany 1920s, later Ambassador to Belgrade 1943–46, Ambassador to Beijing 1946–50, Ambassador to Cairo 1950–55

Strang, William, 1st Baron (1893–1978) British diplomat, Head of the League of Nations Section, Foreign Office 1933–37, Head of Central Department, Foreign Office, 1937–39, Political Advisor to Commander-in-Chief, British Forces of Occupation on Germany 1945–47, Permanent Under-Secretary of Foreign Office 1949–53

Streicher, Julius (1885–1946) prominent anti-Semitic member of National Socialist party, tried and executed at Nuremberg

Stresemann, Gustav (1878–1929) German politician, German Chancellor August – November 1923, German Foreign Minister 1923–29, shared 1926 Nobel Peace Prize following Treaty of Locarno, married **Käte Kleefeld** (1883–1970) in 1903

Strong, Major-General Sir Kenneth William Dobson (1900–1982) British Army officer, Assistant British Military Attaché, Berlin, 1930s, later Director-General of Intelligence at Ministry of Defence 1964–66

Strousberg, Bethel Henry (Baruch Hirsch Strausberg) (1823–84) Prussian railway pioneer and industrialist

Sullivan, Arthur (1842–1900) British composer, best known for his collaboration with W.S. Gilbert

Swaine, Major-General Sir

Leopold (Victor) (1840–1901) British Army officer, Military Attaché at St Petersburg, Constantinople and Berlin 1880s–90s

Sykes, Christopher Hugh (1907–86) British diplomat and author, Hon. Attaché at Berlin 1928–29, later a biographer of Evelyn Waugh

Thomas, Sir Godfrey (John Vignoles) (1889–1968) British diplomat from 1912, First Secretary at Berlin 1913–14, Private Secretary to Edward, Prince of Wales 1919–36, Assistant Private Secretary to King Edward VIII 1936, Private Secretary to Duke of Gloucester 1937–57

Tirpitz, Alfred von (1849–1930) German Admiral, Secretary of State of the German Imperial Naval Office 1897–1916, developer of the German Imperial Navy

Townley, Sir Walter Beaupre (1863–1945) British diplomat from 1885, at Berlin 1898–1900, eventually Envoy Extraordinary and Minister Plenipotentiary at The Hague 1917–19, married **Lady Susan Mary Keppel** (1868–1953) in 1896

Troubridge, Vice-Admiral Sir Thomas Hope (1895–1949) British Naval Officer from 1908, Naval Attaché at Berlin 1936, later Fifth Sea Lord

Tyler House-steward at British Embassy in 1920s, father of **Marjorie**

Tyler, Marjorie British civil servant, typist at British Embassy in 1920s

Ujest, Hugo Herzog von, Fürst zu Hohenlohe-Öhringen (1816–97) Prussian/Silesian general, politician and industrialist

Vansittart, Sir Robert Gilbert (1881–1957) British diplomat from 1902, later Assistant Under-Secretary of State, Foreign Office and Principal Private Secretary to the Prime Minister 1928–30, Permanent Under-Secretary of State, Foreign Office 1930–38, Chief Diplomatic Advisor, Foreign Office, 1938–41, married (2) **Sarita Enriqueta Ward** (1897–1985) in 1931, sister of **Frances, Lady Phipps**, in 1931

Villiers, The Hon. Francis Hyde (1852–1925) British diplomat from 1870, later Assistant Under-Secretary of State, Foreign Office

1896–1905, Ambassador to Brussels 1919–21, brother of **Emily Russell, Lady Ampthill**

Vivian, Lt. Colonel Valentine Patrick Terrel (1886–1969) British security official from Indian Police Service, later Vice-Chief of MI6

Vrancx, Sebastian (1573–1647) Flemish artist, based in Antwerp

Wallace, Richard Horatio Edgar (1875–1932) British author and playwright

Waterlow, Sir Sydney Philip (1878–1944) British diplomat from 1900, later Ambassador to Athens 1933–39

Wedel, Count Georg (1862–1943) German diplomat, Chief of English Department of German Foreign Ministry 1914

Wells, Herbert George (1866–1946) British historian, novelist and social commentator

Wigram, Ralph Follett (1890–1936) British diplomat from 1919, Head of Foreign Office Central Department 1934–36, liaised closely with Winston Churchill over information on Nazi rearmament

Wile, Frederick William (1873–1941) American journalist, Berlin correspondent for the *Daily Mail* and other newspapers 1902–14

Wilford, Michael (born 1938) British architect, worked in James Stirling's practice, won Stirling Prize for Architecture in 1997, architect of new British Embassy in Berlin

Wilson, Sir Horace John (1882–1972) British civil servant, Chief Industrial Advisor to HM Government 1930–39, emissary to Germany on behalf of Neville Chamberlain, 1938

Wilson, May British civil servant, typist at British Embassy, Berlin in 1920s

Winterhalter, Franz Xaver (1805–73) German artist specialising in portraits; a favourite of Queen Victoria and at other European courts

Wirth, Joseph (1879–1926) German politician, Chancellor of Germany 1921–1922

Wolseley, Garnet Joseph, 1st Viscount Wolseley (1833–1913) British army officer, Commander-in-Chief of British Forces 1895–1900

Woolf, Leonard Sidney
(1880–1969) British author and
civil servant, member of the
'Bloomsbury Group', husband
of **Virginia Woolf**

Woolf, (Adeline) Virginia
(1882–1941) British author,
member of the 'Bloomsbury
Group' and close confidante of
Vita Sackville-West, sister of
Vanessa Bell

**Wortley, Edward James
Montagu-Stuart, Colonel**
(1857–1934) British Army officer,
Military Attaché at Paris 1901,
appointed Major-General 1913

Xavier, Mr Chef at British
Embassy, Berlin in 1880s

Zimmerman, Arthur (1864–1940)
German diplomat and politician,
German Foreign Secretary 1916–1

ILLUSTRATION CREDITS

1. Oil on canvas by Ludwig Knaus, 1870. © Stiftung Stadtmuseum Berlin, Photo: Hans-Joachim Bartsch, Berlin

2. Drawing by August Orth, 1867. Architekturmuseum der Technischen Universität Berlin in der Universitätsbibliothek (Inv. No. 14425)

3. Lithograph after August Orth, 1869. Architekturmuseum der Technischen Universität Berlin in der Universitätsbibliothek (Inv. No. B 3431)

4. Watercolour by August Orth, 1867. Architekturmuseum der Technischen Universität Berlin in der Universitätsbibliothek (Inv. No. 14426)

5. Watercolour by August Orth, 1876. Architekturmuseum der Technischen Universität Berlin in der Universitätsbibliothek (Inv. No. 14428)

6. Drawing by August Orth, 1867. ©Architekturmuseum der Technischen Universität Berlin in der Universitätsbibliothek (Inv. No. 14414)

7. Albumen print by Camille Silvy, 2 September 1864. © National Portrait Gallery, London (NPG Ax63776)

8. Albumen *carte de visite* by Numa Blanc, 1860s. © National Portrait Gallery, London (NPG x7897)

9. Photograph by an unknown photographer, c.1870. Architekturmuseum der Technischen Universität Berlin in der Universitätsbibliothek (Inv. No. F 5547)

10. Engraving from *The Illustrated London News*, 22 June 1878. © Illustrated London News Ltd / Mary Evans

11. Engraving from *The Graphic*, 29 June 1878

12. Chromolithograph by 'Spy' [Sir Leslie Ward] from *Vanity Fair*, 28 July 1877, © National Portrait Gallery, London (NPG D 43807)

13. Oil on canvas by Anton von Werner, 1895. © Staatlich Museen

zu Berlin, Nationalgalerie/Klaus Görken

14. Oil on canvas by Viktor Stauffer after Heinrich von Angeli. Woburn Abbey Collection (I.N.1295A), © His Grace the Duke of Bedford and the Trustees of the Bedford Estates

15. Oil on canvas by Viktor Stauffer after Heinrich von Angeli. Woburn Abbey Collection (I.N.1295B), © His Grace the Duke of Bedford and the Trustees of the Bedford Estates

16. Oil on canvas by Oskar Begas, 1871. Deutsches Historisches Museum, Berlin/A. Psille

17. Photograph by an unknown photographer, c.1870. Architekturmuseum der Technischen Universität Berlin in der Universitätsbibliothek (Inv. No. F 5548)

18. Whole-plate glass negative by Alexander Bassano, 1896. © National Portrait Gallery, London (NPG x571)

19. Engraving from Deutscher Architekten und Ingenieuverband, *Berlin und seine Bauten* (1896 edition)

20. Photograph by an unknown photographer, c.1880s. Architekturmuseum der Technischen Universität Berlin in der Universitätsbibliothek (Inv. No. F 5550)

21. & 22. Oils on canvas by William Blake Richmond, 1887. With permission of the Malet Family and thanks to Art UK, © Dillington House, Somerset

23. Engraving from *The Illustrated London News*, 24 March 1888. © Illustrated London News Ltd / Mary Evans

24. Photograph by J. Russell, 1894/ Private Collection / © Look and Learn / Illustrated Papers Collection / Bridgeman Images

25. Engraving from *The Graphic*, 5 April 1890

26. From a photograph by J. Russell, from *The Illustrated*

London News, 25 November 1893. © Illustrated London News Ltd / Mary Evans

27. Chromolithograph by 'Spy' [Sir Leslie Ward] from *Vanity Fair*, 27 March 1902. © National Portrait Gallery, London (NPG xD5411)

28. Oil on canvas by Adolph Menzel, 1878. © Staatlich Museen zu Berlin, Nationalgalerie/ Jörg P. Anders

29. Oil on canvas by Ferdinand Keller, 1893 / Private Collection / © Galerie Bilderwelt / Bridgeman Images

30. From a photograph by J. Russell, from *The Illustrated London News*, 25 November 1893. © Illustrated London News Ltd / Mary Evans

31. Engraving after a drawing by Carl Grote, from *The Graphic*, 10 July 1886

32. Photograph by Topical Press Agency/Getty Images

33. Photograph by F. Albert Schwartz. © bpk/Staatsbibliothek zu Berlin/F. Albert Schwartz

34. From a map of Berlin enclosed with the *Berliner Addressbuch* published by Julius Straube, 1893, showing the Government District

35. Bromide print photograph by Walter Stoneman, 1918. © National Portrait Gallery, London (NPG x167895)

36. Illustration by F.W. Koekoek based on information supplied by F.W. Wile, from *The Illustrated London News*, 15 August 1914. © Illustrated London News Ltd / Mary Evans

37. Chromolithograph by 'Spy' [Sir Leslie Ward] from *Vanity Fair*, 20 April 1899. © National Portrait Gallery, London (NPG D 44597)

38. Oil on canvas by John Singer Sargent, c.1904. Collection of the Birmingham Museum of Art, Alabama, USA (inv. no. 1984.121); museum purchase with funds provided by John Bohorfoush, the 1984 Museum Dinner and Ball, and the Museum Store, photograph by Sean Pathasema, © Birmingham Museum of Art

39. Photograph by an unknown photographer, c.1925. RIBA Collections

40. From *The Illustrated London News*, 12 December 1925. © Illustrated London News Ltd / Mary Evans

41. Oil on canvas by Augustus John, 1925. © The Estate of Augustus John / Bridgeman Images, UK Government Art Collection, London (GAC16337)

42–46. From photographs by J. Russell, from *The Illustrated London News*, 25 November 1893. © Illustrated London News Ltd / Mary Evans

47. Photograph by an unknown photographer, 1922. © Ullsteinbild/TopFoto

48. Album, 'Service of Plate at His Majesty's Embassy, Berlin'; photograph by Ernst Schneider studios, Berlin, for the Ministry of Works, 1930s. © Crown Copyright, The National Archives UK (ref. WORK 68/11)

49. Photograph by Walter Gircke, 1926. © Ullsteinbild/TopFoto

50. Photograph probably by Harold Nicolson, 1929. Collection Adam Nicolson

51. Photograph by H. Wolter, Presse Illustrations Verlag, Berlin, 3 August 1929. © Bodleian Library, University of Oxford (Rumbold Papers, Box 26/2, with thanks to Sir Henry Rumbold)

52. Photograph by unknown photographer, 15 March 1929. Rumbold Family Papers, with thanks to Sir Henry Rumbold

53. Photograph by Verlag Scherl, Berlin, 10 March 1931. From the archives of Roy Export Company Establishment. Scan Courtesy Cineteca di Bologna

54. Photograph by an unknown photographer, 15 May 1932. © Ullsteinbild/TopFoto

55. Photograph by Atelier Balassa, 18 October 1933. © Ullsteinbild/TopFoto

56. Photograph by unknown photographer, 25 March 1935. © Ullsteinbild/TopFoto

57. Photograph by unknown photographer, 26 March 1935. © Ullsteinbild/Topfoto

58. © Crown Copyright, Churchill Archives Centre, University of Cambridge (Phipps Papers, ref. PHPP III 5/11)

59. Press cutting from a German newspaper. Copyright unknown, Churchill Archives Centre, University of Cambridge (Phipps Papers, ref. PHPP III 5/1)

60. Photograph by Atelier Balassa, 13 May 1935. © Ullsteinbild/ TopFoto

61. Photograph from *The Illustrated London News*, 8 February 1936. © Illustrated London News Ltd / Mary Evans

62. Berlin's Government District in a plan probably prepared for visitors to the Berlin Olympic Games, 1936

63. Photograph by Atelier Bieber/ Nather, May 1937. © bpk/Atelier Bieber/Nather

64. Photograph by the Ministry of Works, 1939. © Crown Copyright, Foreign & Commonwealth Office

65. Photograph by Verlag Scherl, Berlin, c.1928. © Bodleian Library, University of Oxford (Rumbold Papers, Box 26/2, with thanks to Sir Henry Rumbold)

66-67. Photographs by the Ministry of Works, 1939. © Crown Copyright, Foreign & Commonwealth Office

68. Photograph from *The Illustrated London News*, 17 September 1938. © Illustrated London News Ltd / Mary Evans

69. Photograph, 28 September 1938. Universal History Archive/ UIG / Bridgeman Images

70. Photograph by the Ministry of Works, 1939. © Crown Copyright, Foreign & Commonwealth Office

71. Photograph by Heinrich Hoffmann, 4 September 1939. © bpk/Bayerische Staatsbibliothek/ Heinrich Hoffmann

72. Photograph, 14 February 1940, by Popperfoto/Getty Images

73. Photograph by Carl Weinrother, 1946. © bpk /Carl Weinrother

74. Photograph, © Ullsteinbild/ TopFoto

75. Photograph, © Ullsteinbild/ TopFoto

76. Photograph, Michael Urban/ Reuters

77. Photograph, © Ullsteinbild/ TopFot

INDEX